SAINTS AND FEAST DAYS
A Resource and Activity Book

The Sisters of Notre Dame of Chardon, Ohio

LOYOLAPRESS.

CHICAGO

LOYOLAPRESS.
3441 N. ASHLAND AVENUE
CHICAGO, ILLINOIS 60657
(800) 621-1008
LoyolaEducationGroup.org

Cover: Detail of Saint Bernardino and Saint Catherine of Siena by Carlo Crivelli, c. 1470–1493. © Burstein Collection/Corbis.

Cover and interior design: Megan Duffy Rostan

Interior art: Yoshi Miyake

Acknowledgments to copyright holders appear on page 476, which is to be considered a continuation of the copyright page.

ISBN: 0-8294-1505-X

Manufactured in the United States of America.

03 04 05 06 07 08 09 10 Bang 10 9 8 7 6 5 4 3 2 1

To Saint Julie Billiart,
spiritual mother of the Sisters of Notre Dame,
in gratitude for her inspiration and example

Contents

Today we rejoice in the holy men and women of every time and place.
—from the Opening Prayer for the Feast of All Saints

Contents

OCTOBER

NOVEMBER

Contents

Contents

Contents

Contents

MAY

Contents

Contents

AUGUST

Contents

Introduction

Looking at a statue cannot possibly give a true impression of the saints. A statue is cold and immobile, while saints are people of action. Use these stories to help the children glimpse the saints as mothers with children tugging at their skirts, fathers instructing their sons, monks praying late into the night, and preachers traveling the back roads of their countries on foot.

The calendar of saints represents men and women from every walk of life, every period of history, and every part of the world. They became saints because they loved. They remind us that it is possible for us to change and grow in the love of God and of others. Through the power of Jesus working in us all, we can become holy and can help the world come to know and love God. Praying to the saints encourages us to live up to our full potential so that we may join them in eternal life.

> We who come after them draw inspiration from their heroic example, look for fellowship in their communion, and in prayer seek their intercession with God on our behalf.
>
> (*National Catechetical Directory* 107)

All men and women are called to holiness. All of us are called to be close to God, to listen and to pray, to respond to Jesus' teachings, whatever the cost, as did the saints. The saints are our companions; we thank God for the example of their lives that makes Christ more present to us, and we ask their intercession.

Our world is, in some ways, very different from the world of the saints, and, in some ways, very much the same. Some saints lived before the writing of biographies was common. Their stories were passed on by word of mouth, and some were naturally embellished. But the substance of the stories is to be considered true. Legends have grown about some of the saints. This does not mean that they are fictional. It literally means they were "to be read" in the Divine Office and are to be understood in the spirit in which they were written. When reading the lives of the saints, remember that their lives and their deaths give purpose and meaning to ours. When we see how God is glorified in them, we are encouraged to strive ever more eagerly to win the crown of everlasting life.

As you and your students read about the saints, you will see one thing over and over: goodness attracts goodness, love begets love. Just as Jesus did, the saints, even hermits and martyrs, attracted followers. Tertullian, an early Christian theologian, said that "the blood of martyrs is the seed of the Church." Unlikely as it seems by worldly standards, you will find that it is true—from the first century through the 21st century, in Europe, Africa, North America, South America, and Far East Asia.

People with a mission to teach or preach or cure the sick found they couldn't do all the work alone. Just as Jesus did, they gathered a group of individuals who shared their ideals and charism and founded religious orders to carry on their good work. Some saints spread the Good News through action (missionaries and social workers), some through words (writers and preachers). Some saints even inspired other saints. A holy person can lead others to sanctity. Let these saints attract your students to goodness and holiness. Let them inspire, awe, console, guide, challenge, and teach the young people in your classroom.

Using This Book

The Church calendar gives special emphasis to the life and teachings of Jesus, from the celebration of his birth through the Paschal Mystery to his sending of the Holy Spirit. Therefore, the year is divided into the seasons of Advent, Christmas, Lent, Easter, and Ordinary Time. Although the Church year begins with the First Sunday of Advent, for ease of use during the school year, this book begins with September feasts.

Traditionally the Church has celebrated the way certain men and women have lived the Paschal Mystery and has honored them as saints. These human beings responded to God through Jesus and overcame their weaknesses and sins through the power of grace. Their lives praise Christ, give hope to his followers, and offer an example for people to imitate.

Saints and Feast Days provides sketches of many saints and feast days celebrated each year by the Church. The suggested activities can help young Catholics see that their own lives offer rich opportunities to become saints too.

Classroom Activities

- Tell, read, or have a student read in class about the saint or feast you are celebrating.

- Make copies of the saint's story and have the children read it at home the night before in preparation for celebrating the feast.

- In the case of summer saints, have children who are named after these saints present information on their birthdays, baptismal anniversaries, or at another suitable time during the year.

- Make a time line as you learn about and celebrate the saints.

- Use a world map to show where the saints lived. Flag the location using pushpins or small sticky notes.

- Keep a saint mural in progress. As each saint is studied, add to the mural. Students themselves might be included in the mural—at least approaching the land of the saints!

- Have the students imagine that they are the saints presented. Ask how they would have felt and what they would have done.

- Have the students write "eyewitness" accounts of an event in the life of a saint. Have each of them choose to be a particular person at the event.

- Encourage students to do additional research on the saints, especially their patrons, and share their findings with the class. These could eventually be assembled into a class booklet.

- On the feast days, use the opening prayer of the Mass for the class prayer.

- Post a calendar that highlights the name days of students as well as their birthdays and baptismal anniversaries.

- After presentations of the lives of the saints, relate their lives to the present day. Stress that living one's faith gives a powerful witness to the world.

- Have the students write their own prayers to the saints or compose a litany of saints. Begin with an intercession to God the Father, Jesus, the Holy Spirit, Mary, Joseph, and then any saints whom they wish to include.

- Activities suggested for the feast of one apostle or early martyr may be equally good for another apostle or early martyr. Use the extra space on the pages to make notes about other activities you would like to try.

- Acquaint the students with the liturgical colors used for various kinds of feast days. For a helpful chart, reproduce the blackline master on page 434.

- Lead the students in a prayer for modern missionaries on the feast of any missionary saint. Use the blackline master on page 435 to make student copies of the Prayer for Missionaries.

Parish or School Activities

- Have each class of children research the saints in the book and choose a patron saint for their class for the year. Based on the biography of the chosen saint, students can determine one way to imitate the virtue of that saint.

- Individual students can check the book for the saint recognized on their birthday and baptismal date. Of the two, they may choose the saint that they feel they could follow. On a school family night involving parents, children could present the saint, their reasons for choosing the saint, and the ways they hope to carry on the saint's mission. Costumes would add color and heighten interest.

- If a parish has a meet-and-share type of activity after Sunday Masses, students could don their costumes from family night and be present to meet and share with parishioners and to answer questions about themselves based on their biography in the book.

- Have students choose a saint from the biographies in the book. Have a partner trace the outline of their figure on a long sheet of butcher paper. They then color and decorate the outline as the saint would have dressed, write the saint's name on the clothes, and cut out the figure. These saints could line the church gathering area or school walls on November 1 or during Lent.

- Each month students could be chosen to write short biographies of one of the saints honored that month. "Publish" their synopses each week in the parish bulletin.

- When new members of the parish are baptized, check the book for the child's patron saint. Send a short biography, the saint's feast day, and a card of congratulations to the newly baptized or the family.

- Using the book as a resource, let children prepare a list of patron saints for various occupations. Publish the list in the parish bulletin close to the feast of Saint Joseph the Worker (May 1).

- For parent night or family night, have students create short plays based on the biographical material in the book. Especially interesting would be plays on pairs of saints, for example, Paul and Barnabas, Peter and Paul, Benedict and Scholastica, Francis and Clare, Vincent de Paul and

Louise de Marillac, Francis de Sales and Jane de Chantal, Hilary and Martin of Tours.

- Have students create a "Who Am I?" booklet or a series of quizzes based on the biographies. These could be published in the parish bulletin with the answers revealed on another page or in the next week's bulletin.

- Encourage families to celebrate the feast days of patron saints in some way:

  Prepare for the celebration by observing a vigil the night before, during which they should read about their patron, read from Scripture, pray the Rosary, or use their own form of prayer.

  Participate in the Eucharist on the feast day of their patron.

  Prepare a special dessert for the day.

  Light a baptismal candle or Christ candle in honor of the saint.

Saint Gregory the Great

(c. 540–604)

September 3

How would you like to be called "the Great?" Try it out: (Your Name), the Great. Today's saint is Gregory the Great. Read his story to find out why he is called "the great."

Gregory lived in Rome during a period of wars, invasions by hostile tribes, famine, and destruction. He was the son of Gordianus, a wealthy Roman senator. Like most of the upper class of his time, he was well educated. But unlike many, he was generous and concerned about the poor.

When he was in his early 30s, Gregory was made the chief prefect, or governor, of Rome. He had long been attracted to the religious life, however, and so left his position before very long. He converted the family estate in Rome into the Abbey of St. Andrew, became a monk there, and founded six Benedictine monasteries on his estates in Sicily. His life of quiet and prayer did not last long; for around 578 he was ordained one of the seven deacons of Rome and sent as the papal ambassador to Constantinople, where he served until 585. When he arrived back in Rome, he was made the abbot of St. Andrew's.

Five years later the pope died, and Gregory was acclaimed pope by the clergy and the people of Rome. Unwillingly Gregory accepted the role. He was the first pope to call himself the "servant of the servants of God." But Gregory was such a good leader that he became known as Gregory the Great.

Because of his political skill, learning, talents, and deep devotion to God, Gregory was able to make peace with the invading Lombards, save the city from famine by reorganizing the property and granaries of the Church, and restore order within the Church itself. Even though there were tremendous problems in Rome, Gregory was able to look beyond his land to the needs of people in foreign lands. He sent a group of monks to England to teach the faith to the people who lived there. So great was Gregory's interest in them that he has come to be called the Apostle of England, even though he himself was unable to travel there to preach.

What really made Pope Gregory great? His achievements were many and had a widespread effect, but Gregory became a saint because of his love for God, which was reflected in all that he did.

ACTIVITIES

BRAINSTORM QUALITIES OF HOLINESS
Discuss how Gregory responded to the needs of his time. Ask the students to brainstorm the qualities a person would need today to be considered a great saint.

LISTEN TO GREGORIAN CHANT
Although Gregory's full influence on the music of his day is debatable, he is sometimes credited with the Church's liturgical chant form, the Gregorian chant. Play some samples of Gregorian chant for the students and get their reactions and opinions.

SING A LITURGICAL SONG
Grades K–3: Simply sing one of the children's favorite songs from your parish liturgy.

PRESENT AWARDS
Gregory is known as a patron of teachers, scholars, and singers. Discuss with the students why these areas are especially related to Gregory. Have them make "_____ the Great" medals or certificates for outstanding teachers, students, and singers.

RESEARCH FATHERS OF THE CHURCH
Along with Augustine, Ambrose, and Jerome, Gregory the Great is considered one of the four Fathers of the Western church. All are included in this book. Have the students discover what is necessary in order to be called a Father of the Church.

VIEW A VIDEO ON MISSION WORK
Gregory supported mission work. During his life he sent groups of monks to evangelize Britain. The practice of sending monks as missionaries was not usual. Show a video on the work being done in the missions today. Many excellent programs are available from the active missionary congregations in the Church.

WRITE TO YOUR BISHOP
In his book *Pastoral Care,* Gregory wrote a powerful description of the qualities and duties of a bishop. Invite the students to find out more about their local bishop. Bring in recent issues of the Catholic newspaper in the diocese and read about some of the activities of the bishop. Encourage the youngsters to respond by writing supportive letters to their bishop.

Catechist's Notes:

_____

_____

_____

_____

_____

_____

Birth of Mary

September 8

We know that everyone has a birthday. The Bible doesn't say anything about Mary's birth, but we know that she was born. Like all parents, Mary's parents—we call them Joachim and Ann—probably took one look at their newborn daughter and knew that she was special.

Joachim and Ann loved God very much, and they were filled with gratitude to God for the gift of a child. They raised Mary as a child of God, teaching her to love and serve God. When the angel Gabriel told Mary that she had been chosen to be the Mother of Jesus, she already had great faith in God. Her strong faith and trust allowed her to say yes to God's plan for her.

We cannot be certain what the future holds for any newborn infant, but we do know that the life of each person has meaning and purpose. When Mary was born, the world did not know who she was. Sometimes others—and maybe even you—don't see how special you are. Maybe you forget that God is calling you, too, right now, to do what Mary did—to bring Jesus into the world.

When we celebrate his mother's birth, we honor Jesus too. Today thank God for the gift of life, and give honor to both Mary and Jesus by showing respect and concern for one another—remembering that God has created each person with love and with a call to something very special in life.

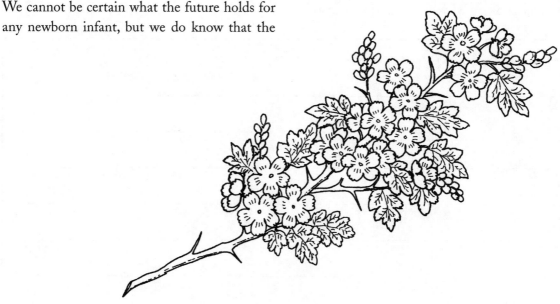

PRAY AND SING

With the children, pray the Memorare; Hail, Holy Queen; or Hail Mary. These prayers may be found on the blackline master on page 436.

Close the class with a hymn honoring Mary.

CELEBRATE MARY'S BIRTHDAY

Grades K–3: Bring in cupcakes or another birthday treat for the children. Light a candle and invite them to sing "Happy Birthday" to Mary.

Grades 3–6: Have the students design a Marian candle, using symbols of Mary such as a lily or an M. Use this candle on the prayer table during the year or for feasts of Mary.

Grades 6–8: The date of the feast of the Birth of Mary, September 8, was used to fix the date of the feast of the Immaculate Conception, December 8. This situation also occurs for the conception and birth of Jesus: the Annunciation on March 25 and the Nativity on December 25. Point this out to the students to reinforce the Church's teaching that life begins at conception.

SHOW ICONS OF MARY

Traditionally this feast is believed to have originated in Jerusalem and was celebrated in the Eastern church before it came to be observed in the Western (sometime around the eighth century). Use this opportunity to share with the students several icons of Mary from the Eastern tradition.

CELEBRATE FEASTS OF MARY

Divide the class into groups, and assign one group to each of the feasts of Mary you plan to celebrate during the school year. Have the students research and present ethnic or national customs honoring Mary. Such presentations may include icons or religious images, samples of music and food characteristic of these celebrations, processions, and so on. Ask the students to be ready to present their plan to you several days before the actual feast.

Catechist's Notes:

_____

_____

_____

_____

_____

_____

Saint Peter Claver

September 9

(1580–1654)

Have you ever been really, really thirsty? Maybe you were hiking or mowing the yard on a hot summer day. Maybe you just came in from the playground or off the basketball court. Think how good a drink of cold water would be. If some kind person brought you water, how would you feel?

Peter Claver was that sort of person. Peter felt he was called to be a missionary. When he was 29 years old, Peter left his home in Spain and went to Cartagena (in what is now Colombia), South America. There he continued his studies and was ordained a priest.

Cartagena was a busy city, but its economic success came from dealing in human misery. Cartagena was the main market for the slave trade in the New World. Hundreds of thousands of people were brought there from Africa, herded into warehouses, and auctioned off to the highest bidder. They had been captured, chained together, crowded onto ships, and neglected during the long journey to South America. The conditions were so terrible that an estimated one-third of the captives died during the journey.

Whenever a ship carrying Africans arrived in port, Peter was there. He would hurry down with a jug of water, and a basket full of medicine, fruit, bread, and clothing. He would greet the slaves by giving them a drink of water. His first concern was to tend to their human needs—to ease their suffering and somehow restore their sense of dignity. He saw the suffering Jesus in the people he served. And he heard in their cry: "What you do for others, you do for me." Peter nursed many back to health and, while they were in warehouses awaiting their sale, he told them that Jesus loved them and gave them the sacraments.

Peter Claver could not eliminate the strong hold that slavery had on society. The hearts and the consciences of many people had been so hardened that they refused to see this evil of slavery in their midst. But Peter did what he could. He tried to be a visible sign that the African slaves were indeed human beings, children of God. By bringing the love of Jesus to them, he was laying the foundations of justice and charity for the future. During his 40 years in Colombia, Peter Claver baptized nearly 300,000 Africans.

A man of deep prayer, unbounded energy, and steady devotion, Peter Claver realized that it was his relationship with Christ that nourished his spirit and gave him the courage to go on when so many problems surrounded his work. When he died the city that had opposed so many of his efforts honored him.

ACTIVITIES

DRAW WORKS OF MERCY

- Peter Claver's life was a vivid demonstration of the works of mercy in action. Review with the students the Spiritual and Corporal Works of Mercy. Have them draw pictures of Peter's ministry, showing how he was involved in these various works.

- Ask the children how they can be modern Peter Clavers. Have them draw pictures of themselves performing one of the works of mercy.

DRAMATIZE WORKS OF MERCY

Read Matthew 25 and let the children dramatize it.

LOCATE SPAIN AND COLOMBIA

Have the students find Spain and Colombia on a globe or map.

DISCUSS RACIAL PREJUDICE

On his solemn profession, Peter Claver signed himself "slave of the black forever." Discuss the problems of racial tensions and prejudice in society today.

PRAY FOR RACIAL JUSTICE

Have the students compose a prayer to St. Peter Claver, asking for his intercession for racial justice.

RESEARCH CONTRIBUTIONS OF AFRICANS

Peter Claver freed 18 Africans to help him in his work and act as interpreters and catechists. Have students research the contributions of native Africans to various cultures. Discuss with the class the need for the various groups in any social structure to help one another.

RESEARCH POPE LEO XIII

Peter Claver was canonized by Pope Leo XIII, who also championed the rights of workers. This pope encouraged missionary activity and the abolition of slavery. Have the students find out more about Pope Leo XIII.

Catechist's Notes:

_____

_____

_____

_____

_____

_____

_____

Saint John Chrysostom September 13

(c. 349–407)

Do you know anyone who is not afraid to speak out against what is wrong, no matter who is involved? Are you that kind of person? People who are willing to stand up for what is right leave their mark on the world. But they also may find themselves with a lot of enemies! John Chrysostom, an eloquent bishop-preacher of the fourth century, certainly understood this.

John lived in Antioch, the city where the believers in Jesus were first called Christians. His father died when John was a child, and so his mother guided his education. A gifted student, John studied under Libanius, a famous orator of his time. Recalling his years as an adolescent, John considered himself too involved in the things of this world. At 18 he experienced some type of religious conversion and began to study the Bible. Three years later, after the death of his mother, John went to join a group of monks living in the mountains. After four years he left them to live the life of a hermit in a cave. After a while he returned to Antioch.

Here others quickly noticed his gifts as a monk, a biblical scholar, an eloquent speaker. Soon he was ordained a deacon, and when he was 39, he was ordained a priest. One role of a priest or bishop is to teach, and teach he did! John was quick to see how greed and lust infected society, and he was not hesitant about condemning it. Of particular concern to him was the widespread indifference to the poor.

In 397 John was made the bishop-patriarch of Constantinople—a position of extraordinary influence. He himself lived a very simple life, giving his wealth over for the building of hospitals, and he set about reforming the clergy and the city. He deposed bishops for buying their way into office. He sold much of the expensive furniture in the bishop's residence and gave the money to serve the poor. He urged other bishops to spend more time in their own areas rather than in the palaces of city officials. He attacked the wealthy for misuse of their riches. He sought to reform the lax clergy, to straighten out the badly managed budget, to rid the land of violence. The list was endless.

Such a champion of charity and justice was he that it was not long before he stirred up the anger of the empress, Eudoxia, and the jealousy of Theophilus, the patriarch of Alexandria. With such enemies mounting an attack against him, John was impeached and exiled. Even though he had the support of Pope Innocent I, the love of the poor, and the devotion of so many others, John was exiled even further and died en route.

John Chrysostom was a powerful prophet of his day, for he was not afraid to speak out against wrong, no matter who was involved. Who are the prophets of today? Who are the prophets in your classroom? Your family? Your group of friends? Might one of them be you?

ACTIVITIES

GIVE SPEECHES

John was given the title *Chrysostom,* meaning "Golden Mouth," because of his eloquence in speaking. Hold a John Chrysostom Day, for which the students prepare speeches dealing with any moral theme relevant to their school, home, or society. Give each participant an award.

READ SCRIPTURE

John was a Scripture scholar, and he devoted time each day to reading and meditation on the Bible. Encourage the students to read the Bible daily for about five minutes.

INVITE A DEACON TO SPEAK

Invite a local deacon or a priest of your parish to speak about the work of a deacon today.

Then, have the students find Scripture passages related to the role of the deacon in the early Church. Acts 6:8–15 describes Stephen, one of the first deacons.

APPLY CHURCH TEACHING TO CURRENT EVENTS

John Chrysostom helped ease tensions in Antioch after a tax riot broke out. The emperor had levied a heavy tax to increase his defense budget, and the people revolted in protest. It was John's first year as a priest, and he interceded, calling for restraint and peace. Such situations still occur. Have the students relate contemporary issues and the directives from the Church regarding such issues. Make newspaper and magazine reports, speeches of the pope and the local bishops, and Internet sources available.

Catechist's Notes:

SEPTEMBER

Triumph of the Cross   September 14

The one symbol most often identified with Jesus and his Church is the cross. Today we celebrate the feast of the Triumph of the Cross. This feast traces its beginning to Jerusalem and the dedication of the church built on the site of Mount Calvary in 335. But the meaning of the cross is deeper than any city, any celebration, any building. The cross is a sign of suffering, a sign of human cruelty at its worst. But by Christ's love shown in the Paschal Mystery, it has become the sign of triumph and victory, the sign of God, who is love itself.

Believers have always looked to the cross in times of suffering. People in concentration camps, in prisons, in hospitals, in any place of suffering and loneliness, have been known to draw, trace, or form crosses and focus their eyes and hearts on them. The cross does not explain pain and misery. It does not give us any easy answers. But it does help us to see our lives united with Christ's.

We often make the Sign of the Cross over ourselves. We make it before prayer to help fix our minds and hearts on God. We make it after prayer, hoping to stay close to God. In trials and temptations, the cross is a sign of strength and protection. The cross is the sign of the fullness of life that is ours. At Baptism, too, the Sign of the Cross is used; the priest, parents, and godparents make the sign on the forehead of the child. A sign made on the forehead is a sign of belonging. By the Sign of the Cross in Baptism, Jesus takes us as his own in a unique way. Today, let us look to the cross often. Let us make the Sign of the Cross and realize we bring our whole selves to God—our minds, souls, bodies, wills, thoughts, hearts—everything we are and will become.

> O cross, you are the glorious sign of
>   our victory.
> Through your power may we share in
>   the triumph of Christ Jesus.
>   *(Prayer of Christians)*

9

ACTIVITIES

LEARN THE PRAYER TO CHRIST CRUCIFIED

Give the students copies of the Prayer to Christ Crucified and pray it together. This prayer may be found on the blackline master on page 437.

RESEARCH THE TRUE CROSS

Encourage the students to do research on Saint Helena and the true cross. Or have them research Constantine, who was emperor at the time of the dedication.

MAKE A CROSS

Have the students construct crosses of their own, using wood, cardboard, foil, stones (pebbles), clay, or any other material available. Or have them make a toothpick cross:

Materials needed:

- at least 79 wooden toothpicks

- a 6" × 9" piece of colored poster board cut in the shape of a cross (dimensions below)

- all-purpose glue

Steps:

1. Cut the poster board as shown:

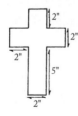

2. Lay five toothpicks on the poster board as shown in the diagram. They form a cross in the center of the cardboard. Glue them down.

3. Glue four more toothpicks down diagonal to the center, as shown in the diagram.

4. Continue to glue toothpicks as shown for each section, alternating thick and thin ends of the toothpicks.

MEDITATE ON THE CROSS

Take the students to the church or prayer room, if one is available, for a short prayer or meditation on the cross or crucifix. Often churches have specially designed crosses and crucifixes. If this is the case, invite someone familiar with the design or church architecture to explain the symbolism of the one there.

Provide Scripture references for meditation (e.g., John 19; Mark 15–16; 2 Timothy 2:10–12) or appropriate music (e.g., "Behold the Wood," or "With What Great Love").

PRAY THE WAY OF THE CROSS

Pray the Way of the Cross with the students, or have them compose their own meditations and drawings for the stations.

Our Lady of Sorrows September 15

How do you feel when your best friend is sad? When you love people very much, you share in all their joys and all their sorrows. When your parents, brothers and sisters, or friends are happy, it is easier for you to be happy too. But when they are sick or suffering, you carry some of their pain in your own heart.

That's how it was for Mary, the Mother of Jesus. When people accepted Jesus and chose to live by his teachings, Mary was filled with joy. But when she saw her Son rejected and hurt, she experienced that pain very deeply. Today we remember Mary's share in the sufferings of her Son, and we call upon her as Our Lady of Sorrows.

When Joseph and Mary presented the infant Jesus in the Temple, Simeon told Mary that a sword would pierce her own soul too (Luke 2:34–35). Because Mary loved Jesus so much, she suffered along with him. Neither complaining nor feeling sorry for herself, she carried these sufferings in silence—knowing that God understood and cared.

Mary is our mother too. That means she rejoices when we draw closer to God. It means she understands our daily pains and sufferings. We may not always understand the mystery of the cross in our lives, but we never have to bear it alone. We are brothers and sisters of Jesus and children of Mary. Today we can turn to Mary with our complaints and our sufferings, with the times we are misunderstood and lonely. She is near to us and will help us. Mary, Our Lady of Sorrows, pray for us.

DESIGN BANNERS OR A MURAL

Traditionally the major sorrows of Mary are listed as seven. Divide the class into seven groups and have each group research one of these incidents in Scripture. Explain to the students that several of the references are not explicit in the Scriptures, but rather come from the traditional understanding of Mary's role in the Passion and death of her Son. Then direct them to work together to illustrate the events to make a mural or to design a banner for each sorrow.

1. The prophecy of Simeon when Jesus is presented in the Temple: Luke 2:33–35

2. The flight into Egypt: Matthew 2:13–18

3. The loss of Jesus in the Temple in Jerusalem: Luke 2:41–50

4. Meeting Jesus on the way to Calvary: Matthew 27:27–31; Mark 15:16–20

5. Mary at the foot of the cross: Matthew 27:45–56; John 19:25–27

6. Jesus is taken down from the cross and placed in the arms of his mother: Luke 23:47–55

7. The burial of Jesus: Matthew 27:57–61; John 19:38–42

LEARN A NEW PRAYER TO MARY

Teach or review with the students several Marian prayers or devotions: the Stabat Mater; the Memorare; Hail, Holy Queen; the Litany of Mary, Mother of the Church; or the Sorrowful Mysteries of the Rosary. You may use the blackline masters on pages 436, 443, and 445.

DISPLAY THE PIETÀ

Show the students either a picture or a replica of Michelangelo's *Pietà*. Display it in the room during the day as a reminder of Mary's love for Jesus and her love for us.

Catechist's Notes:

_____

_____

_____

_____

_____

_____

_____

_____

Saints Cornelius and Cyprian

September 16

(d. 253; 210–258)

Has the beginning of a new school year been hard? Beginnings can be difficult. The beginning years of the Church were, as the lives of Cornelius and Cyprian clearly show. These martyrs confronted heresies, persecutions, and divisions.

The emperor Decius was a severe ruler who believed that Rome could be great only by staying faithful to pagan idols. He decreed that all who would not give up their Christian faith should be killed. Pope Fabian was martyred along with many Christians. Emperor Decius thought that without a pope the Church would fade away, and so he prevented any election of another Bishop of Rome. But the Church did not fade. Instead a group of priests secretly carried on the work. After a year the emperor had to lead his soldiers against invading Goths. During his absence, the Church elected Cornelius pope.

Cornelius had problems from the moment he became pope. Some Christians, led by a man named Novatian, believed that those who had given up their faith during the persecutions could not return to the Church—even if they had repented. Cornelius called a council of bishops to settle the dispute. The council affirmed Cornelius's position as pope and condemned Novatian's view. After two years as pope, Cornelius was arrested and sentenced to banishment. He died in exile.

A close friend and courageous supporter of Cornelius during this time was Cyprian, the bishop of Carthage, near the city of Tunis in North Africa. Cyprian was born in Carthage, the son of pagan parents, and converted to Christianity as an adult. He was extremely intelligent and a powerful speaker. He lived a very virtuous, penitential life and became a priest, and eventually a bishop.

Cyprian was bishop of Carthage for nearly 10 years. After only one year of peace, the persecutions under Decius began, as well as disagreements over what to do with those who gave up their faith during these persecutions. Bishop Cyprian had to deal with a priest named Novatus. Novatus believed that all who had denied their faith should be accepted back with no restrictions. In time the Church took a middle course. When new persecutions broke out under Emperor Valerian, Cyprian was tried for being a Christian. On hearing his death sentence, he exclaimed, "Blessed be God!"

Both Cornelius and Cyprian remained faithful to Jesus and the Church in the midst of difficulties. Although separated by many miles, they were good friends and supported each other in seeking the truth. In their lives we see not only the power of God but also the power of good friendship. They encouraged each other to lead virtuous, self-sacrificing, and loving lives for God. A friend can offer no greater gift.

WRITE NOTES TO FRIENDS

To celebrate the friendship and support Cornelius and Cyprian shared, have students write short notes to their friends, encouraging them to do their best in school this year. End with spontaneous prayers for friends.

ACT OUT TRUE FRIENDSHIP

Ask the students for ways to help friends grow closer to God. List, or have a student list these on the board. Divide the class into small groups and have each group choose one of the ways from the list to role-play. Allow a few minutes for the groups to plan their skits. Then have them take turns acting out the situations for the class.

CELEBRATE RECONCILIATION

The lives of Cornelius and Cyprian show us how the Church has struggled for a deeper, clearer understanding of the Sacrament of Penance. The Church continually tries to discern the mind and spirit of Christ. Have the students discuss the importance of this sacrament in their lives and the need to ask forgiveness from those they have offended. Prepare a short penance celebration or have the students exchange some sign of peace.

INTERVIEW PARISHIONERS

Cyprian was converted largely through the influence of a priest. Have the students interview priests, religious, teachers, or new converts in the parish about the people and things that have influenced their lives and their major decisions. If your parish is involved in a catechumenate program, invite the leaders of this group to come in and explain the importance of community support.

GATHER STATISTICS

A document from Cornelius describes the mid-third century Church at Rome as having 48 priests, 7 deacons, 7 subdeacons, and an estimated 50,000 Christians. Have the students find similar statistics for their own diocese.

Catechist's Notes:

_____

_____

_____

_____

_____

_____

_____

_____

Saint Robert Bellarmine

September 17

(1542–1621)

It is said that Robert Bellarmine was so short he used to stand on a stool in order to be seen in the high pulpits of Europe. But he was a giant in many other ways.

Robert Bellarmine was born into a large Italian family in which prayer and serving others were priorities. From the beginning it was clear that Robert was destined for great things. He attended the Roman College where he was considered a brilliant student. Then he became a professor at Louvain, one of the most prestigious universities in Europe. When he was 28, he was ordained a Jesuit priest. His sermons and his defense of the faith were so powerful that people were attracted to him from all over, and many were eventually converted. He became rector at the Roman College and then the provincial of Naples. But he didn't stop there. He kept right on rising. He was named a cardinal and later became the archbishop of Capua. He was called to Rome to work in defense of the Church against the false teachings of the day.

All in all, Robert Bellarmine was an advisor to five different popes. He was involved in all sorts of controversies. One of the most famous of these involved the teachings of Galileo, the scientist, who was also a friend of Bellarmine.

History shows over and over that great leaders seem to surface during difficult times in the Church. Many of the men Robert Bellarmine knew and worked with also became leaders in the Church. Some, such as Aloysius Gonzaga and Francis de Sales, were also canonized. This is all part of the mystery of the Body of Christ. For those who love and depend on God, there is no challenge too great, no sacrifice too difficult. In our own lives, too, we may find the strength to hold to all that Jesus has taught as we grow in love of him. Today, like Robert Bellarmine, let us use all our gifts for God. May we study hard, pray much, and serve others, so that the world will see how great is our God.

ACTIVITIES

RESEARCH THE PROTESTANT REFORMATION

Robert Bellarmine wrote and taught during the Protestant Reformation (1517–1648), a time of crisis and challenge for the Church. Have the students research some aspects of the Reformation and Robert Bellarmine's role during that time.

MAKE POSTERS

Bellarmine was known as an outstanding student. Have the students discuss the importance of studying their faith in order to witness more effectively to others. Let them design posters illustrating some of the main beliefs of the Catholic faith. Recommend that they refer to the Apostles' Creed or the Nicene Creed as a basis. You might make copies of the Nicene Creed from the blackline master on page 454.

WRITE ESSAYS

Robert Bellarmine wrote a great deal in defense of the faith, and in 1931 he was declared a Doctor of the Church. Have the students consult the Glossary (p. 471) and find out what it means to be a Doctor of the Church. Then ask them to write short essays on some truth of the faith that has come to mean more to them in the past year.

Catechist's Notes:

_____

_____

_____

_____

_____

_____

_____

_____

_____

_____

_____

_____

Saint Hildegard of Bingen

September 17

(1098–1179)

Is music an important part of your life? Saint Hildegard was a musician, among other things. Music was the way Hildegard found to express her vision of the glory of God.

Hildegard lived near the Rhine River in Germany. When she was eight years old, her parents took her to a wise woman named Jutta, who lived in a room attached to the church. Jutta taught Hildegard, and some other girls, how to read the Psalms in Latin and how to do needlework. Hildegard never learned to write.

When Hildegard grew up, she became a nun and the head of the convent. Hildegard composed songs about the love of God for the nuns to sing. She said that she wanted them to sound like angels singing. Her songs were about God's beauty and power in all of creation, about Mary and the saints, and about heaven.

Hildegard was able to express these things so beautifully because God showed her these things. As a child she sometimes told others about her visions, but when she realized that no one else saw the same thing, she kept it to herself. When she was 42 years old, God told her to reveal to the world what she saw and heard.

Still Hildegard hesitated. This amazing woman was not so sure of herself. She had never doubted that the visions came from God, but she worried about what people would think or say.

Again the inner voice told her to speak out. So she did. When the bishop read the first book, *Scivias (Know the Ways of the Lord),* he said that it came from God, and he told her to continue. For the rest of her life she wrote; that is, she dictated to a monk or to several nuns who wrote for her.

In a time when few women wrote at all, Hildegard authored and illustrated major works of theology and contemporary texts on science and religion and on natural healing with plants, trees, and stones. As more and more people heard about Hildegard's wisdom and holiness, they came from all over Germany and France to seek advice and help with ailments of body and soul. She became so famous that bishops, kings, and even the pope consulted her.

Hildegard never took credit herself; everything came from God, who had given her an understanding of the world.

DISCOVER GIFTS TO USE FOR OTHERS

Hildegard used her gift of music to help other people understand God's love. Help the children to think about the gifts God has given each of them. Be ready to suggest something for each student. You may also have the students form small discovery groups. Have the members of each group brainstorm gifts and talents that they see in each member. Then ask each child to write down plans for using his or her gifts to bring others closer to God this week.

COMPOSE SONGS

Have students work together to compose songs that express their belief on a topic about which they are currently learning in religion class.

HAVE AN ARTS FAIR

Have an arts fair entitled "My Vision of Heaven and Earth." Invite the students to express their ideas by painting, sculpting, song, dance, or poetry. Invite families, another class, or the whole school to your exhibition.

LISTEN TO HILDEGARD'S MUSIC

Hildegard composed music back in the 12th century. Her musical compositions were rediscovered in the late 20th century and have been very popular again. Play a selected recording for the students. Be sure to play enough so that they get a good feel for the (probably) unfamiliar sound. Poll the class on whether they think it sounds like angels singing.

Catechist's Notes:

_____

_____

_____

_____

_____

_____

_____

_____

_____

Saint Januarius

(d. 305?)

September 19

Little is actually known about Saint Januarius except that he was a bishop of Benevento (near Naples, Italy) and was probably martyred during the persecutions under Diocletian around 305.

When Diocletian became emperor of the Roman Empire in 284, he knew he would need to divide the land in order to rule better. At first, he did not demand much in the way of homage, but as the number of Christians increased, he feared rebellion and began a series of persecutions. Those who refused to burn incense before a statue of the emperor as proof of their loyalty were executed. Januarius may have been among those who refused to show such worship.

There are a number of legends connected with this saint. According to these stories, Januarius went to visit some Christians who had been imprisoned. He himself was then arrested and condemned to death for being a Christian. Januarius and his companions were thrown to wild beasts in the amphitheater of Pozzuoli, but the animals refused to harm them. Januarius and his companions were beheaded instead, and the blood and body of Januarius were brought back to Naples.

The relics of Januarius have gained more fame than the saint himself. These relics, including a four-inch flask of his blood, have been attracting visitors since the 15th century. Each year the dried blood in the flask is said to liquefy 18 times (usually in May, September 19–28, and in December).

Januarius is regarded as the patron saint of Naples, and his protection is sought when there is the danger of volcanic eruption. Italian Americans celebrate the feast of San Gennaro (Saint Januarius) each year with lively festivals.

ACTIVITIES

REFLECT ON WAYS TO PRACTICE FAITH

Have the students reflect on the need to live their faith even during difficult times. Call their attention to various occasions throughout the day when they have an opportunity to live their faith (e.g., sharing their lunch, resisting the temptation to cheat, reaching out to a new person).

DISCUSS MIRACULOUS EVENTS

You may wish to discuss the purpose of miracle stories such as those that are told about St. Januarius, and also the role of faith without such signs. "The Church also honors the other saints who are already with the Lord in heaven. We who come after them draw inspiration from their heroic example, look for fellowship in their communion, and in prayer seek their intercession with God on our behalf." (*National Catechetical Directory* 107)

RESEARCH MODERN MARTYRS

Have the students research people who have died for their faith in the last century, such as Father Miguel Pro, Father Maximilian Kolbe, and various missionaries.

GO ITALIAN

Celebrate the feast of San Gennaro with some Italian food and music.

Catechist's Notes:

_____

_____

_____

_____

_____

_____

_____

_____

_____

_____

_____

_____

Saints Andrew Kim Taegon, Paul Chong Hasang, and Companions

September 20

(d. 1839–1867)

Today we remember a whole group of courageous Korean Christians—113 martyrs canonized together in 1984. Among them were Andrew, a 21-year-old priest; Paul, a 45-year-old seminarian; Columba Kim, a 26-year-old single woman, and her sister Agnes; and Peter Ryau, a 13-year-old boy. Some 10,000 Catholics were martyred for their faith before religious freedom came to Korea in 1884. Today Korea has nearly 4 million Catholics.

During a Japanese invasion in 1592, a small number of Koreans were baptized. Soon after, Korea cut itself off from the rest of the world. Around 1777, some Confucian scholars decided to follow Christ after reading books brought into the country by Catholics from China. When a Chinese priest secretly arrived about 12 years later, he found 4,000 Catholics who had never seen a priest. Korea's first Christian community was made up entirely of laypeople! Between 1839 and 1867, there were fierce persecutions. One hundred three members of this community were martyred along with three bishops and seven priests from the Paris Foreign Mission Society.

Andrew Kim Taegon was the first native Korean priest. He was the son of converts. His father, a farmer, was also martyred. Andrew was baptized when he was 15. He then attended the seminary in Macao, China, 1,300 miles away from home. After six years Andrew returned to Korea and assumed the job of bringing missionaries into the country secretly. Almost immediately he was arrested, tortured, and beheaded.

In a letter written to fellow Christians, Andrew stated, "We have received baptism, entrance into the Church, and the honor of being called Christians. Yet what good will this do us if we are Christians in name only and not in fact?"

CREATE A BULLETIN BOARD

Involve the students in preparing a bulletin board display entitled CHRISTIANS IN DEED! Post the quote of Andrew Kim from the story. Invite the students to add examples of Christians in action. These may include good examples they see at home or school, notices in the parish bulletin, and articles or photos from the community newspaper.

MAKE ACTION PLANS

Divide the class into small groups to discuss: How can we be Christians in fact? Have the groups report their ideas. Then choose one action for the whole class to practice for the day or week.

LIST WAYS TO BUILD UP FAITH

Andrew Kim was 15 years old when he was baptized. Two of the martyrs were only 13 when they died. Have a class discussion about the challenges Christian teenagers face today. Ask the children to think of how they can strengthen their Christian faith now. Make a list on the board.

MAKE POSTERS

The first Christian community in Korea was formed by laypeople. Have the students make posters showing how laypeople contribute to your parish community.

CONSIDER WHAT FAITH REQUIRES

As a young man, Andrew Kim traveled 1,300 miles from home to study to become a priest. Have a group of students locate cities that are 1,300 miles away from your parish. Draw lines or a circle on a map. With the class, talk about the kind of faith it would take for them to go that far away for six years.

LEARN ABOUT KOREAN CULTURE

If you have a Korean community in your parish or neighborhood, invite some of its members to speak about Korean culture—prayers, music, food, art, and so on.

DISCUSS REPRESSION OF RELIGION

Today there are priests in South Korea waiting for permission to minister and evangelize in North Korea. No one knows for sure how many Catholics live there; perhaps there are about 3,000. They were either baptized before the Korean War (1950–1953) or taught by their parents. Discuss with the class what it would be like to live in a society where they had to practice their religion secretly.

Catechist's Notes:

_____

_____

_____

_____

_____

Saint Matthew

(first century)

September 21

Matthew must have been surprised when Jesus walked up to him and said, "Follow me." He probably fell off the stool in his customs booth!

Matthew, also known as Levi, was a tax collector in the town of Capernaum. Most tax collectors were hated by the Jews because they worked for the Romans, who had conquered the land. A tax collector could use his position honestly or dishonestly. The temptation to use the position to become rich was great. Now do you think the choice of Matthew was surprising?

Yet Jesus chose a tax collector to follow him, to learn from him, and to go out and spread the Good News to others. The call from Jesus was more powerful than the call of wealth. Matthew left his work as tax collector. He invited Jesus to a dinner where other tax collectors (publicans) and sinners were gathered. The Pharisees were upset when they saw this, and they said to the disciples, "Why does your teacher eat with tax collectors and sinners?" Jesus heard them and replied, "Those who are well have no need of a physician, but those who are sick. Go and learn what this means, `I desire mercy, not sacrifice.' For I have come to call not the righteous, but sinners." (See Matthew 9:9–13.)

We know nothing other than that about Matthew from the Scriptures, but we do know that Matthew preached the Good News of Christ, and at least part of the Gospel attributed to him was first written for the Jewish converts in Palestine. There is some uncertainty about where Matthew preached and where and how he died. Some say Matthew went to Persia; some say Syria and Greece, while others say Ethiopia.

Yet we can learn much from Matthew. He was a man who knew quite well the power of money. He knew the comfort it could ensure, the recreation it could buy, the luxury it could provide. But he was wise enough to know what it could not do. Money could never give him that sense of peace deep inside. It could never befriend him when he was lonely or give him the strength and courage to go on when all else seemed lost. Money could never buy him forgiveness or love. But the love of Christ could do all this and more.

ACT OUT THE CALL OF MATTHEW

Grades K–5: Have the children read about the call of Matthew (Matthew 9:9–13) and then act out the scene.

ENTHRONE THE BIBLE

Enthrone the Bible, open to the Gospel of Matthew, and read from it.

PRAY FOR BANKERS

Matthew is the patron of bankers. Pray for those who work with money as their occupation, that they may remain honest and keep a sense of priorities in their lives.

BRAINSTORM AND PRAY ABOUT PRIORITIES

Have the students brainstorm a list of important things that money cannot buy. Then invite them to pray that, through the intercession of Saint Matthew, they may never be fooled into thinking that money can provide the most important things in life, and they will always remember that God will provide all they really need.

SHARE RICHES WITH THE POOR

Decide on a way to share some riches with the poor: collect money for the missions, sponsor a canned goods drive for the hungry, seek donations of clothes and toys for a thrift shop or other group serving the poor.

LOCATE CAPERNAUM

Have the students find Capernaum on a map.

BIBLE STUDY

It is believed that the Gospel of Matthew was written between A.D. 80 and 90. It was written to show that Jesus was the Messiah, the Savior-King foretold by the prophets. In the Gospel of Matthew, there are almost more Old Testament references than in all the other Gospels combined. If there is a Scripture study group in the parish, invite the members in to share what they have learned about the Gospel of Matthew. Have the students look through the Gospel for its Old Testament references.

MAKE SYMBOL BANNERS

There are several symbols for Matthew. Explain them to the students. Then have the students design a banner or cloth for their prayer table.

Symbols for Matthew:

a man: represents the Gospel of Matthew, which begins with Jesus' genealogy, his human family line

seated at a desk: represents Matthew as an author of the Gospel

holding a money box and/or eyeglasses: represents his life as tax collector and reader of account books

Catechist's Notes:

_____

_____

_____

_____

Saint Pio of Pietrelcino (Padre Pio)   September 23

(1887–1968)

The man who would become known as Padre Pio was born in Italy on May 25, 1887, the child of farm workers. He was baptized in the village church the next day and given the name Francesco. Even as a child he knew he wanted to become a priest. When he was 12 years old, he was confirmed and made his first Holy Communion. Three years later he entered the Capuchin Friars, a branch of the Franciscan order, and took the name *Fra Pio* (Brother Pius). In 1910 he achieved his childhood desire and was ordained a priest.

Padre Pio stayed at home with his family for the first six years after his ordination because his lungs were weak and he was in poor health. In 1916 he entered the friary of San Giovanni Rotondo, where he spent the rest of his life.

Shortly after he celebrated his first Mass in 1918, Padre Pio began to experience unusual pains in his hands and feet—pains that corresponded to the wounds suffered by Jesus when he was nailed to the cross. Eventually wounds appeared and Pio's hands and feet began to bleed, and did so for the rest of his life. Wounds of this type are called *stigmata*.

Padre Pio was very devout and spent a great deal of time in prayer, particularly in preparation for celebrating Mass. Feeling that his spirituality brought them closer to God, large crowds of people flocked to attend his Masses, which often lasted as long as two hours.

Great numbers of people also wanted Padre Pio to hear their confessions, and he spent many hours each day doing so. Those who came to him for the Sacrament of Penance said they found great peace in their hearts afterwards.

Padre Pio devoted his life to loving God and helping others to do so. He showed a special concern for the poor, the suffering, and the sick. He opened a 20-bed hospital in 1925. In 1940, with the assistance of Maria Pyle, a wealthy American woman, he began planning to establish a new and much larger hospital near San Giovanni Rotondo. The project was delayed for several years during World War II, but eventually the House for the Relief of Suffering opened. It still serves the poor and suffering.

In declining health at the end of his life, Padre Pio began speaking to his followers over the radio. Despite his fame and his many admirers, he felt himself unworthy and often said, "I only want to be a poor friar who prays." His stigmata disappeared when he celebrated his last Mass, and he died on the following day, September 23, 1968. Padre Pio was beatified by Pope John Paul II in May 1999 and canonized in June 2002. One of his memorable sayings was "Pray, hope, and don't worry."

BRIGHTEN THE LIVES OF HOSPITAL PATIENTS

Padre Pio devoted a great deal of time and effort to serving the sick and suffering. Discuss what students can do to brighten the lives of patients in a nearby hospital or nursing home. Carry out a project such as making prayer cards or tray favors that can be delivered with patients' meals.

LEARN HOW THE MASS HAS CHANGED SINCE VATICAN II

It is evident that Padre Pio had a great love for the Mass. During his lifetime Padre Pio saw Vatican Council II (1962–1965) bring about changes in the way Mass is celebrated. Have students research on line or ask older relatives about the changes that have been made since the council.

EMPHASIZE PRAYERFUL PREPARATION FOR SACRAMENTS

People revered Padre Pio for the amount of time he spent in prayer because they felt his closeness to God added to the meaningfulness of the sacraments he administered. Talk about ways students can make a quiet time to prepare themselves before receiving the Sacraments of Penance or the Eucharist.

RESEARCH SAINT FRANCIS

Padre Pio was a Franciscan priest who embraced the ways of Saint Francis of Assisi (feast day October 4, page 45). Have students research the life of Saint Francis and write a paper telling what they think it was about Francis's life and mission that attracted Padre Pio to follow in his footsteps.

LEARN ABOUT THE CAPUCHIN FRIARS

Encourage students to find out more about the Capuchin Friars, using the Internet or such print resources as the *New Catholic Encyclopedia*. Pose questions such as: Where are the Capuchin Friars located today? How do they live? What is the focus of their work? Schedule a time for the students to report their findings to the class.

Catechist's Notes:

_____

_____

_____

_____

_____

_____

_____

_____

Saints Cosmas and Damian

September 26

(early 300s)

There are some saints of whom we know very little. People from all over the world may honor them. Shrines and churches may be built in their names. But the facts and details of their lives have faded from our memories or their stories may never have been recorded.

Cosmas and Damian are saints like these. Little is known about them except that they suffered martyrdom for their faith in Syria sometime during the persecutions of Diocletian (around 303). We may never know exactly what happened, but we do know that their witness to the faith was so strong that people turned to them for prayerful help and passed their story on to others.

Legends about these two saints abound. According to these stories, Cosmas and Damian were twin brothers, born in Arabia, who went to Syria to study and practice medicine. But they were concerned about more than healing bodies. They brought their belief in Christ to those to whom they ministered. Not only that, but they also served people without charging any fees. Lysias, the governor of Celicia, heard about these

two brothers and he summoned them before him. When Cosmas and Damian proclaimed they were Christians, Lysias had them tortured and finally beheaded. Devotion to these two brothers grew, and many cures were said to have been worked through their intercessions. Later a church in their honor was constructed over the site of their burial. When the Emperor Justinian was sick, he prayed to Saints Cosmas and Damian for a cure. Out of gratitude for receiving this favor, he enlarged the city of Cyr and its church. Numerous other churches were erected for them at Constantinople and Rome. Their names are also included in the First Eucharistic Prayer.

If so little about these saints is actually known, why do we honor them? Part of the answer can be found in tradition. When so many believers continue to honor the memory of martyrs, year after year and all over the world, there is good reason to believe that their lives were true witnesses to the Gospel. People who live and die according to their convictions and faith give hope to the world long after their deaths. Their lives can inspire us and encourage us to be faithful during our little trials and sorrows.

PRAY FOR MEDICAL PROFESSIONALS

Along with Saint Luke, Saints Cosmas and Damian are the patrons of doctors, surgeons, and pharmacists. Lead the students in prayer for all those in the medical profession and those who minister to others in time of sickness.

STUDY ART MASTERPIECES

The stories about Cosmas and Damian have inspired many artists through the centuries. Check local art museums and libraries for possible reprints of these pictures (e.g., one painted by Fra Angelico). Have the children draw pictures of themselves helping people.

MAKE UP TITLES

Cosmas and Damian have been given the name "the moneyless ones" because they did not charge any fee to their patients. Have the students think of some word or phrase by which they would like others to remember them. Have them write this title and why they chose it in their journals. Encourage the students to live up to their ideals.

RESEARCH SAINTS

Ask the students to read the First Eucharistic Prayer and note the saints listed there. Have them each choose one of the saints on whom to research and report.

TALK ABOUT FAMILY SUPPORT

Cosmas and Damian were brothers. Discuss with the students how family support can help them live their faith.

Catechist's Notes:

_____

_____

_____

_____

_____

_____

_____

_____

_____

Saint Vincent de Paul   September 27

(1581–1660)

How much difference can one person make? When you hear the story of Saint Vincent de Paul, you know the answer. One person can make a lot of difference.

Vincent organized charitable groups to provide food and clothing for the poor, started a congregation of priests, helped begin another congregation for women, opened hospitals and homes for orphans and for the aged, established training programs and retreats for seminarians, raised money for the victims of war, and sent missionaries to other countries—just to name a few of his projects!

Vincent did not plan on a life of service and self-sacrifice, but rather on one of security and ease. He grew up in France, the son of peasant farmers. The life of a priest was more comfortable than that of a farmer, so Vincent studied and was ordained.

Little is known about his activities during the first few years after his ordination. Tradition says that during this time, while onboard a ship, Vincent was seized by pirates and sold into slavery in North Africa. Eventually he escaped and made his way to Rome. He returned home to France, and there he was appointed court chaplain to Queen Margaret of Valois. He seemed well on the

way to the life of wealth and comfort. But at the same time, he came to know Pierre de Berulle, who later became a cardinal. Berulle helped Vincent understand more deeply what it meant to be a true Christian. Vincent came face-to-face with himself and his empty goals.

As he became more aware of God's love and his call to serve, Vincent changed the direction of his life. He worked for a year in a small parish in a peasant area and saw how poor the people were. So he organized groups of people who would provide food and clothing for the poor on a regular basis. But Vincent saw another kind of poverty, a spiritual poverty. Many of the people had no real understanding of their faith. So Vincent organized priests who would go out and preach to the people. Eventually this group of priests became the Congregation of the Mission, also known as the Vincentian Fathers.

As Vincent saw the needs of others, he reached out to them. At night he would search the city for abandoned babies, and he founded homes for them. He cared for the prisoners who had been made slaves on the galley ships. He remained good friends with many rich and influential people and involved them in his work with the poor and needy. Vincent de Paul is the patron of all charitable societies.

INTERVIEW PEOPLE WHO SERVE OTHERS

Sometimes we need the help of others to see the needs of those around us. Have the students interview representatives of service agencies in your parish or community about the work they do.

WRITE LETTERS

It is said that Vincent de Paul wrote more than 3,000 letters. Discuss with the students how much good can be done through letter writing (to relatives, to people who need encouragement and care, to newspaper editors). Have the students make cards or write letters to people they know who are sick or lonely, to people in a nearby nursing home, or to policy makers in defense of the poor and in support of programs for the needy.

INVITE SPEAKERS

Vincent de Paul founded two congregations: the Congregation of the Missions (Vincentians) and the Sisters of Charity. If possible, invite members of these communities in for a firsthand presentation of their ministry.

LEARN ABOUT THE ST. VINCENT DE PAUL SOCIETY

Research the St. Vincent de Paul Society, founded in 1833 by Frederic Ozanam. Invite a member of the society to tell the class how it serves the needy. Or visit the local St. Vincent de Paul Society. Have someone explain the purpose of the organization and where and how it distributes goods to the poor.

CELEBRATE GRANDPARENTS DAY

Vincent loved the aged. He never wanted them to be lonely. Have a "Grandparents Day." Let each person in the class invite an elderly friend or relative to class. Have games and activities in which all can share.

MAKE PENNANTS

Vincent's life was the Gospel alive! Find Scripture passages that match some of Vincent's charitable works. Have the students make pennants of these passages and hang them in the school or parish hall.

Catechist's Notes:

_____

_____

_____

_____

_____

_____

_____

Saint Wenceslaus
(907–935)

September 28

A king, a jealous brother, and a plotting mother—it sounds like a fairy tale or a movie plot, doesn't it? But all are part of the life of Saint Wenceslaus. His father, the ruler of Bohemia, was killed in battle when Wenceslaus was young. This left the kingdom in the hands of his mother, who sided with the anti-Christian leaders. Wenceslaus's Christian grandmother, Ludmilla, took over the education of her grandson. Ludmilla was determined that Wenceslaus would be a Christian and that he, rather than his mother, would rule the country. But the grandmother was never to see one part of her dream come true. Some pagan nobles had Ludmilla killed by the time Wenceslaus was ready to assume the throne. Yet Ludmilla had done her work well, and Wenceslaus became a well-educated Christian ruler.

Wenceslaus first made peace with his mother so that he could govern a unified country. He worked in close cooperation with the Church, ended the persecution of the Christians, brought back exiled priests, and built churches. As king, Wenceslaus set an example all could follow. People called him the "Good King" of Bohemia.

He gave alms, was just to rich and poor, visited prisoners, and promoted the religious and educational improvement of his people.

Making peace with the king of the German empire caused opposition. Some of the nobles grew restless and angry because they were ruled by a Christian king. Boleslaus, the brother of Wenceslaus, was jealous that Wenceslaus was king. Taking advantage of the feelings of vengeful nobles, Boleslaus invited Wenceslaus to celebrate with him at a banquet on the feast of Saints Cosmas and Damian. The next morning as Wenceslaus was on his way to Mass, Boleslaus hit him. As they struggled, the friends of Boleslaus ran up and killed Wenceslaus at the chapel door. Before he died Wenceslaus asked God's mercy for his brother. Wenceslaus was recognized as a martyr and proclaimed patron of Bohemia, which is now part of the Czech Republic. His picture was engraved on coins, and the crown of Wenceslaus was regarded as a symbol of Czech nationalism and independence. His life shines as a brilliant example of love of one's country and one's neighbor.

ACTIVITIES

WRITE THANK-YOU NOTES

Ludmilla, Wenceslaus's grandmother, was responsible for his faith. She passed on an outstanding example of Christian life. Suggest that each student write a thank-you note to a person who influenced his or her growth in faith.

LISTEN TO THE CHRISTMAS CAROL AND ADD VERSES

Have the students read or listen to the Christmas carol, "Good King Wenceslaus." You can make copies, using the blackline master on page 438. Talk about the story it tells. What does it say about Wenceslaus's political and Christian life? Why is Saint Wenceslaus associated with Christmas? (The feast of Stephen is December 26.) Invite the children to sing the carol, then to add extra verses about their own Christian witness.

RESEARCH BOHEMIAN CUSTOMS

Let the students research Bohemian Christian customs and explain these to the class. Have them share national or ethnic customs that their families celebrate.

PRAY FOR PEACE

Wenceslaus was a man of peace. Have the students write petitions for peace for their nation, their families, the class, and for inner peace. Invite them to offer their petitions as a class prayer today.

SHARE A SIGN OF PEACE

Wenceslaus wanted to heal the bitter disputes of his people. Have the students reflect on the sign of peace that is given in the Eucharistic liturgy. Ask what it means to them. Ask if they are uncomfortable doing this with a family member or classmate who has hurt them. Add a sign of peace to the class prayer.

Catechist's Notes:

_____

_____

_____

_____

_____

_____

_____

Saint Lorenzo Ruiz and Companions

September 28

(d. 1637)

Lorenzo Ruiz was a man who would have died a thousand times for Christ. Lorenzo's father was Chinese and his mother was Filipino. The family lived in the Chinese section of Manila, in the Philippines. Lorenzo learned Spanish from the Dominicans, for whom he served as altar boy and sacristan. He became a professional calligrapher, writing out documents in beautiful penmanship and recording baptismal, confirmation, and marriage documents in the official books. He also became an active member of the Confraternity of the Holy Rosary and prayed the mysteries of the Rosary each week.

Lorenzo married and became the father of two sons and a daughter. In 1636 the police were looking for Lorenzo because he was thought to have taken part in a murder. To avoid arrest, Lorenzo joined a missionary group of three Dominican priests, another priest, and a layman. Only on the ship did he learn the group was headed for Japan, where Catholics were being persecuted.

In Japan the six men were arrested. After being imprisoned for a year, they were sent to Nagasaki to be tried. Before the Japanese judges, Lorenzo declared, "I am a Christian. I shall die for God, and for God I would give many thousands of lives." As the faithful Christians were tortured, they encouraged one another to be strong. At one point Lorenzo asked whether by giving up the faith he would be freed. When he received no direct answer, his faith grew stronger.

Lorenzo and 15 others were martyred in or near Nagasaki, Japan. The group included two other laymen, two consecrated women, two brothers, and nine priests. Nine were Japanese, four were Spaniards, one was Italian, and one was French. In 1987 they were canonized with 10 others who spread the faith in Japan, the Philippines, and Taiwan.

Lorenzo Ruiz is the first Filipino to be canonized. At the canonization in 1987, Pope John Paul II called him "an improbable saint." Lorenzo shows that you never know where your life is going to lead you. But you do know that you can always follow Christ.

LOCATE COUNTRIES ON A MAP

Have the students locate China, the Philippines, and Japan on a map and explain how each is part of the story of Saint Lorenzo.

TALK ABOUT FAITH

Discuss why some people give up the faith today and what it takes to keep it.

PRINT STATEMENTS OF FAITH

Have the students write or print Lorenzo's statement of faith in their best penmanship.

Or let them choose a type font and print out the quote or their own statement of faith. Provide construction paper and poster board so they can frame their quotes.

DESIGN POSTAGE STAMPS

Have the students do some research on the history of the Church or religious customs in the Philippines. Then have them design postage stamps showing the most interesting thing they learned.

Catechist's Notes:

_____

_____

_____

_____

_____

_____

_____

_____

_____

_____

_____

_____

Saints Michael, Gabriel, and Raphael (Archangels) September 29

God has numerous ways to show his loving concern for us. One of these is through the angels. God has sent angels to intervene in people's lives when they need protection on their way to heaven. The archangels, Michael, Gabriel, and Raphael, are three such messengers.

In art St. Michael is usually pictured as youthful, strong, clothed in armor, and wearing sandals. Biblical accounts of Michael present him as a mighty leader bringing justice and strength. The Book of Daniel describes him as a heavenly prince who stands guard over God's people, helping the Israelites return from their Persian captivity. Michael, whose name means "Who is like God?" is the principal fighter in the battle against Lucifer, or Satan, as related in the Book of Revelation. The early Christians of the second century took courage from these accounts. They believed that Michael's intercession was powerful in rescuing souls from hell. In the fourth century, Emperor Constantine built a church to honor Michael.

Art depicting Gabriel most often shows him as communicating God's message. Biblically he is portrayed in three events as a messenger. In the first he explains to Daniel a vision he had concerning the Messiah. Another time Gabriel comes to Zachary, who is burning incense in the temple, and tells him that John the Baptist will be born. But most people associate Gabriel with the Annunciation and his message to Mary of the birth of Jesus. Gabriel's name means "Strength of God."

The archangel Raphael is pictured as the traveling companion of a young man, Tobiah, who is carrying a fish! A blind man named Tobit sends his son Tobiah on a journey to collect a debt. He asks Raphael (they don't know he is an angel) to be the young man's companion and guide. After an adventure-filled journey, Tobiah collects the debt, finds a bride, and restores Tobit's sight with the fish's gall. You can read the whole exciting story in the Book of Tobit in the Old Testament.

Tobit's family credits the success of the journey and the healing to the presence of Raphael. When they offer Raphael a reward, he announces who he is: "I am Raphael, one of the seven angels who stand ready and enter before the glory of the Lord" (Tobit 12:15). Since it was through Raphael that Tobit was cured of his blindness, the angel's name means "God's healing" or "God has healed."

Because the archangels are very close to God, the Church urges people to pray to them to help them in their needs. In times of temptation, people pray to Michael; to know and carry out God's will, you can call on Gabriel; and travelers and those seeking healing turn to Raphael. In a mysterious and powerful way, the angels protect the Church and her people. They assure us that God cares for and is with us.

LEARN THE PRAYER TO SAINT MICHAEL

Acquaint the students with the Prayer to Saint Michael. You may make copies using the blackline master on page 439. Pray it at the end of class today. Point out to the students that it is a good prayer to know in times of temptation.

READ ABOUT GABRIEL IN SCRIPTURE

Gabriel is the patron of post offices and telephone and telegraph workers because he is God's messenger. Have the students read the accounts in Scripture that record Gabriel's messages and write a statement telling what they were (Daniel 8:15–26 and 9:21–27; Luke 1:11–20; Luke 1:28–38).

WRITE IN JOURNALS ABOUT LIVING FAITH

Raphael brought healing to Tobit's blindness. Explain to the students that we have the ability to see physically and we have the inner ability to see called "insight." Our faith is a kind of insight. Through faith in Christ, we can find real meaning in our lives. Suggest that the students write in their journals things they did today, because of their faith, to help people feel happier.

TALK ABOUT WAYS GOD SENDS MESSAGES

Point out that even though an angel may not appear to us, there are other ways in which God reveals his messages. Ask the students to each write down three of these ways. Then have them share their ideas with a partner.

DO A CROSSWORD PUZZLE

Have the students read or listen to the account about the archangels. Then let them complete a crossword puzzle to see how well they "got the message." Use the blackline master on page 440.

Answers:

Down: 1. Gabriel; 2. Michael; 4. guide; 6. Mary

Across: 3. guardian; 5. Raphael; 7. archangel; 8. Lucifer

LEARN THE MEANING OF NAMES

Each archangel has a name that fits the mission God gave to him. Have the students look up the meaning of their names and relate them to their life or the way they live their faith. Let them tell the others whether they feel their names express their goals and why. You may wish to provide several baby name books from your public library or have the students do research on line. Two books that may help the students discover the Christian meanings of their names are *A Saint for Your Name: Saints for Girls* and *A Saint for Your Name: Saints for Boys* by Albert J. Nevins, M.M., revised and updated by Ann Ball (Our Sunday Visitor, Inc., 200 Noll Plaza, Huntington, IN 46750).

Catechist's Notes:

_____

_____

_____

Saint Jerome

(c. 340–420)

September 30

D o you think you could ever read the whole Bible? How about writing it out—no, not using a computer—with a pen? How long do you think that would take? Saint Jerome did even more. He translated the whole Bible and wrote it out by hand.

Jerome was born in the Roman province of Dalmatia, in the country that is today Croatia. His Christian family was able to send him to Rome at age 12 for a good education. He studied there until he was 20. When he wasn't studying, he enjoyed the spectacles, games, and amusements of Rome. What kept Jerome close to his faith were the frequent visits he made to the catacombs. In his heart was born the desire to imitate the spirit of the holy martyrs. He took his religion seriously and was baptized at age 19—not an uncommon age for Baptism at that time.

When Jerome's studies were over, he followed his desire to live a penitential life. He and several friends lived in a little monastery for three years. Jerome then set out for Palestine, but when he reached Antioch he fell seriously ill. Then Jerome tried living as a monk in the desert. But impure temptations plagued him. To fight off temptation, he studied Hebrew, wrote letters to his friends counseling them in the spiritual life, and copied books by hand.

Eventually Jerome left the desert and moved to Constantinople. He continued his education by studying Scripture under the Greek theologian and preacher Gregory Nazianzen. Jerome liked the sophisticated city and the work. Soon Pope Damasus noticed Jerome's talents and summoned him to Rome to be a papal secretary. The pope also knew about Jerome's love of Scripture, so he commissioned him to translate the Bible from Hebrew and Greek into Latin. Jerome was just the man to do this because he had great knowledge and self-discipline. This was a long, exhausting work. It took him—how many years did you guess—30 years! His translation became the official text of the Catholic Church.

Jerome also guided a group of Christian widows: Paula, Marcella, Eustochium among them, who were practicing a semimonastic life. He gave them lectures on the Scriptures and advised them in their spiritual lives. Some people considered it scandalous that he spent so much time with women. This gossip led Jerome to move these women to Bethlehem. Here Jerome trained Paula and Eustochium to become Scripture scholars, and they assisted him in his research. He continued to write commentaries on the Scriptures.

Jerome sounds like a saint, doesn't he? But you haven't heard the whole story. Jerome's cross was his temperament. He was strong willed and quick tempered. His writings were sometimes explosive. His temper made him enemies wherever he went. His acid pen condemned the rich and reprimanded the lax clergy. He sometimes made biting comments about marriage. To conquer his faults, Jerome prayed and did penance. And he did indeed become a great saint.

DO HOMEWORK WELL

Emphasize that it took Jerome 30 years to translate the Bible, and he did it all by hand. Encourage the students to do their homework this week with the patience and dedication of Saint Jerome.

HONOR THE BIBLE

Jerome reverenced the Word of God. Enthrone the Bible in your classroom. Place candles by it. Take time to read the Bible prayerfully each day.

PROCLAIM SCRIPTURE

It is important for children to learn to proclaim the Scripture effectively. Direct them to find a short passage of the Gospels they like and practice reading it clearly and distinctly. Give each a turn to proclaim the Good News to the class.

MEMORIZE SCRIPTURE

Jerome wanted the Bible to be read by everyone. Have the students memorize a Scripture passage today. Some suggestions are listed below.

Luke 6:37–38	Luke 9:23–25
Luke 6:43–45	Luke 11:9–10

LEARN ABOUT WOMEN IN MINISTRY

Jerome trained women to study Scripture. Some people of his time felt very strongly that women were not capable of being educated. Have the students discover what ministries women may perform in the Church now.

DISCUSS THE IMPORTANCE OF READING THE BIBLE

Tell the students that Jerome's translation was known as the *Vulgate* because it was written in Latin, the common language of the people. Talk about why it would be important for ordinary people to be able to read the Scriptures.

LEARN ABOUT VARIOUS BIBLE TRANSLATIONS

Today there are many translations of the Bible. Have the students find out which translation they use in class and what other translations are available. Have them find out if these modern translations are by a single person, as Jerome's was.

Catechist's Notes:

_____

_____

_____

_____

_____

_____

Saint Thérèse of Lisieux
October 1
(1873–1897)

Thérèse Martin never traveled far from home, never was awarded a medal, never built a hospital, never started a religious community. Yet her autobiography, *The Story of a Soul*, was translated into 35 languages and read by millions. Why was this young woman so popular?

Thérèse proved that we can become saints by doing ordinary things extraordinarily well. She explained "I want to seek a way to heaven, a new way, very short, very straight—the way of trust and self-surrender. . . . I am a very little soul, who can offer only little things to Our Lord."

Thérèse set an example everyone could follow because there was nothing unusual about her life. She was born into a loving and devout middle-class family in France. Her father was a watchmaker, and her mother was a lace maker. Her mother died when Thérèse was four, so Thérèse was raised by her four older sisters. Thérèse had a special place in her father's heart. He called her "my little queen." He would take her fishing with him. Seated on a hill, looking at the beauty of the sky and the meadow, she would pray.

By the time Thérèse was 14, two of her sisters had entered the Carmelite convent in Lisieux. Thérèse also decided to become a nun, and she did not want to wait. Priests and the bishop told Thérèse that she was too young to make such a commitment. But Thérèse was so determined that during an audience with the pope she made a scene, blurting out her request. In the end the bishop let her enter the convent when she was 15.

Thérèse prayed and did the most ordinary tasks of Carmelite life. Her jobs were scrubbing floors, washing dishes, setting the tables, sewing, dusting, and cooking. She helped care for the sick when a flu epidemic spread through the convent.

Thérèse set out to be a saint by what she called the "Little Way." She decided to do every act, even picking up a pin, for love of God. It is not easy to avoid complaining or criticizing, to smile when blamed, and to offer up the dullness of routine. But Thérèse did these things to show her love for Jesus. Hers was a simple way of saying yes to God by doing daily duties well.

Through her autobiography people came to learn about Thérèse's little way. It reveals her struggles and her tremendous love of God. Thérèse's greatest gifts were concentration, which helped her grow in prayer; and determination, which helped build her character. Her crosses were shyness, sensitiveness, and stubbornness.

Thérèse said, "My vocation is love." The Carmalite sisters were not perfect, but she loved them as she loved Christ. This took much faith and sacrifice. Thérèse also loved the Church. She could not go to the missions as she desired, but she offered up her sufferings for missionaries. After intense suffering from tuberculosis, Thérèse died when she was 24. Her last words were "My God, I love you." In 1997 she was declared a Doctor of the Church. In 2002 her relics were taken to countries like Iraq on a peace pilgrimage.

LEARN THE LITTLE WAY OF LOVE

Grades K–2: Sing to the tune of "Here We Go 'Round the Mulberry Bush." This is the way we [sing and do everyday actions], all for the love of Jesus. Examples: wait our turn, smile at you, say our prayers, pass our papers.

Grades 3–8: Have students print "My Way to God" vertically, and then use the letters to list 10 little things they will do to grow closer to God each day.

MAKE FLOWERS

Thérèse is often called "The Little Flower." Her acts of love were like little flowers that she planted in God's garden. Give each child a small strip of paper. Ask the children to write on their papers one act of love they have done or will do today. Have each child wrap his or her paper inside a small square of tissue paper and twist it to make a flower. Secure the flowers with green pipe cleaner stems. Invite the children to place their flowers in a vase on their prayer table.

PRAY TO SAINT THÉRÈSE

Thérèse is usually pictured carrying a bouquet of roses. Shortly before she died, she promised "I will spend my heaven doing good on earth. I will let fall from heaven a shower of roses." Have the children cut pictures of beautiful roses out of gardening catalogs or magazines. On the back let them write prayer petitions (back the pictures with plain white paper if necessary). Scatter the roses on the prayer table.

SEE PICTURES OF SAINT THÉRÈSE

Show the class the portrait of Thérèse painted by her sister Celine or photographs of Thérèse.

PRAY FOR MISSIONARIES AND PRIESTS

- Saint Thérèse is Patroness of the Missions because she prayed and offered sacrifices for missionaries. Ask the students to think of ways they can make sacrifices for the missions today.

- Thérèse also had a great interest in praying for priests. Encourage the students to pray for their parish priests and to make a point of greeting them after Sunday Mass.

PLAN FAMILY TIME

Thérèse's family taught her about love. Help the children think about ways they can build up love in their own families: working together to help others, doing house chores together, having fun together, sharing a meal that everyone helps to prepare. Encourage each child to make a practical plan to present to his or her family. Remind the children that a family shows love more than it talks about love.

TALK ABOUT THE POWER OF LOVE

Thérèse believed charity that begins at home could have long-range effects. From this point of view, discuss with the students the question: "Can the power of love change the world?"

WRITE IN JOURNALS

The book *The Story of a Soul* is really the story of the spiritual journey of Thérèse. Have the students write in their journals what they want to do for Christ right now to show their love for him.

Guardian Angels

October 2

Here is a riddle for you: *I am always with you, but you never see me. I am not God, but I was created by God. I protect and guide you. Who am I?*

God gave us guardian angels to protect and guide us. Saint Jerome wrote that the human soul is so valuable in heaven that every human person has a guardian angel from the moment the person comes into being. These pure spirits, which we can neither see nor feel, play an important role in our lives. Jesus refers to them when he says, "Take care that you do not despise one of these little ones; for, I tell you, in heaven their angels continually see the face of my Father in heaven" (Matthew 18:10).

Angels are messengers from God. The word *angel* comes from the Greek word for "messenger." In a very real way, these powerful spirits point out to us the ways of God. Guardian angels assist us in work or study. In times of temptation, these spiritual beings direct us to do good. Thomas Aquinas said that angels are the most excellent of creatures because they have the greatest intelligence next to God.

Perhaps the guardian angels are best known for protecting us from physical danger, but their main role is to care for the salvation of our souls. It is wonderful to know that God has promised to love, protect, and be with us always. One way he does this is through the care of the angels. Whenever you meet with danger or discouragement, your guardian angel is your personal, heavenly bodyguard. The angels also offer prayers to God for us. Because angels always see and hear God, they can intercede for us. We should love our guardian angels, respect them, and pray to them.

In early Christianity there was no feast for the guardian angels, just one for the archangels. But in the 15th and 16th centuries, the feast of the Guardian Angels was unofficially celebrated in Austria, Spain, and Portugal. In 1608 Pope Paul V made it a universal feast. In doing so, he helped to make us aware of the guardian angels, not just one day in October, but every day of our lives.

LEARN A PRAYER TO YOUR GUARDIAN ANGEL

There are many prayers written to our guardian angels. Two such prayers may be found on the blackline master on page 441.

WRITE A PRAYER OR POEM

Have the students compose their own prayers or poems to the guardian angels. Use a simple form such as a haiku or cinquain. Display these in the classroom. Select one to pray on the feast of the Guardian Angels.

A haiku is a Japanese form of poetry. It consists of three lines. The first line is made up of five syllables, the second line is made up of seven syllables, and the third line, five syllables.

Example:

> Guardian angel
> coming from heaven to earth
> lead me home to God.

A cinquain is a five-line poem, constructed as follows:

line 1: subject of poem

line 2: two adjectives describing the subject

line 3: three verbs telling what the subject does

line 4: a phrase or sentence about the subject

line 5: another name for the subject

Example:

> Angels
> invisible, heavenly
> guide, protect, help
> a gift from God
> friends

SHARE INSPIRATIONS

It is believed the guardian angels have a way of bringing people together in order to do God's work. Mary is "Queen of Angels." She also brings together people who need each other to work for God. Let students share times in their lives when they have met someone who has done something that has influenced them to serve God.

DESIGN SYMBOLS

In art angels have been pictured as chubby cherubs, stately winged guardians, or curly-haired beings playing harps, but these pictures are merely symbols of beings who are in actuality pure spirits. Have the students design symbols that represent angels, and display these. Students may wish to write scriptural passages under their symbols, or use Scripture to find ideas for their symbols. Suggested references are Psalm 103:20; Psalm 138:1; Matthew 4:11; Matthew 18:10; Luke 9:26; Luke 15:10; Hebrews 13:2.

STUDY GREAT ART

Many great artists, especially during the Renaissance, have painted angels in their works. Bring in a variety of art books and let the students find art masterpieces depicting angels. Ask why they think the artist represented the angels as he did.

SHARE STORIES ABOUT "ANGELS"

Encourage the students to ask their parents to tell them about a time when God took special care of their families. Have each student write out his or her story and bind the stories into a booklet. When students read one another's stories, they will see how carefully God cares for each person.

Blessed Mother Theodore Guerin

(1798–1856)

Today people fly from Paris to New York City on the Concorde in four hours. In 1840 Mother Theodore Guerin left France on July 27. She and five other Sisters of Providence traveled by ship, train, steamboat, canal boat, and horse-drawn carriage. They arrived in Vincennes, Indiana, on October 22. The journey across the ocean took 26 days, going overland and by river another six weeks.

Why did the sisters make this long, difficult journey? The bishop of Vincennes begged the superior of the Sisters of Providence in France to send sisters to open schools and to care for poor sick people. Forty-two-year-old Sister Theodore was chosen to lead the group. When the sisters arrived, they went directly to the log cabin chapel in the deeply forested hills. There Mother Theodore dedicated their mission to Mary, and named it St. Mary-of-the-Woods.

Pioneer life is very hard. The sisters struggled to survive the first winter in a drafty little farmhouse. It was very cold, they were very poor, and food was scarce. They worked hard at learning English. By the following summer, they welcomed their first student. Within a year they opened three schools. Other young women saw the good work they were doing and joined them.

The community dealt with many difficulties. Once a fire destroyed their barn and the harvested crops. They faced prejudice against Catholics, especially Catholic religious women. But they persevered. When Mother Theodore died 16 years after the community was founded, the sisters had many schools, two orphanages, and two pharmacies to dispense free medicines to the poor.

As a girl, Mother Theodore was named Anne-Thérèse. She was home schooled by her mother. Her father was an officer in the French navy. When Anne-Thérèse was 10 years old, she knew that she wanted to be a nun. Anne-Thérèse liked to go to the rocky shore near her home to pray. When she was 15, her father was killed by bandits on his way home. After that, Anne-Thérèse took charge of the house and garden, and cared for her sick mother and younger sister.

She joined the Sisters of Providence when she was 25 years old. For years she taught and received a medal of honor for excellence in teaching. She also studied medicine in order to care for people who could not afford a doctor. Then she was assigned to America. She thought there must be someone else who would be much better suited for the job.

Mother Theodore always told her sisters, "Put yourself gently into the hands of Providence." Mother Theodore Guerin was declared Blessed in 1988. She was the right person for this incredible journey after all.

TAKE A TOUR ONLINE

Have the students go online to see the college that grew from the little farmhouse school—St. Mary-of-the-Woods College *(www.smwc.edu)*. It is an outstanding example of what God can do when a person of faith places herself or himself in the hands of Providence.

DRAW YOUR PRAYER PLACE

Remind the children that when Mother Theodore was a child, she liked to pray on the rocky shore near her home. Ask them to think about their favorite place to pray, and then have each student draw a picture of himself or herself in that place.

MAKE A CHART

Mother Guerin's life had two parts—in France and in America. Yet they were connected by her experience. Have the children work in pairs to make a chart showing how Mother Theodore's life in France prepared her for a successful mission in America.

MAKE UP SKITS

Unlike some educators of her time, Mother Theodore believed in gentle discipline for her students. Ask the children to think of common infractions in the classroom and act out skits showing how they could be corrected with fairness and gentleness.

COLLECT FOR CHARITY

The Sisters of Providence suffered from a fire that destroyed their barn and crops. Help the class organize a collection of household items to donate to an organization that helps families recover from a house fire. Call the project God Provides.

WALK IN HER STEPS

Let the children use their imaginations to act out the journey Mother Theodore and the sisters made to America, their first winter of hardship, and starting a school in the wilderness. Simple props and costumes would add to the fun.

Catechist's Notes:

_____

_____

_____

_____

_____

_____

_____

_____

Saint Francis of Assisi — October 4

(1182–1226)

People who met Francis of Assisi had to notice his enthusiasm and energy, his tendency to give playful pats to a wandering animal, and his grateful acceptance of anything that was offered to him. His warmth and his love for people and nature might have given the impression that Francis knew nothing about discipline or suffering. But this would be a false impression.

The son of a wealthy cloth merchant and a devout, loving mother, Francis enjoyed an easy life. His fun-loving way and sunny personality made him very popular. Francis dreamed of becoming a noble knight who would accomplish fantastic deeds. When Assisi and Perugia were at war, Francis had his chance to be a soldier, a defender of right. But the vicious hatred, the fierce fighting, and the humiliation of being held hostage in prison for a year were not what he had expected. Francis began to look for more purpose in life.

One day while he was praying in an old church, Francis heard a voice say, "Francis, go repair my house which, as you see, is falling into ruin." Impulsively Francis rushed home, grabbed bolts of cloth to sell, and took the money to the priest of the church. But the priest refused the money, and Francis's father was very angry with his son. Francis returned the money, gave up his own expensive clothes, and decided that he would rely on his heavenly Father for all that he needed.

For the next few years, Francis worked by hand to repair the little church. Then one day at Mass he heard a reading from the Gospel that helped him understand that he was called to do three things: to be one with his heavenly Father, to work for the Church, and to become as much like Jesus as possible.

He also realized that he was to rebuild not churches, but the Church. All alone he started traveling from place to place, sleeping on the ground, begging for food, preaching about the Father's loving care and the need everyone has to repent and to turn back to God. He tried to convince the rich to live a simpler lifestyle and to create better conditions for the poor. He offered a sense of dignity and respect to the poor themselves. Francis's gentleness and good humor were contagious. Many men joined him, living in poverty and traveling with him, preaching the Good News. So many came that Francis had to write guidelines for their lives, which received the approval of the pope.

Francis wanted more than anything else to become like Jesus because he loved Jesus so much. He tried to be as poor as Jesus was, as humble as he was, and as compassionate toward those who suffered.

At the end of his life, when he was dying, Francis asked to be laid on the ground so that he might be as close as possible to creation, through which he always met his Creator.

PRAISE GOD THE CREATOR

Because Francis recognized God as Creator of all, he called the earth and all creatures to praise and thank God for his care.

- Make copies of the Canticle of the Sun for your class, using the blackline master on page 442. Divide the students into two groups, and have one group read the opening address for each sentence and the other group read the rest of each sentence.

- Ask the students to write an original canticle of nature based on the form that Francis used, (e.g., Praised be You, Lord, for [name creature] who [name job that creature does]).

- Let the students write or print a section of the canticle of Francis neatly on paper and illustrate it. Post the papers in the room or hallway.

TAKE A NATURE WALK

Francis often contemplated the beauty and wonders of nature. Take the students on a nature walk to view rocks, trees, birds, and bugs as Francis saw them—with reverence and courtesy. Have the students carefully record the sights, sounds, smells, and textures that they find. When you return to the classroom, ask each child to write a resolution to respect all life.

LEARN ABOUT FRANCIS AND THE CRÈCHE

To help the poor understand the great love that Jesus has for them, Francis decided to make a life-size scene of the Christmas crib, using real people and real animals. Let the students do research to find the answers to these questions:

1. What is the story connected with Francis's starting the Christmas crib?

2. How did the people respond to his new idea? How do people respond to the crèche, or Nativity scene, today?

3. How have different countries in the world adapted Francis's idea during the Christmas season?

LIST WAYS TO BUILD UP THE CHURCH

At first Francis thought God wanted him to rebuild church buildings. Then he came to realize that God had chosen him to renew the Church, which is the people of God. Direct the students to make a list of ways they can help the parish community. They may want to begin their list with the idea of praying for the parish.

FIND OUT ABOUT FRANCISCANS

So many people wanted to join Francis's way of following Jesus that he founded three orders: The Friars Minor (little brothers); the Poor Clares for religious women; and the Third Order secular for laypersons. Since his time, many Franciscan orders have developed.

- Have interested students make a list of Franciscan orders and find out how each follows the spirit of Saint Francis.

- Invite a member of a local Franciscan group to speak to the class about the spirit of Saint Francis.

PRAY AS FRANCIS DID

When someone asked for his prayers, Francis would pray immediately so that he would not forget about it. Ask the students to think of someone for whom they promised to pray or for whom they should pray for. Take time *right now* to pray for these people.

PROCLAIM THE GOSPEL

The Gospel reading that changed Francis's life was Matthew 10:7–13. Proclaim this passage and discuss with the students how Francis followed Jesus' directions.

Saint Faustina Kowalska

October 5

(1905–1938)

Saint Faustina was born in the 20th century, and canonized in the year 2000. Jesus chose her to deliver to the modern world a message as old as eternity. It is the message of his love for all people, especially sinners. Jesus said to Faustina, "Today I am sending you with my mercy to the people of the whole world." It is his desire to heal the aching world, to draw all people into his merciful heart of love.

On February 22, 1931, Jesus appeared to Faustina as the King of Divine Mercy. He asked her to have a picture painted of him as she saw him—clothed in white, with red and white rays of light streaming from his heart. The rays represent the blood and water that flowed from the side of Jesus on the cross. Under the image are the words, "Jesus, I trust in you."

Many people did not believe Faustina at first. The sisters in her own convent thought that Jesus could not possibly have selected her for this great favor. After all, she was an uneducated peasant girl. Her superiors often refused to give her permission to carry out Jesus' requests. Church theologians, too, doubted her word. Jesus told Faustina that he loved her obedience and that his will would be done in the end.

In June 1934 an artist completed the painting of the Divine Mercy according to her instructions; and it soon became a focus for devotion.

Faustina continued to record in her diary the appearances of Jesus. The diary was translated into English and published in 1987 with the title *Divine Mercy in My Soul.*

Faustina, baptized Helena, had grown up in a poor Polish family of 10 children. When she was 15 years old, she quit school in order to work as a housemaid to help support her family. By the time she was 18, she was sure that God was calling her to a religious life, but her parents objected. So she tried to put it out of her mind. But one night, while the lively polka music was playing at a village dance, Helena saw Jesus, sad and suffering. The very next day she packed a small bag and went to the capital city of Warsaw to join the Sisters of Our Lady of Mercy. There she received the name Sister Mary Faustina.

About 10 years later, Faustina contracted tuberculosis. Soon she was too weak to manage the heavy gardening assigned to her. So she was given the job of gatekeeper. She was able to show mercy to the poor people who came to the convent looking for food. Once Jesus came to the door as a poor young man. After he had eaten the soup and bread Faustina gave him, she recognized him. Jesus told her he had come to experience with great joy her tender love and mercy.

Faustina was canonized by the first Polish pope, John Paul II, on April 30, 2000. The first Sunday after Easter was declared Divine Mercy Sunday.

MAKE A PLAQUE

Have each student make a small plaque with the prayer, "Jesus, I trust in you," to hang in his or her bedroom. Talk about the idea that mercy is what Jesus offers. Trust in his mercy is what he asks of us.

MAKE A JOURNAL ENTRY

Ask the students to recall times when they have been misunderstood or discredited. Have them each write a short journal entry about the experience and conclude with a prayer of trust in Jesus.

OBEY CHEERFULLY

Faustina's obedience was prized by Jesus. Ask the children to follow her example today by obeying their parents and teachers cheerfully.

OFFER TO DO CHORES

Faustina worked as a housekeeper, as a helper in the convent kitchen and garden, and as the gatekeeper. Suggest that the children volunteer to do chores at home or around the school or parish.

MAKE A MERCY WHEEL

The message Jesus wanted Faustina to spread was about God's mercy, but also about the mercy we must show to every human being. He told Faustina that mercy toward others is unquestionable proof of love for him. Jesus gave Faustina three ways of showing mercy toward neighbors: by deed, by word, and by prayer. Discuss these ways of reflecting Jesus' mercy. On the board draw a mercy wheel that is divided into three segments: Deed, Word, Prayer. Have the students suggest specific ways that they can bring mercy to others.

ROLE-PLAY

Let the children act out the scene of Jesus coming to the gate as a poor man to ask Sister Faustina for food. Then have them role-play ways Jesus could come to *them* for help. How would they respond?

COLLECT CLOTHING FOR THE POOR

When Faustina was growing up, her family was so poor that she and her sisters had only one "good" dress among them, which they each had to wear to Mass on Sunday. One girl went to early Mass, came home, and gave the dress to her sister, who wore it to the next Mass, and so on. Organize a collection of clothing for the poor. Suggest that students and their families go through their closets and drawers and bring in clothing they have outgrown or no longer wear. Donate the clothing to the St. Vincent de Paul Society or to a shelter for homeless families.

WRITE PRAYERS OF PETITION

Have the students write prayers of petition for the needs of the children and their families, the school or parish, the Church, the country, and the world. Use the prayers "Lord, have mercy" and "Christ, have mercy" as the responses.

Blessed Marie-Rose Durocher

October 6

(1811–1849)

Have you ever been told you couldn't do something that you really wanted to do?

Marie-Rose Durocher found a way to do what she felt called to do. Of course, God was on her side.

Marie-Rose was named Eulalie when she was born in a village near Montreal, Canada. She was the youngest of 10 children. As she grew up, she wanted to become a religious sister. When she was 16, she went to a convent boarding school, but after a long illness she was not permitted to become a sister because her health was too poor. When Marie-Rose was 18, she went to work in the parish where one of her brothers was a priest. For 13 years she was the rectory housekeeper and hostess. Her goodness showed in the many works of charity she did in the parish so that people began to call her "the saint of Beloeil."

Marie-Rose had had a good education, and so both her spiritual director and the bishop of Montreal encouraged her to found a community of sisters to teach in schools. But Marie-Rose was concerned about the education of poor girls who could not afford to go to school. With two friends, she began a boarding school for 13 girls. In 1843 they founded the Sisters of the Holy Names of Jesus and Mary. Marie-Rose's order was devoted to religious education for the poorest children.

Mother Marie-Rose guided the sisters for six years before she died of tuberculosis on her 38th birthday. She had to deal with poverty, continuing illness, and the difficulties of a new endeavor. But she also had the happiness of accepting many women to share her work and of seeing the children prosper. Her great love for Jesus crucified gave her strength.

Marie-Rose Durocher was beatified in 1982. The Sisters of the Holy Names of Jesus and Mary began a mission in Oregon in 1959 and now work in Canada, the United States, Brazil, Peru, Haiti, and South Africa. They are dedicated to education in faith and are especially concerned for poor and disadvantaged children.

ACTIVITIES

BRAINSTORM WAYS TO SERVE

Have the students brainstorm ways people their age can serve their families, schools, and parish, especially in ways that don't make a big splash. Encourage them to each choose one idea to complete.

ILLUSTRATE THEIR OWN STORY OF FAITH

Have the children draw storyboards or illustrated time lines to tell the story of how they have learned about their faith.

DISCUSS WAYS TO LEARN MORE

Organize the students in small groups to discuss ways they can learn more about the Catholic faith. Ask each group to share its best idea.

TEACH OTHERS ABOUT THEIR FAITH

Explore with the children ways they can assist with religious education in your parish. For instance, they may be partners in the preschool program, help younger children memorize prayers or lists, put on Bible skits, or help with a field trip or a service project.

RESEARCH THE SISTERS' MINISTRY

Have students find out more about the current work of the Sisters of the Holy Names of Jesus and Mary. Their Web site at www.snjm.org is a good place to start.

Catechist's Notes:

Our Lady of the Rosary October 7

Many religions use beads to keep track of prayers. Our Rosary, a circle of beads, is like a garland offered to Mary because we pray a prayer on each bead. This well-loved prayer has its roots in the 150 psalms. People who couldn't read began praying 150 Hail Marys instead, the equivalent of three of our modern rosaries covering the original three sets of mysteries.

The story of the feast of Our Lady of the Rosary is an interesting one. In the 16th century Pope Pius V was having trouble with the Ottoman Turks, who were a real danger to Christianity. After months of disagreements and bickering, he was able to unite Spain, Venice, and the States of the Church in a naval expedition to fight the Turks.

The two navies met in the Gulf of Lepanto in Greece on October 7, 1571. On the same day, the Rosary Confraternity of Rome was meeting at the Dominican headquarters there. The group recited the Rosary for the special intention of the Christians at battle. The Christians defeated the Turks in a spectacular victory and believed it was the intercessory power of the Blessed Virgin that won the victory. Pope Pius V dedicated the day as one of thanksgiving to Our Lady of Victory. Pope Gregory XIII later changed the name to the feast of Our Lady of the Rosary.

The story of the feast of Our Lady of the Rosary focuses on the intercessory power of Mary. It shows that when Christians are in danger, they can go to Mary. And when an individual is in pain, discouraged, or having trouble accepting God's will, he or she can also go to Mary. She will pray to her Son for anyone who calls on her. Anyone who prays to Mary no longer feels alone because she prays with them and for them.

Mary encouraged praying the Rosary in her apparitions. At Lourdes when she appeared to Saint Bernadette, Mary had a Rosary. As Bernadette prayed it, Mary joined in on the Glory Be prayers. At Fatima Mary exhorted the three children who saw her to pray the Rosary for peace.

The Rosary is a deep prayer because as we recite the Our Fathers, Hail Marys, and Glory Bes, we meditate on the mysteries in the lives of Jesus and Mary. No wonder it pleases Our Lady when we pray the Rosary!

ACTIVITIES

LEARN OR REVIEW
THE MYSTERIES OF THE ROSARY
Review the Joyful, Sorrowful, and Glorious Mysteries of the Rosary and the recently added Mysteries of Light. You may use the blackline master on page 443 to make copies of the Mysteries of the Rosary. Divide the class into pairs, and have each pair draw a picture of one of the Mysteries of the Rosary. Hang these up around the room, and have the students explain the mysteries they have drawn.

RESEARCH THE MYSTERIES OF LIGHT
Have students do research online to find out more about Pope John Paul II's addition of the five Mysteries of Light to the Rosary on October 16, 2002.

PRAY THE ROSARY
Pray a decade of the Rosary to honor Mary on her feast day.

INTERVIEW OTHERS
Ask the students to find five people and interview them on why they pray to Mary.

GIVE STUDENTS ROSARIES
Inexpensive Rosaries can be purchased from most religious goods stores. If many students do not have a Rosary of their own, try to obtain a Rosary for each of them.

PRAY A LIVING ROSARY
Join together with other classes to form a living Rosary. Each student represents a bead of the Rosary and leads the group in the prayer.

DO A ROSARY ACROSTIC
Write the word *Rosary* on the board vertically. Ask students to work with a partner to make words that describe qualities of Mary (and themselves) as faithful disciples of Jesus.

seRvice
Obedient
Simple
fAithful
chaRitable
holY

SHARE AN ANECDOTE
Tell the students the story of Knute Rockne, who was one of the greatest college football coaches and a convert to Catholicism. Rockne, who made the forward pass popular, was well known for giving Notre Dame University football teams the ideals of sportsmanship and fortitude. He was killed in a plane crash in Kansas on March 31, 1931. When the rescuers found his body, he had a Rosary still clutched in his hand.

Catechist's Notes:

_____

_____

_____

_____

Blessed Pope John XXIII   October 11

(1881–1963)

This pope is full of surprises, but the fact that Pope John XXIII was a very holy man is not a surprise.

The boy who would one day become leader of the Catholic Church on earth grew up on a small farm in Italy. His name was Angelo Roncalli. He was a very intelligent boy, and he went off to the seminary when he was only 12 years old. But he carried with him a love for life and a place in his heart for common people.

One big surprise was that he was ever elected pope. For one thing he was almost 77 years old. He had had a full career as a seminary teacher, a bishop, an archbishop, and a Vatican delegate in Bulgaria, Turkey, Greece, and France. He—and everyone else—had expected that he would retire quietly as cardinal of Venice, Italy.

Here are some little surprises. About a week after he became pope, he decided he didn't like the custom of the pope eating alone. He hired a cook and started inviting people in for dinner. He enjoyed people, and he didn't want to be far removed from them. He also broke with tradition by going out of the Vatican to the churches of Rome and to visit people in the hospitals and prisons.

He once struck up a conversation with an electrician who was working in his apartment. When he found out how much the man made, he raised the salary of Vatican employees, with more money for those who had more children.

Pope John XXIII liked to laugh and joke. When he went to dress as the new pope, three white cassocks hung ready—small, medium, and large. But this man needed an extra large. Pope John chuckled: "Even the tailors didn't expect me to be pope." He put on the largest cassock, but had to leave a few buttons unbuttoned.

The biggest surprise was that he called all of the bishops to Rome for an ecumenical council. Most bishops had expected him to just keep the Church moving on course for a few years before he died. But Pope John didn't want the Church to be like a musty museum. He wanted fresh air to clear out any staleness, any cobwebs. He said it was time "to throw open the windows so that we can see out and the people can see in." He believed that the Church needs to be in step with the times, able to lead not only Catholics but the whole world to better live out the Gospel. His plan called for renewal in the Church and better relations with other churches.

Pope John was pope for less than five years. The next pope had to continue the Council. But John accomplished a great deal. He was a champion for social justice and the rights of the poor and the working class. He prayed and worked hard for reunion with separated Christians and for peace.

Here is the last surprise. Saints' feast days are usually their day of death, the beginning of new life with God. Pope John's feast is the day he opened Vatican Council II, the beginning of new life for the Church.

KEEP A JOURNAL

When he was 14, Angelo began keeping a diary. He wrote notes, good resolutions, prayers, and personal thoughts. After he died his writings were published as a book, *Journal of a Soul*. Have the students make a journal entry today addressing a concern or need they have or ideas they want to remember. Encourage them to consider keeping a journal as a regular practice. Promise them that it won't be published until they are canonized.

LEARN ABOUT ROMAN NUMERALS

It's hard to ignore Roman numerals when you see this name: Pope John XXIII. Teach or review with the students the basics of reading and writing Roman numerals. Use the popes of the 20th century for practice. Be sure the students know that Pope John XXIII means that 22 popes before him took the name John. By contrast, Pope John Paul I was the first to choose that name. He did it as a sign that he wanted to continue the work and spirit of his predecessors, John XXIII and Paul VI.

EXAMINE EXPERIENCES

His experiences in early life prepared Angelo for his papacy. Share this example with the students.

> When he was a young priest during World War I, Angelo Roncalli worked in a hospital as an orderly and a chaplain. He saw the horror and evil of war. Later he wrote his most famous encyclical, *Peace on Earth,* addressed to all people of good will.

Invite the students to make a list of experiences they have had of which they might make good use when they become adults.

RESEARCH ECUMENISM

For many years Angelo lived and worked in countries where the Eastern churches were influential. He became convinced of the importance of Christian unity and respectful dialog between Catholics and people of other religions. Have the students research the meaning of ecumenism and give short reports about other religions.

Catechist's Notes:

_____

_____

_____

_____

_____

_____

_____

Saint Callistus I
(d. 222)

What would you think of someone who had been born a slave and sentenced as a convict becoming a pope? This did happen to the man who would become Saint Callistus.

Callistus was born as a slave to a Christian master. As he grew to maturity, his master noticed that Callistus had skill in finance. So the master put Callistus in charge of a bank. Some enemies of Callistus falsely accused him of embezzlement. Terrified, though he knew he was innocent, Callistus tried to escape from Rome. He was caught and condemned to the mines of Sardinia. After serving a part of his sentence, he was released so he could get some of the money back. In an effort to recover some of the debts, Callistus went to the moneylenders to plead for his money. He was arrested for fighting and sent back to the mines. Fortunately for him and for the other Christian prisoners, Marcia, the emperor's mistress, won their release.

Pope Zephyrinus recognized the talents of Callistus and gave him a fresh start. The pope made him manager of the burial grounds. Even today the land is named the cemetery of Saint Callistus. Callistus proved himself responsible and was ordained a deacon. Pope Zephyrinus continued to rely on Callistus, in whom he found extraordinary talents for leadership. In a way it is not surprising that Callistus was elected to be the next pope. But Hippolytus and his followers were shocked that Callistus had been chosen. In rebellion this group elected Hippolytus as pope, and he became the first antipope. Now there were two claimants to the papacy.

A *schism*—a split in the Church—went on for 18 years. Callistus knew this could be confusing for the people in the Church, but he also knew what real charity was. He gently tried to encourage Hippolytus to understand the error he had made. At the same time, Pope Callistus tried to make wise and understanding rules for the Church. He worried over rich Christian women who could not find Christian husbands. He taught that marriages between a free woman and a slave were valid. Callistus also knew the struggle of people whose faith was challenged during times of persecution. He understood why some gave up the faith for fear of being killed. Callistus felt there should be mercy for those who had fallen away but repented. The Church has the authority to forgive all sins, said Callistus. This angered Hippolytus, who felt Callistus was too easy on people. Hippolytus wrote bitterly about the pope. But Callistus bore the insults calmly and humbly. Callistus remained steady in his desire to bring peace to the Church. This great man of the Church was martyred in a riot.

FIND OUT HOW POPES ARE ELECTED

It is said that Hippolytus did not believe that the election of Pope Callistus I was valid. Help the students find out how a pope is elected. Assign such questions as:

- Who can elect a pope?

- Who can be elected pope?

- How is the election carried out?

- Do cardinals actually cast the ballots? Explain.

- How many votes does a pope need?

- How secret is the balloting?

- How does one know the election has concluded?

- How will the public learn the identity of the new pope?

- Are the cardinals who are voting allowed to leave the Vatican? Explain.

- When did cardinals first start electing the pope?

- Why have most popes been Italians?

- Can any man be a pope?

PLAN A RECONCILIATION SERVICE

Pope Callistus I was very forgiving. He encouraged the people who had committed serious sin to receive the Sacrament of Reconciliation. Plan a reconciliation service so the students may again participate in the powerful grace of the sacrament.

CONSTRUCT REPLICAS OF YOUR CHURCH

Pope Callistus I knew that loyalty to the Church is important to the believer. Have the students construct replicas of their own parish church out of boxes. Give these directions: Cover a box with plain paper. On the front of the box, draw the entrance to the church. Using construction paper, add to the top any addition such as spire, tower, cross, or dome. On the sides of the box, you may choose to add pictures cut from magazines or newspapers that show various facets of parish life.

LEARN ABOUT EVANGELIZATION

Pope Callistus I proved that no matter how a person starts out in life, he or she can live a life of holiness. Have the students investigate the topic of evangelization in the Church and find out what parishes can do to bring lapsed Catholics back to the faith.

SET UP A PETITIONS BOARD

Callistus knew what it was like to suffer and experience trouble. Start a petitions board. Post a sheet of paper on the bulletin board so students can write petitions for suffering people for whom they would like the class to pray. It is good to remind others to pray for those who are suffering.

Saint Teresa of Ávila   October 15
(1515–1582)

Do you have a favorite word or motto? "Forever!" was Teresa of Ávila's favorite word. She declared that if she made up her mind to love someone, it would be "forever!" It was Jesus who won her heart.

Teresa was born into a wealthy Spanish family. She was endowed with determination, courage, and a vivid imagination. When she was seven years old, Teresa read about the saints and decided that the quickest way to become a saint was to die for Christ. She and her brother Rodrigo ran away to fight the Moors and become martyrs. But their uncle found them and brought them home. By age 12 Teresa was reading stories about knights, love, and chivalry and dreaming about romance and the latest fashions. Teresa was beautiful and charming, and her lively spirit and affectionate nature won her many friends.

After reading the letters of Saint Jerome, Teresa wanted to be a sister. At age 20 she entered a Carmelite monastery.

The Convent of the Incarnation was more like a hotel for upper-class women. The nuns said their prayers, but spent the rest of the time gossiping, entertaining visitors, and vacationing with friends. Teresa gradually took on these ways. Even though it was in her nature to laugh, dance, and carry on lively conversations, Teresa doubted that this was how nuns should live. But for 18 years Teresa lived like this. Then one day, while praying, Teresa noticed a painting of Christ being scourged at the pillar. As she meditated on it, her heart was moved deeply with love. From then on she received special graces and spiritual gifts of mystical prayer and visions.

Soon Teresa felt that God was calling her to reform the way the Carmelites were living. She founded a stricter order of Carmelites. Thirteen women joined the new convent to live in strict poverty for love of Jesus. They slept on straw mats and ate no meat. These nuns did not have visitors, and they earned their income by spinning and by doing needlework. They wore heavy sandals and habits made of coarse brown wool. Some said women would never survive this type of life, but Teresa knew what could be done out of love for God. With God's help and her talent for leadership and organization, Teresa opened 16 more convents. Although Teresa was the superior, she swept floors and cooked meals.

The head of the Carmelite Friars asked Teresa to help reform the monks too. She did that with Saint John of the Cross, a Carmelite friar who became her spiritual director. She also wrote many letters, books about prayer and the spiritual life, and her autobiography.

Teresa's love for God was so great that once she said, "The desire to serve God came to me so intensely that I should like to shout it out and tell everyone how important it is not to just give a little." When Teresa died people remembered her joy, her energy, and her total love for God, whom she had gone to join "forever!"

MAKE BOOKMARKS

In her own prayer book, Teresa kept a card on which she had written this verse:

> Let nothing disturb you,
> Let nothing frighten you.
> All things pass away:
> GOD is unchanging.
> Patience obtains everything.
> Whoever possesses GOD,
>   wants for nothing:
> GOD alone suffices.

Have the students copy the verse onto cards and decorate them with their own designs. If possible, laminate the cards for the children to use as bookmarks.

RESEARCH DOCTORS OF THE CHURCH

Teresa of Ávila, Catherine of Siena, and Thérèse of Lisieux are the three women who are called Doctors of the Church. Direct the students to find out what it means to be named a Doctor of the Church.

PERFORM SKITS ABOUT LEADERSHIP

Once Teresa was assigned to return to the Convent of the Incarnation as prioress, or superior. The nuns did not want her because they liked living the easy way. Teresa placed a statue of Mary on the chair of the prioress with the keys to the convent and announced that Our Lady was in charge. Before long Teresa won the respect and loyalty of the nuns. Have the class brainstorm situations in which children their age may be in charge. Then have small groups put on skits showing how they could be leaders who serve and who would earn the respect and loyalty of others.

TRY TO BE CHEERFUL

Teresa once remarked that she did not like gloomy saints. Recommend that the students try to be cheerful today in her honor, especially when things don't go their way.

MEDITATE ON THE PASSION OF JESUS

Teresa loved to meditate on the passion of Christ because it showed how much Jesus loved everyone. Suggest that the students read the Passion from one of the Gospels today.

Catechist's Notes:

_____

_____

_____

_____

_____

_____

_____

Saint Hedwig

October 16

(c. 1174–1243)

Have you ever heard the expression "the power behind the throne"? It is an old saying meaning that a queen has great influence over her husband, the king. This was true of Hedwig. Born the daughter of a count, Hedwig was educated in a monastery. At age 12 she married Henry I of Silesia, a region in Europe that is now part of Poland. Henry was 18. In the 1100s this was the usual age for marriage. The couple had seven children.

Henry succeeded his father to the throne. Even though a woman in Hedwig's position was expected to do nothing more serious than needlework, Henry depended on Hedwig to help him with the administration of the country. Henry admired Hedwig, not only because she was a beautiful woman, but because her virtue was outstanding. He recognized her qualities of fortitude, prudence, and remarkable insight. The most remembered incident of her great influence occurred when Henry was at war with Conrad of Masovia. Henry was captured by surprise at a church service. With great courage Hedwig persuaded Conrad to return her husband.

But throughout the land, the queen was loved more for her gentleness and kindness to the poor than for her political undertakings. She founded a hospital for lepers. The doors of her castle were open to travelers, the homeless, the sick and dying. It is said that Hedwig would go out herself to serve the poor. In the evenings she would visit their cottages. Late at night she would darn their clothes. Early in the morning Hedwig would rise and pray for the kingdom. She did all this while taking very good care of her own family. Hedwig invited Franciscans, Dominicans, and the first convent of nuns, Cistercians, to build monasteries in the kingdom.

Hedwig was greatly distressed when two of her sons disagreed over land given them by their father, and they went to war against each other. Yet she bore this sorrow and the death of her son Henry with patience. The people of her kingdom loved her so much that they considered her a saint even when she was alive.

ACTIVITIES

MAKE BANNERS

It is told that Hedwig would deny herself shoes in winter rather than see a poor person cold and barefoot. Review the spiritual and corporal works of mercy. Have each student make a banner depicting how he or she can live out one of the works of mercy.

FIND NEWSPAPER ARTICLES

As a leader of her country, Hedwig set the example of how a queen could be concerned for others. Ask the students to look through recent newspapers and cut out articles that report positive things people are doing in the world to help one another.

RESEARCH MEDIEVAL TIMES

Hedwig lived during medieval times. Have the students do projects on medieval life. Understanding the flavor of Hedwig's historical setting will help them understand the saint.

LEARN ABOUT THE FAITH IN POLAND

Hedwig is one of many saints who made the Polish country strong in faith. Find out how the people of Poland kept the faith alive throughout decades of Communist rule.

Catechist's Notes:

_____

_____

_____

_____

_____

_____

_____

_____

_____

_____

_____

Saint Margaret Mary Alacoque

October 16

(1647–1690)

Have you ever promised something "with all your heart"? What did you mean by that? When we speak of our heart, we often mean it to represent our whole person and all the love we can give. That is why the heart seems a fitting symbol for God's unending, always forgiving love.

More than 300 years ago, Jesus revealed his great love for all people to Margaret Mary Alacoque. And he used the image of the heart as a symbol of his love. His message was "See this Heart which has loved so much and received so little love in return. Tell everyone that I really love them and I want to be loved in return. If you love me, pray and sacrifice for those who do not believe in my love or do not care about my love."

Jesus asked Margaret Mary to tell everyone about the Sacred Heart of Jesus. This was a difficult job because the false teaching of Jansenism was very popular at that time. According to this heresy, Jesus did not die for all human beings, but only for those predestined to be saved. When Margaret Mary tried to explain that Jesus died for everyone out of love, she met with opposition from all sides—theologians of the Church, parents of students whom she taught, even the sisters of her convent, became hostile and made life difficult for her. People did not believe that God would reveal his love so powerfully to someone like Margaret Mary.

Margaret Mary was born into a refined, well-known French family, but she had an unhappy childhood. Her father died when she was eight years old. After his death her mother tried to collect money that people owed her husband, but she did not succeed. Without any income mother and daughter were forced to share the farm with greedy relatives who treated them miserably. Margaret Mary once said that her greatest pain at this time was to see her mother suffer and not to be able to help.

When she was 24, Margaret Mary entered the Visitation convent of Paray-le-Monial. When she was assigned to help take care of the sick nuns, she was criticized for being slow, clumsy, and impractical. But she also was known to be humble, honest, patient, and kind. Two years later, Jesus revealed his love to her as the Sacred Heart. Father Claude de la Colombière was one of the few people who believed Margaret Mary. He gave her encouragement and spiritual guidance. Gradually Margaret Mary, who returned kindness for criticism and patience for rejection, won the confidence of those around her. In 1765 devotion to the Sacred Heart was approved by the pope for liturgical observance, 75 years after Margaret Mary's death.

COPY A SCRIPTURE VERSE

In the Old Testament, God revealed his merciful love to the sinful nation Israel. And in the New Testament, Jesus revealed the love of God for all, fishermen, tax collectors, widows, sinners, the poor, and the sick.

Grades 1–4: Have children copy Matthew 11:29: Jesus said, "Learn from me; for I am gentle and humble of heart."

Grades 5–8: Have students find a quote in Scripture that reveals God's love for them and copy it onto a heart-shaped paper.

HELP PEOPLE IN NEED

To identify with the Heart of Christ is to want what Jesus wants and to love as Jesus loves. Followers of Jesus want to help people who are in spiritual or material need. Have students write or e-mail Catholic Relief Services about current projects and find out how they can help. The mailing address is Catholic Relief Services, 1011 First Avenue, New York, NY 10022. The online address is www.catholicrelief.org. Send students to www.catholicrelief.org/kids. This site provides information and interactive games for children as well as teachers' resources that include games, activities, and lesson plans.

PLAN A PRAYER SERVICE

One of the devotions that evolved from Jesus' message to Saint Margaret Mary was the Holy Hour of Reparation. People agreed to meet and pray for an hour to make up to Jesus for all the people who didn't care about God's love and ignored it. Have the class plan a prayer service to pray for people who do not believe in God's love for them. Possible readings are Ezekiel 34:11–16; Hosea 11:1–9; Isaiah 49; Romans 5:5–11; Ephesians 1:3–10, 3:14–19; Philippians 1:8–11; Luke 15:1–10, 11–32; John 15:1–8, 9–17, 19:31–34.

LEARN ABOUT DEVOTION TO THE SACRED HEART

Have the students research devotions to the Sacred Heart: First Fridays; the feast of the Sacred Heart; consecrations to the Sacred Heart; the enthronement of the Sacred Heart; the use of short prayers such as "Jesus meek and humble of heart, make my heart like yours"; the votive Mass for the Sacred Heart; and related songs and prayers.

Catechist's Notes:

_____

_____

_____

_____

_____

Saint Ignatius of Antioch — October 17

(d. 107)

Every person's life affects others. If Ignatius of Antioch were alive today, he would tell us that. Up to the moment of his death, Ignatius was influencing the lives of others for the better.

Ignatius was converted from paganism to Christianity in Syria. He became the second bishop of Antioch, a successor of Saint Peter. In 107 the Emperor Trajan visited Antioch and tried to force the Christians to renounce their religion. At this time Ignatius gave the best witness a bishop can ever give his people. He allowed the company of soldiers to bind him in a rickety cart and lead him to Rome for martyrdom. So great was the witness of his faith and courage that, as his cart rolled into the different towns en route to Rome, the local bishop and delegations of Christians would come to meet him and encourage him. Polycarp, the Bishop of Smyrna, received him with great honor, for he saw the holiness of Ignatius and cherished his friendship.

On his long journey as a prisoner, Ignatius composed seven letters to the churches he left behind. The Church today is fortunate to have those letters because they give valuable insight into the growth of theology in the early Church. In his letters Ignatius praises the brotherly love and support he experienced on his way to Rome. He insists that the people of the Church give obedience to their local bishop. "Wherever the bishop is, there let the people be, for there is the Catholic Church" (Smyrna 8.1–2). He urged that nothing be done concerning the Church without the approval of the local bishop.

Ignatius loved the Eucharist and wrote that Christ was really present in the Blessed Sacrament. Of himself he said, "I am the wheat of Christ, may I be ground by the teeth of beasts to become the immaculate bread of Christ." He asked his people to gather around the Eucharist as a community and care for "the widow, the orphan, the oppressed, as well as those in prison, the hungry and the thirsty" (Smyrna 6.2). Ignatius renewed the people's courage by reminding them of the presence of Jesus in the Church and in each member. That is why Ignatius called himself "the bearer of God." Ignatius was martyred by being devoured by wild beasts in the arena.

WRITE LETTERS TO THE BISHOP

Ignatius emphasized the important role of the local bishop in the Church. Review with the students the role of the bishops in the Church. Have the students write letters to their local bishop(s) expressing appreciation for him and his work for the Church.

ROLE-PLAY

Role-play the scene of Christians coming out to meet Ignatius on his journey from Antioch to Rome. Challenge students to think about what they would like to ask him and how he might answer them.

REFLECT ON SCRIPTURE

Luke 9:23–24 was a passage Saint Ignatius took seriously. Have the class reflect on this Scripture passage. Ask the students to think about how Jesus is asking them to follow him today. Remind them that "denying themselves" and "losing their lives for his sake" can mean thinking of others more than themselves.

VISIT THE CATHEDRAL

Cathedra means "chair." The church where the bishop presides is called the cathedral because of the presence of the bishop's chair. It is a sign of his leadership. But the cathedral belongs to everyone in the diocese. Plan a visit to the cathedral of your diocese and let the students discover why it is an important part of the diocese.

WRITE A LETTER TO SAINT IGNATIUS

Have the students pretend that Ignatius is alive today and write a letter to him telling how they live their faith and how they encourage others to do likewise.

Catechist's Notes:

_____

_____

_____

_____

_____

_____

_____

_____

_____

Saint Luke

(first century)

October 18

Can you imagine what it would have been like to travel with Saint Paul on his missionary journeys? Exciting, certainly. Paul's mission was to bring the Good News to the Gentiles. He carried a wonderful new message of hope and salvation in Christ throughout the Roman Empire. The mission was dangerous too. Paul and his companions were beaten, thrown into prison, run out of town, and shipwrecked. Luke could tell you all about it. And he did!

Christian tradition recognizes Luke as the "beloved physician," as Paul calls him, who was a co-worker and companion of Paul. Luke wrote firsthand accounts of Paul's missionary journeys. Luke is the author of a two-part work telling the story of Jesus and the early Church. His Gospel gives us a look at the compassionate, forgiving Christ. In the Acts of the Apostles, he gives us valuable data describing the post-Resurrection Church.

But we have little information about Luke himself. Luke's aim was to tell us who Jesus was. He did a masterful piece of work.

Since Luke's Gospel is written in excellent Greek, it is thought that Greek was his native language. He was probably a Syrian from Antioch. Luke was a writer who was careful about his sources. His writing is concrete and shows detail. His is a story of human interest and human sympathy. In his Gospel we see the gentleness of Jesus as he heals the widow of Naim, speaks to the penitent woman at his feet, and comforts the weeping women on his way to the cross. It is Luke who includes the parables of mercy: the Good Samaritan and the Prodigal Son. The repentant thief is also his addition. Luke's pagan origins probably gave him open-mindedness to all peoples. Samaritans, lepers, publicans, soldiers, public sinners, shepherds, and the poor all find a special place in his Gospel.

Luke also writes about Jesus as a master of prayer. Often Jesus is portrayed going alone to speak to his Father or helping his disciples to pray. Luke presents the disciples as happy to give all, leave all, and suffer all joyfully, as he himself did. Luke's writings make it clear that he was a man who placed all his faith and trust in Jesus.

ACTIVITIES

READ SCRIPTURE REFERENCES

Have students find references to Luke in Scripture: Colossians 4:14; Philemon; 2 Timothy; and passages in Acts in which the author uses the pronoun *we:* Acts 16:10–15, 20:6–16.

DISCOVER THE JOYFUL MYSTERIES IN THE GOSPEL

Luke is the evangelist who wrote the most about Mary. Have the students find the sources of the Joyful Mysteries of the Rosary in the first chapters of Luke and make a list of these passages from Scripture.

BE HEALERS

Remind the children that Luke was a physician. Suggest that they find a way to make one person feel better today.

MAKE A MURAL OF LUCAN THEMES

The Gospel of Luke has several distinguishing themes. List them on the board. Ask the students to look through the Gospel and find stories that fit these themes. Have each student draw an example and then make a mural of the drawings. The themes are

> Love of the Poor and Lowly
> Joy
> Salvation for All
> Mercy
> Prayer
> Discipleship

PERFORM A DRAMA

Have the students adapt a story from the Acts of the Apostles for classroom theater. Props and costumes may be used. Appropriate choices include the cure of the crippled beggar (Acts 3:1–10), Stephen's martyrdom (Acts 7:54–60), Philip and the Ethiopian (Acts 8:26–39), Saul's conversion (Acts 9:1–19), the deliverance of Paul and Silas from prison (Acts 16:25–34), and Paul raising a dead man to life (Acts 20:7–12).

MAKE CHRISTMAS CARDS

Luke is considered the "Christmas Evangelist" because the stories of Jesus' birth are found in his Gospel. Have the class make Christmas cards by drawing or pasting appropriate pictures on construction paper and writing Lucan quotations beneath them.

FIND SYMBOLS OF EVANGELISTS

Each of the evangelists, or Gospel writers, has a traditional symbol: Matthew (man), Mark (lion), Luke (ox), John (eagle). The ox was chosen for Luke because his Gospel is very down-to-earth. In addition the Gospel of Luke begins with the story of Jesus' birth in a stable. If your parish church features these symbols in art, take the students to the church and have them locate the symbols.

Catechist's Notes:

_____

_____

_____

Saints Isaac Jogues, John de Brébeuf, and Companions October 19

(d. 1642–1649)

Why would eight of the most talented and dynamic men of 17th-century France volunteer to be missionaries in the wilderness of North America? Six Jesuit priests—Isaac Jogues, John de Brébeuf, Gabriel Lalemant, Noel Chabanel, Charles Garnier, and Anthony Daniel—and two laymen—Rene Goupil and John de Lalande—did just that.

By 1632 the Jesuits had established a mission center in Quebec to minister to the Huron people. The Huron nation was made up of 20,000 people who lived in 30 villages. The missionaries had to travel extensively in this new land, through dense forests as well as by rivers. They learned the Huron language and lived among the people.

But the missionaries' culture and religion were very different. Their differences made the Huron distrust them. When the Huron first saw the black robes of the Jesuit priests, children went running to their mothers, afraid that the missionaries were sorcerers. And the missionaries were not accustomed to the Huron way of life, which revolved around their hunting season and the attacks of their enemies, the fierce Iroquois. The Frenchmen suffered from cold and heat and sleeping in smoke-filled rooms.

Yet they carried on. John de Brébeuf founded schools among the Huron and wrote a catechism and dictionary in their native language. Noel Chabanel, a brilliant professor of languages in France, had a great deal of trouble with the Huron language, but he made a vow to stay and try, in humility, to do the work of God. Rene Goupil and John de Lalande gave their time without any pay. Charles Garnier would walk 30 or 40 miles to baptize a single child.

All these efforts seemed to be useless. The Huron people were polite, but generally ignored the Christian missionaries. After years of kindness, unselfishness, and perseverance, the missionaries had about 2,000 converts. Then the Iroquois, who resented the French and blamed them for a smallpox epidemic, attacked the missionaries. Rene Goupil was struck down while baptizing a baby. Anthony Daniel was at Mass when he was shot with arrows. He told his Huron friends to flee, saying, "I will stay here. We will meet in heaven." The Iroquois admired the bravery of John de Brébeuf so much that after his death they drank his blood and saved his heart for the chief to eat. They believed that by doing this they could gain some of his courage.

Isaac Jogues, who had been captured and tortured by the Iroquois, was able to escape back to France. Later he bravely returned to America. This time when on a peace mission to the Iroquois for the governor of New France, he was accused of bringing a bad harvest, and they took his life.

ACTIVITIES

OFFER UP SUFFERINGS

Even though the Iroquois considered the missionaries to be enemies, they marveled at their courage. Encourage the students to offer up their complaints silently today in imitation of these heroic martyrs.

DO A CHORAL READING

In 1642 Father John de Brébeuf wrote a Christmas carol as a gift to the Huron people. He composed the song in their own language, using a popular French melody. Have the students illustrate or do a choral reading of the carol, which may be found on the blackline master on page 444.

MAKE A NATURE COLLAGE

The French missionaries tried to reach the Huron by appealing to their love of and reverence for nature. Let each student make a poster using a collage of pictures of nature from magazines, natural objects, and a verse of a psalm that praises God in his creation.

READ ABOUT BLESSED KATERI

Blessed Kateri Tekakwitha belonged to the Iroquois Nation. She was born just 10 years after the Jesuit martyrs died. Have the students read her story (feast day July 14, page 353) to find out how the sacrifices of the missionaries bore fruit.

PRAY FOR MISSIONARIES AT MASS

When Isaac Jogues escaped to France, his left hand had been mutilated. Pope Urban VII gave him special permission to continue to preside at the Eucharist, saying, "It would be a shame that a martyr of Christ not drink the blood of Christ." Plan a Mass for missionaries or include intercessions for them at a Mass. You may wish to include the prayer for missionaries from the blackline master on page 435.

Catechist's Notes:

_____

_____

_____

_____

_____

_____

_____

_____

Saint Anthony Claret

October 24

(1807–1870)

Do you ever wonder what you will do in life? It took Anthony Claret a long time to discover all the many gifts God had given him. Anthony grew up in a large family in Spain. His family was poor but hardworking. Weaving was a family trade that Anthony learned. His earliest memories were the family praying the Rosary together and going to church.

By age 21, Anthony had been educated and was in much demand as a weaver. He imagined himself, however, as a Carthusian monk or a foreign missionary. On the advice of the bishop, he attended the diocesan seminary and was ordained a priest. First Anthony was sent as a pastor to a small mountain village. There were many sick people there, so he studied medicine. Anthony also found out that he had power to read people's thoughts.

Anthony began preaching throughout Spain, spreading devotion to the Immaculate Heart of Mary and reviving devotion to the Eucharist. A popular preacher, he realized that people could be reached through the printed word as well. Anthony published a book, *The Catechism Explained*. The bishop of the Canary Islands read the book and invited Anthony to preach for a year on the islands. Anthony was delighted to at last be a missionary.

When Anthony returned to Spain, he founded a congregation called the Missionary Sons of the Immaculate Heart of Mary, or "Claretians." Here, he thought, was where he wanted to concentrate his efforts, but, surprisingly, God had other plans. Anthony was assigned as Archbishop of Cuba, a turbulent island that had not had an archbishop for 14 years. Many Cubans had relaxed their Christian standards. Most priests and political leaders were happy without an archbishop in charge. Anthony set vigorously to work, encouraging priests in their vocations, preaching in all of the churches, and spending hours doing what he did best—hearing confessions and guiding people to Christ.

He challenged the political system of Cuba by working for updated farm methods and credit unions. Anthony wanted the people to own their farms and market their crops. He believed that stable material conditions would lead to good family life. He made political enemies by giving instruction to slaves. On 15 occasions, enemies tried to assassinate him.

After eight years, Anthony was just getting things in order in Cuba when he was called back to Spain to be Queen Isabella II's confessor. Unhappily he obeyed. He soon opened a religious publishing house and wrote more than 200 books and pamphlets. In 1886 a revolution took place. All those associated with the court were accused of treason. Anthony fled to Rome, where Vatican Council I was in session. Here he brilliantly defended the pope's infallibility. Afterward he retired to a Cistercian monastery in Spain and stayed there in solitude until his death. An outstanding and humble leader, Anthony is called the spiritual father of Cuba.

SHARE THE GOOD NEWS

Anthony Claret wrote and published books as one way of sharing his faith with many people.

- Have the students research how the Good News is communicated today: Catholic newspapers, magazines, books, newsletters, radio, television, videos, films, Web sites, billboards, church signs, and so on. Let them share information and examples they find.

- Order several subscriptions to a Catholic magazine the children would enjoy. Let them read and pass along the magazines each month.

- Divide the class into small groups to discuss ways that they can share the Good News of God's love with others.

- Set up a Catholic library in the classroom. Stock it with newspapers, magazines, and books.

FIND OUT ABOUT THE CLARETIANS

Saint Anthony Claret, like the first apostles, was "on fire with God's love." This is the motto of the men who continue his work of bringing the Good News of God's love to everyone they meet. Have the students research the Claretian Missionaries on the Internet.

ILLUSTRATE THEIR GIFTS

Anthony Claret discerned and used many gifts of God for the good of others. Read the story of Anthony Claret aloud or have the students read it. Ask them to choose the part of the story with which they identify most. Lead them to reflect on the dreams or gifts they have. Finally ask the students to write one gift vertically down the center of a sheet of drawing paper. On one side they should draw themselves using that gift to help others now. On the other side have them illustrate themselves using the gift to help others in the future.

BEGIN A PROJECT

Anthony faced many difficulties in bringing Christ's healing to Cuba. So he started in small ways that had a potential for growth. With the students determine an area or situation in your class, school, parish, or neighborhood that needs healing or reconciliation to the will of God. Decide on a small way to begin to help. If you need seed money for a project, collect nickels, dimes, and quarters or soft-drink cans to recycle.

RESEARCH RELIGIOUS FREEDOM

Anthony Claret was a pastoral bishop who cared about human dignity and religious freedom. Help the class find examples of ways Pope John Paul II also took deliberate action on this Gospel teaching.

Catechist's Notes:

_____

_____

_____

_____

Saints Simon and Jude   October 28

(first century)

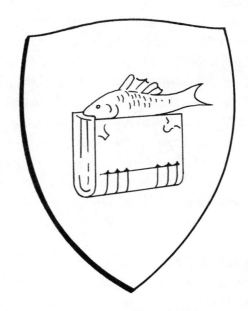

How do you feel when you are chosen to do something important? Honored, surprised, nervous? Some of the apostles must have felt as you do.

After spending much time in prayer, Jesus decided to choose 12 men, 12 rather unlikely candidates, who would be his apostles and proclaim the Kingdom of God to all people.

Simon the Zealot was one who was called. The Zealots were a Jewish group who believed that the promise of the Messiah meant a free and independent Jewish nation where they would never have to pay taxes to the Romans again. Some Zealots were also very concerned that the spiritual ideals of their religion be kept. But others in the group acted more like modern-day terrorists by raiding, killing, and inciting riots. Simon was known as "the zealot" to distinguish him from Simon Peter.

At the same time, Jesus called Jude Thaddeus, brother of James, most likely a fisherman by trade. Along with 10 other men, these two followed Jesus, lived with him, fled when he underwent his Passion, and rejoiced when he rose from the dead. At Pentecost they were filled with the Spirit and a burning desire to spread the Good News to all. Jude traveled to Mesopotamia to preach, and Simon went to Egypt. Eventually they both ended up in Persia, modern-day Iran. There they worked together evangelizing the people until they were both martyred. These two unlikely candidates for apostleship finally witnessed to the risen Lord with their lives.

Traditionally Saint Jude the Apostle is identified with the author of the Letter of Jude in the New Testament. He has also come to be known as the saint of hopeless cases.

ACTIVITIES

DESIGN PERSONAL SHIELDS

Symbols have traditionally been associated with both apostles. Jude has been pictured with a club, which may have been the instrument of his death, and with a flame over his head to show the Spirit's influence upon him at Pentecost. Simon is pictured with a fish, symbol of the early Christians' identification with Christ. (In Greek, the initials for "Jesus Christ, God's Son, Savior" spell the word for "fish.") Both saints also have special shields. Jude's shield is red with a sailboat that has a cross on the mast. Simon has a shield bearing a book with a fish resting on it. Have the students design personal shields with symbols and pictures for their own faith and lives. Display the shields around the room.

MAKE PRAYER PETITIONS

Saint Jude in modern days has come to be known as the saint of hopeless cases. Invite the students to pray for people in need of hope. Gather in a prayer circle and light a candle in the center. Take turns offering short prayers, for example: "That the Lord will strengthen my Aunt Sarah through the intercession of Saint Jude, we pray." The students respond, "Lord, hear our prayer."

LEARN ABOUT ST. JUDE HOSPITAL

Have students use the Internet to find out about St. Jude Children's Research Hospital in Memphis, Tennessee: why it was founded, the work that is done there, how people can help. Then hold a video drive for the children at St. Jude's. Collect child-friendly used videos and make computer-generated labels telling who each video is from. Send them to the hospital with a card made by the class for the patients to enjoy.

MEDITATE ON A SCRIPTURE READING

Read the following passage as a guided meditation. Point out that Saint Paul understood that God chooses the very people that others look down upon. He taught this to the Corinthians, saying, "Consider your own call, brothers and sisters; not many of you were wise by human standards, not many were powerful, not many were of noble birth. But God chose what is foolish in the world to shame the wise; God chose what is weak in the world to shame the strong; God chose what is low and despised in the world" (1 Cor. 1:26–28a).

Catechist's Notes:

_____

_____

_____

_____

_____

All Saints

On the feast of All Saints, we honor those men and women who—whether they've been canonized or not—have led lives of heroic virtue that set an example for all Christians. They have truly witnessed to their faith. Although no two saints are alike (in fact, no two people are exactly alike), there are certain qualities that they all share.

Saints are big dreamers. They make the impossible seem possible. They do not let their weaknesses or those of others hold them back from doing good. They believe that with God on their side, no one and nothing can stop them.

Saints are go-getters. They believe what is written in the Gospel: give all, turn the other cheek, love God above all, feed the hungry, clothe the naked, sin no more, follow Jesus. They don't wait for someone else to do good first. They jump right in.

Saints are love-bringers, in big and little ways. They try to see Christ in every person and in every situation.

The big dreamers, the go-getters, the love-bringers—we've read about them, we've heard about them, we've celebrated their feasts. But today we celebrate all the saints together—the ones we know and the ones we don't. These are the people who help us believe that love is the most important thing in the world. Their lives tell us that what matters most in life is not what we earn or own, not the job we have or the people we know. What really matters is how much we love God, others, and ourselves, and how well we show that love in all we do.

Perhaps there are big dreamers, go-getters, and love-bringers among your friends. Perhaps you are one of those special people who want to make this world a better place. Perhaps you are someone racing toward heaven with joy. Know that it begins with little things: a smile, a helping hand, a prayer. This is the road to sainthood.

Let us pray today.
> Father, all-powerful and ever-living
> God,
> today we rejoice in the holy men
> and women
> of every time and place.
> May their prayers bring us your
> forgiveness and love.

> We ask this through our Lord
> Jesus Christ, your Son,
> who lives and reigns with you and
> the Holy Spirit,
> one God, for ever and ever.
> *(Opening Prayer from*
> *the Feast of All Saints)*

ACTIVITIES

HONOR THE SAINTS

Choose one of the following ways to celebrate all of the saints. Leave the display up until the feast of Christ the King.

- Have each class or homeroom select a saint as its class patron. Let the students decorate the door to the classroom in honor of their patron saint.

- Have the students draw their favorite saints on cardboard, cut them out, and either glue them on a long sheet of shelf paper to hang in the hall or post them on a large bulletin board, creating a mural of saints.

- Let the students design banners to celebrate the goodness of Christians they know who are becoming saints.

IMITATE THE SAINTS

Have the students pretend to be their patron or favorite saints. Then ask them, as that saint, to write a letter to the class about how young people today can live the Gospel more completely. Read several letters during each religion class for the rest of the month.

WRITE FRONT PAGE NEWS

Have the students research their own patron saint and/or the patron saint of the parish. Then ask them to write and lay out the front page of a newspaper as a report. Give the students the following directions:

1. Read several books or articles on your saint. Take notes as you read, especially on events that might make good "front page news." Include notes about such things as the type of clothing worn at the time your saint lived. Be sure to put title and page number references in your notes in case you need to check the information.

2. After you have completed your research, choose one event from the saint's life and write your headline story. Use your notes about other events to write shorter stories for the front page. Write headlines for your stories.

3. Organize all your articles and prepare a rough layout of your page, arranging the articles in columns. Pictures and/or drawings may be included, as in actual newspapers.

4. Print your name in the lower right-hand corner of the front page.

5. May this activity help you make a new friend!

FIND OUT MORE ABOUT CANONIZATION

Encourage the students to find out and report on (a) how a person is nominated for canonization, (b) the process of becoming a saint, and (c) what it means to be proclaimed a saint by the Church.

Catechist's Notes:

_____

_____

_____

_____

All Souls

We believe that death can separate us from the people we love only for a while. We are still united with them in the Communion of Saints. We remember the people we knew and loved who have died. We save pictures and mementos of the loved ones. On the anniversaries of their deaths, we might bring flowers or plants to their graves as signs of our continuing love and prayers.

On this feast of All Souls, and throughout the entire month of November, we recall our deceased relatives, friends, and all the faithful departed who may yet be waiting for the full joy of heaven in purgatory. We pray for them, remembering that likewise these people being purified have the power to intercede for us too.

Christians have always prayed for those who have died and have had Masses said for them. Anniversaries of death have been regarded as "birthdays" to a new life. Praying and offering sacrifices for those in purgatory is based on Scripture. Judas Maccabeus "made atonement for the dead, that they might be delivered from their sin" (2 Maccabees 12:46).

In the 11th century, Odilo, who was an abbot at Cluny and later a saint, required that the monks pray for all the dead on the day after All Saints. Soon this custom spread. Hispanics celebrate this Day of the Dead with colorful customs and much festivity.

ACTIVITIES

LEARN A PRAYER FOR THE DEAD

Teach the students the traditional verse and response that the Church uses to pray for the faithful departed.

> Eternal rest grant to them, O Lord,
> and let perpetual light shine upon them.
> May they rest in peace.

PRAY FOR THE DEAD

Cut out of large construction paper a cross or a crown. Pass it around and have the students list deceased relatives, friends, or others for whom they would like everyone to pray. Keep the cross or crown in the classroom prayer corner near the enthroned Bible for the entire month of November.

VISIT THE CEMETERY

If there is a cemetery attached to the parish and easily accessible, take the students through it on a pilgrimage of prayer. Pray especially at the graves of those relatives or friends of students. Have the students make gravestone rubbings and note memorial verses on the markers. Some cemeteries have special sections for infants, and you might wish to point this out to the students. If the situation allows, you might involve the students in a cemetery beautification project: pulling weeds, clearing away areas near markers, picking up debris, and so on.

SHARE FAMILY OR LOCAL CUSTOMS

Depending on the needs and sensitivities of the students with whom you are working, consider having a sharing session of different family customs concerning showing respect for the dead. There are some funeral directors who provide excellent programs and explanations concerning such rites of passage and mourning. Find out what is offered locally to determine if something appropriate for your class is available.

GO TO MASS

Find out the schedule of Masses for the day and provide a listing for the students and their families.

Catechist's Notes:

_____

_____

_____

_____

_____

_____

Saint Martin de Porres November 3
(1579–1639)

Difficult times can make a person bitter or better. You may think: Why me? Why did this happen to me?

Martin de Porres had his share of troubles, but he never let them turn him into a mean person. He was born in Lima, Peru, the son of a Spanish nobleman and a freed woman from Panama. Martin's father did not stay with or support the family for long. Martin, his mother, and his sister Juana made a living for themselves. Even in the midst of his own poverty, Martin cared for the needs of other poor people. He often gave away his money or food.

When he was 12 years old, Martin became an apprentice to a barber/surgeon. He learned not only to care for hair but also to heal and mend ill and broken bodies. When he was 15, Martin entered the Dominicans as a lay brother. Nine years later the community asked that he make full religious profession.

All his life, Martin chose to do only the lowest tasks. He was known to pray long hours, and he took care of the needs of those around him. Martin's care extended beyond the walls of his own residence. He cared for sick people throughout Peru. He handled the community's distribution to the poor. He founded an orphanage and a hospital, and he also ministered to the slaves brought from Africa. In all of this he was known for his humility, kindness, and gentle manner.

Martin is sometimes pictured holding a mouse or collecting mice from a church drawer. The scene originated from the story that Martin found a little mouse in a trap. The mice had been nibbling away at the priests' vestments. Martin made a deal with the mouse. "Run along, little brother," he whispered, "and tell your friends to stay out of the monastery. From now on I will feed you outside." Martin released the mouse, and soon all the mice were seen running from the church. The closest they came to it was the garden where Martin would feed them daily. It is also said that Martin kept a hospital for dogs and cats at his sister's house. Other stories of Martin's way with animals abound!

Martin spent most of his days as the head of the infirmary, caring not only for the sick brothers, but the people of Peru who came for help.

Martin was canonized in 1962 by Pope John XXIII and was named the patron of interracial justice. At that time John XXIII said, "He excused the faults of others. He forgave the bitterest injuries, convinced that he deserved much more severe punishments on account of his own sins. He tried with all his might to redeem the guilty; lovingly he comforted the sick; he provided food, clothing, and medicine for the poor; he helped, as best he could, farm laborers and Negroes, as well as mulattoes, who were looked upon at that time as akin to slaves. Thus, he deserved to be called by the name the people gave him: Martin of Charity."

ACTIVITIES

COMPOSE BALLADS

Have the students compose ballads about the charity of Martin de Porres. Students may wish to work with partners.

PUT ON A PLAY

Let the children act out scenes from the life of Saint Martin. If you have a large class, check other books for additional scenes illustrating Martin's kindness to people and animals. If possible, invite another class in for the show.

DISCUSS PREJUDICE

Discuss how racial prejudice is built on ignorance and fear. This same ignorance and fear can keep people from reaching out to others even in their own neighborhood or even in their own classroom. Discuss ways the students can become more alert to prejudice of any kind and how they themselves can be more hospitable to others.

LIST WAYS TO CARE

Martin did great things right in his own hometown. Have the students think of ways they can be more caring in the situations in which they find themselves every day. Make a master list on the board.

LOVE THE EUCHARIST

Martin was especially devoted to the Holy Eucharist. Remind the students to make frequent visits to the church and before the Blessed Sacrament when they are able. Remind them also to prepare well to receive Christ in the Eucharist and to spend time in prayer of love and gratitude.

Catechist's Notes:

Saint Charles Borromeo   November 4

(1538–1584)

Have you ever heard the expression, "To whom much is given, of him much is expected?"

Charles Borromeo was highly gifted. By the time he was 21, he had received his doctorate degrees in civil and canon law. Within the year he was called to Rome by his uncle, Pope Pius IV, and made a cardinal and administrator of Milan. The list of his duties and responsibilities at that time is long and impressive. As secretary of state at the Vatican, Charles was in charge of all the papal states. He also worked closely with his uncle at the Council of Trent, when many topics were discussed that led to heated arguments. Several times it seemed as though the council would break up and everyone would return home. But Charles, working behind the scenes, helped keep people together.

When Charles was 25, his older brother died. Usually this meant that the next oldest son would take over as head of the family. But Charles decided instead to be a priest. Shortly after he was ordained, he was made the bishop of Milan. Although his uncle wanted him to remain in Rome, Charles felt the need to be with his flock in Milan. It was in Milan that his talents and his holiness really became apparent, for more than any other individual at the time, he tried to make the decrees and changes of the Council alive in his diocese.

He traveled throughout his diocese constantly, even into the hills and mountains of Switzerland. He set up orphanages, hospitals, homes for neglected women, seminaries, and colleges. He sought to reform the lives of the clergy and the religious orders of the day. He started a group of priests called the Oblates of St. Ambrose (now the Oblates of St. Charles) to help him in his work. Charles was also instrumental in establishing what is now known as Solemn Annual Exposition, a way to honor the Blessed Sacrament.

In 1576 a plague broke out in Milan, and with it came famine. So many people were ill and dying that even the city officials fled the area. But Charles did not. He stayed with the sick and ministered to them. He himself ate very little and slept only a few hours a night. He sold all he had and even borrowed large sums of money so that he could continue to feed the 60,000 to 70,000 people who came to him for help.

Although Charles Borromeo demanded much from the priests and religious he worked with, he never asked of them anything he himself was not willing to do. Sometimes it is easier to see what should be done or how others can improve than it is for us to make the effort ourselves. Today, like Charles Borromeo, try to do what you know is right, and do not judge those around you.

LIST CHALLENGES OF LEADERSHIP

When people try to do the right thing, they may find opposition to their efforts. Charles Borromeo once attempted to reform a certain religious order. They were so angry that they hired an assassin to kill him. An attempt was made on his life during his evening prayers, but he was not injured. Have the students list the challenges and dangers of being a true leader: a leader in school, at home, in the neighborhood, on teams, or in clubs.

WRITE A CINQUAIN

Charles Borromeo had many interests as a young man. He enjoyed hunting; he played the cello; he liked chess. Have the students compose a cinquain about themselves that tells others who they are and what they like to do. Encourage them to include their faith.

A cinquain is a poem, constructed as follows:

>*line 1:* subject of poem
>
>*line 2:* two adjectives describing the subject
>
>*line 3:* three verbs telling what the subject does
>
>*line 4:* a phrase about the subject
>
>*line 5:* a noun that is another name for the subject

Example:

>Mrs. Fisher
>smiling, patient
>welcomes, prays, encourages
>loves kids and God
>catechist

LEARN ABOUT LEADERS WHO OVERCAME DIFFICULTIES

Writers tell us that Charles Borromeo had a slight speech defect, so he spoke seldom and in very low tones. This did not stop him from becoming a great spiritual leader. Encourage the students to read biographies of other leaders who overcame or worked around difficulties. Have each student give a one-minute report. Point out that everyone has some kind of handicap—what matters most is how we use what we have.

RECOGNIZE CATECHISTS

Charles Borromeo is the patron of catechists. He worked hard to improve religious education in the parishes of his diocese. He also helped write the catechism used in his day. Have the children make medals or awards for all catechists in your parish or school. If possible, have the children present the medals or awards personally.

Catechist's Notes:

_____

_____

_____

_____

_____

Dedication of Saint John Lateran

November 9

In the earliest days of Christianity, those who believed in Jesus and followed his way met in private homes to hear his teachings and to celebrate the Eucharist. It was a long time before it was safe for them to use public meeting places or to build churches. When the Christians were no longer persecuted for their faith, they used their talents to the fullest and built beautiful churches honoring God. A palace owned by a noble Roman family named Laterani, built sometime before the fourth century, eventually became the property of the Emperor Constantine. Constantine had recognized Christianity as the religion of the empire, and he donated the palace and other buildings on the site to the Church. This became Rome's oldest church. It was given the title the Basilica of the Savior, but later was dedicated to John the Baptist. It was then known as St. John Lateran.

We normally think of St. Peter's and the Vatican as the traditional home of the popes, but this was not always so. St. John Lateran was the home of the popes—the center of the Catholic world—for many years. Twenty-eight popes were buried there, and it is still considered first in rank of all the basilicas. Although our pope now lives at the Vatican, St. John Lateran is considered his cathedral as the bishop of Rome. The dedication of this basilica is a happy occasion for all the Church because it reminds us of our beginnings, our roots, and our unity. It stands as a monument to God and all that he does through his Church.

On this day it is good to be grateful for our own parish church and the cathedral of our diocese. A good way to express our gratitude is to spend some quiet, prayerful time in church.

RESEARCH BASILICAS

Technically a basilica is a large rectangular building with supporting columns and a roof. In ancient times these buildings were used as meeting halls, markets, and courtrooms. Now, however, only certain structures may be designated as religious basilicas. There are four major basilicas in Rome: St. John Lateran, St. Peter (Vatican), St. Paul (outside the city walls), and St. Mary Major (founded by Pope Liberius). The part of St. John Lateran that was formerly the palace is now a museum.

Have the students research these basilicas, contact local libraries or art museums, or search the Internet to secure pictures of other famous basilicas.

VISIT THE CATHEDRAL

A cathedral is the main, or mother, church in a diocese, where the bishop presides, preaches, teaches, and leads in prayer. It does not have to be the largest church in the diocese, but it is the church where the bishop carries out a major part of his ministry. Take the students to the cathedral. Suggest they try to sketch it. Have them note the position of the bishop's chair (the *cathedra*) and any significant artistic symbols. Contact the cathedral ahead of time to see if brochures are available and if a guide can accompany the group. Encourage the students to discover more about their own parish church and its history. Recommend that they find and interview older members of the parish about the history of the church as they know it.

CONSTRUCT MODELS

Have the students design and build replicas of their cathedral or the parish church, or design a new church. They can use any of a variety of materials, such as cardboard, wood, clay, sugar cubes, or Styrofoam.

Catechist's Notes:

_____

_____

_____

_____

_____

_____

_____

_____

Saint Leo the Great

(d. 461)

Do you remember Gregory the Great? There is one other pope who earned the title *Great*—Leo I. Leo was pope about 100 years before Gregory was born.

Leo lived in Rome and became a deacon. In that position he had many responsibilities. Already other church leaders looked to him for advice and for explanations of the mysteries of the faith. Leo was even sent to settle arguments between commanders and leaders. He was in Gaul on just such a mission in 440 when Pope Sixtus III died, and Leo was elected the new pope. There was much work awaiting him, but Leo went right to the task. Leo helped the Church stay united at a time when it was being attacked inside by false teachers and outside by warring tribes.

In 452 the Huns, a fierce tribe led by Attila, marched toward Rome, ready to destroy it. Pope Leo himself went out to meet Attila and was able to stop him from entering and destroying the city by agreeing to pay tribute to him every year. Three years later another tribe, the Vandals, marched on Rome. Leo also met with their leader, Genseric. But this time Leo was only able to stop them from burning the city. For two weeks the Vandals pillaged and looted Rome while the people sought shelter in the churches. Leo helped rebuild the city.

Afterward he sent priests to Africa to minister to those who had been captured by the Vandals.

Leo is often remembered for his famous writings and explanations of the faith, especially during the Council of Chalcedon. His words were so powerful that the 600 bishops gathered there felt they had heard Saint Peter speaking through Leo.

ACTIVITIES

WRITE A HOMILY

Pope Leo's sermons dealt with everyday needs and problems. Have the students select an ordinary problem or need and write advice about it in the form of a homily.

SUPPORT THE PASTOR

Have the students work together to send a card of encouragement and support to their pastor. Ask a small group of volunteers to make a card, and let everyone add his or her signature. Invite the pastor to your classroom today or hand deliver the card.

GET SOME PERSPECTIVE

Leo was pope for 21 years, one of the longest and most significant terms in the early Church. Have students find out about other popes who served the Church. Who was pope the longest? the shortest? How long has the present pope served? What names were chosen most often? From what countries did the popes come? How many popes have there been?

DEFINE *PRUDENCE*

Prudence is a virtue often associated with Pope Leo. Ask the students to define prudence and give an example in the life of Leo where this virtue was evident.

DECLARE A DAY OF PRAYER

Declare today Pray for the Pope Day in your class. Compose and pray a special prayer for the current Holy Father.

ROLE-PLAY

Have the students act out the meetings of Leo with Attila the Hun and with Genseric and the Vandals.

Catechist's Notes:

_____

_____

_____

_____

_____

_____

_____

_____

_____

Saint Martin of Tours
November 11
(c. 316–397)

Goodness cannot be hidden. It can't be locked behind monastery walls or disguised by rough and shabby clothing. Martin of Tours was a good and holy man, and people from far and wide could recognize this. He was born in what is today the country of Hungary and was raised in Italy. His parents were pagans, and his father was an officer in the army. Because he was the son of an officer, Martin was expected to join the army, too, which he did when he was 15 years old. But at the same time, he had been drawn to Jesus and his teachings and had become a catechumen—a person who is preparing to become a Christian.

A famous story is told about Martin. When Martin was 18 and stationed in Amiens (in Gaul, now France), he was making his rounds one cold winter evening. As he entered the city gates, he saw a beggar shivering in the cold. Having nothing else to give, Martin cut his own cloak in two and wrapped half of it around the poor beggar. That night in a dream Martin saw Christ wearing the cloak. Martin was baptized soon after that.

But being both a Christian and a soldier did not work for Martin. He could no longer seek to hurt anyone in war or battle. When he was 23, he refused to arm himself for battle. This came to the attention of the emperor. Martin was accused of being a coward and was thrown in prison. He was soon released, however, since the enemy in the meantime had sent a messenger seeking peace. Now Martin was free to give his life to the true battle—the battle against evil. He went to study under St. Hilary, the bishop of Poitiers. Martin returned home and converted his mother, although his father never converted. Martin fought heresy and was beaten and driven out of towns for trying to teach the truth. But he never gave up.

Eventually he returned to Gaul and founded a monastery, probably the first one there. He lived there for 10 years, but his reputation for goodness and holiness had grown so much that when the bishop of Tours died, the people there would not be satisfied until Martin was made their bishop. Reluctantly he was ordained bishop in 371. He traveled throughout the area, meeting the people, teaching them, and curing them. He destroyed pagan temples and the sacred groves. But he also sought the quiet of a prayerful community. So he founded another monastery to train more priests to help him bring the Gospel to the people.

When Martin died he was immediately honored as a saint, one of the first who was not a martyr to be so honored. So popular is this saint that his shrine at Tours is one of the most visited places of pilgrimage in all of Europe. He is known as the Apostle of Gaul, one of the patron saints of France, the patron of soldiers and, at the same time, a true patron of peace.

RETELL THE STORY

Prepare the children to work together in small groups. Let each group choose one of these options:

- Act out the story of Martin and the beggar.

- Depict the story by constructing a diorama—a three-dimensional scene in a box on its side.

- Draw a large picture of Martin hiding so as not to be made bishop. According to legend, his pet goose gave away his hiding place by honking.

WRITE ABOUT A GOOD FRIEND

Much of what we know about Martin of Tours comes from a biography of him written by his close friend Sulpicius Severus. True friends are able to see both strengths and weaknesses in each other. Ask the students to write a paragraph about an event in the life of one of their friends that shows one of the best characteristics of that friend—one that could even qualify him or her as a "candidate for goodness." Share these stories.

LEARN ABOUT THE RITE OF CHRISTIAN INITIATION OF ADULTS (RCIA)

Martin was a catechumen. In the early church, this was one step in the process of conversion and preparation for Baptism, Confirmation, and Eucharist. This rite has been revived in the Church. Ask a parishioner who is involved in the RCIA to explain the catechumenate to the students.

RESEARCH THE HISTORY OF THE PARISH

Some say it was Martin who first conceived of the organization of settlements into parishes. Have the students find out more about their parish: its founding date, former pastors, current pastoral team, membership, active organizations, parish council, and so on. Make posters or an illustrated time line to display in the parish hall or church gathering area.

Catechist's Notes:

_____

_____

_____

_____

_____

_____

_____

Saint Frances Xavier Cabrini

(1850–1917)

Have you ever moved to a new city or a different state? Did you, or would you, feel lost and alone until you got settled and made new friends? Imagine what it is like for the thousands of immigrants each year who make their way to other countries, hoping to find a brighter future in a new land. Many of these people have their hopes dashed, and they lose their way. It was to people such as these that Mother Frances Cabrini came.

Francesca Cabrini was born in northern Italy. Her parents, Agostino and Stella, owned a prosperous farm. They were a loving family and deeply religious. In the evenings Papa Cabrini would read stories to the children about the work of the missionaries. Francesca enjoyed these stories and hoped to become a missionary herself.

After completing school and receiving a teacher's certificate, Francesca taught for a while and was then asked to take over a nearby orphanage, the House of Providence. Francesca gathered around her the small group of women who would soon become the Institute of the Missionary Sisters of the Sacred Heart. She chose as patrons of the community Saints Francis de Sales for teaching and Francis Xavier for missionary work. Her hope was to travel to China and the East. She went to Rome for approval of her order, and Pope Leo XIII did indeed bless her and her work. But he insisted, "No, not to the East, but to the West."

People in the mother country had heard of the hard times that had befallen the Italians who had gone to the United States and South America looking for jobs and prosperity.

And so Mother Frances Cabrini set sail for New York with six sisters on March 23, 1889. When they arrived, they discovered that they had no place to stay. They often were without money or lodging, but somehow God provided. Soon Mother Cabrini established hospitals, schools, and orphanages. The sisters went to the major cities where the Italian immigrants gathered. The sisters taught them skills, cared for their needs, and comforted some of them in prisons. In 35 years Mother Cabrini founded nearly 70 institutions for helping the needy, the poor, the abandoned, and the ill. In 1909 she became a naturalized citizen of the United States.

She continued her work at an amazing pace. She crossed the ocean 30 times, even though she was deathly afraid of water, each time bringing more sisters. She established homes in a number of cities in the United States, as well as in Central and South America.

Mother Cabrini died rather suddenly in Columbus Hospital, which she had founded in Chicago. Only the day before, she had been wrapping presents and helping with plans for a Christmas party for the children. She was the first United States citizen to be canonized.

SHARE STORIES OF SAINTS

Frances Cabrini was inspired by the stories she heard as a child. Have older students select short stories about the saints to read to younger children. Set up a story-sharing time with the younger students so they, too, can learn to dream of serving others in Christ's name.

OFFER A PRAYER FROM THE LITURGY

Use this prayer of the Church at the end of class today:

> God our Father,
> you called Frances Xavier Cabrini from Italy
> to serve the immigrants of America.
> By her example, teach us concern for the
> stranger, the sick, and the frustrated.
> By her prayers, help us to see Christ
> in all the men and women we meet.

REACH OUT

Have the students design and make greeting cards for sick or elderly people at home, in hospitals, and in nursing homes. Make arrangements to visit a home for children, bringing games and prizes.

CATCH THE MISSIONARY SPIRIT

Have the students research and make short reports on what missionaries are doing in the world today, including your own diocese. If Missionary Sisters of the Sacred Heart work in your area, consider inviting one or two of them in as guest speakers. Encourage the students to pray and sacrifice for the success of the Church's missionary efforts.

ILLUSTRATE FRANCES'S BOATS

When Frances Cabrini was a young girl, she would make paper boats and fill them with tiny violets. She sailed these little boats down the canal near the home of her uncle. The flowers represented missionaries going out to bring the Good News of Jesus to the world.

- Have the students draw pictures illustrating this event or others in the life of Frances Cabrini.

- Help the children make a bulletin board display of a sailboat. Let them make and add paper flowers. Say a prayer for all missionaries and for immigrants who are looking for a new home and a better life.

Catechist's Notes:

_____

_____

_____

_____

_____

_____

_____

Saint Albert the Great   November 15

(c. 1206–1280)

You probably know that many saints were priests and sisters, teachers and nurses, even kings and queens. Did you know that one saint was a leading scientist of his time?

He is known as Albert the Great. So devoted to God and such a seeker of truth was he that he saw the whole created world before him, waiting to be discovered, recorded, and taught. Albert is the patron of scientists, philosophers, and students.

Albert came from a noble military family in Germany. He studied at the University of Padua. It was there that he became acquainted with the Dominican Order. After some hesitation he became a Dominican—even though his family was against it. He continued his studies and went on to become a famous and gifted teacher. One of his most famous pupils was Thomas Aquinas. Albert seemed to be interested in everything—biology, chemistry, physics, astronomy, geography, economics, politics, logic,

mathematics—all of this plus theology, Scripture, and philosophy. But nonetheless his life was not centered on science; it was centered on God. For Albert all these different areas displayed most beautifully the wonderful plan and providence of God.

When he was 48, Albert was named the provincial superior of the Dominican Order. Three years later he resigned his post so that he could devote more time to study. Then he was appointed bishop of Regensburg. Because he traveled his diocese on foot, he was known as "Bishop with the Boots." After two years he was able to go back to writing and teaching until his death. For Albert life was filled with wonders to discover—whether it was the life cycle of a spider or developing the theory that the world was round. If creation is so wonderful, how much more wonderful is the Creator! Albert the Great is a model of the kind of scientists and faith-filled men and women the world needs today.

ACTIVITIES

EXPERIMENT

Conduct a fun science experiment or group projects. Older students may help younger ones if necessary. Let everyone get "hands on."

DEDICATE SCIENCE FAIR

If your school sponsors a science fair, have it renamed in this saint's honor, for example, Albert the Great Expo.

DISCOVER SCIENCE

Let the students enjoy a nature walk. Or devote time to the care of the environment, for example, planting trees or spring bulbs, picking up debris, or preparing a bird feeder.

MAKE WORD WEBS

Have the students make word webs to illustrate Albert's many interests. Ask the youngsters what would go in the center circle (God). Then let them add circles emanating from the center. In each circle have them write fascinating facts they know or find out about each subject, or questions they have. Be sure to display the finished webs.

Catechist's Notes:

_____

_____

_____

_____

_____

_____

_____

_____

_____

_____

_____

_____

Saint Margaret of Scotland

(1045–1093)

Some people feel they have done enough for the poor and needy when they have given money. But for Margaret of Scotland—a busy wife, mother, and queen—giving money was never enough. She was right there with the poor, washing their feet and making sure they had food to eat and clothes to wear. Only after all the others were cared for would she herself eat and rest.

Margaret was born into a noble family and raised in the royal court in Hungary. When she was 12, she was sent to the English court of Edward the Confessor. There she was further educated. But when the Normans conquered England, Margaret, her mother, brother, and sister tried to return to Hungary. Their ship was blown off course, and they landed in Scotland. They were warmly welcomed by King Malcolm III. The king fell in love with the beautiful and gentle Margaret. They were married in 1070.

Scotland was a rough country, and although Malcolm was a good man, he was more of a soldier than a gentleman. Margaret helped him become a virtuous, gracious leader. They had eight children—two girls and six boys—and all of them grew to love the poor and care for them just as their parents had before them.

Margaret was known for her prayerfulness as well as her charity. She would rise early in the morning to go to the castle chapel before

another busy day began. Her most prized possession was her prayer book. She gathered a group of women together to study and discuss the Scriptures and to embroider vestments and fine altar cloths. She called Church councils to encourage observance of Lent, respect for the Eucharist, and keeping Sunday holy.

The queen was often approached by beggars, and she gave them money and clothes. She helped ransom the English who had been captured, and she set up homes and hospitals for strangers, the sick, and the poor. She and her husband would go to the church in the middle of the night during Lent and Advent. On the way home, they would wash the feet of six poor people and give them money. At home Margaret would personally feed nine orphans who were brought to her daily.

Her concern was for all her people. She brought a love of the arts and education to the people, and they loved her in return. So well did she teach her children to love God that they are believed to be primarily responsible for two centuries of progress and peace in Scotland.

Margaret died four days after her husband Malcolm. In 1250 she was canonized and later declared patroness of Scotland. People today still look to her example. She saw Christ in the poor and did not wait for someone else to take care of their needs. She was there—and led others to loving service as well.

PRACTICE REVERENCE IN CHURCH

It was recorded that when Margaret went to church, she was quiet and extraordinarily reverent. Remind the students of the importance of respect and awareness of God's presence as they enter a church. Review with them the use of the blessing with holy water and reverent genuflection.

MAKE FAMILY BOOKLETS

The power of family training and love was evident in Margaret and Malcolm's family. Their youngest son, David, was acclaimed a saint by Scottish people. Have the students make a "My Family" booklet, illustrating the members of their families, describing their family schedule, mealtime at home, holiday customs, and so on. Suggest that they also show examples of family love, service to others, and faith in God.

DECORATE A BOOK COVER

King Malcolm himself never learned to read, but he saw how much his beloved queen, Margaret, treasured her book of psalms. Malcolm had the finest craftsmen in the country decorate her favorite books with gold and precious jewels. Let the students make decorative covers for their Bibles or religion books. Provide a variety of fabrics, paper, stickers, beads, and "jewels" to stimulate their imaginations.

CONDUCT A COURTESY CAMPAIGN

Margaret did much to civilize Scotland. Have the students brainstorm a list of actions that show good manners and courtesy. Ask them to explain the reasons or thinking behind each action. Lead them to the root reason— respect for God's creatures shows respect for God. And, as children of God, all people are in justice due respect. Have the students make campaign-type posters to advertise good manners and courtesy.

REVIEW CHURCH LAWS

Margaret worked to educate the Celtic clergy and the people. She encouraged the meeting of synods and helped bring back a proper understanding of the Lenten fasts, the need to receive Holy Communion, and the proper marriage laws. Review with the students the Duties of Catholic Christians. You may wish to use the blackline master on page 467.

Catechist's Notes:

_____

_____

_____

_____

_____

_____

Saint Gertrude
(1256–1301)

The most important thing we know about Saint Gertrude is that she loved God and was very aware of God's love for her. When she was five years old, Gertrude was placed in the care of the Benedictine nuns at Helfta, in Germany. Under the leadership of a holy abbess also named Gertrude, their monastery was a center of holiness and intellectual activity. Saint Mechtildis was put in charge of the young girl. Gertrude became a charming person who loved to study.

Later Gertrude herself became a nun at Helfta and eventually was made abbess. When she was 26, Gertrude began having deep mystical experiences; she would be so caught up in God that she became unaware of those around her. She also had the gift of miracles. Her life from that point on revolved around the study of Scripture, prayer, spiritual reading, and the liturgy of the Church. She copied and translated many books and wrote her own in Latin. Besides being a theologian, Gertrude was known for her charity and humility.

Gertrude's holiness flowed in part from her great devotion to the Sacred Heart, the symbol of Jesus' love for the human race. Gertrude carried her love for Christ to others through the prayers that she wrote and through the journal of her mystical experiences.

NOVEMBER

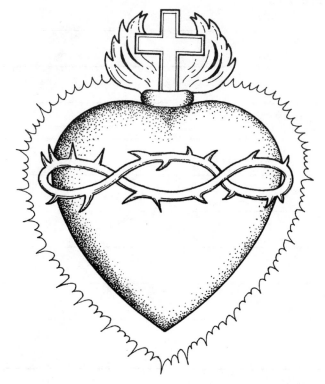

ACTIVITIES

MAKE LOVE TREES

One of Gertrude's deepest experiences was the love of the Sacred Heart. Remind children that the Sacred Heart is a symbol of the great love of Christ. Have the students make heart-shaped love trees, and on each heart write one way they will show love today.

Directions

1. Fold an 8½" × 11" sheet of paper in half. On the fold trace three half-hearts, with the hearts becoming progressively larger.

2. Cut out the outlined hearts, being careful not to cut through the folded edge. Decorate the edges of the hearts. In the middle of each of the three hearts, have the students write ways they will show love today.

3. Attach the heart structure to pink or red construction paper, 9" × 12", and add stem, leaves, and base, using markers or green paper. You might print on the base the title "Letting My Love Grow and Grow."

WRITE IN JOURNALS

In the Bible the heart is understood as the center of the whole life of a man or a woman. Have the students read the following passages and reflect on them by writing in their journals: John 15:9; John 13:34; Matthew 12:35.

LOCATE THE WEST INDIES

Gertrude is the patroness of the West Indies. Have the students locate the islands on a map or globe and pray for the people who live there.

Catechist's Notes:

_____

_____

_____

_____

_____

_____

_____

_____

Saint Elizabeth of Hungary

(1207–1231)

Have you ever felt misunderstood or judged unfairly? Few people have understood what that means more than Elizabeth of Hungary.

Elizabeth's father was Andrew II, the king of Hungary. Her marriage was arranged very early, and at the age of four she was sent to Thuringia (now part of Germany) for education and eventually marriage. When she was 14, she married Louis, the ruler of Thuringia. They loved each other deeply, and they had three children. Even at so young an age, Elizabeth showed a great love for God and the poor. Louis supported her in all she did to relieve the sufferings of the poor and sick. But Louis's mother, Sophia, his brother, and the other members of court resented Elizabeth's generosity. Elizabeth dressed in simple clothes rather than the royal robes expected of someone in her position. For this she was taunted and mocked by the royal family. But she was deeply loved by the common folk. Louis loved her and defended her.

After six years of marriage, Louis went to fight in the Crusades, but he got sick and died on the way. When Elizabeth heard of his death, she was grief-stricken. Louis had been her husband, her best friend, and her loyal supporter. Now she was without him. At the same time, her in-laws accused her of poorly managing the finances of the kingdom, and finally forced her and her children out of the palace. They were left homeless and poor. For a while they found refuge in a pig barn. Finally Elizabeth and her children were taken in by her uncle, the bishop of Bamberg. When her husband's friends returned from the Crusades and saw Elizabeth's plight, they helped restore her to her rightful place in the palace. But rather than enjoying the comfort and ease of royal life, Elizabeth increased her service to others. When Elizabeth died at age 24, the people acclaimed her sanctity, and she was canonized only four years later.

Elizabeth is often pictured with red roses filling her cape. According to legend, she went out with loaves of bread to feed the poor. Her mother-in-law saw her and took hold of her cape to see what she was carrying. What she found was not bread, but roses! Because of this story Elizabeth is considered the patroness of bakers.

Saint Elizabeth had suffered much, but she had loved much too. She was a devoted wife and mother. Her life is a beautiful example of all the Gospel calls us to be—loving, caring, and forgiving.

FEED THE HUNGRY

Saint Elizabeth carried out the corporal work of mercy to feed the hungry. Engage the students in this work through one or more of the following activities:

- Have a bake sale. Students may sell home-baked goodies to other classes in school or religious ed, or to parishioners after each Sunday Mass. Donate all proceeds to a charity that feeds the hungry.

- Have the children decorate grocery bags to be used at a food pantry. Encourage them to use seasonal art or cheerful designs.

- Encourage student volunteers to help serve or clean up after the coffee hour following Sunday morning Mass.

AID LOCAL CHARITIES

Elizabeth is the patroness of the Franciscan Third Order and of all Catholic Charities.

- Explain what a third order is. If such a group is active in your parish, consider inviting a speaker to tell the children what they do.

- Help the students find out about services that are offered through Catholic Charities in your diocese and how the children can help.

BEAR WRONGS PATIENTLY

One of the spiritual works of mercy is to bear wrongs patiently, as Elizabeth did. Ask the students to give examples of how they have been or may be called to do this.

Catechist's Notes:

_____

_____

_____

_____

_____

_____

_____

_____

_____

_____

_____

Saint Roque Gonzalez and Companions

November 17

(d. 1628)

How do you react when you see something that in not fair? Do you figure it's none of your business? Or do you try to make it right? Roque Gonzalez tried to make it right.

Roque was born in Asuncion, the capital city of Paraguay in South America. His family was of Spanish nobility, and his brother was a governor of Asuncion. Roque became a priest. At that time Spanish conquistadors (conquerors) were enslaving members of native tribes, taking them from their homes, and forcing them to work in the silver mines of Peru. Even though both the Spanish rulers and the Church condemned the treatment of the natives, the practice continued.

Roque wanted to find a way to change the system. He joined the Jesuit Order and helped come up with a plan. In order to protect the Guarani natives of Paraguay, the Jesuits gathered them together to live in communities called reductions. These settlements were like small, protected villages. The Guarani had their own mayor and council. The priests lived and worked with them, and taught skills such as farming, weaving cotton, and building boats.

The Guarani also learned arts and crafts, including making musical instruments, painting manuscripts, and printing books. At the same time, they were instructed in the faith, and many were baptized. The Jesuits ran into strong opposition from the Spanish authorities but were backed by the Church.

Roque headed the first settlement in Paraguay and founded six others. Within 10 years the Jesuits had established a chain of settlements in Paraguay, Argentina, Brazil, and Uruguay. Two Spanish Jesuits who worked closely with Roque were Alonzo Rodriguez and Juan de Castillo.

One of their last settlements was in southern Brazil, in an area that was controlled by Nezu, a powerful native chieftain. Nezu became alarmed that the Jesuits were undermining his authority. He organized a raid on the settlement of All Saints in which Roque Gonzalez and Alonso Rodriguez were killed. Juan de Castillo was killed two days later at the reduction dedicated to the Assumption of Our Lady.

Roque Gonzalez was beatified in 1934. He and his companions were canonized in 1988.

CELEBRATE

Roque Gonzalez is the patron saint of preserving native traditions. He enabled the Guarani to celebrate holy days of the Church by incorporating aspects of their tradition: colorful decoration, dancing, and loud noise. After a solemn Mass, they would have games, bonfires, fireworks, and the music of native flutes. Take time today for some activities the children especially enjoy.

RING BELLS

Roque was hanging a bell at the Church of All Saints when he was attacked from behind and killed. Hang or place a small bell in your prayer space. Use it to call the children to pray today. Or organize a procession with the children ringing hand bells.

WRITE RELIGIOUS VERSE

Roque was a man of many talents, and he used every one of them to help others. He composed hymns and compiled a catechism in rhyming verse to help teach religion. Have the children write short religious verses about whatever they are studying in religion class this week. Compile the verses into a small booklet, make copies, and distribute them to the class.

SEEK JUSTICE

Have the students look through newspapers and magazines to find examples of injustice or exploitation going on in the world today. Discuss ways people of faith can bring justice to each situation.

Catechist's Notes:

_____

_____

_____

_____

_____

_____

_____

_____

_____

Saint Rose Philippine Duchesne

November 18

(1769–1852)

Rose Philippine was born in France, but from the very beginning it seems she was destined for America. She was named for Saint Rose of Lima, who was the first saint of the New World. A Jesuit missionary who had worked in Louisiana visited the Duchesne home and told stories about the Native Americans. Young Rose's imagination and interest were sparked.

Rose attended a school taught by the Visitation sisters. When she was 17 and her family was looking for a husband for her, Rose told them she wanted to become a Visitation sister. Her family objected, but Rose joined the community. When the French Revolution forced religious communities to leave their convents, Rose returned home but continued to live as a religious. She cared for the sick, visited prisoners, and taught.

At that time Madeleine Sophie Barat was starting the Society of the Sacred Heart, a new community of sisters. At the age of 33, Rose joined them. She expressed a wish to go to America as a missionary, but it wasn't until she was 49 years old that her dream came true. She and four other sisters were sent at the request of the bishop of St. Louis. They spent 11 weeks crossing the ocean before landing at New Orleans, and seven weeks on the Mississippi to reach St. Louis.

Rose was dismayed to discover that there was no work with Native Americans in St. Louis. In fact the sisters' arrival was unexpected. The bishop sent them to a log cabin on the frontier, where they opened the first free school for girls west of the Mississippi. With courage and trust in God, Rose Philippine and the sisters educated poor children. Eventually Rose founded six convents from St. Louis down to New Orleans and several schools in Missouri and Louisiana.

When Mother Duchesne was 71 years old, she was allowed to resign as American superior. Father Pierre de Smet was asking the sisters to open a school for the Potowatomi Indians in Sugar Creek, Kansas. Mother Duchesne asked to go. Although she could not speak the language or teach, she could pray. In Kansas she spent four hours every morning and four hours every evening praying in the chapel. The Potowatomi called her Woman-Who-Prays-Always. There is a story that one day when Mother Duchesne was kneeling in prayer a child placed kernels of corn on the skirt of her long habit. He came back hours later and found the kernels unmoved.

When her health failed, Mother Duchesne returned to St. Charles, Missouri. There she lived a simple life of prayer and penance until her death. She was canonized in 1988.

FILL A PRAYER JAR

Place a glass jar and a basket or bowl of kernels of corn (can be unpopped popcorn) on the prayer table. Talk with the children about how important Mother Duschesne's prayer was to the mission in Kansas. Ask the children to pray for the success of current missionary work of the Church in your area. Invite them to drop a kernel of corn into the jar each time they pray for missionaries.

USE A MAP TO RETELL THE STORY

Have the students locate on a map the cities Grenoble, France; New Orleans, Louisiana; St. Louis and St. Charles, Missouri; and Topeka, Kansas, as they retell the story of Mother Duschesne.

LEARN A POTOWATOMI GREETING

Mother Duchesne learned English when she came to America. But she was never able to master the Potowatomi language. Teach the children a phrase of the Potowatomi. TA-NI-KI DO-DAM NIC-CON means "How do you do, my friend?" The class may want to post this sign on the classroom door for the day.

FIND OUT ABOUT OTHER FIRSTS

Have students find out more about other Catholic firsts in the United States: the first bishop, the first church, the first saint, the first Catholic school.

SUPPLEMENT THE STORY

Suggest that a group of interested students read about Saint Madeleine Sophie Barat, who founded many schools, and give a short lesson or skit about her for the rest of the class.

DISCUSS DREAMS AND REALITY

Mission life was not the glamorous adventure Rose Philippine had imagined as a child. Once she had to travel on a riverboat with yellow fever patients. After tending to the sick, she contracted the disease. When she was put ashore at Natchez, Mississippi, the only lodging available was the bed of a woman who had just died of the fever. Ask the students to tell about times when their dreams or ideals came up hard against reality. Talk about why Mother Duchesne would continue under such conditions. Discuss what faith is really calling us to do.

Catechist's Notes:

_____

_____

_____

_____

_____

_____

_____

Dedication of the Churches of Peter and Paul

November 18

The basilicas of Saint Peter (at the Vatican, where the pope lives) and Saint Paul in Rome are important because they honor these apostles. The basilica of Saint Peter is the largest in Christendom today. It is used for most major ceremonies although St. John Lateran is the pope's cathedral. St. Peter's basilica was built over Peter's tomb. The basilica of St. Paul was erected on the Ostian Way and honors the place where he was martyred.

Peter, the former fisherman and witness to the Resurrection, was entrusted with the leadership of Christ's Church. He steered it through its crucial first years. Paul, the apostle to the Gentiles, founded and guided many of the early churches. Through his preaching and letters preserved in Scripture, he helped shape the theology of Christianity.

The basilicas of these two giants of the faith are important also because they give the people of God a sense of what Christianity is all about. Peter and Paul gave their lives to spread the good news that God has redeemed his people. Century after century, saints and sinners alike have found peace and joy in the Church and in her sacraments. Today, as we celebrate the Eucharist in our parish churches, we are united with the community of believers all over the world. There is but one Lord, one faith, one Baptism—and we rejoice that we are one people of God.

LEARN ABOUT SAINT PETER'S

Select a few volunteers to go to the library or search the Internet, find pictures of the basilica of Saint Peter, and then use the pictures as they point out to the class interesting details of the structure, including mention of some of the various statues inside. If any of your students have been to Rome, they may have pictures, videos, or slides to share with the class.

BEAUTIFY THE CHURCH

Both basilicas, Saint Peter's and Saint Paul's, were completed in the fourth century under Popes Sylvester and Siricius. Both basilicas were later destroyed and reconstructed. Have the students launch a beautification program for the parish church and grounds. Let them clear out and arrange storerooms, polish church materials, plant flowers, and so on.

REFLECT ON CEMETERIES

The basilicas of Saint Peter and Saint Paul honor the tomb or place of martyrdom of these apostles. Have some students research the excavations under Saint Peter's, which identified the place of Peter's burial in an old Roman cemetery. Discuss the custom of decorating cemeteries as a sign of respect for those who have died. Encourage the students to pay such respect when their families make memorial visits to the grave sites of deceased relatives and friends.

LEARN ABOUT YOUR PARISH

Invite the pastor or an associate to give a talk on the history of your parish church. Many parishes keep photos or parish annals available for use in such presentations.

Catechist's Notes:

_____

_____

_____

_____

_____

_____

_____

_____

_____

Presentation of Mary

How would you answer someone who asked, "Why do we pray to Mary? Why does the Church honor Mary with special feast days?" Pope Paul VI said to us that Mary was to be honored and imitated because in her own life she fully accepted the will of God and did it. We ask her to pray for us so that we can accept God's will for us.

The feast of the presentation of Mary dates back to the sixth century in the East and the 15th century in the West. It is based on an ancient tradition that says Mary was taken to the Temple in Jerusalem when she was three years old and dedicated to God. What we celebrate on this day is the fact that God chose to dwell in Mary in a very special way. In response Mary placed her whole self at the service of God. How does this relate to you?

Through the sacrament of Baptism, God chooses to live in you through grace and the Holy Spirit. You become a temple of the living God. Every moment since your Baptism, God invites you to be open to his grace and to dedicate yourself to him, as Mary did.

Perhaps you were taken to church and baptized when you were very young. How can you say yes to God now? How can you dedicate yourself to God's will for you? Each time you celebrate the Eucharist, you have the opportunity to present yourself to God. During the presentation of the gifts (bread and wine), you can present yourself to God too. You can offer everything you do with love, and everything you accept from God with thanksgiving. During the Eucharistic Prayer, you can unite yourself with the offering of Jesus, who gave his life to God.

NOVEMBER

PRAY A LITANY

With the students, pray the Litany to Mary, Mother of the Church. Use the blackline master on page 445 to make copies for the class.

SERVE OTHERS

Encourage the children to serve others in honor of Mary, the first and most faithful disciple of the Lord. First talk about ways they can put the needs of others before their own, such as listening to what others have to say in conversation, giving someone else first place in line, and helping at home. Then give each child a small piece of paper. Have the children each write one way a person their age could be a disciple and give service to others. Collect the papers in a box. Pass the box around the room. Have the students each draw a slip of paper. Encourage them to practice for one week what is written on the slips they have drawn.

DEDICATE YOURSELF TO GOD

Today's feast also commemorates the dedication of the Church of Saint Mary, which was built in Jerusalem near the site of the Temple. Have students draw outlines of one another. Have each one label the drawing The Church of Holy _____ [his or her name]. Ask them to write inside the outline some ways they will dedicate themselves to God.

FIND THE FOCUS OF EACH FEAST

All feasts of Mary are closely related to the mysteries in Christ's life. Challenge older students to explain how each Marian feast points to Christ as the center of Mary's life. The feasts of Mary are

September 8	Birth of Mary
September 15	Our Lady of Sorrows
October 7	Our Lady of the Rosary
November 21	Presentation of Mary
December 8	Immaculate Conception
December 12	Our Lady of Guadalupe
January 1	Mary, Mother of God
February 2	Presentation of the Lord
February 11	Our Lady of Lourdes
March 25	Annunciation of the Lord
May 31	Visitation
May	Immaculate Heart of Mary
July 16	Our Lady of Mount Carmel
August 15	Assumption
August 22	Queenship of Mary

PRAY A RESPONSORIAL PSALM

Psalm 50 is a Scripture selection for the liturgy for this feast. Pray Psalm 50:1–15 as a responsorial psalm. Use verse 14 as the psalm response: Offer to God a sacrifice of thanksgiving.

SING A FAVORITE SONG

Today sing a Marian song or hymn that the children like.

Catechist's Notes:

_____

_____

_____

Saint Cecilia

(late 200s?)

We really know very little about Saint Cecilia, although stories abound. She lived in Rome in the second century during the time of great persecutions. One story dates back to the fifth or sixth century, when she was a popular saint. We are told that as a young girl Cecilia wanted to give her life to God. Her parents forced her to marry a noble pagan youth named Valerian. He had so much respect for Cecilia that he let her remain a virgin as she desired. In time she converted him and his brother Tiburtius to the faith. All three of them died as martyrs.

According to a story about Cecilia's martyrdom, the officials unsuccessfully tried to suffocate her in her own house. Then an executioner tried to behead her. He struck her with his sword three times but did not sever her neck completely.

She lived three days. Before she died she asked to have her house dedicated as a church. Cecilia was buried in the catacomb of Callistus. Remains thought to be her body are now buried under the altar of the basilica of Saint Cecilia.

Cecilia is often pictured with a musical instrument—a small organ, a harp, or a viola.

One legend says that while the musicians played at her wedding, Cecilia sang to the Lord in her heart. She is the patroness of musicians. The feast of Saint Cecilia is a reminder that the Church has always recognized the value of music and song. Some thoughts and feelings are best expressed in music.

Cecilia's name is mentioned in Eucharistic Prayer I.

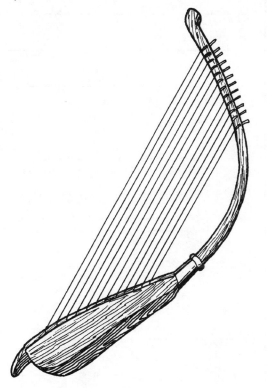

NOVEMBER

ACTIVITIES

SING A PSALM

Jesus and his disciples sang psalms of Passover on the night before he died. Read Matthew 26:30. Sing one of the psalms that is used in your parish liturgy.

RESEARCH THE CATACOMBS

Have the students look up information about the catacombs where Saint Cecilia's remains were found. Her remains were taken to Rome, where a basilica was built in her honor. The students might also research the basilica of Saint Cecilia.

ENJOY A CONCERT

Since Cecilia is the patroness of musicians, schedule a band concert, choir performance, or sing-along assembly in her honor. Some students may wish to compose original songs or music and perform them.

BE A MARTYR

The word *martyr* means "witness." Some martyrs witness to their faith by dying. We also witness to our faith by the way we live. Ask the students for examples of people, famous or not, who give their lives for the faith by following the Gospel.

Catechist's Notes:

_____

_____

_____

_____

_____

_____

_____

_____

_____

_____

Saint Clement of Rome

November 23

(d. c. 100)

Saint Clement I was the third pope of the Roman Church after Saint Peter. Very little is known about Saint Clement. He succeeded Cletus as bishop of Rome around the year 92, and his reign lasted until 101.

Even though we have few biographical facts about Clement, we do know that he wrote a very important letter to the Corinthians while he was pope. The city of Corinth had a large Christian population, but it also had a number of problems. During Clement's time a group of people in Corinth refused to follow the legitimate Church authority there. They split off from the main group of believers. But when part of the Church is divided, the whole Church suffers. Clement, as the shepherd of the Church, wrote to the people explaining the role of authority, the role of the people, and encouraging peace and harmony. He begged them to stop their jealousies and quarreling. So powerful and clear was the letter that in some places in the early Church it was ranked next to the accepted books of Sacred Scripture. It is one of the earliest Christian documents we have outside the New Testament. Clement was martyred for the faith. He was the first theologian known by the title Father of the Church. The basilica of Saint Clement is in Rome.

LEARN MORE ABOUT THE POPE(S)

After Peter's martyrdom, the Church was led by Linus, then Cletus, and then Clement.

- Some students would find it fascinating to look at a list of popes through the centuries. They could discover some unusual names, the names that were used most often, some very short tenures, and some that were quite long. Most important, they will see the continuity from Peter to the present.

- For students who like current events better than history, post a picture of the present pope. Invite the students to bring in other pictures, summaries of his letters or statements, and articles about his activities and travels to add to the display.

TALK ABOUT FACTIONS

Ask the students to read 1 Corinthians 1:11–16 and explain the problems that had arisen. Paul reminded the people that there is only one Christ, and so factions are out of place. Clement, too, had to deal with the problem of factions. Let the students discuss how they would handle the problem of groups of Christians opposing one another. Discuss with them the problems connected with forming cliques in classes, schools, and neighborhoods.

MAKE A MONTAGE

Have the students make a montage together, using one or more symbols of the pope:

a tiara: a beehive-shaped circular headpiece of three crowns, one above the other, with a cross on the top and two lappets hanging down the back

a triple cross: the papal cross has three crossbars

a church

a papal coat of arms

a mitre: the ceremonial headdress worn by bishops that is similar to the tiara

CHOOSE PATRONS

Clement is the patron of marble-workers, stonecutters, and mariners. One story about him relates how he made a miraculous spring of water flow for some convicts with whom he worked. Another story states that an anchor was tied around his neck and he was drowned, but the sea opened up to reveal the angels burying him in a marble tomb under the seas. From these stories certain groups have taken Clement as their special patron. Ask the children to jot down their hobbies or other interests, or the occupation they would like to have some day. Have them use the Internet or resource books to find a saint that might be an appropriate patron.

Catechist's Notes:

_____

_____

_____

_____

Saint Columban

(d. 615)

Zeal is a word we associate with missionaries and people on fire with the love of God. Zeal can win many followers for Christ. It can also stir up enemies— people who do not want to hear how their lives must change. Columban, one of the greatest Irish missionaries who labored in Europe, was a man filled with zeal. He came to know the joy and hardships of working for Christ.

Columban was born in Ireland before the middle of the sixth century. He entered a monastery, and led a life of prayer and study for 30 years. Then in the year 591, he and 12 companions were sent to Europe as missionaries. They made their way through France, Switzerland, and eventually Italy. Everywhere they went they established the monasteries that were to become the centers for Christianity, learning, and prayer throughout Europe.

Columban wrote a strict rule for these monasteries, and he tried to reform the lives of the clergy, the nobility, and the laypeople. He attacked abuses and evil wherever he saw them. He spoke out loudly against the immorality that was so common among the royalty. Finally he was exiled for pointing out the sins of the king and for criticizing the local bishops because they did not speak out against him too.

While Columban was being deported, he was shipwrecked and ended up in Italy, where he found refuge. While he was there, he founded a monastery in Bobbio, and it was there that he died.

ACTIVITIES

WRITE A RULE

Columban is known for the strict monastic rule he wrote. Have the students draft 10 or so rules for everyday Christian living or try to write the rules for living together as a Christian community.

RECEIVE AN IRISH BLESSING

Play some Celtic music in the background today in honor of Columban. Bless the children with this traditional Irish blessing at the end of the day.

> May the road rise to meet you.
> May the wind be always at your back.
> May the sun shine warm upon your face.
> May the rains fall softly upon your fields.
> And, until we meet again,
> May God hold you in the hollow of his hand.

LEARN FROM MISTAKES

Saints are not born saints. Nor does holiness guarantee that one will make no mistakes. Even Saint Columban made some mistakes. Have the students discuss the positive aspects of making mistakes. Discuss the obligation the students have to study, pray, form Christian consciences, and then live faithful and true lives.

EXPLORE MISSIONARY COMMUNITIES

Help the students find out about a missionary community such as Maryknoll or the Columban Fathers. They might use the Internet and/or write for material. Explain that besides foreign missionaries, there are home missionaries such as the Glenmary communities, who work in their own country.

Catechist's Notes:

Blessed Miguel Agustín Pro

(1891–1927)

On November 23, 1927, Father Miguel Pro, a lively, fun-loving young Jesuit, faced a firing squad with a small cross in one hand and a Rosary in the other. He had refused a blindfold and had asked only for time to pray. Not long before, he had offered his life to God for the faith of the Mexican people.

Miguel Pro was born in Guadalupe, Mexico, one of 11 children of a mining engineer. He joined the Jesuits in 1911, a year after a persecution began in Mexico. While Miguel was in the novitiate, soldiers broke into the building and set fire to it. The novices were sent to study in other countries. Miguel, dressed as a peasant, fled to California. Then he was sent to Spain, Nicaragua, and Belgium, where he was ordained. Study was hard for Miguel, who suffered from a stomach illness.

In 1926 Father Pro returned to Mexico City where the government banned public worship. Priests ministered secretly, celebrating Mass in homes, preaching, baptizing, and hearing confessions. Father Pro usually lived with his parents. He rode his bicycle, distributing Communion at prearranged places and providing clothing for the poor. Disguised as a mechanic, an office worker, or a beggar, he courageously served the Catholic Mexicans.

Father Pro's quick thinking helped him in many narrow escapes. Once, when the police were following him, he turned a corner and saw a woman he knew. He winked at her and took her arm. When the police turned the corner, they saw only a loving couple walking.

In November 1927 an assassination attempt was made on a Mexican general. A bomb was thrown from a car that had once belonged to Father Pro's brother. Police arrested Father Pro and his two younger brothers. These brothers were members of the National League for the Defense of Religious Rights, but they had had nothing to do with the assassination attempt.

When the man behind the plot heard that Father Pro had been arrested, he confessed. But to teach Catholics a lesson, with no trial, Father Pro and his two brothers were condemned to death. Reporters, photographers, and others were invited to a special execution.

One of the officers who had captured Father Pro led him out of jail to be executed. He begged Father to forgive him. Miguel put his arm around him and said, "You have not only my forgiveness but my thanks." He also softly told the firing squad, "May God forgive you all." Father Pro heard the guns being cocked. With arms spread as if on a cross, he shouted, "Long live Christ the King!" before a bullet silenced him. One of Miguel's brothers was also shot. Although the government forbade a public funeral, thousands came to Father Pro's wake. He was beatified in 1988.

ACT OUT SCENES

Have small groups act out scenes from Miguel Pro's life: fleeing the country as a student, celebrating a secret home Mass, a narrow escape, arrest.

PRAY FOR RELIGIOUS FREEDOM

Talk about the blessing of religious freedom. Pray to Blessed Miguel for all the people in the world today who are trying to live their faith.

LOOK FOR SIGNS OF SANCTITY

His fellow Jesuits referred to Miguel as "the brother who is convinced that God wants him to be a saint." Ask the students to speculate on what made the Jesuits form that opinion. Then ask the students for signs that a student today is serious about becoming a saint. If they start to sound too pious, have them think back to Miguel Pro's personality and story. List adjectives that describe him. Then continue the discussion.

REPORT ON MODERN MARTYRS

Ask interested students to find out about more recent 20th-century martyrs and give short oral reports to the class. You might begin in El Salvador with six Jesuits and their housekeeper and her daughter; lay missioner Jean Donovan and Sisters Ita Ford, Maura Clarke, and Dorothy Kazel; and Archbishop Oscar Romero.

Catechist's Notes:

_____

_____

_____

_____

_____

_____

_____

_____

_____

_____

Saint Andrew Dung-Lac and Companions

November 24

(d. 1798–1862)

The story of the martyrs of Vietnam is the story of the Church in Vietnam. Its history has been marked by the cross and includes several severe persecutions of Catholics. Pope John Paul II canonized together 117 Vietnamese martyrs who had been beatified in four groups from 1900 to 1951. Andrew Dung-Lac, a parish priest, is one of them. Of the 117 martyrs, 96 were Vietnamese, 11 were Spanish, and 10 were French. The group included 8 bishops, 50 priests, and 59 lay Catholics.

The Portuguese brought the faith to Vietnam. In 1615 Jesuits opened the first permanent mission in Da Nang to minister to Japanese Catholics who had been driven from Japan. The king of one of the three kingdoms of Vietnam banned all foreign missionaries. Priests went into hiding in Catholic homes.

Later, in the 19th century, three more persecutions occurred—one because the emperor thought that Christians were in favor of his son, who was rebelling against him. Foreign missionaries, too, were martyred. The last to be martyred were 17 laypersons, one only nine years old. That year, 1862, a treaty with France gave religious freedom to Catholics. Persecutions continued, however.

In the 20th century, Catholics from North Vietnam fled to South Vietnam in great numbers. The Church now in Vietnam is strong and committed to the faith. Vietnamese Catholics and Catholics worldwide have been inspired by the Vietnamese martyrs, who were canonized in 1988.

GET A HISTORICAL PERSPECTIVE

Have students compare the dates of the martyrs of Korea and the martyrs of Vietnam. Then have them find out what was happening in the Church in the United States during that same time.

LEARN ABOUT VIETNAMESE-AMERICAN CATHOLICS

Have interested students do some research on Vietnamese Catholics in the United States. Where do they live? What are their religious traditions? Do they have religious communities of priests, brothers, and sisters?

LIST ACTS OF FAITH

Remind students that faith is shown not only by dying for it but by living for it. Brainstorm and make a list of things they do as a result of their faith. Have each student copy the list and star the actions that are difficult for him or her.

SING ABOUT FAITH

Together sing a song about faith from your parish hymnal, such as "How Great Thou Art," "We Walk by Faith," or "Without Seeing You."

GRAPH CATHOLIC POPULATION

Have the class research the distribution of Catholics in the world today. Record numbers on a world map, or have each student make a bar or circle graph showing percentages.

Catechist's Notes:

_____

_____

_____

_____

_____

_____

_____

_____

_____

_____

Saint Andrew

(first century)

November 30

Imagine two men fishing. They were not standing in a cool mountain stream with fancy fly-fishing gear. They were working. Their boat was small. Their hands were callused from grasping and throwing the heavy fishing nets. Their faces were beaten by sun and storm.

On this morning, as usual, they were out in their boat not far from shore, casting a net into the Sea of Galilee. A man called out to them—he seemed to know who they were—brothers Simon and Andrew, sons of Jonah. "Come follow me," he said. "I will make you fishers of men."

This invitation was as compelling as it was puzzling. We don't know whether the fishermen asked questions or how hard the decision was. We do know that both Simon and Andrew left their nets behind and became disciples of Jesus. That day their entire lives changed forever. It was not such an ordinary morning after all.

Andrew originally was a disciple of John the Baptist. Then one day John identified Jesus as "the Lamb of God." Andrew followed Jesus to the place where he was staying and remained with him all day. He was one of the first disciples. Andrew not only followed Jesus himself, he seemed to take a special delight in bringing others to Jesus.

- After spending the day with Jesus, Andrew told his brother Simon, "We have found the Messiah," and he brought Simon to Jesus. (John 1:35–42)

- It was Andrew who noticed a boy in the crowd with the five barley leaves and two fish that became a meal that fed over 5,000. (John 6:1–15)

- It was Philip and Andrew whom the Greeks approached when they wanted to see Jesus. (John 12:20–22)

Although we do not know much more about Andrew from Scripture, these few events indicate he was a man who was easy to approach, a man faith-filled and loyal—the kind of man you could trust.

Tradition holds that later Andrew preached in northern Greece, Epirus, and Scythia (what is now the southern part of Russia), and that he was probably crucified at Patras in Greece around the year 70. Andrew is the patron saint of Russia and Scotland.

The name *Andrew* is a Greek name meaning "courageous" or "manly." As a man who gave his life to follow Christ, he certainly lived up to his name. Through his intercession, may we live up to our calling as Christians.

ACT OUT SCRIPTURE SCENES

Have the students act out these scenes from Scripture in which Andrew is mentioned: Mark 1:16–18 and Matthew 4:18–20; Mark 1:29-31; John 1:35–45; John 6:1–15; John 12:20–22. Older students may wish to write and follow scripts.

BE DISCIPLES

Distribute or have each student cut two fish shapes out of construction paper. Ask students to write on one fish one way they will follow Jesus today. On the other fish they should write one way they will bring others to Jesus. Invite the children to place their fish in a net or basket on the prayer table.

USE GEOGRAPHY

Andrew and Simon Peter were from Bethsaida in Galilee. Help the students locate Bethsaida on a map. Point out to them the three geographical areas: Galilee (northern), Samaria (middle), and Judea (southern). If slides or photos of these areas are available, show them to the students. Each area can be recognized by its land and vegetation, from the fertile greenness of Galilee to the barren rockiness of Judea.

Have students work together to make a relief map of the Holy Land.

CREATE DIORAMAS

Have children make dioramas of the fishing scene and Jesus calling Simon and Andrew to follow him.

MAKE PERSONAL SYMBOLS

In the 15th century, artists began picturing Andrew with the saltire, or X-shaped cross, which has become his traditional symbol. The fish and the fisherman's net are other symbols associated with Andrew. Ask the children to draw a symbol for themselves that tells about one of their natural gifts, accomplishments, or ways of serving others.

Catechist's Notes:

_____

_____

_____

_____

_____

_____

_____

_____

Christic the King

(Last Sunday of the Church year)

Ordinary Time

Can you imagine a wheel without a center? A center is necessary for balance and for smooth running. Some people, however, try to live without a center. The feast of Christ the King reminds us that Jesus is our center. He is the beginning and the end. This feast comes on the last Sunday of the Church year, just before Advent. It is a fitting way to end the Church year.

Jesus is a descendant of King David, the greatest king Israel ever had. Jesus is the King whose birth the prophet Isaiah foretold:

For a child has been born for us,
a son given to us;
authority rests upon his shoulders;
and he is named
Wonderful Counselor, Mighty God,
Everlasting Father, Prince of Peace.
His authority shall grow continually,
and there shall be endless peace
for the throne of David and his kingdom.
He will establish and uphold it
with justice and with righteousness
from this time onward and
forevermore.

(Isaiah 9:5–6)

When Pilate asked Jesus, "Are you the King of the Jews?" Jesus replied, "My kingdom does not belong to this world." Soldiers put a purple cloak on him, set a crown of thorns on his head, and mocked him as a king. On the cross the sign over his head stating his crime read, "Jesus of Nazareth, King of the Jews." Ironically his accusers were right.

Jesus is the King who will come at the end of the world. The Gospel describes this: "When the Son of Man comes in his glory, and all the angels with him, then he will sit on the throne of his glory" (Matthew 25:31). Jesus is the great victor described in the Book of Revelation as riding on a white horse with the name written on his robe and on his thigh, "King of Kings and Lord of Lords" (Revelation 19:11–16).

We celebrate Christ not only as King of the world and nations, but as King of our families and of our hearts. The kingdom of Christ is within each of us. Every time we try to make something else the center of our lives, we get thrown off balance. Jesus, the Shepherd-King, loves us and is always ready to guide us.

DRAW CROWNS

Have the students draw a crown of thorns and a kingly crown and use them as part of a prayer service in honor of Christ the King.

TALK ABOUT CHANGE

The feast of Christ the King was established by Pope Pius XI in 1925 to worship Christ's lordship over all the universe. At that time, it was celebrated on the last Sunday of October. Now, it comes on the last Sunday of the Church year. Point out to the students that since the Church is living and growing, it can change in some respects. Suggest they interview parents, grandparents, or others about how the Church has changed and how it has remained the same.

PARTICIPATE IN MISSION

With Christ as our King, we all belong to one family. Involve the students in mission activities so that they may share in the responsibilities, as well as the blessings, of this worldwide family.

CELEBRATE IN SONG

Sing songs from the missalette or parish song book for Christ the King.

PRAY THE ROSARY

The feast of Christ the King has much in common with the feast of the Ascension, where Christ is crowned in glory and honor. Have the students pray the second Glorious Mystery of the Rosary to prepare for this feast.

Catechist's Notes:

_____

_____

_____

_____

_____

_____

_____

_____

_____

_____

_____

Saint Maria Clementine Anuarite Nengapeta

December 1

(1939–1964)

Think of the choices you have made today. You probably made easy decisions like what to eat for breakfast or which shoes to wear to school. If you have the same kind of cereal every morning or you wear the same shoes to school almost every day, maybe it didn't even seem like a choice. It was a habit, a choice you make often.

Maria Clementine had to make a very difficult decision. But, because she was in the habit of pleasing God in all of her actions, she didn't have to think a long time about it.

Maria Clementine lived in the Republic of Congo, in Africa. She was baptized when she was four years old, along with her mother and one of her sisters. From the very beginning, Maria listened carefully when her teachers talked about God and how to live as a Christian. She developed good habits and the virtues of obedience, generosity, purity, and faith.

When she was 15, Maria Clementine chose to give her whole life to God by becoming a sister. Told at first that she was too young, she eventually stowed away on a truck that was taking postulants to the convent and was allowed to join the Holy Family sisters. Her parents were present when she took her vows and gave two goats to the convent in her honor. Later, however, her mother would urge her to leave the convent to come home and help support the family. But

Maria remained in the convent for 10 years, joyfully praying and working with the sisters. She was willing to do unpleasant chores that others avoided, but she sometimes lost patience with those who had shirked their duties.

At this time there was political upheaval in the country as two groups vied for power. The rebels suspected the native-born monks and nuns of collaborating with foreigners. On December 1, 1964, Maria and a small group of sisters were being moved by force, supposedly to another convent, when they were stopped by a troop of soldiers. The soldiers began to harass the sisters, and two colonels began competing for Maria Clementine even though she had vowed she would never give herself to a man. One of the colonels began beating Maria. When she said, "I forgive you, for you do not know what you are doing," he became so furious he had her stabbed and then shot and killed her.

People admired her courage and strength. But Maria Clementine would have told you that it was not a hard decision to make. Her love was very strong because she had been making loving choices all of her life.

Maria Clementine was buried in a mass grave with other prisoners, but later her body was moved to a cemetery near the Isiro cathedral. She was canonized in 1999, becoming the first Congolese woman saint.

MAKE A LIST

Have the students brainstorm a list of choices or decisions they have made today. Then go back and have them check the ones that were based on faith or love of God.

EXERCISE

Lead the class in some calisthenics. Get the students talking about the kind of exercise they do regularly and why they do it. Explain that just as physical exercise keeps their bodies strong and healthy, spiritual exercise makes their spirits strong. Tell them that another word for spiritual strength is *virtue*. Ask them what they would consider spiritual exercise: prayer, celebrating the Sacraments of Eucharist and Penance, living the virtues of faith, hope, and charity, and so on.

EXPLORE VOCATIONS

Have the students interview a religious order priest, brother, or sister to learn his or her vocation story. You might invite one of them to class to tell the story of God's call. Have the class prepare questions beforehand, such as the following: When did you realize you had a religious vocation? How did your parents and friends react? What have been challenges for you as you answered the call?

Catechist's Notes:

_____

_____

_____

_____

_____

_____

_____

_____

_____

_____

_____

_____

Saint Francis Xavier

December 3

(1506–1552)

Francis Xavier had to choose between a life of popularity, prestige, and pleasure and a life of dedication, sacrifice, and love. Which do you think he chose?

Francis was the youngest son of the chief counselor of Spain. Private tutoring highlighted his great intelligence. Eventually he studied at the University of Paris, where he became a teacher of philosophy. His career led to honor, and he accompanied it with an active social life.

Ignatius Loyola, a retired artillery captain, was a student at the same university. Ignatius recognized Francis's talents. He saw the ambition that made Francis a great athlete, as well as a good teacher. He saw Francis's ability for leadership, his strong pride, and his extravagant generosity. For his part Francis did not like Ignatius and mocked him for his disciplined lifestyle. Ignatius's response was "For what will it profit them if they gain the whole world but forfeit their life?" (Matthew 16:26).

Challenged by Ignatius, Francis saw that the energy, ambition, and talent he was using to further his career could be better used to teach people about God's love. With five others, he joined Ignatius as one of the first members of the Society of Jesus (Jesuits). Their mission was to serve the Church wherever needed.

At this time there was a need for missionaries in the East Indies. Ignatius assigned two men there. Before the ship sailed, one man became ill and Francis was sent instead. On the five-month journey across the ocean, Francis was constantly seasick. The food spoiled, and the water became contaminated.

In India Francis evangelized in a new way. He started with children. He went down the street, ringing a bell and gathering the children. He told stories and taught them religious songs. Then he went to the poor, the sick, the overworked, and the prisoners. He lived among them and gained their confidence. By the example of his life, Francis introduced them to the teaching and life of Jesus. Then, when he preached, they understood his message. Francis converted thousands before he sailed to Japan to spread the Gospel.

Letters Francis wrote reveal the hardships and the loneliness he endured. Many Christians he converted were robbed, killed, or carried off as slaves by pagan leaders. Foreign merchants, greedy and cruel, also caused problems. But Francis continued undaunted. His dream was to bring Christianity to the people of China too.

En route to China, Francis developed a high fever, and the sailors on the boat became frightened. They took him off and laid him on the shore of a nearby island. The island was so close to China that Francis could see it. But he never got there. A fisherman found him as he lay dying, and took him to his hut.

ACTIVITIES

Saint Francis Xavier / December 3

LEARN ABOUT MISSION WORK TODAY

Francis Xavier was declared copatron of the missions, with Saint Thérèse of the Child Jesus, in 1927. Invite a missionary to speak to the class about his or her experiences, or show a mission video. Permit the students to ask questions afterward, then have them discuss the following:

1. What ideas or insights on missionary life did you gain?

2. Compare missionary work today with the ministry of Francis Xavier.

3. What qualities should a missionary have?

LEARN THROUGH SONG

Francis Xavier used songs as an effective teaching method.

- Have the students read the lyrics of popular religious Christmas carols and discuss ways they might be used in teaching others about the Christian faith.

- Have the children make up new Christmas carols by putting their own words to simple tunes they know. You may wish to have the children work in small groups, then take turns teaching their carols to the other groups.

BEGIN A SERVICE PROJECT

Bring mission magazines to class. Have the students look through them and list organizations they would like to support. Help the class choose one cause and decide on a project: something to make and sell (stuffed toys, note cards, cookies, etc.) or jobs to do to raise funds. Send the money to the organization that was chosen.

MAP FRANCIS'S MISSIONARY JOURNEY

Have the students trace Francis's missionary journey on a map. You might want them to compare Francis's journey with Paul's missionary journeys.

WRITE AN ESSAY

Write this quote on the board: "For what will it profit them if they gain the whole world but forfeit their life? Or what will they give in return for their life?" (Matthew 16:26). Have the students paraphrase these questions, putting them in their own words. Then have them each compose an essay, giving examples as they answer the second question.

Catechist's Notes:

_____

_____

_____

_____

_____

Saint John of Damascus

December 4

(late 600s–mid 700s)

John grew up in the rich, luxurious court of the Muslim ruler of Damascus, where his father was a wealthy Christian court official. In order to make sure John had a solid Christian foundation, his father employed a brilliant Sicilian monk named Cosmos, who was a war captive, to teach John. Cosmos schooled the boy in science and theology, in the Greek and Arabic languages, and in the culture of Islam. Then John was ready to assume a high place in the government, which he did. But the spirit of the Muslim rulers was turning against Christians, so John left his position in the government and became a monk in Jerusalem. The date of his death is uncertain. Some think he may have lived to be 104 years old.

We know about John's faith through his writings. In them John explained the mysteries of the Christian faith, such as the Trinity, the Incarnation, the Real Presence in the Eucharist, and Mary's Assumption. One book he wrote is an important source on the teachings of the Greek Fathers of the Church. John was also a poet and hymn writer. Some of his songs are summaries of the truths of faith.

Perhaps John is most famous for his opposition to the heresy of the Iconoclasts. The Iconoclasts claimed that it is superstitious to have religious images. They wanted to destroy all religious icons, pictures, and statues. The Iconoclasts were supported by the Eastern Christian Emperor Leo III. John of Damascus defended the use of sacred images. He explained that the respect given to them is really given to the person they represent. If you look around an Orthodox Church today, you will see that John won the debate. For all of his efforts to defend the faith, John of Damascus was named a Doctor of the Church in 1890.

BEGIN A CHRISTMAS ART PROJECT

Since Christmas is coming, you may wish to have the students work on a nativity scene.

- Make an Advent calendar. After showing a number of depictions of the birth of Jesus, have each child draw a manger scene. Tell the children to leave a clear sky above the scene. Have them draw a star in the sky for each remaining day of Advent. For the rest of Advent, on each day that they pray or do a kind deed, they may color a star. If you prefer, give each child a sheet of gold star stickers to use instead.

- Make a nativity triptych, popular in Eastern art. It is a three-part picture, with the main focus in the center. For example, the children may draw the Christ Child in the center, with Mary and Joseph on each side. Or the Holy Family could be in the center, with shepherds on one side, and angels on the other. Have the children plan their work today and continue the project until Christmas break.

- Have the children make nativity sets out of clay or papier-mâché, or by dressing clothespin dolls. This project could be started today and finished by Christmas.

LEARN ABOUT EASTERN CHURCHES

Assist the class in looking up information on the Eastern churches in communion with Rome. If there is an Eastern Catholic church in the area, invite someone to come in to explain this tradition.

DRAW RELIGIOUS IMAGES

The use of sacred images, which John of Damascus defended, has always been popular in the Church. Take a walk with the students around your school, parish, and church. Ask the children to be quiet and look at everything. You may stop and talk about sacred images you see, or simply ask the children to be observant. Then let each child choose a favorite image to draw.

FIND SCRIPTURE IN SONG

Have the students look through a parish hymnal or listen to contemporary religious songs to see how song writers can use messages from Scripture to instruct and encourage people in their faith.

PRAY THE HAIL MARY

John of Damascus had a great devotion to the Blessed Virgin. Pray the Hail Mary together today.

Catechist's Notes:

_____

_____

_____

_____

Saint Nicholas

(d. mid-300s)

December 6

The feast of Saint Nicholas is celebrated in many countries around the world. He is the national patron of Greece, Sicily, and Russia. His image appears in stained glass windows, frescoes, and carvings, and about 400 churches in England alone are named for him. Parents name their children Nicole, Nicolette, Nikki, Nick, Claus, and Cole in his honor. He is one of the most popular saints in the Church.

Yet we actually know very little about Saint Nicholas. He was a fourth-century bishop in Lycia, which was southeast of Turkey. How did he become so popular for so many years in so many different countries? Good question!

The answer is that many stories have been told about Saint Nicholas. In them he is always generous in helping the poor and reaching out to those in need, as Jesus did. People love good stories, and people loved hearing about Bishop Nicholas.

In one story Nicholas frees three unjustly imprisoned officers, and in another saves three innocent boys from death. One of the best known stories concerns a poor man who was unable to provide the usual dowries for his three unmarried daughters. Knowing they might be forced into prostitution, Nicholas devised a plan to save the girls. One night he took a bag of gold and tossed it through an open window into the room where the man was sleeping— perhaps it landed in the man's shoe! Then Nicholas hurried away so that no one would know who had given the gold. Not long after this, Nicholas heard that the eldest daughter had gotten married. Twice after that, Nicholas repeated his secret gift, and each time one of the daughters was able to marry. But the last time that he threw a bag of gold into the window, the poor father was waiting for him and thanked him over and over.

In the Netherlands, Germany, and Switzerland, children put out their empty shoes on the eve of Saint Nicholas's feast, hoping that they will receive presents. In America and England, the legend of Saint Nicholas has evolved into the modern-day Santa Claus, who brings presents on Christmas Eve.

DECEMBER

ACTIVITIES

Saint Nicholas / December 6

PLAN GOOD DEEDS

Remind the students that a good way to prepare for Christmas is to be kind and generous toward others. Their good actions truly help to bring Christ into our world.

- Have the class brainstorm a list of acts of kindness that could be done in secret either at school or at home. Encourage the children to try to do one anonymous act of kindness each day for a week in imitation of Saint Nicholas.

- Busy parents need "elves" to help with cleaning, shopping, wrapping, babysitting, and so on, as they get ready to celebrate the holidays. Have the children make service coupons to give to family members.

IMITATE SAINT NICHOLAS

Suggest that the students make a card or bring in a treat for children in a lower grade. Then, at recess, let the students put these surprises on the children's desks.

ENJOY A TREAT

Make Saint Nicholas cookies, or give another type of treat to your class in honor of Saint Nicholas.

Catechist's Notes:

_____

_____

_____

_____

_____

_____

_____

_____

_____

_____

Saint Ambrose

(c. 340–397)

Have you ever been asked to do something you weren't sure you could do? This happened to Saint Ambrose.

The new bishop of Milan was to be elected by the people. Ambrose, who was governor, attended the election for two reasons. He knew there might be disagreements and felt responsible for keeping the peace. Since Ambrose was preparing for Baptism, he was also interested in who would be bishop. During the election, fighting broke out. No one could agree on who the bishop should be. Ambrose stood and pleaded for peace in the assembly. During his speech a voice cried out, "Ambrose for bishop!" Ambrose was shocked. The crowd took up the cry, shouting, "Ambrose for bishop!" Ambrose begged them not to elect him, but he could not silence them. Over the next several months, Ambrose was baptized, ordained, and consecrated bishop.

Ambrose was well prepared for the office of bishop. He came from a wealthy Roman family. His father was a chief officer in the Roman military. Not only had Ambrose received the finest education in Rome, he had been raised in a good Christian household. His sister became a nun. Ambrose had followed in his father's footsteps when he entered political life. In 370 he became governor, with his headquarters in Milan, Italy. Ambrose administered strict and fair justice. He was a courageous leader. He was also strong in his Christian faith and prepared to be baptized as an adult.

After his election as bishop, Ambrose turned his attention from political government to church government. Immediately he gave a share of his family's money to the poor and encouraged others to do so. He simplified the bishop's household and freed the place of expensive finery. He took a firm stand in controversial matters of Church and state. When conflicts arose with the ruling family, Ambrose told the people, "The emperor is in the Church, not above it." Even the rulers must obey the laws of God.

On more than one occasion, Empress Justina sent soldiers to force Ambrose to go along with her wishes. Ambrose had to defend his cathedral against attack, but the people stood by their bishop, and the army had to back down.

Later Emperor Theodosius, to get revenge for the murder of several officers, had a town of 7,000 people destroyed. Ambrose warned Theodosius that he would be excommunicated if he did not do public penance. People were astounded that Ambrose would do this. They were speechless when Theodosius knelt at Ambrose's feet, humbly accepting forgiveness.

When Ambrose died at age 60, he was mourned by the people. He had been a zealous pastor, a champion of the poor, a teacher of the faith, and a practical, fatherly priest. Ambrose had been like Christ, a good shepherd.

WRITE A HOMILY

Through the homilies of Ambrose, Saint Augustine was led to the faith. Ambrose knew the importance of the Sunday homily for teaching the people about God.

- Have the students study the readings for the coming Sunday and compose their own homily.

- Encourage the students to listen closely to the Sunday homily and write down the major points. Discuss how the priest or deacon taught about Christ.

SING A CLASS FAVORITE

To honor Saint Ambrose's feast and his skill at composing church hymns, have the class select a favorite religious song to sing today.

DEFEND WHAT IS RIGHT

Ambrose always defended the teaching of the Church in matters of right and wrong. Have the class give examples of issues in which the Church today must defend Gospel values (examples: abortion, euthanasia, human rights, marriage and the family, capital punishment, war, racial prejudice). Then have students give examples of times when a person their age may have to stand up for what is right.

LEARN ABOUT CATECHUMENATE

Ambrose was a catechumen in the Church before he was baptized. Introduce the students to how the Rite of Christian Initiation of Adults is being implemented in your parish. If possible, invite catechumens to share their experiences with the students. With the class, pray for the people who are in the process of initiation.

Catechist's Notes:

_____

_____

_____

_____

_____

_____

_____

_____

Immaculate Conception   December 8

If you were given a saint's name at Baptism, that saint is your patron saint. The saint whose name you choose at Confirmation is also your patron saint. A patron is a saint or angel chosen by a person, a group, or by the Church as a protector and model. Patron saints show us by their example how to be open to God and how to follow Jesus more faithfully.

Countries have patron saints also. Here is a little quiz.

Who is the patron saint of Ireland? (*Patrick*)

Who is one patron saint of Russia? (*Nicholas*)

Who is the patron saint of the United States?

If you answered, "Mary, the mother of Jesus," you are right. In 1846 the bishops of the United States asked Mary to watch over our country and its people in a special way. They also chose one particular title and feast of Mary—her Immaculate Conception.

Do you know why a diamond sparkles? The stone is cut so that it acts as a prism, separating light into an array of brilliant colors. In much the same way, Mary's life reflects God's grace and shows us the beautiful privileges and gifts that God gave her.

The title of the Immaculate Conception recognizes Mary's privilege of coming into the world free from sin. Through the power of Jesus' death and resurrection, every human being can be freed from sin at Baptism. Through that same power, Mary was always free of sin, even from the very first moment of her life.

On December 8, the Church celebrates this special privilege given to Mary. At the liturgy we thank God for all the blessings he has given to the people of our country. And we can thank Mary for watching over and protecting our people.

In response to the grace of God, Mary offered to God an obedient, loyal love. She always chose to do God's will. In this, Mary gives us an example of holiness to imitate.

> Father,
> you prepared the Virgin Mary
> to be the worthy mother of your Son. . . .
>
> Trace in our actions the lines of her love,
> in our hearts her readiness of faith.
> Prepare once again a world for your Son
> who lives and reigns with you and the
>   Holy Spirit,
> one God, for ever and ever.
> *(Opening Prayers for the Mass of the
> Immaculate Conception)*

ACTIVITIES

RESEARCH THE NATIONAL SHRINE

Have students write to the National Shrine of the Immaculate Conception, Fourth and Michigan Avenues, Washington, DC 20017, or go online for information on the shrine.

WRITE PETITIONS

To appeal to Mary as patroness of the United States, have the students write petitions for the needs of the country, especially for the rights and dignity of every human being. Have them make their petitions through the intercession of Mary.

MAKE BANNERS

Let the students make small door banners for each classroom door. They may cut out the capital letter *M,* decorate it with symbols of Mary such as a lily or white candle, and post one next to every classroom door as a reminder of this feast day.

SCRIPTURE STUDY

Ask the students to look up Scripture readings for the feast of the Immaculate Conception: Genesis 3:9–15,20; Ephesians 1:3–6,11–12; Luke 1:26–38. Have them discuss why these particular readings were chosen.

PRAY AN ACT OF CONSECRATION TO MARY

Encourage the students to pray an Act of Consecration to Mary daily. Distribute copies of the blackline master on page 436.

> My Queen, my Mother! I give myself entirely to you, and to show my devotion to you I consecrate to you my eyes, my ears, my mouth, my heart and my whole being. Wherefore, good Mother, as I am your own, keep me, guard me, as your property and possession.
> Amen.

Catechist's Notes:

_____

_____

_____

_____

_____

_____

_____

_____

Saint Juan Diego

(1474–1548)

A beautiful picture of Mary can be seen on a cloak above the main altar in the Basilica of Our Lady of Guadalupe in Mexico City. The cloak belonged to Juan Diego, an Aztec who lived more than 450 years ago.

Juan Diego and his wife, María Lucía, converts, walked 14 miles to religious instructions and Mass every Saturday and Sunday. On December 9, 1531, when Juan was a 57-year-old widower, he was walking to Mass. A beautiful lady dressed as an Aztec appeared. She told him she was the Immaculate Virgin Mary, the Mother of the true God. She desired to have a shrine there at Tepeyac Hill so that she could show her love for people. She said, "Ask for my help. Here I will listen to people's prayers and I will help them." Mary asked Juan to tell the bishop of her desire.

The bishop didn't believe him, so Juan returned to the lady and suggested she send a better speaker. Mary told Juan that she chose him for this work and that she would bless him for helping her. Juan revisited the bishop. This time the bishop told him to ask his lady for a sign that she was the Mother of God. When Juan did, Mary told him to return the next day for a sign.

The same day Juan's Uncle Bernardino became ill, and Juan stayed home to care for him. When his uncle was dying, Juan went for a priest. On the way he met the Holy Virgin. He apologized for not meeting her the day before. Mary replied, "Now listen to me. Do not let anything bother you, and do not be afraid of any illness, pain, or accident. Am I not here, your Mother? Are you not under my shadow and protection? What more could you want? Don't worry about your uncle. He is well already."

Mary then sent Juan to the top of the hill to gather the flowers growing there. Juan knew that nothing grew on that rocky hill, let alone in winter. However, he did as the Lady said. Juan found gorgeous roses! He picked them and brought them to Mary, who arranged them in his cloak that María Lucía had made from cactus fibers. Mary told Juan to take them to the bishop.

When the bishop saw Juan, he asked what he had in his tilma. Juan opened it, letting the roses fall. Imagine the bishop's surprise at seeing roses in winter! Yet he saw an even greater miracle: on Juan's cloak a beautiful, life-size image began to appear. Juan gasped. It was his Lady! The bishop cried out, "The Immaculate!" Then he knelt and with tears asked the Blessed Mother's pardon for not believing Juan.

On that same day, Mary appeared to Juan's uncle and cured him. Uncle Bernardino went to the bishop and told how he had been cured.

Juan Diego remained poor, simple, humble, and devoted to the Eucharist. He spent the next 17 years traveling throughout central Mexico, bringing others to the faith and delivering Guadalupe's message that Mary loves us and wants to help us. Juan Diego was beatified in 1990 and canonized in 2002.

HELP THE POOR

Mary, the Mother of God, showed great concern for the poor. Help the children plan and carry out an Advent fundraiser. Send the money you collect to an organization such as Catholic Relief Services. Have students write or e-mail Catholic Relief Services about current projects and how they can help. The mailing address is Catholic Relief Services, 1011 First Avenue, New York, NY 10022. The Web site is *www.catholicrelief.org*.

HONOR OUR LADY OF GUADALUPE

Display the image of Our Lady of Guadalupe in your classroom through December 12—the feast of Our Lady of Guadalupe. Bring in roses to place near the image, or have the children make roses out of tissue paper or colored cellophane.

ACT OUT THE STORY

Let the students act out the story of Juan Diego. Get everyone involved. "Extras" are needed as onlookers at the bishop's palace and visitors to the modern basilica.

TELL THE STORY

Suggest that the children each tell at least one other person the story of Our Lady of Guadalupe, in honor of Juan Diego, who spent the rest of his life telling the marvelous story.

OTHER ACTIVITIES

See the Feast of Our Lady of Guadalupe (December 12) for other activities that are appropriate for this day.

Catechist's Notes:

_____

_____

_____

_____

_____

_____

_____

_____

Our Lady of Guadalupe

December 12

Just three days ago, on December 9, the Church celebrated the feast of Saint Juan Diego.

On December 9, 1531, a 57-year-old Aztec, Juan Diego, saw the Blessed Mother on a hill in Mexico City. She told Juan to have a church built in her honor. When Juan went to ask Bishop Zumarraga about this, the bishop did not understand the Indian dialect—and he did not believe in the vision Juan described.

Three days later, on December 12, Mary appeared again to Juan Diego, and this time she gave him a sign for the bishop. "Take these roses to the bishop," she said, as she arranged in his cloak beautiful roses she had Juan Diego pick from the hillside although it was winter. When he was admitted into the bishop's room, Juan Diego opened his cloak, and out dropped the roses. On the cloak there remained an image of Mary as she had appeared to Juan Diego.

The image of Mary on the cloak is known as Our Lady of Guadalupe for an interesting reason. On that same day, Mary appeared to Juan's uncle and cured him, giving him a message for the bishop, saying that she would "crush the serpent's head." The bishop did not understand the Indians' language. The Indian word for "crush the serpent" sounded to him like "Guadalupe," the name of Mary's shrine in Spain. Thinking that the Virgin wanted the new shrine to have the same name, the bishop called her Our Lady of Guadalupe.

Mary appeared to Juan Diego dressed as an Aztec woman to show her love and compassion to an oppressed group of people. Mary had heard the prayers and pain of these people, and she came to give them hope.

Mary's visit to Guadalupe is a reminder that God will remember his mercy for all people. In Mary's song of joy, the Magnificat, she praised God because he has put down the mighty, exalted the lowly, filled the hungry, and sent the rich away empty. People honor Our Lady of Guadalupe because they recognize her motherly concern for them.

On December 8, we celebrated the feast of the Immaculate Conception of Mary, patroness of the United States. Today the Church celebrates Mary as patroness of the Americas.

DISPLAY THE IMAGE OF GUADALUPE

Obtain a picture of Our Lady of Guadalupe and post it in the classroom. Be sure the children understand that the cloak of Juan Diego with the image of Our Lady is displayed above the main altar in the Basilica of Our Lady of Guadalupe in Mexico City. Bring in roses to place near the image, or have the children make roses out of tissue paper or colored cellophane.

COLOR THE PICTURE

Using the blackline master on page 446, make copies of the image of Our Lady of Guadalupe for the children to color. Display the pictures today and then let the children take them home to tell their families the story of today's feast.

WRITE A POEM OR PRAYER

People honor Our Lady of Guadalupe because they recognize her motherly concern for them. Invite the children to write a poem or prayer to Mary, their Mother.

ILLUSTRATE THE BEATITUDES

Mary showed through her appearance at Guadalupe that Christ brings salvation to those who are poor in spirit and live according to the Beatitudes. Give the students drawing paper and have them illustrate ways they might live the Beatitudes (Matthew 5:3–10) today.

LEARN MEXICAN CUSTOMS

Pope Pius XII stated that the Virgin of Guadalupe was queen of Mexico and patroness of the Americas. Have the students find out about special celebrations and customs Mexicans have to honor Mary.

VISIT A MARIAN SHRINE

Let the students research shrines of Our Lady, such as the ones at Knock, Mexico City, Lourdes, Fatima, Czestochowa, and Medjugorje, as well as shrines located in your own diocese or region. Have students share information and pictures they find with the class by making posters or a virtual tour on a computer program. If possible, plan a pilgrimage to a nearby shrine.

OTHER ACTIVITIES

See the feast of Saint Juan Diego (December 9) for other activities that are appropriate for this day.

Catechist's Notes:

_____

_____

_____

_____

_____

_____

Saint Lucy

(d. 304)

Do you remember the parable of the 10 bridesmaids who waited for the bridegroom to come? It is told in the Gospel, Matthew 25:1–13. The bridesmaids brought oil lamps to light their way, but only five wise ones carried flasks of oil for refills. The ones who were able to keep the light burning were permitted to enter the wedding banquet with the bridegroom; the others were left out in the dark.

Lucy, whose name means "light," kept the light of her faith burning and now enjoys the eternal wedding banquet of heaven.

Lucy was a young woman who was martyred for being a Christian. She died at Syracuse in Sicily during the persecution of Roman emperor Diocletian. The fact that she is mentioned in Eucharistic Prayer I of the Mass indicates the great respect that the Church has for her.

One story about Lucy portrays her as a young Christian who struggled against the pagan influences of her friends and of society. Because of her deep love for Jesus, Lucy vowed to remain unmarried. When the man she was engaged to marry found out, he reported her to the government for the crime of being a Christian. She then had the opportunity to prove her faithfulness to Christ by giving her life for him.

Lucy's feast is celebrated during the season of Advent, when we wait for the coming of Christ our Light. Various customs have developed around her feast. In Scandinavian countries young girls dress in white dresses with red sashes, symbolizing virginity and martyrdom. They carry palms, symbolizing victory, and wear crowns of candles on their heads. In Sweden the girls dressed as Lucy carry rolls and cookies in procession as songs are sung. A Hungarian custom is to plant a few grains of wheat in a small pot on St. Lucy's feast. By Christmas there will be little green sprouts—signs of life coming from death. It symbolizes the fact that, like Lucy, we enter new life—an eternal wedding feast—when we die.

Perhaps because Lucy's name means "light," she is the patron of eyes.

DECEMBER

ACTIVITIES

ACT OUT A PARABLE
Have the children act out the parable of the 10 virgins, Matthew 25:1–13.

RESEARCH ADVENT CUSTOMS
Older students may enjoy researching other Advent customs from around the world and giving oral or poster reports.

DONATE FOOD
According to a legend the people in Lucy's country were starving at one time. She prayed with them for help. As they prayed, a ship sailed into the harbor carrying enough wheat for everyone. Encourage the students to contribute to food drives during Advent or even to organize such a drive.

CELEBRATE ADVENT LIGHT SERVICE
Let the students prepare and celebrate a short Advent light service. Use Scripture readings, prayers, and songs about light. If possible, light a candle or an Advent wreath.

SHARE CHRISTMAS CUSTOMS
Have students share Christmas customs of their own family or national heritage.

MAKE CANDLES OR LAMPS
As reminders to the students to keep their lights burning, help them make or decorate candles or have them make lamps out of clay.

Catechist's Notes:

_____

_____

_____

_____

_____

_____

_____

_____

_____

_____

_____

Saint John of the Cross

December 14

(c. 1542–1591)

John of the Cross was locked in a cell six feet wide and ten feet long for nine months, with no light except that which filtered through a slit high up in the wall. He later forgave the men who had imprisoned him. How could he do that? He explained, "Where there is no love, put love, and you will find love."

John's father had been disowned by his wealthy Spanish family when he married a poor weaver rather than a woman of equal economic status. Living in poverty proved to be too much for him, and he died shortly after John was born. John spent much of his youth in an orphanage, where he was clothed, fed, and given an elementary education. At the age of 17, he found a job in a hospital and was accepted into a Jesuit college. In 1563 he entered the Carmelite Order. Eventually he enrolled in another university, where he did so well that he was asked to teach a class and to help settle disputes.

When he met Teresa of Ávila and learned from her about the reform of the Carmelite Order, John decided to help with it. As part of this decision, he wore sandals instead of shoes and lived very simply in prayer and solitude. In 1577 the attitude toward the reform shifted.

John was caught up in a misunderstanding and imprisoned at Toledo, Spain. During those months of darkness in that little cell, John could have become bitter, revengeful, or filled with despair. But instead, he kept himself open to God's action, for no prison could separate him from God's all-embracing love. During this time he had many beautiful experiences and encounters with God in prayer. Later he would describe these experiences in poetry. In 1578 John escaped to southern Spain to join the reformed Carmelites. There he held leadership positions and wrote reflections on his experiences, which showed his deep spirit of prayer. When he became ill, he chose to go to the city of Ubeda, where no one knew him. It was there that he died.

ACTIVITIES

EMPHASIZE THE SPIRITUAL

Discuss with the students some spiritual (nonmaterial) ways to celebrate Christmas. Encourage each child to choose one way that he or she will personally undertake.

REFLECT ON REACTIONS

John of the Cross knew how to change painful situations into blessings. Ask the students to think of times in their lives when they have been misunderstood, misjudged, or wronged. Have them consider the ways they have responded to these situations. Has their general response been to

- defend themselves
- blame others
- hold in anger and ignore the situation
- acknowledge their faults
- apologize for failures
- ask God to show them possible causes and creative ways of responding?

Ask the students to prayerfully reflect on how they can respond to such situations in the future. Conclude with the Sign of the Cross.

WRITE POEMS

Have the students write diamantes in honor John of the Cross, a poet of the soul. A diamante is a poem that moves from one idea to its opposite, as John turned suffering into blessing. A diamante resembles a diamond in form and is usually composed of seven lines.

line 1: one-word subject

line 2: two adjectives describing the subject

line 3: three participles (*-ing* words) describing the subject

line 4: four nouns. The first two pertain to the subject, the second two pertain to the opposite or new subject

line 5: three participles describing new subject

line 6: two adjectives describing new subject

line 7: new subject

Example:

Saint John of the Cross
Suffering
betrayed, imprisoned
dying, forgiving, praying
pain, darkness, light, gladness
living, trusting, praying
mystic, poet
Blessing

PLAN A DAY OF RENEWAL

John of the Cross was involved in reform and renewal. Have the students plan a day of renewal for their class. Have them discuss the following questions:

- What are the goals of a renewal?
- What are our needs?
- What could the theme be?
- What topics could be chosen for talks, discussions, or videos?
- Who would he a good speaker?
- What activities would match the theme?

PRAY IN SILENCE

John of the Cross is known for his life of deep prayer. Have the students spend some silent prayer time in church. Have Bibles and a variety of prayer books available.

Saint Peter Canisius

(1521–1597)

Have you ever thought about who wrote your religion book? Many people share the credit: theologians, teachers, writers, editors, artists, photographers, designers, consultants, and publishers. Today's saint wrote one of the first catechisms.

Peter's father intended him to marry well and follow a legal career. But after making a retreat under the direction of Peter Faber, one of the first Jesuits, Peter Canisius decided that God was calling him to serve as a Jesuit—a member of the Society of Jesus. Peter entered the order and began his studies for the priesthood. He was a brilliant student who easily mastered his subjects. His gifts of preaching and teaching were soon recognized, and he was appointed rector of a college. Though Peter's gifts were mainly intellectual, he was a man of incredible physical energy. He was often seen visiting the sick or prisoners in his free time.

Bigger tasks were awaiting him at this time when the Reformation was splitting the Church. By 1552, parishes in Vienna were without priests. There had been no ordinations for 20 years, and monasteries were empty. Peter was sent to Germany, where his work for the Church won him the name "the Second Apostle of Germany" after Boniface. Peter worked tirelessly, teaching, diplomatically handling the problems of the Church, and bringing back Catholics who had fallen away from the practice of their faith. He showed gentleness and zeal in caring for the sick during the great plague.

People loved him so much that he was offered the position of archbishop. Peter refused, but administered the diocese for one year.

Peter felt the need to strengthen the faith of the people. He did much scholarly writing to defend the faith. He became the advisor to Popes Pius IV, Pius V, and Gregory XIII. He attended two sessions of the Council of Trent. But one of his greatest concerns was that the middle-class and the poor understand the Gospel and the teachings of the Church. For this reason he wrote a catechism in a question-answer style, which included a calendar of saints and feast days. The faith was explained in a way ordinary people could understand. Eventually this catechism was translated into 15 different languages. Peter valued Catholic education and the Catholic press as important means for spreading the faith. His enthusiasm for the apostolic work of the Jesuits attracted many young men to the priesthood. He saw the need for strong, faithful priests and worked hard so that the clergy received a better education and were carefully selected. Some of his letters to Catholic leaders who showed little interest in the Church were stern and critical, yet genuinely positive. Peter lived in an age of confusion within the Church, yet he never despaired or became discouraged because he was constantly united with Christ.

After suffering a paralytic seizure, he continued to write religious books for six more years with the aid of a secretary. For his contribution to catechesis, he was named a Doctor of the Church.

DECEMBER

ACTIVITIES

INTERVIEW PARENTS

Peter Canisius promoted religious education. Have the students interview their parents about why they think Catholic religious education is important. Let the students write up their interviews and read them to the class.

ASK QUESTIONS

Prepare a question box in which the students can submit questions about theology or living the Catholic faith. When you have several good questions, answer them for the class.

MAKE BOOKMARKS

Peter Canisius was remembered for his writings, especially for his catechism. Have the students make bookmarks for their religion books and design them with religious symbols or Scripture quotes.

PRAY FOR THE POPE

Peter Canisius loyally supported the Holy Father throughout his life. Have the class offer a prayer for the Holy Father during class today. Ask the students what they know about the present pope. Ask what they think his prayer intentions might be today.

PROMOTE VOCATIONS

As in Peter's time, we need more priests. Pray with your students for vocations to the priesthood and religious life. Tell them that they have a responsibility to foster vocations. Suggest that they speak about the possibility of a vocation to people who have the qualities needed. Lastly, encourage students to consider whether God is calling them to serve him and the Church in these special ways.

Catechist's Notes:

_____

_____

_____

_____

_____

_____

_____

_____

_____

Saint John of Kanty

December 23

(1390–1473)

John of Kanty was known and loved for his spirit of generosity. There is a story that makes the point. Once robbers stopped John and demanded his money. He gave them all he had. When they had left, he realized he still had two coins sewn in his cloak. John ran after the robbers and gave them the coins. The thieves were so shocked that they returned all they had taken. The story is certainly unusual, but it makes you think, doesn't it? Do you have opportunities to be generous with your money? How about with your time or your talents? Remember how the thieves returned all the money to John? Well, God promises to gives back to you all you give, plus more! Jesus said: "Give, and it will be given to you. A good measure, pressed down, shaken together, running over, will be put into your lap; for the measure you give will be the measure you get back" (Luke 6:38).

John grew up in Poland and became a priest and teacher at the University of Kraków. He was a serious man who taught well and was hard on himself. He was patient and kind to his students, who respected and loved him in return. There were some members of the faculty, however, who were jealous of John and had him removed. John was sent to do parish work, but he was not acquainted with these duties and responsibilities, and he found it a heavy burden. Although the people liked John for his generous and energetic spirit, he was not successful as a parish priest.

Again John returned to the university to teach the Scriptures. The material he taught the students was not remembered as much as the holiness of his life. Everywhere he was known for his humility and spontaneous generosity. He gave everything to the poor and kept only the clothes he most needed. Four times he made a pilgrimage to the Holy Land, carrying his luggage on his back. When John died at age 83, people claimed he was already a saint.

ACTIVITIES

PRAY FOR PEOPLE OF POLAND AND LITHUANIA

Saint John of Kanty is a patron of Poland and Lithuania. Help the students locate these countries on a map. Explain that they are places where the Catholic faith had been strong for centuries, but was suppressed when these countries were under Soviet rule. Today pray for all Catholics in these countries, especially for priests, teachers, and students.

GIVE ALMS

John of Kanty was known for his almsgiving. He knew that Jesus wanted people to give material goods and to serve others—even to the point of sacrifice. Assist the students in a work of charity that involves service or monetary sharing that stretches them a bit.

BE GENEROUS

Saint John showed that a person's life speaks louder than words. Encourage the students to be extra generous today in the time they spend with someone, in helping someone, or in thinking of another person's feelings above their own.

LEARN ABOUT THE HOLY LAND

Discuss why John went to the Holy Land. Invite someone who has made a pilgrimage there to share the experience with the students, or show them slides or a video about Israel.

Catechist's Notes:

_____

_____

_____

_____

_____

_____

_____

_____

_____

_____

Christmas

December 25

God, who loves us so much and who wants our love in return, sent his Son to become man and to make visible his love for us. God wanted so much for us to be with him that he became one of us. This is the greatest Christmas present—God's presence on earth.

Everyone knows the story of the first Christmas—of Mary and Joseph searching for a place to stay in Bethlehem, of Jesus being born and laid in a manger, of his birth being announced by angels and indicated by a special star. His love shows itself in his becoming like us in our weakness and in suffering all the limitations of being human. The real depth of His love, though, was manifested in the mission he came to accomplish—to suffer and die for our sins so that we might be free.

It is God's great love that the Church celebrates with sparkling lights, color, and song during this season. His love leads people all over the world to forgive, to give and receive gifts, to rejoice at being home with their families, and to sing Christmas carols. People who understand this feast want to make God's love more visible in their lives. They want to be more welcoming to strangers, more caring about family and friends, and more forgiving of past hurts. The angels' message of joy and peace from that first Christmas is true even today.

See, I am bringing you good news of great joy for all the people: to you is born this day in the city of David a Savior, who is the Messiah, the Lord. . . . Glory to God in the highest heaven, and on earth peace among those whom he favors!

(Luke 2:10–11, 14)

The name *Christmas* comes from the Mass of Christ. On Christmas three separate liturgies are celebrated: a Mass at midnight, one at dawn, one during the day. The Christmas season last 12 days, until the feast of Epiphany. We can never celebrate the Incarnation enough!

COMPARE CAROLS AND SCRIPTURE

Have the students study the lyrics of familiar religious Christmas carols and compare them with the Gospel accounts of the first Christmas. Direct the students to make a list of carols and match them to Scripture references.

REFLECT ON APPROPRIATE WAYS TO CELEBRATE

Discuss with the students some spiritual (nonmaterial) ways to celebrate Christmas, such as praying special prayers, calling or visiting someone, and sharing gifts.

MAKE SCRAPBOOKS

Let each student prepare a scrapbook that his or her family can use during the Christmas holidays. Pages may be labeled and decorated along the edges. Possible titles for pages may include the following: Advent Events, Christmas Preparations, Family Favorites (such as the favorite cards, cookies, carols, ornaments, and gifts of each member of the family), Christmas Day, What Christmas Means to Me, How Jesus Comes Through the Kindness of Others. Have students allow room on the pages for written paragraphs, photos, Christmas cards, and drawings.

SHARE CHRISTMAS GREETINGS

Ask the students to find out how to say "Merry Christmas" in different languages. Post these in the room and use them to greet one another.

DISCUSS PRICELESS GIFTS

Ask the students to think of gifts they might give family and friends other than the usual purchased gifts. Suggestions might include homemade gifts, coupons for service, or charitable donations made in the person's name.

Catechist's Notes:

_____

_____

_____

_____

_____

_____

_____

_____

Saint Stephen

(first century)

After Pentecost the small group of Spirit-filled Christians began preaching the Good News of Jesus and converting people throughout Jerusalem. At this time there were two groups of Christian converts from Judaism. One group was the Palestinian Jews who decided to follow Christ, and the other was the Greek-speaking Jews, called Hellenists, who decided to be Christians. In the daily distribution of funds or food, some widows in the Hellenist group felt that they were treated unfairly. The apostles didn't have the time to wait on tables because they had been commissioned to preach the Gospel.

To solve the problem, they called the disciples to a meeting and had them choose men to be in charge of the daily distribution. The apostles prayed over these men, who would become the first deacons, and laid hands on them. This delegation of work freed the apostles to care for the spiritual needs of the people. One of the first deacons was Stephen, a man filled with the Holy Spirit and with faith. Besides his job of overseeing the distribution to the poor, he also preached. A group of Jewish Hellenists strongly resented Stephen's preaching about salvation through Jesus. Finally the situation became so tense that they found witnesses to falsely testify that Stephen had committed blasphemy.

Stephen was arrested and brought before the Sanhedrin. He knew that this Jewish court had a great deal of power and that the odds seemed to be against him. But Jesus had said, "When they hand you over, do not worry about how you are to speak or what you are to say; for what you are to say will be given to you in that hour; for it is not you who speak, but the Spirit of your Father speaking through you" (Matthew 10:19–20). Stephen believed that he would be helped by the Holy Spirit, and he wasn't afraid.

Stephen made two major points in his speech. First he showed that God can be found everywhere, not just in a single place like the Temple and not just in a single person like Abraham. Second he demonstrated how from the beginning, the Israelites had consistently rejected God's messengers, the prophets, and God's chosen servants. And now they rejected and killed God's Son who had been sent to them.

Those who were listening to Stephen were blinded by an anger so strong that they didn't even wait for the normal court proceedings. They rushed toward him, dragged him out of town, and stoned him. His last words were "Lord, do not hold this sin against them" (Acts 7:60).

Stephen was the first person to be killed for Christ. After his death a bitter persecution started, and many Christians fled from Jerusalem. Saul, who had approved of Stephen's death, became very active in persecuting Christians. Perhaps it was the courageous witness of Stephen that eventually enabled Saul to find the strength to turn to Christ and follow him.

DECEMBER

ACT OUT SCENES

Help the students locate the story of Stephen in Acts 6 and 7. Have them act out several scenes from his life.

MAKE CROWNS

The name *Stephen* means "crown." Stephen won the crown of martyrdom by his death for speaking the truth about Christ. Have the children make paper crowns to wear during class today.

PROCLAIM A FORGIVENESS DAY

As Stephen died, he forgave his enemies—following the example of Jesus. Proclaim a Forgiveness Day in honor of Saint Stephen. Offer students these possibilities:

- Decide to say a kind word or do a kind deed for someone who has hurt them.

- Consider if there is anyone in their lives from whom they need to ask forgiveness—someone they have hurt. Encourage them to work for reconciliation.

- Pray that they may become channels of forgiveness as Jesus and Stephen were. Students may write their own prayers or use this one:

Jesus, help me to imitate Saint Stephen. Every hurt that I have ever experienced—heal that hurt with your love. Every hurt that I have ever caused to another person—please heal that hurt also. I choose to forgive and be forgiven. Remove any resentment or bitterness from my heart and fill the empty spaces with your forgiving love. Thank you, Lord. Amen.

Catechist's Notes:

_____

_____

_____

_____

_____

_____

_____

_____

_____

Saint John the Apostle   December 27

(first century)

Have you ever thought it would be easier to be a disciple of Jesus if you could hear and talk to Jesus in person?

John, traditionally the youngest apostle and the only one not married, had the experience of living with Jesus. He walked at his side, watched him perform miracles, listened to his teaching, asked him questions, shared experiences with him, and received signs of his great personal love. After Jesus had ascended to his Father, John had many memories to pass on to others.

According to Matthew's Gospel, John was sitting in a boat mending nets with his older brother James and his father Zebedee when Jesus came by and called them to follow him. John and his brother James said yes to the call. And this was the beginning of a great adventure, a truly life-changing experience.

Much of what we know of John's life comes to us through the Gospels. John and his brother James were called Sons of Thunder, possibly because of their fiery tempers. One example of this came when the people in a Samaritan town would not accept Jesus. James and John wanted to call down fire from heaven to destroy the town. Jesus had to correct their thinking.

In the Gospels John is a close companion of Jesus. The Gospel of John calls him "the one Jesus loved." John had the privilege of being with Jesus at crucial times. With Peter and James, John witnessed the miracle of Jairus's daughter coming back to life. Again with Peter and James, he saw the glory of Jesus' transfiguration. Jesus also invited these three to be closer to him than the other apostles during his Agony in the Garden, when it was night and there was no show of miracles or glory. John stood at the foot of the cross of Jesus, too, faithful to the end.

After Jesus had sent the Holy Spirit upon the apostles, we read in Acts how John continued to respond to the challenge of Jesus' call. One day he and Peter cured a lame beggar in the name of Jesus and were promptly arrested and kept in jail overnight. The next day the religious leaders listened to their message about Jesus' Resurrection and were amazed that these uneducated fisherman were so confident and could speak so convincingly. When the leaders warned them never to teach in the name of Jesus, both Peter and John said, "Whether it is right in God's sight to listen to you rather than to God, you must judge; for we cannot keep from speaking about what we have seen and heard" (Acts 4:19–20).

At another time Peter and John returned to Samaria to pray that the Holy Spirit would come down upon the Samaritans. This was quite a different request from the one John made earlier to call down fire to destroy a Samaritan town. Friendship with Jesus really changes a person, and John had been learning to live like Jesus all those years.

LOVE ONE ANOTHER

There is a story handed down in tradition about Saint John. When he was very old, the people had to carry him to where the Christians had assembled to worship. And each time he preached, he gave the same homily: "Little children, love one another." The people grew tired of hearing the same thing each time, and they asked him if he could talk on a different topic. But he said that this is the Lord's Word, and if they really did this, they would do enough.

Grades K–3: Tell this story and write John's homily on the board. Divide the class into small groups to make up skits to show how they can "love one another" every day. Let each group perform for the class. Then have each child copy John's homily on drawing paper and decorate it.

Grades 4–8: Have the students find quotes about love in the Gospel of John and the Letters of John. Instruct them to choose and copy one quote on drawing paper and decorate the edges. They may glue or tape yarn on the back of the paper so that it can be hung like a banner. Suggest that the students hang their banners on doorknobs or other appropriate places at school or home.

CELEBRATE THE LIGHT

The Gospel of John uses a theme of darkness and light. Help the students plan and celebrate a prayer using this theme. For example: Have everyone form a large circle. Darken the room. Light a large candle in the center of the circle.

Grades K–4: Read John 1:1–5 slowly. Give each child a personalized paper candle on which you have written "[Name], shine in the darkness." Have the children color the flame with markers.

Grades 5–8: Have a student read the Prologue (Chapter 1) of Saint John's Gospel slowly. If fire regulations permit, have each student hold an unlit taper. At each line have one student walk up and light his or her taper from the large candle. Or have the students light battery-powered candles. Open and close the prayer service with a verse or two of an appropriate song that students choose from the parish hymnal or a recording.

READ MORE ABOUT JOHN

John and his brother James asked to have the highest rank in the kingdom Jesus was forming. They wanted to have more power than any of the other apostles. Have students read the story in the entry for James (feast day July 25, page 367).

WRITE A LETTER TO JESUS

John—and the other apostles—had a close relationship with Jesus. The stories of the saints tell us that this is also true of many men and women down through the ages who have welcomed the invitation to friendship with Christ. Have the students reflect on their relationship with Jesus. Then ask them to write a letter to Jesus in their journals, sharing recent experiences they've had and their feelings about the experiences.

Saint Thomas Becket   December 29

(1118–1170)

What is more important than friendship? What is stronger than loyalty? Faithfulness to Jesus.

Thomas was a tall, handsome, young legal clerk. He had a magnetic personality and made friends easily. His keen business sense was soon noticed by Archbishop Theobald, who brought him to Canterbury. The bishop found Thomas to be a master of speech and debate, and able to solve problems. At his recommendation Thomas was made chancellor of England. Thomas loved his new power and position. He lavishly spent his money on clothes, entertainment, hunting, and good times. A strong friendship developed between the king and the chancellor.

Henry II had one ambition—complete control of his kingdom, which included the Church. He needed an archbishop who would support him, and Henry believed Thomas was the man for this. When Thomas heard of the plan, he protested, saying, "If you make me archbishop, you will regret it." But Henry was king, and Henry had his way. Thomas became archbishop of Canterbury.

With the responsibility of leading the people of God, Thomas drastically changed. To Henry's surprise, Thomas resigned as chancellor. He sold his mansion and went to live in a monastery. He sold his rich clothes and furnishings, gave the money to the poor, and adopted a simple and holy lifestyle. The faithful servant of the king became the faithful servant of the pope. Thomas would be a loyal archbishop. His commanding personality was the same, but more noticeable were his generosity and determination to protect the Church. Thomas opposed Henry's taxation of the Church. He refused to let Henry decide who would be given Church positions and stopped the king's effort to control the Church.

The king had expected their friendship to continue. But Henry did not know the strength of Thomas's conscience. Hurt and embittered, the king turned on the archbishop and threatened imprisonment and death. Thomas fled to France and took refuge in a Cistercian monastery for six years. Both Thomas and the king appealed to Pope Alexander III. The pope condemned some of Henry's demands, and Thomas returned to England. He felt God wanted him to defend the truth there, even if it would cost him his life.

For a while the Church and the state were at peace. Then Henry had bishops who supported him crown his son—an infringement of the rights of the archbishop of Canterbury. The pope excommunicated these bishops, and Thomas upheld his decision. One night in a rage, the king expressed a wish to be rid of the archbishop. Four knights rode to the monastery where Thomas lived. An argument took place, but Thomas refused to disobey the pope. Going to the cathedral to pray, Thomas insisted the doors remain unbolted, despite the monks' pleas to lock them. The knights entered the cathedral and murdered Thomas near the high altar by the bishop's chair. His last words were "I accept death for the name of Jesus and for the Church."

ACTIVITIES

ROLE-PLAY

Have the students come up with situations in their own experience in which friendship or loyalty is tested. Talk about what part conscience plays. What are the consequences? Then have the students role-play some of the situations or draw storyboards showing a resolution.

MAKE A PILGRIMAGE

Soon after Thomas's death, miracles were reported to occur at his tomb, and many pilgrimages were made to his gravesite. In *The Canterbury Tales,* a famous book by English poet Geoffrey Chaucer, the characters are all on a pilgrimage to the Shrine of Saint Thomas Becket. Discuss with the class the purpose of a pilgrimage—to petition or praise God or a particular saint. Then organize a pilgrimage to a shrine or church nearby. Prepare a prayer service to use during your visit.

LIVE GOSPEL VALUES

Thomas Becket lived according to his conscience as enlightened by the Gospels and the teachings of the Church. Have the students write down four Gospel values they feel people their age should live by. Suggest that students keep their list in a private place and read it daily as an examination of conscience to renew themselves in living the Gospel.

Catechist's Notes:

_____

_____

_____

_____

_____

_____

_____

_____

_____

Holy Family

(Sunday after Christmas)

Christmas Season

A family is a special gift of God to each of us. A family is a result of God's love made visible through the special love of a man and a woman for each other. We need family. We need to accept the support and love given by family members, and we need to share our support and love with them.

On the feast of the Holy Family, we celebrate the family life of Jesus, Mary, and Joseph. These three people lived for God and loved and supported one another. The Holy Family is a model for all Christian families.

The Scripture readings for the Gospel on this feast occur in a three-year cycle, which means that one of three Gospels is read on this feast. Each of the Gospel accounts has a message for today's families. The first one shows the obedience of Joseph to the angel's command to leave for Egypt and Mary's cooperation with her husband. Just as these two parents showed fidelity to each other, so all Christian parents should live in fidelity and mutual support.

The second reading shows Joseph and Mary bringing the infant Jesus to the Temple to present him to the Lord. There Simeon prophesies that Jesus came for both Israel and the Gentiles. Just as Joseph and Mary showed Jesus to the world, so all Christian families, by their living example, should give witness to Christ.

The third Gospel reading tells of 12-year-old Jesus traveling with his parents to the Temple, but not returning with them. When his parents find him, he returns to Nazareth with them and is obedient to them. In a Christian family all family members should respect one another and work together in a loving way.

On this feast take a new look at your family—a look of appreciation for its strengths and a look of understanding for its weaknesses.

ACTIVITIES

PRAY FOR FAMILIES

Have the students think about what they want most for their families.

Grades K–4: Give each child a strip of light-colored construction paper and a pencil or marker. Ask the children to write their petitions on the paper. Let them come forward one by one, offer their prayer, loop their prayer strip, and staple or tape the strips together to form a prayer chain. Display the chain in your prayer area. If your parish has a statue of the Holy Family, gather there for the prayer, and hang the chain there for the Christmas season.

Grades 5–8: Suggest students write a prayer in their journals, asking God to help their families. Close with a litany for families. The response may be "Bless my family, Lord."

> Because they accept me just as I am . . .
>
> Because they rejoice at my success and comfort me in failure . . .
>
> Because they encourage me when I'm discouraged . . .
>
> Because they share their love with me . . .
>
> Lord, I am not always grateful for my family. But today, I thank you for each one *(pause for students to name family members)* and ask you to bless their lives. Amen.

MAKE PLAQUES

Have each child make a plaque for his or her family. Students may use the following verse:

> My family is my family, special to me.
> I love and support them, as they do for me.

They may draw the faces of family members, or their own design, around the verse. Encourage students to hang the plaque in their kitchen or family room at home.

PLAN A FAMILY MEAL

Encourage the children to help prepare a family meal or arrange a family gathering. During this gathering they may ask each family member to tell the others one thing that most people don't know about him or her.

RATE THEMSELVES

Have the students rate themselves according to the following checklist:

Scale
1 never
2 seldom
3 sometimes
4 often
5 every day

_____ I pray that the members of my family will grow in love for one another.

_____ I do my share of the work at home.

_____ I speak respectfully to the other members of my family.

_____ I thank the other members of my family for the things they do for me.

_____ I praise the other members of my family for the things they do well.

Solemnity of Mary, Mother of God

Do you ever feel that some things are worth fighting over? Way back in 431, there was a bitter controversy among theologians over the role of Mary in the Church. So the bishops held a meeting, called a council, at Ephesus, a city in Greece. Its purpose was to correct the errors that Nestorius, the bishop of Constantinople, was teaching about beliefs of the Church. Cyril of Alexandria conducted the assembly of 150 bishops. They debated the question, Who is Mary in God's plan?

In the end the bishops declared that Mary was to be called *Theotokos*, a Greek word that means "God-bearer." They said that Mary is really the Mother of Jesus and Jesus is really God. So it must be said that Mary is the Mother of God. The Council of Ephesus confirmed an ancient belief of the Church. The oldest Christian greeting of Mary was proclaimed when Mary's relative Elizabeth called her "Mother of my Lord." When Elizabeth welcomed Mary, she recognized both the great privilege God had given Mary and Mary's great faith in accepting it. No one heard the Word of God and believed it more than Mary. Jesus was able to enter human history because Mary made a gift of herself to God in faith.

For centuries Mary has been praised because she believed. She is Mother of God because of her faith in God. The Solemnity of Mary, Mother of God, celebrates Mary's faith and trust in God alone. The Church wants us to call on Mary, Mother of God, and ask her to help strengthen our faith. She will listen and answer our prayers. The Church wants us also to imitate her faith. As we honor Mary today, we rely on her to help us grow in faith and trust in her divine Son.

PRAY THE MEMORARE

One of the earliest prayers to Mary is from the fourth century. A revised version of this prayer is called the Memorare. Give the students a copy of the prayer and encourage them to memorize it. The Memorare is included on the blackline master on page 436.

DISPLAY A VARIETY OF IMAGES

Throughout the year bring in a variety of pictures, icons, or statues of Mary. Display these on the prayer table. Let the students appreciate the ways that people have visualized the Mother of God.

MAKE RESOLUTIONS FOR PEACE

January 1 is recognized also as a day of prayer for world peace. How fitting because we are celebrating the Mother of the Prince of Peace! Help the students to understand that they can work for world peace by beginning with themselves. Encourage them to make a class resolution to be kind and considerate to others at home, on the playground, and in the cafeteria.

PRAY FOR ISLAMIC NATIONS

The Islamic authors have always honored Mary as the mother of a great prophet. Have the class pray today to Mary, Mother of God, that she may help reconcile the wars and suffering in Islamic nations.

WRITE AND DECORATE A PRAYER FOR MOTHERS

When we celebrate Mary as Mother of God, we celebrate the privilege of motherhood and family. Suggest that the children write a prayer to Mary, asking her to help their mothers this year. Have the children write their prayers on good paper in their best handwriting, then decorate the page and give it to their mothers.

Catechist's Notes:

_____

_____

_____

_____

_____

_____

_____

_____

Saints Basil the Great and Gregory Nazianzen

January 2

(330–379; 330–389)

Friends are great. Do you know that a true friend helps you be your very best self?

Basil and Gregory were close friends. In one way they were opposites. Basil was a man of action who needed projects to challenge his organizational abilities and who enjoyed a stimulating university life. Gregory was a quiet and scholarly man. But in their faith and work for peace and Church unity, they were the same.

Basil traveled in the East and studied monastic life. He decided to form his own monastic group with his own rule, and Gregory joined him. Their community life was divided between liturgical prayer, study of Scripture, and manual work. The rule allowed monks and nuns to operate hospitals and guest houses and to do other good work outside the community. Basil's principles still influence Eastern monasticism.

The two friends lived monastic life for about five years. Then Gregory returned home to care for his aging father, a bishop. In those times priests could marry. Gregory was ordained a priest and took on the duties of his father's diocese. In 374 Basil was made Bishop of Caesarea. The Church called on Basil to refute the Arian heresy, which claimed that Jesus was not God. The Emperor Valens had promoted the heresy. Basil believed the Church must be independent of the emperor and spoke out in defense of the Church, preaching morning and evening to large crowds. He practiced what he preached. When famine struck he used his own money to organize a soup kitchen and served people himself. Basil even built a town.

Basil wrote letters. He decided who would be ordained, assisted with prison reform, and warned leaders when punishments were too harsh. Basil corrected clergy who were causing scandal and advised his relatives about which subjects to take in school. He wrote for the Church, to oppose the Arian heresy, and to clarify the doctrines of the Trinity and the Incarnation. Basil knew that if truth were to triumph, faithful bishops were needed in every diocese. When one town, known for its fighting, was falling away from the faith, Basil ordained Gregory bishop and sent him there. This caused a rift in their friendship, but they were reconciled later.

When the Emperor Valens died, the city of Constantinople had been under Arian leadership for 30 years. The bishops nearby begged Gregory to come and restore the faith. There Gregory made his house a church and preached powerfully on the Trinity. Gradually he brought back the true faith.

When Basil died at the age of 49, he was mourned even by strangers and pagans. Gregory spent his last years reading, writing his autobiography, and enjoying his gardens.

NAME THAT TEACHING

Both Basil and Gregory were defenders of the faith. Write the following words on slips of paper and put them in a hat or basket. Use additional words or teachings so you have one for each student in the class. Have each student draw a paper. Ask the students to explain the belief they drew without saying the word, and let the class guess the word. Give them a short time to prepare their explanations.

Incarnation	Trinity
Catholic Church	Creed
Theological Virtues	Prayer
Ten Commandments	Heaven
God the Father	Beatitudes
Jesus Christ	Sacraments
Holy Spirit	Blessed Mother

An option is to list the words on the board and have students use the words to make matching tests or crossword puzzles. Then have students exchange tests or puzzles and try to solve them.

GET ACQUAINTED WITH THE CATECHISM

Show the students that the Church still explains and defends the faith. If the students are not already acquainted with the Catholic *Catechism*, introduce it. You may wish to have them look up some of the words or teachings listed in the activity above. You may also bring in some papal encyclicals or pastoral statements issued by the bishops. Even though these writings may be too difficult for the students to understand, it is good that they know about them.

RECALL THE HELP OF A FRIEND

Invite the students to tell or write about a time when a friend helped them follow the teaching of the Church and do what was right.

REFLECT ON SAINT BASIL'S WORDS

Read to the class this selection from Basil's writings:

> The bread you do not use is the bread of the hungry: the garment hanging in your wardrobe is the garment of him who is naked, the shoes that you do not wear are the shoes of one who is barefoot; the money that you keep locked away is the money of the poor; the acts of charity that you do not perform are so many injustices that you commit.

Have a time of silent prayer to reflect on this. Then discuss its meaning with the class.

TELL ABOUT FAMILY SUPPORT

Seven members of Basil's family became saints: his grandmother (Macrina the Elder), father (Basil the Elder), mother (Emiliana), two brothers (Gregory of Nyssa and Peter of Sebaste), a sister (Macrina the Younger). Suggest that the students read more about this holy family. Then invite them to tell or write about how their families have helped them live their faith.

Saint Elizabeth Ann Seton

(1774–1821)

Do you know who was the first person born in the United States to be declared a saint? She opened the first American Catholic parish school and orphanage. She also founded the first American religious community of women. This person was Elizabeth Ann Bayley Seton.

Elizabeth was born two years before the Declaration of Independence. Her father was a prominent New York physician. He did not attend church, but by his example he taught his daughter to love and serve the poor. Her mother and stepmother were devout Episcopalians who taught Elizabeth the value of prayer and reading the Scriptures. Elizabeth's education and training prepared her for New York high society. At the age of 19, she married a handsome, wealthy businessman, William Seton. Furs and satins, parties and plays, an abundance of friends and money—all were part of the young couple's life. Will and Elizabeth were very much in love, and they loved their three girls and two boys.

Then in 1803 Will Seton's business went bankrupt and his health failed. The Filicchi family in Italy invited the Setons to visit so that Will could recuperate in the warm, sunny climate.

The ocean voyage was rough. Then, because of a yellow fever epidemic in New York before the Setons left, the Italian government kept them isolated in an old fort for six weeks. If they did not get yellow fever, they would be allowed to enter Italy. Will Seton grew worse in the cold, damp room. Elizabeth, with the help of a Filicchi servant, cared for him. Finally they were released, but in a few weeks Will was dead.

Elizabeth, widowed at 30 with five small children and many medical bills, returned to New York. While she was in Italy, the Filicchi family had taught her about the Catholic faith. Back in New York she began to attend St. Peter's, the only Catholic church in the city. When Elizabeth made her profession of faith in 1805, her family and friends turned against her, and she was on her own.

Elizabeth opened a Catholic boarding school for girls in Emmitsburg, Maryland. Women with the same ideals came to help her, and the school grew. In 1812 Elizabeth and these other women became a religious community, the Daughters of Charity of St. Joseph. From then on, these sisters served in hospitals, homes for the aged, orphanages, homes for the mentally challenged, and in schools.

As a religious sister, Elizabeth continued to cherish and guide her children. Her two sons joined the navy. Her daughters became nuns.

ACTIVITIES

BECOME TEACHERS

Let students become teachers for a day in honor of Elizabeth Seton. They may help out in a class of younger children or prepare to teach part of your next class.

VIEW A VIDEO

Show a video about the life of Saint Elizabeth Ann Seton and let the students discuss it. Encourage them to read a book on her life and to research her community.

MAKE A MINIMURAL

Divide the class into small groups. Give each group a long strip of paper, six inches deep. Have the children divide the events of Elizabeth Seton's life and together create a minimural featuring this American saint.

MAKE MOBILES

Have the students make a mobile using symbols for the different experiences and roles that Elizabeth Seton had and for the places she lived. Ask students to take one finished mobile to each class in the building and explain the story of Elizabeth Seton's life. Or have the students take their mobiles home and explain her life to their families.

INTERVIEW MOTHERS

Elizabeth Ann Seton always considered herself a mother. She never stopped praying for her children or trying to help them. Have the students interview their mothers (or those who act as mother for them) on being a mother. Give them time in class to brainstorm possible interview questions, such as

- What's it like to be a mother?

- What goals do you have for your children?

- What do you see as a mother's role in passing on the Christian faith to her children?

Catechist's Notes:

_____

_____

_____

_____

_____

_____

_____

_____

Saint John Neumann

(1811–1860)

January 5

He was so short that people laughed when they saw him riding his horse, for his feet did not reach the stirrups. He was not very good-looking. He was a quiet man, not one to charm a crowd or draw attention to himself. He was not a Church leader who pleased influential people. But John Neumann was true to God and to himself.

Born and educated in Bohemia, John was interested in botany and astronomy as well as Church matters. By the time he was 25, he knew six languages and was a trained seminarian. Since there were many priests in his country, John came to the United States in 1838—with one suit of clothes and one dollar in his pocket.

The bishop of New York ordained John and sent him to the German-speaking people clearing the forests around Niagara Falls. John traveled on horseback from mission to mission, visiting the sick, teaching catechism, training teachers to take over when he left. He was busy but lonely, and felt the need for community life.

So John entered the Redemptorist Order. As a novice he was moved so frequently that he wondered if the order really wanted him. Finally they allowed him to make his vows. He eventually was made the superior of the American branch of the order. John felt unqualified, but under his direction the Redemptorists became leaders in the parochial school movement. He served as a parish priest in Baltimore until he was made bishop of Philadelphia in 1852. There was great opposition to his appointment.

The influential, wealthy Catholics wanted a bishop who was a gentleman. The Irish wanted a bishop who was an Irishman. Some people wanted a bishop who would overlook their unchristian behavior. John received a very cold reception when he went to Philadelphia. While it hurt him deeply, John decided that he would just be himself and do the best job he could. But his resolution did not make the criticism stop.

He also found himself confronted by the Know Nothings, a political group determined to deprive foreigners and Catholics of their civil rights. They burned convents and schools. John became so discouraged that he wrote to Rome requesting a transfer, thinking someone else might do a better job in Philadelphia. But he was told to stay at his job—which he did!

In eight years the number of Catholic schools in Philadelphia grew from two to a hundred. John brought in many teaching orders of sisters and Christian brothers. For the German immigrants he published two catechisms and a Bible history in German. He also wrote many articles for Catholic newspapers and magazines.

Bishop John Neumann died suddenly while walking down the street. After his death people began to praise his many hidden virtues. This unassuming, often unpopular man who worked so hard for God was declared a saint in 1977.

ACTIVITIES

GATHER HISTORICAL DATA

John Neumann lived in the United States between 1836 and 1860. Have the students research other developments in the Catholic Church at this time, especially the Catholic school system in other parts of the country. Tell them to look for significant historical events that may have influenced the growth of Catholic schools. Then allow them time to share their information with the class.

EVALUATE EXPECTATIONS OF OTHERS

John Neumann would not have been an effective leader or an honest person if he had tried to live up to the unrealistic expectations of others instead of being true to himself. Suggest that the students make a list of all the things that others expect of them. Have them put a check next to the ones that would make them more like Jesus.

MAKE POSTERS

John Neumann's major contribution to the Catholic Church was in education. Let the students make posters to show how their school or religious education program is giving them a Catholic education—helping them to learn Christ's message, to live in a faith community, and to serve others as Jesus did. The posters may be displayed in the school hallway or parish church.

REVIEW AND REWARD

It is said that Father John made learning religion very sweet. When he came into a class he would ask the children questions and reward correct answers with a piece of candy from his pocket. Conduct a review session, with correct answers meriting a piece of candy. Be sure each child is rewarded!

Catechist's Notes:

_____

_____

_____

_____

_____

_____

_____

_____

_____

Epiphany

Christmas Season

(January 6 or the Sunday between January 2 and January 8)

The solemnity of the Epiphany of the Lord is considered to be one of the oldest feasts of Christianity. It was celebrated as far back as the second century in the Eastern Church. In the East the feast meant the adoration of the Magi, the baptism of Christ, and the miracle at Cana. At each of these events, there was some manifestation of Christ's divinity. The word *epiphany* means "manifestation" or "revelation." On this feast the Eastern Church blesses holy water.

In the West the feast came to mean the visit of the Magi. Here it refers to God being made known in the person of Jesus to the Magi, who represent all nations. Matthew records the event in his Gospel. Some astrologers—advisors to Eastern kings—traveled to Jerusalem from the east. They followed a star that they believed would lead them to an infant who would be King of the Jews. When they found the child

with his mother, they fell on their knees and offered him gifts of gold, frankincense, and myrrh. The Fathers of the Church later interpreted these gifts as symbolic of the royalty (gold), divinity (incense), and suffering (myrrh) of Christ.

The readings for the feast emphasize the universality of God's power, love, and presence to all people. Jesus is Light of the Nations—all nations. Jesus has come for all because there are no limits to his love, and he will bring all people to his Father.

The feast reminds us that we are responsible for sharing the Church's gifts, especially the gift of Christ to the world. We are to have an ecumenical outlook. We are to reach out in prayer, sacrifice, and active charity with the vision that God's kingdom is for everyone.

ACTIVITIES

REFLECT ON THE GOSPEL

Matthew's Gospel contains themes of proclamation (God is with us!), acceptance (God is welcomed!), and rejection (God is rejected!). Let the students read the account of the Magi (Matthew 2:1–18) and discuss how these themes are exemplified.

CELEBRATE WITH SONG

Let the students sing songs about the Magi: "As with Gladness Men of Old," "We Three Kings," "Shepherds and Kings," "Do You See What I See?", "Winter, Cold Night," "Come Weal, Come Woe," "Song of Good News."

SHARE A TREAT

Share crown-shaped cookies or a cake in the shape of a crown as an Epiphany treat.

MAKE EPIPHANY SYMBOLS

At first the early Church considered Epiphany a day to celebrate three feasts: adoration of the Magi (Matthew 2:1–18), the baptism of Jesus (Mark 1:9–11), the miracle at Cana (John 2:1–12). Let the students read each of these accounts. Give each student three paper circles and have the students draw a picture or symbol for each theme. Then have them attach the three circles together. Post the Epiphany symbols.

RESEARCH CUSTOMS

Since the Middle Ages it has been a custom to remember the feast of the Epiphany by writing initials of the Magi (Caspar, Melchior, and Balthazar) and the date with blest chalk above the doorways:

$$\dagger \, C \, \dagger \, M \, \dagger \, B \, \dagger$$
$$2004$$

You may wish to have a priest do this over the classroom doorway. Have students look up Epiphany customs used around the world and share this information with one another.

VIEW *AMAHL AND THE NIGHT VISITORS*

Encourage students to watch Gian Carlo Menotti's opera *Amahl and the Night Visitors* (about the visit of the Magi). This is sometimes on television during the Christmas season, or you might obtain a video and watch it in class.

Catechist's Notes:

_____

_____

_____

_____

_____

_____

Blessed André Bessette

January 6

(1845–1937)

The most unexpected people can be saints. André Bessette was sickly all his life. He failed at every job he tried. He could barely read or write. Yet he became famous and well loved for his holiness.

André, the eighth of twelve children, was born near Montreal, Canada, and baptized Alfred. His parents, who were French-Canadian, died early. André was adopted when he was 12 years old and became a farmhand. Later he tried being a shoemaker, a baker, and a blacksmith, but he was unsuccessful. Then André joined the Congregation of the Holy Cross, but at the end of a year, he was told to leave because of his bad health. However, a wise bishop convinced the community to allow André to remain. Brother André became the doorkeeper at the College of Notre Dame and served in that position for 40 years.

André had a statue of Saint Joseph on the windowsill in his room. André spent many hours praying during the night. Soon it was discovered that André had healing powers. He would visit the sick, pray with them, rub them with oil, and they would be cured. Before long, throngs of people were coming to him for healing and spiritual direction. André would say, "It is Saint Joseph who cures. I am just his little dog." André ministered to people eight to ten hours a day. In the meantime four secretaries were kept busy handling the 80,000 letters André received each year.

The Holy Cross community had tried for many years to buy a piece of land nearby. André buried a medal of Saint Joseph on the property, and suddenly the owners sold the land. Then André raised money to build first a small chapel there and then a church. For years he cut students' hair for five cents and saved the money. At the church he received visitors. Cured people left behind their crutches and canes. It took 50 years to build Saint Joseph's Oratory, which is probably the world's main shrine to Saint Joseph. More than 2 million people visit the oratory every year.

André let God work through his weakness to accomplish great things. He became known as "the Miracle Man of Montreal." He was beatified in 1982.

ACTIVITIES

START A CLASS PROJECT

Remind the students that for years Blessed André cut hair for five cents a head. Little by little, the money added up. Start a class project to collect money for a children's shelter. Suggest that the students do chores or extra jobs in their homes or neighborhood for a nickel and contribute their earnings. At the end of the school year, involve the students in adding up the money and sending or delivering it to their chosen charity.

TAKE A VIRTUAL TOUR

Have the students go on line to see pictures and find more information about Saint Joseph's Oratory in Montreal.

CELEBRATE ANOINTING OF THE SICK

Arrange for the class to attend a communal Anointing of the Sick service at your parish. Perhaps one of the students has a relative who would want to celebrate this sacrament.

MAKE GET-WELL CARDS

Talk about how the children can be healers right where they are, right now. Family members, schoolmates, neighbors, or parishioners may be sick, elderly, or lonely. People need emotional and spiritual healing as well as physical healing. Provide art materials to make get-well cards. Encourage the children to hand deliver or mail the cards as soon as possible.

RESEARCH THE GIFT OF HEALING

Some students may be interested in giving a report on the gift of healing in the Church today.

WRITE A POEM OR HYMN

Have the children work individually or in small groups to compose a poem or hymn honoring either Saint Joseph or Blessed André, who shows us the power of Joseph.

Catechist's Notes:

_____

_____

_____

_____

_____

_____

_____

_____

Baptism of the Lord — Christmas Season

(Sunday after Epiphany)

Have you ever attended an inauguration or watched an inauguration ceremony on television? When a president of the United States has been newly elected, he participates in a formal ceremony of inauguration and presents an inaugural address. In this speech he explains his role in leading the country, and shares his hopes and his plans for the future. Jesus' baptism was similar to an inauguration.

One day Jesus was standing in a crowd listening to John the Baptist. John always challenged his listeners to turn their backs on their sinful way of life and turn to God. A sign that a person really wanted to live according to God's way was his or her public baptism by John. When a person stood beside John in the water, everyone in the crowd expected that person to change for the better. After all the people had come forward that day to be baptized, Jesus came forward. This was confusing to John the Baptist. He knew that Jesus did not need to change the way he was living. But the Gospel records that when Jesus was baptized, a very important thing happened—some signs showed that the Father and the Spirit were in intimate connection with Jesus.

Jesus was anointed for his mission just as Isaiah had written: "The spirit of the Lord God is upon to me, because the Lord has anointed me" (Isaiah 61:1). Jesus quoted the rest of that passage to explain his mission when he spoke to his neighbors at Nazareth:

He has anointed me to bring good news to the poor. He has sent me to proclaim release to the captives and recovery of sight to the blind, to let the oppressed go free, to proclaim the year of the Lord's favor.

(Luke 4:18–19)

Jesus, who did the Father's work, was always one with the power of the Father and the Holy Spirit. After rising from the dead, Jesus sent the Holy Spirit upon his disciples at Pentecost. Then their work of spreading the Good News of Jesus began.

Jesus' baptism by John was his inauguration for his mission to save all people from their sins. This mission would result in Jesus' Passion and death on the cross, to be followed by his Resurrection from the dead. The Gospel records that on his way to Jerusalem, he spoke about his Passion and death as a baptism. "I have a baptism with which to be baptized, and what stress I am under until it is completed!" (Luke 12:50).

The source of grace received in Christian Baptism is the death and Resurrection of Christ Jesus. Through the power of the Holy Spirit, we have been baptized into Christ's death (the death that saved us) and have become God the Father's adopted children. As baptized members of the Christian community, we also have a mission—to spread the Good News of Jesus by the way we speak and act. When we celebrate the feast of Jesus' baptism, we can also celebrate our own initiation, our own Baptism.

JANUARY

REPORT ON JESUS' BAPTISM

Have the students write "eyewitness" accounts of Jesus' baptism, using one of these Gospel accounts as a basis: Matthew 3:13–17; Mark 1:9–11; Luke 3:21–22. Have them choose to be a particular person at the event: John, a sinner, a passer-by, one newly baptized.

FIND OUT ABOUT THEIR OWN BAPTISM

Ask the students to discover as much as they can about their own baptismal day. Have them design a poster or collage that illustrates the important facts and the interesting details of their special day. Have them bring to class pictures and other remembrances. Take time for each person to share his or her findings with others.

LEARN ABOUT THE SYMBOLS OF BAPTISM

Have the students list the symbols used in the Rite of Baptism: signing on the forehead, candle, water, oil (catechumen and chrism), white robe, and so on. Discuss with them the significance of the symbols. Finally, have each student design a prayer card for a newly baptized person, using the symbols of Baptism and the words: "You have been baptized in Christ."

RENEW THE PROMISES OF BAPTISM

At the end of the lesson, let the students renew their baptismal promises, following the formula used at the Easter Vigil or at the Mass for Confirmation.

STUDY THE RCIA

The Rite of Christian Initiation for Adults (RCIA) has been reintroduced into the life of the Church. This rite was originally used in the early Church as a process of conversion and preparation for Baptism, Confirmation, and Eucharist. To familiarize the students with this rite:

- Assign different students to research and report on the various rites of the catechumenate: entrance, exorcisms and blessings, rite of election, and so on.

- Ask students to find examples of different baptismal fonts in pictures or in actual churches. Discuss what the design and decoration say about the Church's understanding of Baptism.

- Have students discover how their particular parish meets the needs of those who wish to join the Catholic Church.

- Have students discover more about the RCIA by interviewing someone who has been involved in it. Allow them to share their findings with the class.

- Show the video "This Is the Night: A Parish Welcomes New Members" (Liturgy Training Publications, 1992 [30 minutes]). Have the students discuss new information or insights they have gained.

Catechist's Notes:

_____

_____

_____

Saint Marguerite Bourgeoys

(1620–1700)

Saint Marguerite Bourgeoys Catholic Church in Brookfield, Connecticut, was founded in 1982, the same year Marguerite was canonized. Marguerite is a fitting patron for a new Catholic parish.

As a young woman in France, Marguerite joined a group of women who did charitable work. Marguerite's work was teaching in the poorest part of her hometown, Troyes. Then the governor of Ville Marie, a village in what is now Canada, visited his sister in Troyes. He was looking for teachers to start a school. In June 1653, 33-year-old Marguerite boarded the ship for America. Three months later she arrived in the village that would grow into Montreal.

Marguerite had no students. Life was so hard for the settlers that children seldom lived to reach school age. So Marguerite worked in the hospital. Five years later she opened her first school in a stone stable.

Marguerite believed that education was for everyone, and she included girls, poor children, and Native American children. Besides reading, writing, and arithmetic, she taught home management, music and art, and religion. Marguerite worked with the whole family to address both spiritual and social needs.

When young women from France came to make lives for themselves in the New World, Marguerite became their guardian. She took them in and taught them skills to run a home in the wilderness. Then she helped them find husbands and witnessed their marriage vows. She was later called "the Mother of the Colony."

As the number of colonists increased, Marguerite set up schools throughout the territory. She returned to France three times to invite other women to join the Congregation de Notre Dame, which she had founded. Marguerite and her sisters survived poverty, a war with the Iroquois, a fire that devastated the village, and disease.

Marguerite was also responsible for the construction of the first permanent chapel in Montreal—Notre Dame de Bon Secours (Our Lady of Good Help). The present chapel on that site is still a place of pilgrimage, especially for sailors. Many have left models of boats to hang in the chapel as thanksgiving to God and Our Lady for their safe journeys.

Marguerite's inspiration was Mary, who hurried to Judea to help her aged relative Elizabeth, who was pregnant. Mary went without hesitation to serve, and that is what Marguerite wanted to do. Most sisters at the time lived apart from the world. Marguerite said her sisters should be "daughters of the parish." She thought that they should live with the people, pray in the parish church, and be free to go wherever needed.

JANUARY

ACTIVITIES

EVALUATE CHOICE OF PATRON

After reading about Marguerite, help the class make a master list of the reasons she is a good choice for patron saint of a parish. You may also wish to have the students recall or read the life of the patron saint of your parish. Make a similar list of why your patron may have been chosen.

RESEARCH WORK OF SISTERS

Today more than 2,500 sisters of the Congregation de Notre Dame are serving others in North America, Latin America, Japan, and Cameroon. Have the students find out more about the work of these daughters of Saint Marguerite.

ACT IT OUT

Let the children act out the story of Saint Marguerite. Some simple costumes and props will make the experience more memorable.

PRAY FOR THE PARISH

Lead the children in extemporaneous prayers for the people of Saint Marguerite Bourgeoys parish on the feast day of their patron saint.

HELP FELLOW PARISHIONERS

Provide a number of parish bulletins or newsletters. Ask the students to find groups in the parish who are ready to serve where they are needed. Have them brainstorm parish needs or interview parish staff to learn about needs and decide how they could help fellow parishioners.

THINK ABOUT THE NEEDS OF OTHERS

Ask the children if they think young people or families from other countries coming to the United States today would need much help. Brainstorm the kind of help they might need. Find out about the aid available to refugees in your diocese.

Catechist's Notes:

_____

_____

_____

_____

_____

_____

_____

_____

Saint Hilary

January 13

(315–367)

This saint was charged with disturbing the peace! Yet everyone who knew Hilary said he was a friendly, charitable, and gentle man.

Hilary was born to pagan parents of Poitiers, France. After studying philosophy and the Greek and Roman classics, Hilary married. He and his wife had one daughter, Afra. Hilary's studies led him to read the Scriptures. He became convinced that there was only one God whose Son became man and died and rose to save all people. So Hilary, with his wife and daughter, was baptized into the Christian faith.

The people of Poitiers were impressed with the example of Hilary and chose him to be their bishop in 353. He was an able administrator, and a pastor and bishop who spoke out against Arianism. He warned the people of this heresy that denied the divinity of Christ. When the Emperor Constantius II wanted Hilary to sign a paper condemning Athanasius, the great defender of the faith, Hilary refused. The emperor was furious and exiled Hilary to Phrygia in Asia Minor.

In exile Hilary did even greater good through his preaching, writing, and suffering. During this time he requested a debate with the Arian bishops. Fearing Hilary's strong arguments, the Arians begged the emperor to send Hilary home. The emperor, believing Hilary was also undermining his authority, recalled him.

Hilary's writings show that he could be fierce in defending the faith, but in dealing with the bishops who had given in to the Arian heresy, he was very charitable. He showed them their errors and helped them to defend the truths of the faith.

Though the emperor called him "disturber of the peace," Saints Jerome and Augustine praised him as "teacher of the churches."

ACTIVITIES

RECOUNT PERSONAL EXPERIENCES

Hilary was a mentor to a young man who also became a saint—Martin of Tours. Have the students share experiences in which their actions have strengthened another or another has strengthened them.

MAKE A BANNER

Hilary had strong faith convictions and defended the faith fearlessly. Ask the students to read what Saint Paul teaches Timothy about faith in 2 Timothy 1:6–14. Then have the students make a banner about faith, using a verse from Scripture and symbols.

LIST ACTS OF FAITH

Love of his faith directed Saint Hilary's life. Have the students make lists of all the things they do—or do not do—because of their religious beliefs. Which list is longer? Why?

PRAY FOR THE BISHOP

Review with the students who their bishop is. If possible, show a picture of the bishop to the students. Discuss the good things the bishop of their diocese has done. Remind them to pray for the bishop at Mass when his name is mentioned in the Eucharistic Prayer.

Catechist's Notes:

Saint Anthony

(c. 250–356)

Have you ever admired someone so much that you wanted to be just like him or her? To some the lifestyle of Saint Anthony may seem uninviting. But Anthony has a message for anyone who wishes to know God.

Anthony was born in Egypt. He disliked school and its social atmosphere. At age 20, when his parents died, he did not welcome the thought of taking care of a large home and property. He decided to take the Scripture teaching "Sell all that you own and distribute the money to the poor" literally. First Anthony made sure his younger sister's education could be completed in a community of holy women. He then sold all his possessions and left for a life of complete solitude in the desert. There Anthony found an elderly hermit who taught him about a life of prayer and penance. For 20 years Anthony lived in isolation, alone with God. He did penance by eating bread and water once a day at sunset. The devil tempted him during these years. But Anthony relied on God's power over the evil one. Anthony's unusual life did not make him harsh, but instead made him radiant with God's love and full of caring and compassion.

Stories of Anthony's holiness spread, and people began to come to the desert to learn from him how to become holy. Many of his sayings and stories about him were written down to teach people how to live holy lives. One story was about three men who visited Anthony every year. Two would discuss their hopes and their spiritual life with Anthony. The third never said anything. After many years Anthony said to the third man, "You often come here to see me, but you never ask anything." The man replied, "It is enough to see you, Father."

Some admirers who came wanted to stay, so Anthony—at age 54—founded a type of monastery consisting of scattered hermitages near one another. Anthony wrote a rule that guided the monks in a life of silence, prayer, and manual work. Later when Anthony heard of the persecutions of the Christians by the Emperor Maximinus, he wanted to die a martyr. At age 60 he left the desert to minister to the Christians in prisons, fearlessly exposing himself to danger. While doing this work, he realized that a person can also die daily for Christ by serving him in ordinary ways with great love. So he returned to the desert to his life of prayer and penance. However, his life of solitude was again interrupted when at age 88 he had a vision about the harm Arian followers were doing to the Church. Anthony went to Alexandria to preach against the heresy. During this time Anthony worked miracles and won converts.

At age 90 another vision sent Anthony searching the desert for Paul, the first hermit. These two holy men met and spoke of the wonders of God. Anthony is said to have died peacefully in a cave at age 105. The impact he left on the world is tremendous. Anthony taught us that through solitude and penance we do not move away from those in the world but come closer to them.

FIND SOLITUDE

Anthony reminds the world of the need for solitude. Plan a "hermit time" for the class. Take the students to church or a quiet place outdoors for a silent time of about 15 minutes. Let them spread out and find their own space. Allow them to read from the Scriptures, write in their journals, or read the life of a saint. Encourage them to share what they learned from their solitude.

REMEMBER GOD'S WORD

When the Emperor Constantine wrote Anthony, asking him to pray for him, people were impressed—but Anthony wasn't. He explained, "Don't be surprised that the emperor writes to me. He's just another man as I am. But be astounded that God should have written to us, that he has spoken to us by his Son." Share this idea with the students. Then ask them to look through the Gospels and find something that Jesus taught or said that they think everyone should know and remember. Give them time to memorize their verse. Then have students recite their verses for the whole class.

REFLECT ON THE SIGN OF THE CROSS

It is said that Anthony triumphed over the power of the devil many times by making the Sign of the Cross. Discuss with the students the value of this prayer. We make the Sign of the Cross before we pray to compose ourselves and focus on God. In temptation we make the Sign of the Cross to be strengthened. It is also a sign of blessing that God may sanctify us. It is a sign of faith in the Trinity, Incarnation, and Redemption. It may also be a sign of offering ourselves—mind, will, and entire body. Ask the students to be conscious of these things when they make the Sign of the Cross. Encourage them to slowly make the Sign of the Cross immediately on waking each morning. Have them make it reverently at the end of class.

OFFER UP DIFFICULTIES

Anthony found out that God doesn't want everyone to die in persecutions. God sometimes asks the daily offering of unrewarded kindnesses and sacrifices. Remind the students to quietly offer up any difficulties for love of God.

PRAY SHORT PRAYERS

Anthony said that when he stopped during his manual work to think of God, his love of God grew stronger. Teach the students several short prayers such as "My Jesus, mercy," "My God I trust in you," and "Jesus, Mary, Joseph." Encourage them to pray one of these prayers silently during the day.

Catechist's Notes:

_____

_____

_____

_____

Saints Fabian and Sebastian

January 20

(d. 250; d. 288)

Fabian was a pope, and Sebastian was a soldier in the Roman army. What do they have in common?

The traditional story told about Saint Sebastian is that he was an army officer who was condemned to death for his belief in Jesus. His fellow soldiers shot him with arrows. Surviving this, he was clubbed to death. The only actual fact we have is that Sebastian was an early Christian martyr during the reign of Emperor Diocletian.

More is known about the life of Fabian, who was pope in 236, when the political situation was very unstable. Philip, an ambitious and ruthless man, killed Emperor Maximus and made himself emperor. Later he regretted his own violent behavior and changed the government policy from persecution of Christians to tolerance for Christians. He even gave Fabian permission for Church authorities to own property. For the first time, being a Christian was officially legal. But this easy life for the Christians did not last long.

Philip was killed by his own lieutenant, Decius, who became the next emperor. Decius believed that his empire could be saved only if the pagan customs of ancient Rome were restored. He reversed Philip's policy by sending an edict that commanded the death penalty for all who would not give up following Christ. Pope Fabian showed to whom he gave his loyalty by dying for the faith. Following his example, many Christians died as martyrs. However, the years under Philip had softened the dedication of many of Jesus' followers. In a moment of terror, many denied their faith in Christ.

Decius was pleased. He hoped that without a pope and with so many Christians defecting, the Church itself would disband and then disappear. But he didn't realize that a power stronger than the power of human beings was protecting the Church. Jesus said, "I am with you always, to the end of the age" (Matthew 28:20).

Soldier and pope, Sebastian and Fabian were faithful followers of Christ, faithful until death.

ACTIVITIES

DRAMATIZE THE STORY

Have the students choose roles and act out scenes from the life of Saint Fabian. You will need students to be Fabian, Emperor Decius, the emperor's messenger who announces the edict, faithful Christians, soldiers who arrest Christians, unfaithful Christians, and soldiers who question and intimidate the Christians. Include a scene in which the Christians try to encourage one another in being loyal to Christ.

WRITE A STORY

Ask the students to imagine that they are living during a time of persecution. Have them consider what their response would be if they were arrested for being a follower of Christ. Tell them to write a short story about the situation and their response. Let the students share the stories with the class or post them.

SEARCH FOR MARTYRS

See how many early Christian martyrs the students can name. List the names on the board. Have the students construct word searches or other word puzzles using these names.

Catechist's Notes:

_____

_____

_____

_____

_____

_____

_____

_____

_____

_____

Saint Agnes

January 21

(c. 300)

Today's saint assures us that holiness does not depend on age. Agnes, a 12- or 13-year-old girl, willingly gave her life out of love for Christ.

The traditional story of Agnes is that she was beautiful, and many men wanted to marry her. She refused each one because she wanted to be a bride of Christ. One of her suitors was so angry that he reported to the governor that she was a Christian. The governor summoned Agnes to the palace. He threatened her with torture and punishment. Agnes looked at the instruments of torture with heroic calmness. The governor then had her sent to a house of prostitution, but everyone who saw her courage was afraid to touch her. One man who looked at her lustfully was struck blind, but Agnes prayed for him, and he regained his sight. The governor, seeing that Agnes was determined to remain a virgin, had her condemned and executed. Saint Ambrose wrote that she went to the place of execution more cheerfully than others go to their weddings.

Early art depicts Saint Agnes as a young girl praying with arms outstretched. Since the sixth century she has been shown with a lamb in her arms or at her feet.

ACTIVITIES

CHOOSE A PERSONAL SYMBOL

Saint Agnes is often pictured with a lamb for two reasons: (1) because her name is similar to the Latin word for lamb, *agnus;* (2) because the lamb is young and innocent, and therefore a symbol of purity. Ask the students to choose a symbol for themselves, something that tells about them and the way they wish to follow Christ. Have them design holy cards for themselves, either hand-drawn or computer generated.

RESEARCH OTHER MARTYRS

Saint Agnes is named in Eucharistic Prayer I, along with several other saints. Distribute missalettes and have the students find this reference in the prayer. Encourage them to do some research to find out what these saints have in common and why they are so honored.

PLANT A SEED

The courageous example of martyrs like Agnes helped strengthen the courage of others. Have the students write on cards how they can grow in Christian courage and place these cards by the Bible. Then let them plant a seed in a pot and place it by the Bible. As the class checks the seed's progress, point out that the slow, steady growth of the plant symbolizes their slow, steady efforts to grow in Christian courage.

DISCUSS CHALLENGES TO CHASTITY

Saint Agnes, one of the most famous and well-loved saints, has always been regarded as a special patron of purity. Discuss the challenges to purity and virginity young people face in our time. Talk about how they can be strong and not cave under pressure. Encourage the students to pray to Saint Agnes in times of temptation.

Catechist's Notes:

Saint Vincent

(200s)

The stories that spread about Saint Vincent may or may not sound impossible. It is clear that he was willing to accept great suffering because of his great love of God. Augustine praised Vincent in one of his sermons, and centuries later the glorified accounts of his sufferings were gathered to form this story.

Vincent was trained and ordained a deacon by Valerius, Bishop of Saragossa, Spain, in the third century. These were dangerous times to be a Christian, for the Roman emperors had written edicts that made being a Christian punishable by death. When the Emperor Dacian discovered Bishop Valerius holding Christian services, Dacian had Valerius imprisoned. Vincent was caught visiting the bishop and was put in prison. The emperor refused to give food to either of them. Both men were so cheerful and strong in their suffering that the emperor banished Bishop Valerius and had Vincent tortured on the rack. Vincent accepted and endured this suffering for love of Christ. Seeing that the torturers had failed to weaken Vincent's courage, Emperor Dacian ordered that the torturers be beaten.

Dacian then told Vincent that Dacian would spare his life if he would hand over the sacred books to be burned. Vincent refused and, in fury, Dacian ordered Vincent to be roasted on a gridiron. Again Vincent suffered patiently and survived. It is said that Dacian wept with rage and had Vincent thrown in a dungeon filled with broken pottery. Vincent was so calm and heroic that he converted the jailer. The emperor, at his wits' end, finally had Vincent confined to life in prison. Friends of Vincent came to console him, cleanse his wounds, and pray with him. Vincent died there in the bed his friends had made for him.

Vincent's story teaches about the spirit of Christian courage. Here is a man who welcomed pain, suffering, and death as a chance to show his love for Christ. What are you willing to do?

JANUARY

ACTIVITIES

INVITE A DEACON TO SPEAK

Vincent served as a deacon. Invite a deacon to explain his role in the Church and how a man becomes a deacon.

MAKE A CHART

Have the students read Acts of the Apostles 6:1–7 to discover the role of deacons in the early Church. Make a chart comparing their role with the role of deacons today.

GET IN TOUCH

Encourage the students to visit, write a note, or send a greeting card to someone they know who is suffering or lonely. They might make their own cards.

STOP WHINING

Suggest that the students imitate Valerius and Vincent by accepting without complaint the little difficulties and annoyances that come their way today. Remind them that they can offer up suffering for a special intention, such as for the poor souls in purgatory or for world peace. By doing this they praise God and become stronger people.

Catechist's Notes:

_____

_____

_____

_____

_____

_____

_____

_____

_____

_____

_____

Saint Francis de Sales
January 24
(1567–1622)

Francis de Sales knew how to maximize his efforts. He used creative approaches to spread God's Kingdom to the widest number of people most effectively.

Francis was born into a family of nobility and enjoyed many advantages. He studied at the University of Paris for six years and then went to the University of Padua, where he received a doctorate in civil and canon law. Besides being well educated, Francis was a skilled swordsman who enjoyed fencing, an expert horseman, and a superb dancer. He was expected to take up a career in government and to marry well. But through his studies, Francis had gradually grown in a life of prayer and decided to share his love for God with other people by being a priest.

Francis and his cousin Louis, who was also a priest, volunteered to work in Chablais, where religious wars were taking place. They visited homes, preached the Word of God, and sought new converts. The work went so slowly that after four months, Louis became discouraged and left. Then Francis needed to multiply his efforts. He began to write and distribute a weekly essay explaining some doctrines of faith. For two years he had these essays printed and passed them on to as many people as possible. Why was this a new tactic? In Francis's time the printing press was thought to be mainly a means of preserving the best thoughts of the past. It only gradually occurred to people that it could be used to bring new ideas to people and to encourage them to follow Christ.

Francis preached with power and charm in a simple, clear language. His gentleness and love were so appealing that he drew many hearts to God. The final result of his printing and preaching was that the majority of the Chablais inhabitants accepted the Catholic faith.

When Francis was appointed bishop of Geneva, he discovered other ways to maximize his efforts for the Lord. First he worked with the priests. He encouraged the active priests and made sure that candidates for ordination were fit for this vocation. In this way Francis helped form good leaders for the Church. Second he gave laypeople an active part in spreading the Kingdom. When visiting each parish, he celebrated the sacraments, instructed the people, and set up catechism classes for the young people. The classes would be held every Sunday and holy day, and he trained laypeople for the role of teaching them. To help people grow in their relationship with God, Francis often had individual conferences with them and gave spiritual guidance.

In 1610 Francis helped Jane Frances de Chantal found the Visitation sisters, an order of religious women. Once again his efforts multiplied. To reach more people, Francis wrote books.

For his writings Francis was declared a Doctor of the Church and the patron of journalists and writers. For his gentleness and patience and for his dedication to bringing others to the love of God, he was declared a saint.

JANUARY

ACTIVITIES

IMAGINE NEW WAYS TO SHARE THEIR FAITH

Francis was creative in his efforts to build up the Kingdom of God. Ask the students to report on "new" ways of spreading the faith. What ways were new in the last century? (Modern textbooks, television, films and videos, CDs, and Internet sites.) Ask the students which media they have used. Encourage them to imagine and share new ways they may be able to use in 20 or 50 years.

LEARN ABOUT CATHOLIC PUBLISHING

Francis de Sales is the patron of Catholic journalism. Bring in a variety of Catholic periodicals, newspapers, and pamphlets for the students to look at. Encourage them to research various organizations involved in the ministry of publishing Catholic material.

WRITE A CLASS PRAYER

Francis is also the patron of writers. Have the students compose a class prayer to Saint Francis. Make copies of the prayer to put in students' English composition notebooks or journals.

PUT ON SKITS

Francis was well known for his gentleness and patience to everyone, no matter how tired he was or how bothersome the person was. He has been credited with the saying "You can get more flies with honey than you can with vinegar." Have the students rephrase this quotation in their own words and then think of examples that prove it to be true. Let them get into groups and do skits to show how their example would work.

MAKE NEW YEAR'S RESOLUTIONS

One of Francis's books shows that everyone can grow in holiness—not just priests and nuns. Suggest that the students make New Year's resolutions about growing in holiness. Have them write in their journals.

Catechist's Notes:

_____

_____

_____

_____

_____

_____

_____

Conversion of Paul

"So if anyone is in Christ, there is a new creation: everything old has passed away; see, everything has become new!" (2 Corinthians 5:17). Paul was able to write about a person becoming a new creation because he had an experience that made him a new man.

Paul had two names. As a Roman citizen, he was given the name Paul. He lived in Tarsus, a center for Greek culture. The Greek influence appears in Paul's letters when he writes about wrestling, military drills, parades, and games. As a Jew of the tribe of Benjamin, he was called Saul. Saul learned the strict traditions of the Pharisees. At the age of five, he probably knew Jewish law. At the age of six, he may have started school in the synagogue and studied Scripture. He probably went to the temple college in Jerusalem at the age of 15 and studied under an excellent teacher. Most rabbis then married and learned a trade. While Paul never had a wife, he did learn the work of tent making and used it later on in life.

To Saul, Christianity was a threat to Judaism. After he watched Stephen murdered for his faith, Saul became a leader in the movement to stamp out Christianity. Zealously he went into homes and dragged Christians to prison.

Then one day, when Saul and his companions set out from Jerusalem intent upon harassing the Christians of Damascus, a phenomenal thing happened. A great flash of light appeared, and he fell to the ground. He heard a voice say, "Saul, Saul, why do you persecute me?" And he said, "Who are you, Lord?" And he said, "I am Jesus, whom you are persecuting" (Acts 9:4–5). At this moment the Resurrection of Jesus overwhelmed Saul. He knew that Jesus was alive—risen from the dead! And somehow Jesus was present in Christians. Saul entered Damascus helpless, led by the hand of one of his companions, because he had been blinded by the experience. Following the direction of the Spirit, he was baptized and regained his sight.

For three years Paul lived in the Arabian desert, letting go of his old way of thinking and allowing the new life of Christ to be built up within him.

From Arabia, Paul returned to Damascus to preach that Jesus was the Son of God. The Jewish community had expected help in destroying Christianity. Seeing that he was a traitor, they plotted to kill him. Discovering the plot, Paul had the disciples lower him in a basket over the city wall so that he could escape!

Then he went to Jerusalem to meet the apostles. Paul stayed there, preaching fearlessly in the name of Jesus.

This is only the beginning of Saint Paul's mission. From the Acts of the Apostles and his letters, we gain an idea of the scope of his journeys, the extent of his writings, and the intensity of his suffering and his joy.

JANUARY

ACTIVITIES

ACT IT OUT

The story of Paul's conversion is dramatic.

- Let the students dramatize the story of Paul's life up to and including his conversion. Or have some students prepare a dramatic reading of Paul's conversion (Acts of the Apostles 9) and present it to the class.

- Have the students rewrite the incident, putting the story in a modern setting, and act it out.

- Let students write the story of the conversion of someone they know or someone they have read about.

WRITE BEFORE-AND-AFTER ACCOUNTS

Have the students fold a sheet of paper in half. On one side have them write two diary entries that might have been written by Paul before his conversion experience. On the other side have them write two diary entries that Paul might have written after his conversion. Post the results.

MAKE A JOURNAL ENTRY

Have the students think about any times in their own lives when they received a "miniconversion," a new insight into God or themselves (e.g., after celebrating penance, during a crisis, while praying quietly). Suggest they write about the experiences in their journals.

CREATE A FRIEZE

Have the students choose scenes from the story of Saint Paul to illustrate. Invite students to cut out the pictures and mount them on a long sheet of paper.

Catechist's Notes:

_____

_____

_____

_____

_____

_____

_____

_____

_____

Saints Timothy and Titus

January 26

(first century)

Think of all the ways you are a helper: at home, at school, to your friends, at Church. Today's saints are two important helpers.

Saints Timothy and Titus lived when the apostles were dying and Gentile Christians were beginning to take roles of leadership. Both men knew Paul well and were his traveling companions. They were bishops of newly converted communities, but the role of bishops was not clearly defined yet. They administered a large area and traveled in and out of a number of the Christian communities.

Timothy's father was a Gentile, and his mother was Jewish. Timothy had studied Scripture as a young man and was converted by Paul, who was on a missionary journey to Lystra in Asia Minor. Paul needed a traveling companion at the time because Barnabas and Mark had left him. Timothy was willing to help. He was ordained to the ministry and sent as Paul's representative to the Thessalonians, Corinthians, and Ephesians. Acting as envoy for Paul was difficult because he sometimes met trouble in the communities. However, Timothy proved capable enough for Paul to make him bishop of Ephesus. Paul wrote several pastoral letters to Timothy and praised Timothy's enthusiasm and example. In these letters Timothy was told that as a bishop he was to correct teachers of false doctrine and appoint bishops and deacons.

Timothy must have been a good friend of Paul's because Paul begged him to come to comfort him in prison in Rome. Seeing Paul's courage in suffering must have consoled Timothy later when he underwent martyrdom himself. Timothy opposed pagan festivals and was killed by pagans with stones and clubs.

The other young bishop and companion of Paul was Titus. Titus is mentioned in one of Paul's letters to the Corinthians. Paul tells that he had gone to Troas and was worried because he did not find Titus there. He then went to Macedonia where there was trouble among the Christians. Paul writes, "But God, who consoles the downcast, consoled us by the arrival of Titus" (2 Corinthians 7:6). Paul's trust in Titus's competence as a peacemaker and administrator was evident. Titus smoothed out difficulties between the Corinthians and Paul. He organized the Church in Crete as its first bishop. He corrected abuses, appointed bishops, and worked for the Church in an energetic, efficient, and decisive manner. Titus died in Crete when he was 93.

Both of these bishops were given instructions by Paul for teaching and governing the Christians. Under their wise guidance and example, the early church grew stronger. Their feast is fittingly celebrated the day after that of their great friend, Paul.

ACTIVITIES

READ ABOUT TIMOTHY

Let the students look up the following descriptions Paul gives of his traveling companion, Timothy: 1 Corinthians 4:17, Philippians 2:19–20, Romans 16:21, and 2 Timothy 1:4–5.

READ THEIR MAIL

Have the students read the letters of Paul to Timothy and Titus. Ask them to list the characteristics of a good bishop.

MAKE BOOK JACKETS

Let the students make book jackets for the Letter to Timothy or the Letter to Titus.

Have them write a short summary of the letter on the back of the jacket.

WRITE A NEW CHAPTER

Have the students write an imaginary "unwritten" chapter of the adventures of Paul that include Timothy and Titus.

COMPARE BISHOPS NOW AND THEN

Conduct a class discussion of how the roles of bishops today are the same as or different from the time of Timothy and Titus. Find out what they know about their own bishop.

Catechist's Notes:

_____

_____

_____

_____

_____

_____

_____

_____

_____

_____

_____

Saint Angela Merici

(1470–1540)

Today we hear a lot about family values and family education. Angela Merici was talking about this more than 500 years ago. Angela, it turns out, was a woman of vision. "Convert the woman and one converts the family," said Angela Merici. Her goal was to restore strong Christian family life, especially through the good education of future wives and mothers.

Angela did not have a perfect family life herself. She was orphaned early in life. She lived for some years with her uncle's family and grew into a simple, charming woman of good looks and capable leadership abilities. Her faith led her to become a member of a Third Order, to dedicate herself to good works and to prayer. Angela received a vision in which it was revealed "Before your death, you will found a society of virgins at Brescia." For 10 years Angela waited patiently for God to help her know what to do. A sign came when the Patengoli family invited her to Brescia to keep them company because they had recently lost two sons in death. After she lived in Brescia for a short time, her eyes were opened to the needs of the city. Deprived girls were unable to get an education, for only rich people and nuns were educated. This distressed Angela. She began catechetical work for these girls, but the task was overwhelming for one person.

At 57 years of age, she formed a religious group of 28 women who shared her goal. Angela decided to call her group the Company of St. Ursula. Saint Ursula was the patron of medieval universities, and Angela had great devotion to this saint who was a leader of women. The work Angela undertook was difficult because women in religious communities at that time were not permitted to leave their convents to teach or care for the sick, except in emergencies. Men's communities such as the Dominicans and Franciscans already were actively engaged in such charitable works, but women's orders were not.

To accomplish her dreams, Angela's sisters received permission from Rome to live in their own homes and devote themselves to every type of corporal and spiritual work of mercy, with emphasis on education. They would teach young girls to read and write, and prepare them for what they needed to know about a Christian home and marriage. Her sisters wore lay clothes and met once a month for a day of prayer and discussion on their ministries.

Forty years later Charles Borromeo asked the sisters to become a religious community and to live together in a convent rather than in their own homes. Gradually they began to wear distinctive habits and were known as the Ursulines. Angela Merici was a woman of vision. She was the first to form a religious order of women that served God outside the cloister. Her vision of serving God in an active manner was followed by many groups of religious women who teach, nurse, and minister for the Kingdom.

JANUARY

ACTIVITIES

MAKE FLOWCHARTS

Angela's dream was to use education as a means for building up the faith and for social reform. Christian education would lead to strong Christian families, and the good moral values of these families would help the Church and society. Divide the class into small groups. Ask each group to work together to develop a flowchart showing how a particular Christian teaching could follow Angela's plan.

HEAR ABOUT THE URSULINES

If there is an Ursuline community in the area, invite a sister to speak to the class about the life and spirit of Saint Angela.

LIST COMMUNITIES

Today there are many communities of women who actively minister in the Church. Have the students list the names of the communities they know and the ministries in which they engage. Challenge them to research secular institutes, Third Orders, and associate programs.

CELEBRATE FAMILY DAYS

Have the students make a list of all the birthdays and anniversaries in their families. Encourage them to post this list in their bedrooms and remember to do something cheery for each family member on his or her special day.

CHECK THE BULLETIN

Angela's goal was to strengthen Christian family life. Have the students check the Sunday bulletin to find out what their parish does to strengthen family life.

DO WORKS OF MERCY

Review with the students the spiritual and corporal works of mercy. Ask them to select one that they could practice in or with their families that week. Set a time when they can report back on their efforts.

Catechist's Notes:

_____

_____

_____

_____

_____

_____

_____

Saint Thomas Aquinas
January 28
(1225–1274)

Have you ever wondered about God? Who is God? What is God like? Young Thomas Aquinas thought about God a lot. Thomas came from a wealthy ruling family in Italy. At age five he was sent to the Benedictine monastery at Monte Cassino in hopes that someday he would be abbot. But King Frederick II was having military troubles and sent his troops to occupy the monastery as a fortress. Thomas then went to the University of Naples. It was there that he came into contact with the Dominicans. Their lifestyle of prayer and study fascinated him, and he was determined to join them. His family was shocked that Thomas, who was a nobleman, would join a group of poor friars. His mother sent his brothers after him, and they pursued, kidnapped, and then forced Thomas to stay for over a year at a family castle. But nothing would shake his resolution to enter the Dominicans. Finally his family gave up, and in 1244 he joined the order. In the following years he enjoyed studying, teaching, and writing.

Thomas first studied under Albert the Great, a great scientist, and he profited immensely from the scientific precision of Albert's studies. But he preferred theology. Thomas is well known for his writings in philosophy and theology.

Thomas's most famous work, the *Summa Theologica,* contains five volumes of his thought on all the Christian mysteries. It is said that no one has equaled the depth of understanding and the clear reasoning that Thomas showed. He was a brilliant man and had extraordinary powers of concentration. He reportedly never forgot anything he read, and he had the ability to dictate to four secretaries at the same time on different subjects. But this intellectual giant of a man was very humble. He insisted that his learning was due more to prayer than to genius.

While saying Mass on December 6, 1273, Thomas received a revelation from God. After that he stopped writing completely. Thomas said that all he had written was so much straw after what he had seen.

Thomas died at the age of 49 on his way to the Council of Lyons, France, which Pope Gregory had asked him to attend. He had been an advisor to kings, a writer of masterpieces, a counselor to popes, and a teacher of classics. But most of all, Thomas was a servant of God. Saint Thomas is a Doctor of the Church and called "the angelic doctor" for his purity and knowledge.

ACTIVITIES

WRITE A PRAYER

Pope Leo XIII declared Saint Thomas Aquinas patron of Catholic schools. Have the class compose a prayer to Saint Thomas and use it for the whole school today.

PRAY TO SAINT THOMAS

Encourage the students to pray regularly to Saint Thomas to help them in their studies.

FIND SAINT THOMAS'S PRAYER

Locate the prayer Saint Thomas wrote in honor of the Blessed Sacrament, "O Saving Victim," and pray it. This prayer is sung during Benediction.

LEARN ABOUT THE DOMINICANS

Ask the students to find out why the discipline of study is a characteristic of the Dominican Order. Why did Saint Dominic believe this was important?

DEEPEN FAITH

Have the students choose an aspect of their faith they'd like to know more about and then research it and write a brief report.

Catechist's Notes:

_____

_____

_____

_____

_____

_____

_____

_____

_____

_____

_____

Saint John Bosco

(1815–1888)

Do you know the story of Oliver Twist? During the industrial revolution in Europe, hundreds of orphaned or destitute boys flocked to the cities to find work. They lived poorly (six or seven in a small room), were paid little, and worked long hours. With no family or religious training, these boys often turned to thievery. John Bosco could have lived like that if it hadn't been for his hard-working and devout mother.

John was the youngest son of a peasant family in Italy. His father died when John was two, so he was brought up by his mother. The family lived in extreme poverty, and there was no possibility for higher education. Once a priest, Saint Joseph Cafasso, noticed John's intent face as he listened to a homily. The priest questioned John and discovered he had a remarkable memory. When he heard that John wished to be a priest, he encouraged him to enter the seminary. With shoes and clothes provided by charity, John arrived at the major seminary in Turin. It proved to be a perfect place for John, who was a natural leader and gifted with initiative.

Father Cafasso saw John's talent for working with youth. He showed John the jails and slums of Turin and encouraged him to use his gifts to keep the young people out of trouble. John began to invite the poor city boys on Sunday outings in the country. The day would start with Mass, which was followed by breakfast and outdoor games. The afternoon would include a picnic, a catechism lesson, and closing evening prayers.

The groups of boys grew. John made each boy feel needed and important. He respected every boy and used gentle discipline instead of harsh punishment. One day a week was not enough. He wanted the boys to live in an environment that would help them to be good, study, work, and pray.

Eventually John was able to get a house for himself and 40 boys, with his mother as the housekeeper. There he held workshops to train boys to be shoemakers and tailors. Within six years there were 150 boys in residence. Besides learning a trade, the boys got a religious education. John encouraged them to receive the sacraments often. He taught them to play musical instruments, to perform in plays, and to engage in sports. Often when John went to the villages to preach and celebrate the sacraments, he took along boys to provide entertainment. His reputation as a preacher became well known. He wrote and printed books on Christian faith for boys, using his own printing press.

John lived during times in Italy when the state did not favor the Church. For four years assassins were after him. Once they tried to shoot him while he was teaching, and at other times tried to poison him and attack him on the street. But so successful and honest was John's work with boys that even enemies of the Church changed their minds and supported him.

When John Bosco died, 40,000 people came to his wake. He is called the patron saint of boys.

JANUARY

RESEARCH THE SALESIANS

In 1859 John started a religious congregation that would serve the Church by helping poor boys. John Bosco admired Francis de Sales so much that he named the group the Salesians. Today the Salesians are an international community, with two provinces in the United States. Have the students find out if the work of the Salesian priests and sisters is similar to that of John Bosco.

BEFRIEND YOUNGER CHILDREN

St. John Bosco always considered himself a friend of youth. Have the students invite a younger class to their classroom for games or a student dramatization of a life of a saint. Perhaps a treat could be provided.

SING TO MARY

St. John Bosco had a devotion to Mary, Help of Christians, and wanted to build a church in her honor. When the contractor started to build the church in 1863, John made his first payment. "Here is all I have," he said, "but Our Lady will provide what is necessary for the church." He put in the man's hand 40 cents. The rest of the money came. John's trust in Mary and in God's Divine Providence led him to do great things. Have the students dedicate their day to Mary, Help of Christians, by singing a song in her honor.

START A CHEERFUL CLUB

When John Bosco was in the seminary, he started a club called the Cheerful Club. No one was allowed to say or speak in an unchristian way. Each one had to do his studies and be cheerful. Try John Bosco's club in the classroom this week.

Catechist's Notes:

_____

_____

_____

_____

_____

_____

_____

_____

Saint Brigid of Ireland

February 1

(c. 450–523)

At first it might seem that you would not have anything in common with Brigid. Her world was much different from yours. For one thing, her father was a pagan chieftain and her mother was a Christian slave. Before Brigid was born, her mother was sold to a druid (a pagan priest). Does anything sound familiar yet? Brigid lived with her father, but did the work of a slave. She ground corn, tended sheep, milked cows, and made butter. And she is said to have healed lepers.

Brigid also liked to have a good time. She enjoyed music and conversation. She had a bubbly personality. She welcomed people warmly to her home and always provided refreshments. In fact Brigid was famous for her hospitality and her generosity.

How generous was Brigid? Brigid was so generous that her father was afraid he would go broke. Brigid was in charge of her father's household. She was a hard worker and a good manager. She was obedient and kind. But if Brigid saw someone in need, she held nothing back. She never turned away anyone who came to their door looking for food. She was so generous that one day her father couldn't take it anymore. He decided to sell her to the king of Leinster. Perhaps the king could afford her! Brigid remained outside the castle gate while her father went inside to negotiate the deal. As she waited, a beggar approached her. Brigid had nothing to give him. But the poor man was very hungry. Brigid saw her father's mighty battle sword, which he was not allowed to take into the castle. In a characteristic burst of generosity, Brigid gave the sword to the beggar. When Brigid's father came back and discovered what she had done, he hauled her before the king, offering her action as proof that he could not keep Brigid. The king, a Christian, asked Brigid why she had given away her father's most prized possession. Brigid explained that nothing was too precious for Christ. The king told his guards to find the beggar and buy back the sword. He sent Brigid home with her father with the command not to curb Brigid's charity.

Brigid, ever generous, wanted to give her whole life to God and to share her love and joy in Christ with others. She formed communities of Christians to work, pray, and serve others. In her community they were no longer slave or free, but all free to do the work of charity. Her monastery at Kildare, a double monastery that included both men and women, was surrounded by the homes and workshops of artisans and became famous for the beautiful bells, crosses, chalices, and illuminated books produced there.

So what do you have in common with Brigid? Only the most important thing—being loved by Christ with a love that is great and generous, eternal and unchanging.

FEBRUARY

WELCOME OTHERS

Make a large welcome sign to hang on the door before the children come to school or class. When they are settled, ask how many noticed it and how it made them feel. After talking about their experience in welcoming others, ask the children to grade themselves on how they welcome new students to class or new students in school.

- Invite the children to add their names or smiling faces to the welcome sign. Leave it hanging on or near the door to welcome everyone to the room.

- Ask the students to find out how new people are welcomed into your parish. Let them make greeting cards to be sent or given to new parishioners.

BLESS THE CLASSROOM

In Ireland Saint Brigid crosses made of woven straw are often hung near the door as a sign of Christian welcome and hospitality. On her feast day, homes are traditionally blessed. Invite the children to gather at the doorway of the classroom and pray this blessing:

> May God give his blessing to this place.
> God bless this room from ceiling to floor,
> from wall to wall.
>
> In the strong name of the Triune God
> all evil be banished,
> all disturbance cease,

God's Spirit alone
dwell within these walls.

We call upon the Sacred Three
to save, shield, and surround
this building, this room,
this hour, this day,
and every day.

HONOR CHRIST IN THE POOR

Brigid's guiding light was "To honor Christ, for Christ is in the body of every poor man." Print her motto on a large poster board. Have the students look through newspapers and magazines for pictures of people who are poor, that is, in some kind of need, physical or spiritual. Let them cut out the faces they find and glue them around the motto to make a collage.

CREATE ART

Celtic art styles that originated at monasteries like Kildare have become very popular. If possible, show the children some actual items, or illustrations from books or religious goods catalogs. Invite the children to make beautiful crosses to hang in their homes. Provide a variety of materials to spark their creativity, such as beads, aluminum foil, gems, sequins, and yarn. This could be an ongoing project to be completed for the beginning of Lent.

Catechist's Notes:

_____

_____

_____

_____

Presentation of the Lord   February 2

Does it seem that Christmas was a long time ago? Today's feast is like another little Christmas. Forty days ago we celebrated the feast of Christmas, the birth of Jesus. According to the law of Moses at the time of Christ's birth, for 40 days after the birth of her son, a woman was excluded from public worship. Then on the 40th day, she would bring an offering of a pigeon or a turtledove to the Temple. It was also customary to bring an offering of thanksgiving and praise to God for the safe birth of the child. This offering would be a young lamb or, if the couple was poor, another pigeon or turtledove could be substituted.

And so we read that when Mary and Joseph went to the Temple for the purification, they took the child Jesus to "be consecrated to the Lord," and they offered a pair of turtledoves or two young pigeons, the offering of the poor. They were careful to observe all that the law required.

While this is an ancient feast in the Church, it is interesting that the name of the feast has gone through several stages. In the fourth century in Jerusalem, the feast was celebrated on a different date and was called simply "the 40th day after the Epiphany." By the sixth century it was known in the Eastern church as "the meeting of Jesus and Mary with Simeon." By the seventh century in Rome, it was named the "Purification of Mary." Because of the central act of the feast, today the Church calls it the "Presentation of the Lord in the Temple."

Today we celebrate Jesus' offering of himself to his Father as the Savior of all people. The symbolism of the Jewish feast, emphasizing the purifying of the mother and the offering and buying back of the child, has been given a greater meaning. Mary did not need the rites of purification, and God's Son, Jesus, did not need to be "consecrated" or ritually "redeemed." But by God's plan, Mary and Jesus obeyed the Mosaic law. This ceremony was an act of deep love for them.

In the Gospel of Luke, we read that there was a man named Simeon in the Temple of Jerusalem at that time, a man "righteous and devout. . . . It had been revealed to him by the Holy Spirit that he would not see death before he had seen the Lord's Messiah" (Luke 2:25–26). When Simeon saw the child Jesus, he took the child into his arms and prayed, "Master, now you are dismissing your servant in peace, according to your word; for my eyes have seen your salvation, which you have prepared in the presence of all peoples, a light for revelation to the Gentiles and for glory to your people Israel" (Luke 2:29–32).

The coming of Jesus was a light for all to see—a light breaking upon a dark, sinful world. Another name for this feast is Candlemas. Candles are blessed on this day, and the liturgy suggests a candlelight procession representing the coming of Christ as the Light of the World. Today is a day to remember that we, as Christians, are to be lights in this world too.

FEBRUARY

DISCUSS OBEDIENCE

Discuss with the students the difficulties involved in obedience. Ask for examples of some laws or rules they find hard to obey. Point out that in Jesus and Mary, we have a clear example of obedience.

BLESS CANDLES

Have the students participate in the blessing of the candles and in the procession in the parish if possible. Recommend that they check to see if their families have any blessed candles available at home. If not, encourage them to get some for the family.

PRAY A DECADE OF THE ROSARY

Remind the students that this feast is also recalled in the fourth Joyful Mystery of the Rosary. Pray it together with the class.

BRING CHRIST TO OTHERS

Mary brought Christ to others. Have the students plan ways to bring the story of the feast (Luke 2:22–40) to a younger class through booklets, puppet shows, skits, or songs.

LEARN CUSTOMS

Inform the students about the customs that surround the celebration of this feast. In Europe, if the weather is bad and the skies are cloudy on Candlemas, it means summer will come early. If the sun shines for most of the day, then 40 days of cold and snow are expected to follow. In North America the weather predictions associated with Candlemas have been ascribed to Groundhog Day, also occurring on February 2.

DECORATE CANDLES

Have the students decorate large candles for the blessing. They might use flowers, holy pictures, or liturgical symbols. The decorations can be glued onto the candles, or, if the students are making their own candles, the decorations can be sealed right into the wax.

SING A HYMN ABOUT LIGHT

Sing songs written about Christ the Light: "We Are the Light of the World," "Christ Is the World's True Light," "The Light of Christ," "I Am the Light," "The Lord Is My Light," "This Little Light of Mine."

Catechist's Notes:

_____

_____

_____

_____

_____

_____

_____

Saint Blase

February 3

(d. c. 318)

If you are already familiar with Saint Blase, it is probably through the blessing of throats—a tradition on his feast. Various stories about Saint Blase and actual episodes in his life have been woven together to form the picture we have of him.

Blase was the bishop of Sebaste (in what is now central Turkey). He was martyred sometime around 318 under the persecutions of the Emperor Licinius. About 400 years after his death, various stories began to be told about him—especially in France and Germany, where he became very popular.

According to tradition, Blase had been a doctor before he was ordained a priest and later a bishop. When the persecutions broke out, he fled to the mountains and lived the life of a hermit. Here he cured and tamed the wild animals. One day hunters discovered Blase and took him back to the Governor Agricolaus, who sentenced Blase to death. Many people came out to see him on his way to prison. One woman ran up to Blase and pleaded with him to cure her son, who was choking to death on a fish bone. Blase prayed over the boy, who was saved. In prison Blase was condemned to darkness, but a friend secretly brought him some candles. (The candles used for the blessing of throats remind us of these wax tapers smuggled to Blase in prison.) Blase was cruelly tortured and finally beheaded.

Blase is the patron of those with throat diseases. He is also invoked to protect animals against the attacks of wolves. In fact he is patron of wild animals, wool combers, and wax makers. In some areas people pray to him for fair weather too.

We are often concerned about our physical ailments. But there are spiritual ailments that should be of great concern to us too. If we call on Saint Blase to protect us from sickness of the throat, let us also call on him to help us speak the truth at all times. Today and always, let our words be true and kind, reflecting the goodness and kindness of God our Father.

RECEIVE THE BLESSING OF THROATS

The blessing of throats with two candles began during the 16th century. Besides the connection with the candles Blase received in prison, the feast of Saint Blase follows the Presentation of the Lord (Candlemas), when candles for liturgical use are blessed. After providing an explanation of the purpose of the blessing, invite the children to have their throats blessed. It is important that they understand that a blessing demands an openness of faith on their part. This is the blessing the Church uses:

> Through the intercession of St. Blase,
> bishop and martyr,
> may God deliver you from every
> disease of the throat
> and from every other illness:
> In the name of the Father, and of the
> Son, and of the Holy Spirit.

The one receiving the blessing responds:

> Amen.

CHOOSE HEAVENLY HELPERS

Blase is one of the Fourteen Holy Helpers. This list of "helpers" originated during the Middle Ages and names patrons for almost every aspect of life. Have the students look up these Fourteen Holy Helpers. Then have them choose two or three saints they want to have as their personal friends on earth. Ask them to write an explanation of why they chose the particular saints and how these saints will be their "helpers."

SHARE BREAD

In Europe there is a custom of giving blessed bread, called Saint Blase sticks, on this day. People eat a piece of this bread when experiencing a sore throat. Today bless some bread sticks and share them among the students. Then have them learn about an international organization such as Food for the Poor or a local soup kitchen. During Lent this year, collect money for one of these charities so that bread may be shared with the poor.

Catechist's Notes:

_____

_____

_____

_____

_____

_____

_____

Saint Agatha

(mid-200s)

She is the patroness of nurses, foundrymen, miners, jewelers, and Alpine guides. She is invoked against fire, earthquakes, famine, thunderstorms, and volcanic eruptions. In Italy her feast day is celebrated with fireworks displays. Who is this popular saint? Agatha.

Many stories are told of Agatha. According to these, she was born of noble parents. Her reputation for loveliness and kindness was widespread and came to the attention of Quintian, governor of Sicily. Quintian put her into prison for being a Christian, and there she underwent extreme tortures before she died.

We know for certain that Agatha was a martyr. She probably suffered death at Catania, in Sicily, during the persecutions under Decius from 240 to 251. Although Agatha lived in Sicily, devotion to her was so widespread and so fervent that her name came to be included in the Mass in Eucharistic Prayer I. We know that Agatha has long been honored for her great courage in suffering and in remaining pure for the sake of Christ.

A year after Agatha's burial, Mt. Etna erupted. People prayed to her and claimed that her intercession stilled the volcano. Popular art represents Agatha as holding a plate, a burning coal, or a house in flames.

We, as Christians, need the example of others. We need to see those around us living according to the faith. We need to see people who love Jesus so much that they are willing to carry their own crosses for him. And if we need to see others do all this, then they, too, need to see us do it. God chooses the weak so that we may rely on him and let him work through them. Like Agatha, may we be strong followers of Christ.

FEBRUARY

NOTE TO THE TEACHER

Students may be curious about pictures of Saint Agatha or about popular accounts of her life. Teachers should, therefore, know some of the details connected with her martyrdom. All the stories make mention of her tortures. According to these accounts, Agatha was forced to live in a house of prostitution, her breasts were cut off, and she was rolled in hot coals. She is often pictured holding a plate on which her severed breasts are lying.

To understand the kind of tortures suffered by Agatha, it is helpful to know that Roman law forbade the killing of virgins. Before death, they had to be subjected to attacks on their virginity. The Church names them virgins because of their firm determination to remain pure for the love of Christ.

WRITE ANNOUNCEMENTS PROMOTING CHASTITY

Ask the students to name some of the challenges to chastity that young people face today. Discuss with them the importance of remaining pure and of understanding the role of modesty in this regard. Then divide the class into small groups. Ask each group to write and deliver a 30-second public service announcement for television promoting youth modesty or chastity.

GAIN INSIGHT ON PRIORITIES

People have always feared natural disasters such as fires, earthquakes, and floods. On Saint Agatha's day in the Middle Ages, especially in the southern part of Germany, important items that could be destroyed by fire were blessed. Candles were also blessed on this day. Ask the students to list the five things they would most desire to save from destruction. After their lists have been made, compare them. Help the students to try to understand their priorities in life according to their lists.

PRAY FOR A CHRISTIAN ATTITUDE

Lead the students in a prayer:

Lord,
You have promised us the power to rise above our smallness—
    not by grasping power or wealth,
    nor by basking in the light of
    others' glory,
    nor by seeking glory of our own—but
by realizing how well loved we are—
    your own cared-for children,
    heirs with Jesus to your Kingdom,
    brothers and sisters of the risen Lord.
Free us, Lord, from our worldliness.
Amen.

Catechist's Notes:

_____

_____

_____

_____

Saint Paul Miki and Companions

February 6

(d. 1597)

In 1549 Francis Xavier and other missionaries were allowed into Japan, which had been closed to foreigners for centuries. They were able to bring the Good News of Christ to the Japanese. Many people became Christians, including the Shoguns, the lords of the various areas. Then Hideyoshi took command in place of the emperor. At first he tolerated the missionaries and Christians. But then he sensed a spirit of unity among them and feared they would try to take control of his government.

Hideyoshi issued a decree on July 25, 1587, to banish all missionaries and destroy the churches. Some missionaries left; others went into hiding and exchanged their priestly clothes for the clothes of the people so that they could continue to minister to the Christians.

On December 8, 1596, Hideyoshi arrested three Japanese Jesuits, six Franciscans, and 17 Japanese laymen. They were condemned to death by crucifixion. The charge: attempting to harm the government. But the real reason was that they were Christians. Among them were Louis, age 10; Anthony, age 13; Thomas, age 16; and Gabriel, age 19. The best known is Paul Miki, a Japanese of aristocratic family, who was a Jesuit and an excellent preacher. The martyrs included teachers, doctors, carpenters, acolytes, priests, and brothers.

The 26 men were tortured and then forced to walk more than 300 miles, from Miako to Nagasaki, through snow and freezing streams. Along the way they preached to people who came out to see them. They sang psalms of praise and joy. They prayed the Rosary and told the people that such a martyrdom was an occasion of rejoicing. Finally on February 5, they reached Nagasaki where 26 crosses awaited them. It is said that they ran to their crosses, singing. They were bound to the crosses with iron bands at their wrists, ankles, and throats. Then they were thrust through with two lances. Many people came to watch. Hideyoshi and his soldiers had hoped the example would frighten other Christians. Instead it gave them the courage to profess their faith too.

Hideyoshi died in 1598, and for a few years the persecutions stopped. But by 1612, they had begun again. Christians were beheaded, burned, drowned, and tortured. There are some 3,100 known martyrs from these years. It is believed there were thousands of others. By the mid-17th century, Japan closed its doors to foreigners again. Surely Christianity would die out there. But in 1858, after France and Japan had signed a treaty—in part permitting Christianity in Japan—returning missionaries found thousands of Christians in Japan, especially around Nagasaki. For 200 years the faith had been carried on in secret.

Today we celebrate the 26 martyrs of Nagasaki. Other martyrs of Japan have been beatified and await canonization.

ACTIVITIES

Saint Paul Miki and Companions / February 6

FORGIVE YOUR ENEMIES

From his cross Paul Miki forgave his persecutors and told the people to ask Christ to show them the way to be truly happy. Give the students a short time to reflect on the unhappiness caused by sin. Lead them to ask God to forgive their sins and in their hearts to forgive those who have hurt them.

MAKE CROSS SYMBOLS

For the Japanese Christians, the cross and the Passion of Jesus were powerful symbols of their faith. Display the cross prominently in the classroom. Have the students make crosses out of twigs and wire (or yarn) and then exchange them with other students as reminders that we are all to share in the Cross of Christ.

DRAW PICTURES OF RELIGIOUS PRACTICES

Some of the history of the persecutions has been recorded on Japanese tapestries and silk drawings.

- Have the students find out more about Japanese culture. What particular difficulties might they encounter as present-day missionaries to the East?

- Have the students draw pictures of current religious practices in their own parish that could one day be used by others as a recorded history of their church.

DRAW AND HONOR RELIGIOUS IMAGES

One way to identify Christians during the persecutions was the "tread" picture. These pictures were plates depicting the crucifixion of Jesus, the nativity, or other mysteries of the Church. Persons suspected of being Christians were ordered to tread (walk) on the pictures. Those who refused to show such disrespect for the articles were condemned. Remind the students that we show respect to religious articles because of the sacred persons or objects they represent. Have the students draw religious pictures on paper or foam plates and hang them in a place of honor.

PROCLAIM YOUR FAITH

The martyrs sang and prayed, loudly and joyfully. Ask the students to compare their enthusiasm for song and prayer with that of the young men of Nagasaki. Encourage the students to proclaim their faith by participating wholeheartedly in the liturgy.

PRAY THE STATIONS OF THE CROSS

Accompany the students to the parish church to pray the Stations of the Cross. Let this prayer be a reminder that Jesus was the first to suffer in order to give courage to all his followers who suffer for him.

Catechist's Notes:

_____

_____

_____

_____

Saint Josephine Bakhita   February 8

(1869–1947)

She was called Bakhita. She was a Sudanese girl of the Daju people, about nine years old when she went out to a field to pick herbs. Without warning she was kidnapped by Arab slave traders. When they asked her name, the frightened girl remained silent, so they called her Bakhita, which means "the lucky one." She certainly did not feel fortunate at the time. Bakhita and another girl escaped and spent the night crouching in a tree to avoid a hungry lion. But they were recaptured and taken to the market in El Obeid. After two owners mistreated her, Bakhita was taken to the slave market in Khartoum. There she was bought by an Italian official who was returning to Italy. The family treated her well and eventually gave her to the Michieli family in Genoa, who needed a babysitter for their young daughter Mimmima. By this time Bakhita was 14 years old. The Michieli family owned a hotel near the Red Sea and planned to have Bakhita work there when Mimmima was older. Then Mr. and Mrs. Michieli had to return to Africa on business, and they arranged to have Bakhita and Mimmima stay with the Canossian sisters in Venice. Bakhita later said that the minute she walked in the door she felt that at last she had returned home.

She was called Josephine. At the convent Bakhita began to know the God whom she already loved. She had felt the presence of God even when she otherwise felt abandoned. Now she was overwhelmed to learn that this God, who made the sun, moon, and stars that she so admired, also loved her. When Mrs. Michieli returned 10 months later for her daughter and slave, Bakhita refused to go with her. She said that it was her desire to stay with the sisters. Mrs. Michieli was not happy with this decision, but Bakhita was of legal age, and according to Italian law, a free woman. Bakhita was baptized and given the Christian name Josephine. She was filled with happiness, and her eyes shone with tears of joy. She kissed the baptismal font where she became a daughter of God. Finally Josephine knew who she was.

She was called Mother Moretta. Josephine became a Canossian sister and was then called Mother Josephine. For the next 50 years, Josephine served the community as a cook, seamstress, and doorkeeper. The people who met her at the door affectionately called her Mother Moretta, "our black mother." Each morning when the little children came to school, Josephine placed her hand gently on their heads. The children loved the sound of her sweet, melodic voice, and everyone loved her bright, warm smile. She often asked people to pray for those who do not know God. She finally considered herself the lucky one, fortunate to know and love God.

She was called Saint. In the year 2000 Josephine Bakhita was canonized by Pope John Paul II.

ACTIVITIES

PRAISE THE MASTER OF CREATION

From her childhood Josephine wondered who could have the power to be the master of the sun, the moon, and the stars. She said that she felt a great desire to know and pay homage to the master of these beautiful things.

- Today pray St. Francis's Canticle of the Sun with the class. Use the blackline master on page 442 to make copies for the students.

- Have the children make a mural of creation, contributing illustrations of their favorite creatures.

ENJOY MUSIC OF AFRICA

Play some Sudanese or African music as background for your class activities today. Or let the children use rhythm instruments to accompany their prayer.

VOLUNTEER TO BABYSIT

In honor of St. Josephine, suggest that the children volunteer to babysit for younger siblings, relatives, or neighbors. Or a group may assist with child care in the parish nursery during Mass or a meeting.

CELEBRATE BAPTISM

- Take the children to the baptismal font in your parish church. Discuss what the design and decoration say about the Church's understanding of Baptism. See if they can tell you why they take holy water when they enter the church. (It is a reminder of their Baptism, when they first entered into membership in the Church.) Have them practice taking holy water and signing themselves reverently.

- Place a small holy water font near the entrance of your classroom door for the children to use.

RENEW BAPTISMAL PROMISES

After learning about Saint Josephine, invite the students to renew their baptismal promises, following the formula used at the Easter Vigil, or, for younger children, a short version.

Do you reject Satan?
I do.

And all his works?
I do.

And all his empty promises?
I do.

Do you believe in God, the Father Almighty, creator of heaven and earth?
I do.

Do you believe in Jesus Christ, his only Son, our Lord,
who was born of the Virgin Mary,
was crucified, died, and was buried,
rose from the dead,
and is now seated at the right hand of the Father?
I do.

Do you believe in the Holy Spirit,
the holy Catholic Church,
the communion of saints,
the forgiveness of sins,
the resurrection of the body,
and life everlasting?
I do.

Saint Miguel Febres Cordero

February 9

(1854–1910)

How would you like to have a teacher who was described like this: He was kind to everyone and treated all of the students, rich or poor, the same. He liked to be with the students, and they liked to be with him. All of the children in the school loved him. That is exactly what a student said about today's saint.

Miguel was born in Cuenca, Ecuador, where his family was influential in politics. As a child he suffered from a disability that kept him from standing and walking like other children. He could not stand alone until he was five years old, when it was said he experienced a vision of Our Lady. Miguel was educated at home until he was 14, then went to a school taught by the Christian Brothers. He was a gifted student, and when he was only 17, he published the first of many books, a textbook on Spanish grammar.

Miguel joined the Christian Brothers and became a teacher for 32 years in Quito, the capital of Ecuador. As a teacher he was always looking for new ways to present the material. He wanted to make the lessons and the work more pleasant for the students. He laughed with them and was understanding and patient.

Brother Miguel continued writing, too, and his scholarly works in literature earned him academic honors in South America and Europe. But Brother Miguel did not think he was very important. He thought the most important ones were his students. Most important of all was preparing young men to receive their First Communion.

In 1907 Miguel was called to the Motherhouse in Belgium to translate some books. On the way he stopped for a short visit in New York City. From Belgium he went to a school in Spain where young men were preparing to become Christian Brothers. In 1909, during the Spanish Revolution, the school came under attack. Brother Miguel took the Blessed Sacrament from the chapel and led the novices across the bay to safety in Barcelona. He died of pneumonia less than a year later, and his body was shipped to Ecuador for burial. The people welcomed him home with a great procession through the streets of Quito. Pope John Paul II canonized him in 1984.

FEBRUARY

PRAY FOR TEACHERS AND STUDENTS

Help the children make a prayer chain. Begin by listing the names of all the teachers on the board. Ask volunteers to print these names on strips of colored paper. Let other volunteers take the name strips and make loops, then staple or tape them together to make a paper chain. Have each student print his or her name on a strip of paper and add it to the chain. If you wish, invite other classes to add on their names, and drape the long chain in the hall. Ask the students to pray a short silent prayer for teachers and students as they add the names; when the prayer chain is completed, offer a prayer for the school or parish community.

THANK A TEACHER

Ask students to think of their favorite teacher or catechist. Encourage them to write a note or make a card to thank that person. Let students hand deliver the mail if the teachers are in the building, or help them find addresses if the teachers are elsewhere.

HELP YOUNGER CHILDREN
PREPARE FOR FIRST COMMUNION

Brother Miguel loved to prepare classes for First Communion. Engage older students in helping children who are preparing for First Communion. The older students may help with projects and practice, answer questions, sit with the youngsters at a school Mass, share memories of their own First Communion day, and talk about what First Communion meant to them and what receiving the Eucharist means to them now.

HAVE A PROCESSION

Honor Saint Miguel with a procession around the classroom or down the hall. If necessary, explain to the children that a procession is a religious movement, more of a prayer than a parade. Instruct the children to walk slowly and maintain order, to sing and keep in mind what they are doing. Today, have the children sing a Eucharistic hymn they know by heart. When you arrive at your destination—a statue of Mary, your prayer table, the tabernacle in church—lead a short prayer asking Saint Miguel to pray for all of the students, that they may each find the best way for them to follow Jesus.

DESIGN A STAMP OR MONUMENT

In 1954, on the 100th anniversary of Brother Miguel's birth, the government of Ecuador issued a postage stamp and put up a monument to honor Miguel Febres Cordero for his service to God and country. Have the students design a stamp or a monument for themselves showing something great they would like to achieve for God.

Catechist's Notes:

_____

_____

_____

Saint Scholastica

(c. 480–547)

February 10

Sometimes we can learn big lessons from small events. Although we know very little about Saint Scholastica, we do have one recorded event that teaches us much. Pope Gregory the Great wrote a collection of stories and events about the saints called the *Dialogues*. He devoted the entire second book of the *Dialogues* to Saint Benedict. It is from that collection that we learn of a simple and loving event in the lives of Saints Scholastica and Benedict.

Scholastica was the twin sister of Benedict. Benedict had spent some time studying in Rome, but then decided to devote all his life to the search for God. He first organized several clusterlike community dwellings, but finally established a very important monastery at Monte Cassino. Scholastica founded a community of religious women at Plombariola, about five miles south of her brother's monastery. Benedict directed the progress of these women, so Scholastica must have been the abbess there.

Scholastica and Benedict visited together only once a year. They would go to a small house near their monasteries, for no women were permitted at Monte Cassino. On one occasion Benedict, with several of his monks, met Scholastica at the house. They spent the day praying and speaking of God and the spiritual life. After they had eaten, they continued their conversation late into the night. When Benedict said he had to return to his monastery, Scholastica begged him to stay and talk a while longer. Benedict refused, saying that his rule required that the monks be in the monastery at night. Heartbroken at his refusal, Scholastica folded her hands, put her head on the table, and quietly wept and prayed. While she was praying, a terrible storm began, a storm so terrible that no one could venture out into it. "God forgive you! What have you done?" Benedict exclaimed to his sister. She explained that since he had refused the favor she asked, she had turned to Almighty God instead and he said yes. What more could Benedict say? They continued their conversation and prayer until morning, and then Benedict and his monks left. Three days later Scholastica died. They had enjoyed their final conversation. Benedict told the monks that he saw her soul, like a dove, ascend toward heaven. He had her buried in the tomb he had built for himself.

We may not know much about Scholastica's early life, about her penances or powerful virtues, about her hopes and her dreams. But we do know that she valued people more than things. She knew it was important to listen to and care about others. And she also knew how to pray. So complete was her trust in God that she turned to him often. She placed her problems and her hurts in his loving heart. And that made all the difference. From this small event, we know all we need to know to become saints: love God, love others.

FEBRUARY

ACTIVITIES

BE KIND TO SIBLINGS

Declare the day Kindness to Brothers and Sisters Day. Have the students make cards of appreciation, plan to do something extra-special for their brothers and/or sisters, or prepare I'm Glad You're You coupons:

> Because I'm GLAD YOU'RE YOU,
> I want to make this day special for you by
> _____
> _____
> Signed,
> _____

You may use the blackline master on page 447 for this activity.

MAKE PRAYER POSTERS

Scholastica offered a powerful prayer to God. Remind the students that two-second prayers offered often throughout the day help keep us aware of God's loving presence and concern for us. Have the students make small prayer posters to display in the room to help themselves learn and remember to pray short prayers often. A number of suitable prayers may be found on the blackline master on page 448.

ROLE-PLAY WAYS TO BE THERE FOR OTHERS

One lesson Scholastica teaches us is the importance of being available to people when they are in need. Have the students suggest situations in which someone their age can do this. List them on the board. Then have the students work with partners or in small groups to role-play some of the situations. Encourage the students to make special efforts to be aware of the needs of others throughout the day and to take time to listen to people.

MAKE VALENTINES

Benedict and Scholastica loved each other and loved God. Much of their closeness and warmth must have come from their family experiences. Give the students time and materials to make valentines for family members. Suggest that they offer special prayers for their relatives too.

Catechist's Notes:

_____

_____

_____

_____

_____

_____

Our Lady of Lourdes

Each year over 2 million people make their way through the mountainous country of southeastern France to Lourdes. They come seeking cures, hoping to find answers, believing, and praying. At Lourdes these pilgrims pray in the church, wash in the baths from the flowing stream, and walk, sing, and pray in the processions. There the people recall the Lady dressed in white, with a blue sash, yellow roses at her feet, and a Rosary on her arm—the Blessed Virgin Mary.

On February 11, 1858, Mary appeared here to 14-year-old Bernadette Soubirous. This was the first of 18 visits, many of them with up to 20,000 people present. When Bernadette asked the Lady's identity, she replied, "I am the Immaculate Conception." Just four years earlier the pope had proclaimed it a dogma that Mary was conceived immaculate, without original sin. The Blessed Virgin, through Bernadette, had come to call sinners to a change of heart. Her message was a request for prayer and penance. She also instructed Bernadette to tell the priests that a chapel was to be built on the site and processions held.

On February 25, 1858, the Lady told Bernadette to dig in the dirt and drink of the stream. Bernadette began to dig, and after several attempts she was able to find the water to drink. The water continued to flow from where she had dug with her hands until it was producing over 32,000 gallons of water a day—as it still does. Three days later, a mother who had two paralyzed fingers was cured in those waters. Since then there have been over 5,000 cures recorded, but less than 100 of them have been declared miraculous by the Church. Most of these have taken place during the blessing with the Blessed Sacrament.

There are daily reports of cures, but most people discover that the greatest blessings of Lourdes happen not to the body but to the soul, the spirit, the very heart of the people who go there.

Today we celebrate the feast of Our Lady of Lourdes. We may never travel to Lourdes and join in the processions, but we can know always that we have a Mother to help us and lead us to her Son, Jesus. And so we pray to her:

God of mercy,
we celebrate the feast of Mary,
the sinless mother of God.
May her prayers help us
to rise above our human weakness.

We ask this through our Lord Jesus Christ,
   your Son,
who lives and reigns with you and the Holy Spirit,
one God, for ever and ever.

(Opening Prayer, Proper of Saints, February 11)

ACTIVITIES

SING A HYMN

The song "Immaculate Mary" is known also as the Lourdes hymn. It is used in procession at the shrine. Have the students sing this hymn as a closing prayer.

PRAY THE ROSARY

One message to Bernadette from the Virgin Mary was to pray the Rosary. Review the Rosary with the students. Then pray the Glorious Mysteries together with the class. You may use the blackline master on page 443 to make copies of the Mysteries of the Rosary.

RESEARCH LOURDES AND OTHER SHRINES

Have the students go on line to research Lourdes and other major shrines of Our Lady, such as the ones at Knock, Guadalupe, Fatima, Czestochowa, and Medjugorje, as well as shrines located in your own diocese or region. Have them make posters or virtual tours on a computer program as a way of sharing information and pictures they find.

REVIEW THE MEANING OF THE IMMACULATE CONCEPTION

The dogma of the Immaculate Conception had been defined by Pope Pius IX just four years before the first apparition at Lourdes. When Mary identified herself using this title, it further strengthened this teaching of the Church. Review with the students the significance of the Immaculate Conception, (i.e., that Mary, in view of the role she would have in salvation history, was free from original sin from the moment of her conception).

DISCUSS MIRACULOUS CURES

Cures at Lourdes are declared miraculous only after a very careful review by the Church and by a board of international doctors, some of whom are not even Christian. Discuss with the students why the Church would be so cautious about this.

Catechist's Notes:

_____

_____

_____

_____

_____

_____

_____

Saints Cyril and Methodius

(825–869; 826–884)

February 14

I t is hard to keep going when others seem to be against you, isn't it? Some people just give up once things become difficult—but the real saints in the world do not give up.

Cyril (whose name was Constantine before he became a monk) and Methodius were brothers, born in Thessalonika, Greece. Cyril, a brilliant philosopher, studied at the university in Constantinople. He was ordained a priest. His brother Methodius, for five years the governor of a Slavic section of the empire, later became a monk. In 861 these two brothers were sent as missionaries to one of the regions of Russia. They learned the language of the people before they went and were able to lead many people to Christ.

Later, in 863, Cyril and Methodius were sent to Moravia, which is in Eastern Europe. They prepared well for their work. With their knowledge of the Slavonic tongue, they began translating the Gospels into the language. To do this, Cyril devised a special alphabet (still used in Russia and in some Slavonic countries), and so he also helped promote Slavonic literature in general. And the brothers always showed love and respect for the people. Cyril and Methodius ministered to the people as one of them, and they celebrated the Mass and gave homilies in Slavonic. But some German bishops at the time were suspicious of these two from "the East." They accused the missionaries of many things,

so that in 869 Cyril and Methodius were called to Rome to defend their actions. They did this so well that not only were they told to continue preaching and using Slavonic in the liturgy, but they were also to be consecrated bishops. They could then ordain to the priesthood the candidates they had helped. Cyril died before he could be consecrated bishop; Methodius was consecrated and he returned to Moravia. There some German bishops continued to hurl accusations at him until he was deposed by a German synod and imprisoned. Methodius was released two years later by order of the pope, but the tensions continued. Again, in 878, he was called to Rome to defend his actions, and again he was approved. For the rest of his life, Methodius was to endure the anger and misunderstanding of the German clergy.

Something deep within Cyril and Methodius kept them going. Love of God, love of the people, love and knowledge of the Scriptures they had worked so hard to translate—all of these played a part in their determination.

At Baptism you, like Cyril and Methodius, received many gifts through the power of the Holy Spirit dwelling within you. One of those gifts was fortitude, or courage. It made all the difference in the lives of Cyril and Methodius. It could make all the difference in your life too.

FEBRUARY

LEARN ABOUT PRAYERS IN LATIN

Today it is considered a normal thing to have the Mass celebrated in your own language. But it was not always that way. In fact when Cyril and Methodius began to celebrate the Mass and give homilies in the language of the people, they were suspected of being heretics. There is, however, a value in knowing a common language. In the Church, Latin is that type of language. In large multinational gatherings, such as at Lourdes or the Vatican, common prayers may be said in Latin. Let the students become acquainted with these prayers. Make copies of the blackline master on page 449.

- Make sure the students know the Sign of the Cross; use it occasionally in class.

- Play a recording of the "Ave Maria" as the students follow along with the words.

- Have the students write out the English words of the Lord's Prayer to parallel the Latin words.

LOCATE SLAVIC COUNTRIES

Cyril and Methodius are called the apostles of the Slavs and are honored by Russians, Serbs, Ukrainians, Bulgarians, Czechs, Slovaks, and Croatians. Have the students locate the homelands of these groups of people on a map to see the extent of the influence of Cyril and Methodius.

DISCUSS CYRILLIC ALPHABET

Cyril developed a Slavonic alphabet. However, the Cyrillic alphabet often associated with him was developed by his followers, who continued his work after his death. Ask the students why it would be important for people to read the Scriptures in their own languages. If you wish, show the students—or let them find on the Internet—a sample of the Cyrillic alphabet. The Russian language is still written using the Cyrillic alphabet.

ACCEPT OTHERS

Cyril and Methodius exemplified some of the best procedures in missionary work: trying to understand the people and their particular culture rather than imposing on them a foreign culture or tradition. It is easy to want others to change rather than to accept them as they are. Discuss with the students the importance of loving and accepting people as they are.

REVIEW THE GIFTS OF THE SPIRIT

Review with the students the gifts of the Holy Spirit they received at Baptism, which are sealed and strengthened in Confirmation. Talk about how Cyril and Methodius used the gifts of the Spirit and about how young people today can use these gifts.

Catechist's Notes:

_____

_____

_____

Blesseds Francisco and Jacinta Marto

February 20

(1908–1919; 1910–1920)

What do you like to do on a sunny spring afternoon? On a beautiful Sunday afternoon, May 13, 1917, three children were laughing and chatting as they kept watch over their families' sheep. This afternoon they were building a playhouse out of brush and rocks. Suddenly a bright light flashed. They thought it was lightning. Then it flashed again. They saw a ball of light descend upon a shrubby little evergreen tree. Within the light was a beautiful woman dressed in white.

The children were Lucia dos Santos, who was 11 years old, and her cousins Francisco Marto, nine, and his sister Jacinta, seven. These children lived in Portugal, in a small village near Fatima. The shining woman told them not to be afraid and that she was from heaven. She told them she would return on the 13th day of each month for six months, and she asked them to meet her at this place, the Cova da Iria.

Many people, including Lucia's family, did not believe the children. People laughed, ridiculed, harassed, threatened them and put them in jail for two days. But nothing could change the truth.

Through that summer, on the 13th day of each month, the Blessed Mother Mary appeared to the children. Each time more and more people accompanied them to the Cova. Each time Mary told them to pray the Rosary for peace in the world, to sacrifice for sinners. She said they would suffer, but she would be their comfort. On October 13, the day of the last apparition, more than 70,000 people were waiting. This time the Lady of the Rosary asked them to build a chapel on the rocky hillside. Then the entire crowd witnessed a remarkable sight. The sun seemed to dance in the sky. It was spinning like a top and shooting off brilliant colors of the rainbow, transforming the countryside. Suddenly the sun dropped treacherously close to earth. People dropped to their knees, and the sun just as quickly returned to its place in the sky.

You might think that, of course, if the Blessed Mother of God appears and speaks to you, you are a saint. But that is not necessarily true. What is true is that Mary chose to come to children who the year before had been visited by the Angel of Peace, children who had listened to the angel's message and prayed the prayer the angel taught them. They responded to Mary in the same way. They listened to her and tried to do everything she asked. They prayed the Rosary and offered sacrifices for sinners and for the conversion of the world. They were children who wanted to please God with all their hearts, and that is why the Church has declared them Blessed.

Two of the three children—Francisco and Jacinta—died within a short time, as the Lady had said they would. They were beatified on May 13, 2000. At that time Lucia dos Santos was a Carmelite nun in Portugal.

PRAY THE ROSARY

Review with the children how to pray the Rosary and the Mysteries of the Rosary. You may wish to use the blackline master on page 443.

- Pray a decade of the Rosary with the children today.

- Provide beads and string and let the children make rosaries for themselves.

OFFER A SACRIFICE

Francisco and Jacinta eagerly made little sacrifices as our Lady asked them to do. However, some sufferings were given to them. One was the accusations of their neighbors. Another was the crowds of people who began to follow them around and question them. Last were the painful complications of influenza. Remind the students that they should also offer their suffering to God. They will be misunderstood and laughed at. They will be annoyed and pestered by other people. They will have aches, pains, and sickness. Give them a moment to think about what they can offer to Jesus today.

REFLECT ON THE EUCHARIST

Both Francisco and Jacinta longed to receive their First Communion. Francisco received the Eucharist the day before he died. When Jacinta was ill, the priest promised her he would come the next morning, but she died during the night. Lead the children to reflect on what receiving Jesus in Holy Communion means to them. Give them time to write about this in their journals.

Catechist's Notes:

_____

_____

_____

_____

_____

_____

_____

_____

_____

Chair of Peter

Whenever the pope, the Bishop of Rome, speaks out on an issue or delivers a teaching, his words are recorded, printed, and meditated upon. Whenever the pope cautions world leaders, pleads for peace, or condemns discrimination and social injustice, people listen. The pope travels where other leaders dare not go; he speaks freely about issues that others fear to discuss. What makes the world stop and listen to this particular shepherd of Christ's flock?

The answer lies both in Scripture and in tradition. In the New Testament, Peter is named first among the apostles of Jesus: he was often their spokesman and leader; he was the first to preach after Pentecost, the leader in defending Christ and his message to rulers who opposed him. Peter was at the Transfiguration and in the garden. Peter proclaimed, "You are the Christ," and Christ in turn singled out Peter, calling him *Cephas,* which, like *Peter,* means rock:

"And I tell you, you are Peter, and on this rock I will build my church, and the gates of Hades will not prevail against it. I will give you the keys of the kingdom of heaven, and whatever you bind on earth will be bound in heaven, and whatever you loose on earth will be loosed in heaven."

(Matthew 16:18–19)

Jesus gave Peter a threefold commission of love and ministry:

When they had finished breakfast, Jesus said to Simon Peter, "Simon son of John, do you love me more than these?" He said to him, "Yes, Lord; you know that I love you." Jesus said to him, "Feed my lambs." A second time he said to him, "Simon son of John, do you love me?" He said to him, "Yes, Lord; you know that I love you." Jesus said to him, "Tend my sheep." He said to him the third time, "Simon son of John, do you love me?" Peter felt hurt because he said to him the third time, "Do you love me?" And he said to him, "Lord, you know everything; you know that I love you." Jesus said to him, "Feed my sheep."

(John 21:15–17)

From the first the "primacy" of Peter has been recognized. It is a sign of Christ's love for his Church and his presence and protection.

On the feast of the Chair of Peter, we celebrate our unity as a Church. The title of the feast refers to the chair from which a bishop presided and gave homilies, a symbol of his authority. When the title refers to St. Peter, it recalls the supreme teaching power of the Prince of the Apostles and his successors. It is from the chair that the pope teaches, guides, and shepherds the flock of Christ. On this feast let us pray for the Church and especially for our pope, that God may protect him and give him the strength, courage, and wisdom he needs to guide us.

FEBRUARY

BECOME FAMILIAR WITH EPISTLES

Two letters were written by Peter. This might be a good time to introduce the students to these letters and to all the letters referred to as "universal" or "catholic" because they are not addressed to any specific church: James, 1 Peter, 2 Peter, 1 John, 2 John, 3 John, Jude. Provide some time during the day, for the students to quietly read one or two of these letters.

COLLECT NEWS ITEMS ABOUT THE POPE

Have the students bring in articles about the pope, his travels, his teachings, and his interests. You may wish to encourage them to read biographies of the recent popes.

HOLD A PRAYER SERVICE

Help the students plan and conduct a prayer service for the pope, the bishops, the priests, and the deacons. Make it part of a vocation-awareness day. The students might wish to write letters to the clergy, expressing their prayerful support.

RESEARCH PETER IN SCRIPTURE

Have the students locate Scripture references relating to Peter. What qualities of a leader does Peter have? What other qualities did he have to overcome in order to give better witness to Christ? Suggest that the students act out a scene from Peter's life as found in the Acts of the Apostles.

FIND SAINT PETER IN ART

Peter is often represented in art with a set of keys, with a ship or fish, with a cock (representing his denial of Christ), dressed in a toga or as a pope or bishop, or as being crucified head down. Have the students find pictures with these representations or have them draw their own.

LEARN ABOUT THE VATICAN

Show the students photographs or a video of the Vatican.

LEARN ABOUT ANCIENT ANTIOCH

Tradition indicates that Peter was the bishop of Antioch before he went to Rome, where he was martyred. Have the students locate Antioch on a map and do research on why it was an important city in the early Church.

FIND SCRIPTURE SYMBOLISM IN THE PARISH CHURCH

The words inscribed on the base of the dome of Saint Peter's are from Matthew 16:18. Ask the students to study their parish church for Scripture references.

Catechist's Notes:

_____

_____

_____

_____

Saint Polycarp

(c. 60–155)

February 23

Do you ever wonder what it was really like in the time of Christ? Suppose you could ask one of the apostles of Jesus. What would be your first question?

Polycarp was a disciple of John the apostle. Polycarp bridged the gap between the disciples who lived with Jesus on earth and those who would know and love Jesus by faith. Although we know few details about Polycarp's life, we know a great deal about his martyrdom. It is one of the earliest recorded accounts of a Christian martyr.

While still quite young, Polycarp became the bishop of Smyrna (in what is now Turkey) and as such was one of the most respected leaders in the first half of the second century. Ignatius of Antioch and Irenaeus spoke highly of him, and the people loved him very much.

Polycarp was so highly respected that he was sent as the representative of the churches in Asia Minor to Rome to discuss with Pope Anicetus the date for the celebration of Easter. East and West had chosen separate dates for the celebration of this major feast. When a compromise could not be reached, Pope Anicetus did not demand Polycarp's agreement, nor did Bishop Polycarp encourage any schism, or division, between the groups over the issue. They sought in charity to leave the two separate dates for the time being, and then together they celebrated the Eucharist.

Polycarp was a Christian leader in a pagan world. He spoke with clarity and simplicity, fearless in his love for and defense of Christ, even though persecutions raged around him. He sought only to hand on the message he had been given by John, who had seen and heard and really followed Jesus Christ. Even as Polycarp himself prepared for martyrdom, his joy and his confident trust were evident to all those around him.

Polycarp was seized for being a Christian. He was threatened and pressured in many ways, yet he explained to his captors that he had followed Christ for 86 years. Persecution and death would not tear him away from Jesus now. So Polycarp was led into the stadium at Smyrna. The crowd demanded that he be left to the lions, but instead he was sentenced to death by fire. He was finally killed by the sword in February 155, and his body was burned. A group of Christians took his remains and buried them.

The community of believers celebrated the anniversary of his death with great joy, for in Polycarp they had seen an outstanding example of love and patience. He had held strong and had won—not an earthly treasure that could rust or corrode, but instead he had won the treasure of eternal life. Polycarp, along with Ignatius of Antioch, Clement of Rome, and a few others, is remembered as an Apostolic Father—one who was a disciple of the apostles.

FEBRUARY

ACTIVITIES

RESPECT DIFFERENCES

Bishop Polycarp and Pope Anicetus accepted diversity in the Church. Their respect for differing customs is something from which we can learn today. Challenge the students to evaluate how they solve disagreements among themselves or how well they accept the customs and styles of other people.

FIND IMAGES OF CHRIST

People are usually interested in learning about what life was like in the time of Christ and during the early years of the Church. Many people have also wondered what Christ really looked like. Images of Christ—most of them symbolic—have been collected throughout the centuries. Suggest that students do some research and display copies or reproductions of the art they find.

WRITE PRAYER PETITIONS

In his letter to the Church at Philippi, Polycarp stressed patience after the example of Christ, following the Gospels, almsgiving, and prayer for kings, rulers, enemies, and persecutors. Have the students write and offer petitions related to each of these topics.

IMAGINE CONVERSATION BETWEEN JOHN AND POLYCARP

Ask the students to imagine and write a conversation between the apostle John and his disciple Polycarp. Then ask them to imagine and write a conversation between Bishop Polycarp and a group of young people in the second century. Have volunteers read or role-play their conversations for the class.

Catechist's Notes:

_____

_____

_____

_____

_____

_____

_____

_____

Saint Katharine Drexel   March 3

(1858–1955)

What would you do with a few million dollars? In 1889 newspaper headlines read "Gives Up Millions." The article told about Katharine Drexel, an heiress from Philadelphia.

Katharine's father was an international banker, and her mother died soon after Katharine was born. When her father remarried, he chose a wonderful mother for his daughters. The Drexels were very rich and even had a private railroad car. They were also devout Catholics—they had a private chapel in their home. They made good use of both the railroad car and the chapel. Katharine received an excellent education, she traveled, and she made her debut into society. Her father and stepmother set good examples of prayer and charity for Katharine and her two sisters.

When Katharine's stepmother became ill with cancer, Katharine nursed her for three years until she died. Through this experience Katharine began to think about her own values in life and about becoming a nun. Then after visiting the western part of the United States, she became concerned about the Native Americans.

Soon after while on a tour of Europe, Katharine met Pope Leo XIII. She asked him to send more missionaries to the American West to help her friend Bishop James O'Connor. The pope asked, "Why not be a missionary yourself, my child?"

Katharine and her sisters visited the Sioux reservations in South Dakota, where they had been supporting mission schools. After much thought and prayer, Katharine knew that this was where her heart was. She joined the Sisters of Mercy in Pittsburgh to make a two-year novitiate. When she was 33, Katharine made her vows as the first Sister of the Blessed Sacrament. Her order was dedicated to sharing the Gospel and the life of the Eucharist among Native Americans and African Americans. The old Drexel summer home in Pennsylvania was the sisters' first convent.

After three-and-a-half years of training, Mother Drexel and other sisters opened a boarding school in Santa Fe, New Mexico. She spent her life and millions of dollars on her work. In the end she had established 50 missions for Native Americans in 16 states, a system of Catholic schools for African Americans, 40 mission centers, and 23 rural schools. She had also made the Church and the country more aware of the needs of the poor and had spoken out against racial and social injustices.

No doubt Mother Drexel's greatest educational achievement was founding Xavier University in New Orleans, the first university for African Americans in the United States. A heart attack at the age of 77 forced Katharine to retire. She spent the next 20 years praying for the sisters who carried on her work. She died at the age of 96. She was beatified in 1988 and canonized on October 1, 2000.

ACTIVITIES

PLAN A SERVICE PROJECT

Katharine Drexel had a strong devotion to the Blessed Sacrament. In the Eucharist, Jesus gives himself totally. Katharine gave not just her money but her entire life. Challenge the children to think about how they could give of themselves to show their love. Help them plan a service to their families, school, or parish community.

CELEBRATE DIVERSITY

Discuss with the class how the Native American and African American cultures contribute to the richness of the Catholic Church.

- Listen to a recording of African American spirituals and talk about this rich musical tradition.

- Have children choose slides or other photographs to illustrate a Sioux prayer. You may make use the blackline master on page 450 to make copies for the class.

PRAY FOR LOVE

Together pray for an end to prejudice and racism.

RAISE MONEY

Have a fundraiser—a car wash, a pizza or sandwich sale, a rummage sale—and contribute the profits to an organization that promotes the welfare of Native American, African American, or Haitian peoples.

Catechist's Notes:

_____

_____

_____

_____

_____

_____

_____

_____

_____

Saint Casimir

(1458–1484)

March 4

Casimir is claimed as the patron of two countries—Poland and Lithuania. A prince of Poland, Casimir had natural gifts of leadership and idealism. Casimir was highly disciplined and eager to learn. Under the influence of an exceptional teacher, John Dlugosz, Casimir learned to love God and tried always to live by his conscience.

By the time Casimir was 13, his virtue and integrity were so well known that the nobles in Hungary, dissatisfied with their king, wanted Casimir as ruler. Casimir's father equipped him with an army and sent him to the Hungarian border to take over the country. As young as Casimir was, he could see the problems facing his troops. Their pay was low and soldiers were deserting. As Casimir surveyed the situation, he saw he was clearly outnumbered by the enemy, and the battle would be a waste of lives. Moreover, he learned that Pope Sixtus IV had sent an emissary to his father to try to stop the takeover. So Casimir returned home with no kingdom to his name. Casimir's father felt angry and disgraced. To punish his son, he banished him to a nearby castle for three months.

Casimir went as directed and continued to study and pray. During this time he made a serious resolution never again to be involved in war; instead, he would govern by peaceful means. Casimir also decided to remain unmarried. This decision further frustrated his father when Casimir refused to marry the daughter of the Emperor Frederick III.

Casimir governed Poland for four years while his father was occupied in Lithuania. During this time everyone admired his prudence and commitment to justice. When he was 26, Casimir went on an important mission to Lithuania. While he was there he died of consumption, a lung disease, and was buried at the cathedral in Vilnius. As he had requested, a copy of the hymn "Daily, Daily, Sing to Mary" was placed in his hands. Casimir had a great love for Mary and often recited this long hymn, part of which is still sung today. Many miracles were reported immediately after Casimir's death, and he was venerated as a saint.

Casimir's life reminds us how important it is to have a well-formed conscience and to live by our convictions. Though a prince, Casimir saw that his first duty was to God.

LIVE THE BEATITUDES

After Casimir had witnessed the horrors of the battlefield, he resolved to rule by peace.

Grades K–3: Talk about how it is sometimes hard to do what is right. Have the children draw a picture of themselves doing the hard but right thing.

Grades 4–8: Write the beatitude "Blessed are the peacemakers" on the board. Have the students brainstorm what this teaching requires of them. Then have small groups prepare to act out how to be peacemakers in their own lives.

PRAY FOR STRONG FAITH

For a time Poland and Lithuania were part of the USSR and religion was severely restricted. The Cathedral of Vilna, where Casimir was buried, was turned into a museum and art gallery, and his remains were transferred to a parish church. But the people of these countries still honor him. Have the students locate Poland and Lithuania on a map and pray for Catholics who live there, that they may have the courage to witness to their faith.

LEARN PRAYER FOR PEACE

Casimir should make us more aware of our own quest for peace. Have the students copy The World Peace Prayer onto a card. Laminate the cards. Or make a large prayer card for your prayer area. Pray the prayer often as a class.

> Lead us from death to life,
>   from falsehood to truth.
> Lead us from despair to hope,
>   from fear to trust.
> Lead us from hate to love,
>   from war to peace.
> Let peace fill our hearts,
>   our world, our universe.

HONOR MARY

Following Casimir's love and respect for the Mother of God, place a picture or statue of Mary in your prayer area or decorate your image of Mary. Pray the Hail Mary or sing a Marian hymn together today.

Catechist's Notes:

_____

_____

_____

_____

_____

_____

_____

Saints Perpetua and Felicitas

March 7

(d. 203)

Have you ever kept a diary or journal? Have you ever read the journal or diary of a famous person? Perpetua wrote a diary during her last days, while she awaited execution. Her diary, along with an eyewitness account of her death, is one of the oldest, most reliable histories of a martyr's sufferings. This account was passed down generation after generation to encourage other Christians to witness to the world with their lives—to teach others that wealth, popularity, convenience, pleasure, and power are not the most important things in life. What is greater than life itself is knowing Jesus and being loyal to him.

Perpetua's diary records the events that took place in Carthage, Africa, in the year 202, when the Emperor Severus issued an anti-Christian edict forbidding anyone to be baptized and thereby become a Christian. At that time Perpetua was 22 years old and a catechumen studying to become a Christian. She was arrested along with four other catechumens, including Felicitas, a slave woman, who was about to give birth to a child. All were tried and sentenced to be thrown to the wild beasts in the amphitheater during a national holiday. Their deaths would be scheduled along with sports events and various games.

During the days before their execution, their teacher, Saturus, voluntarily joined the catechumens so that he might die for Christ with them. Perpetua's father, a wealthy pagan, endeavored to make his daughter change her mind. He pleaded with her to offer sacrifice to the pagan gods so she could be freed from imprisonment, but she refused. While they were awaiting death, Perpetua and her companions were baptized. Shortly before the scheduled execution, Felicitas gave birth to her child and was free to join her companions in the arena.

On the day of their execution, the martyrs left their prison "joyfully as though they were on their way to heaven" and entered the amphitheater, where they were killed before the cheering crowd.

What enabled these Christians to face death so courageously? During childbirth, Felicitas had cried out in pain, and when someone asked her how she would ever endure the suffering of martyrdom, she replied, "Now it is I who suffer what I am suffering; then, there will be another in me who will suffer for me, because I will be suffering for him."

ACT AS CHRISTIANS

When her father was pleading with her to deny her faith in Christ, Perpetua said, "Father, do you see this water jar standing here? Could one call it by any other name than what it is? Well, in the same way, I cannot be called by any other name than what I am—a Christian." Have the students role-play this conversation between Perpetua and her father. Then ask them to think of a situation they will be facing in the next few days, a situation in which they will have an opportunity to act as Christians. Have them picture the place and the persons involved, and visualize their responses to the situation. Explain that when people know they are going to face difficult situations, it sometimes helps if they go through the coming events mentally and decide on the Christian responses they want to give.

- Invite the students to role-play a conversation or situation in which they choose to act as Christians.

- Ask the students to draw storyboards illustrating the situation they imagined.

SUPPORT FAMILY FAITH

Perpetua's mother and one brother were already Christians, and another brother was a catechumen. In her family Perpetua found support for her own faith.

Let the children tell ways their families support and encourage them in their efforts to live Christian lives. Also ask them how they can assist the other members of their families. Put two columns on the board, one labeled My Family Helps Me and one labeled I Help My Family. Have the students, as a group, list ways that families help members be faithful Christians.

MAKE SIGNS OF ENCOURAGEMENT

Perpetua, Felicitas, and their companions went to martyrdom rejoicing. Have the students look up Scripture passages that refer to the joy of suffering for Christ. Then have them choose a quotation, print it on a sheet of heavy construction paper, and decorate it. Post these papers to remind the students that they also can offer their sufferings for Christ in joy. Here are some references:

2 Corinthians 12:9–10	Colossians 1:12
Galatians 6:14	Colossians 3:4
Philippians 1:30	1 Peter 1:6–7
Philippians 3:8–10	1 Peter 4:13
Philippians 4:13	

WRITE NOTE CARDS

After Perpetua had been attacked by a wild beast, but while she was still alive, she said to her Christian brother who was watching from the crowd, "Stand firm in the faith, love one another, and do not let our sufferings be a stumbling-block." By her own words and example, Perpetua wanted to encourage her brother to be strong. Ask the students to think of someone who has recently given them a good example. Have them write a note of appreciation to that person.

DISCUSS PREJUDICE

"As many of you as were baptized into Christ have clothed yourselves with Christ. There is no longer Jew or Greek, there is no longer slave or free, there is no longer male and female; for all of you are one in Christ Jesus" (Galatians 3:27–28). Perpetua was a wealthy free woman; Felicitas was a slave. Yet, both realized that in Christ they were one and equally important. Consider with the students the types of prejudice. Discuss ways to combat prejudice.

Saint John of God

(1495–1550)

March 8

John of God was a saint of such extremes that some people thought he was crazy! John was a Spanish soldier who had given up religion and turned away from God. The wild life he led gave him a bad reputation. When he left the military at age 40, he returned to the work he did as a boy—herding sheep in Spain. Thinking about his past life, he believed he was a miserable sinner. John decided to make a radical conversion. He vowed to go to Muslim North Africa and free Christian slaves. He imagined himself dying as a martyr. It took his confessor months to convince John that this plan was not wise. Gradually John settled on a more prudent plan—to sell religious books in Granada, Spain. This project he successfully managed, but he was still not content; his spirit was restless.

One day John went to hear John of Ávila preach, and the sermon struck home. John's impetuous nature again showed itself, for he felt he must do something at once to show the world he had converted. John began publicly beating himself in remorse for his sins; he ran through the streets, tearing his hair and gave his books away so frantically that people threw stones at him. John was committed to a mental institution. When John of Ávila heard the effect his words had had on John, the great preacher hurried to the hospital. The preacher calmed John and persuaded him that rather than going to such extremes, he should spend his great energy caring for the sick and poor. This idea seemed reasonable to John, who wanted to love God. John left the hospital and rented a house near Granada. Out into the streets he went to find the penniless and the homeless, the lepers, the lame, the insane, the paralyzed, and those who were dumb and deaf. What a hospital he soon had!

At first John went begging to find enough money to support these poor, but soon people gave him money, food, and supplies because they were so impressed with his charity. John led a life of total giving and constant prayer. Once when a fire broke out in the house, John ran back into the burning building countless times, carrying the sick out on his back. When unemployed men came to his back door, he found them work. When the archbishop called John to his office because people complained that John kept tramps and prostitutes in his hospital, he was silenced by John's humility. John fell on his knees, saying, "I know of no bad person in hospital except myself, who am unworthy to eat the bread of the poor." His ceaseless energy and wholehearted goodness attracted so many helpers that soon he had a flourishing hospital. Later these helpers formed a religious community called the Brothers Hospitallers.

John of God died from a disease he caught while saving a drowning man. Before dying, John went carefully over all hospital accounts and appointed a capable leader to take his place. He died kneeling before the altar in the hospital chapel. John's lifelong conversion encourages us never to give up trying to love God more deeply. Though it takes struggles to live the Gospel, perseverance brings a heavenly reward.

MAKE NAME PLAQUES

The bishop of Puy once invited John to supper. The bishop was so impressed by John's humility that he called him "John of God." Pass out half sheets of paper and have the students design their name and a title as a plaque. Encourage them to choose titles of a religious nature. Have them write the reasons for their choices on the back of the paper. A sample follows:

Joe the Charitable

Front

Jesus showed us how to love
his Father and others.
I want to be like him.

Back

VISIT A HOSPITAL

John of God is the patron of hospitals. Have the class visit a hospital. Perhaps the students could prepare songs or skits for the children there and present them at a scheduled time.

HAVE A BOOK FAIR

John of God was a promoter of religious books. Have a religious book fair at your parish, or let the students volunteer to help in the parish library. Today there are many interesting books on the lives of holy people. Have the class select a saint from whom they would like to learn, and read a section of his or her biography to them every day.

PRAY FOR THE POOR

Saint John of God is a good saint to imitate for peace and justice. Read his words to the class: "[My hospital] receives the elderly and children, pilgrims and travelers. We offer them fire and water, salt and cooking vessels. We receive no payment, but Christ provides. When I see so many of my brothers and sisters suffering beyond endurance or oppressed in body and spirit and I cannot help, I grieve indeed but I trust in Christ, for my heart is sure of him." Have the students pray to John of God for the unemployed, the suffering, and the destitute.

INTERVIEW HEALTH PROFESSIONALS

Suggest that the students interview someone who works in a hospital to find out why this person serves people. Have them write their interviews for in the school newspaper.

Catechist's Notes:

_____

_____

_____

_____

Saint Frances of Rome
March 9
(1384–1440)

When Lorenzo Ponziano of Rome brought Frances, his beautiful bride, to the altar, his family and the wealthy of the city were in awe. Not only did he marry one of Rome's most charming and gentle maidens, but one who was virtuous. Frances, who was 13 when she married, was different from the other rich girls. Her mother had taught her how to pray and love the poor, as well as how to manage a large household.

Though she had wished to be a nun, Frances obediently married. She was young and spirited, and dressed herself in the silks, velvets, and jewels of the family to please her husband, who dearly loved her. She also loved him and willingly took care of her duties at the castle, but Frances was sometimes lonely and yearned to serve God in the poor. One day her sister-in-law Vanozza discovered Frances crying and confided that she, too, had the same desires. They made a plan to care for the poor. Frequently Frances and Vanozza left the palace in simple dresses and veils to care for the sick in the hospitals and to distribute goods to the poor. Lorenzo's family and relatives were horrified when they found. The wealthy, proud aristocrats ridiculed the young women.

But Frances persuaded Lorenzo to allow her to continue to serve the needy. Frances was a marvelous mother to their growing family. She supervised the education of her children and spent long hours caring for them. When her mother-in-law died, Frances took charge of the household. She treated the servants so well that they did their work more carefully and attended church more often. Though Frances prayed much, she always cared for her family first.

Frances met with many trials. When floods and famine crippled Rome, Frances opened her house as a hospital and distributed food and clothing. Her father-in-law was outraged and took away the keys to the supply rooms. But he relented when he saw the corn bin and the wine barrel miraculously replenished after Frances finished praying. Natural disasters were followed by wars. When Rome was invaded, Frances endured the kidnapping of her husband and the deaths of three of her children. The wars brought plagues and hardships. Again Frances opened her home as a hospital and drove her wagon through the countryside to collect wood for fire and herbs for medicine. She was seen everywhere, burying the dead, nursing the sick, serving the poor, and patiently taking upon herself the hardest, most disagreeable work.

When the wars ended and Frances's husband returned, she founded the Oblates of St. Mary. This was a congregation of women who lived in their own homes and served the poor. Later the Oblates lived a community life, but Frances did not join them until after Lorenzo had died and her children were grown. Frances was a ray of hope and joy during the disasters that struck Rome in the early 1400s. To the city she was another Christ.

ACTIVITIES

PRAY TO GUARDIAN ANGELS

For many years Frances was aware of her guardian angel who protected her on dangerous charitable missions. Remind the students to pray to their guardian angels to protect them and their families from all harm. Review the prayers to the guardian angels on the blackline master on page 441.

LEARN ABOUT PASTORAL MINISTRY

Today many laypeople serve others as Frances did. Invite a parishioner who is involved in pastoral ministry to speak to the class. Help the children list the many ways Catholic laypeople can work to help others.

BE KIND TO EVERYONE

Frances was scorned by her son's beautiful but violent-tempered wife. But when this daughter-in-law fell seriously ill, Frances nursed her back to health and converted the girl through kindness. Encourage the children to be kind to those who irritate them.

BE KIND TO MOTHERS

Frances was a loving mother who taught her children to be good Christians. Encourage the students to do something to give extra rest to their mothers when they are especially tired or not feeling well.

EAT SOUP

Frances began a soup kitchen to aid the poor. During Lent, especially, the students could have a soup-only lunch. The money saved by having soup instead of a regular meal could be given to the missions.

DEMONSTRATE WORKS OF MERCY

Review the corporal and spiritual works of mercy. Discuss how Frances lived out the works of mercy. Have older students plan original skits about each work of mercy to perform for younger students.

Catechist's Notes:

_____

_____

_____

_____

_____

_____

_____

_____

Saint Louise de Marillac — March 15
(1591–1660)

"What God wants will be done in his good time." These words of Louise de Marillac came true for her.

Louise was born near Paris, France. Her father belonged to the aristocracy; she never knew her mother. When Louise was four years old, her father remarried. Louise wasn't accepted by her stepmother. She was sent to school at a Dominican convent where her aunt was a nun. At this time Louise desired to become a nun too.

Louise's father died when she was 13, and her life changed completely. There was no money for her education, so Louise had to live and work in a boarding house. There she learned domestic skills and the use of herbal medicines.

When she was 22, Louise married Antoine le Gras, the secretary to the Queen of France. Soon a son, Michel Antoine, was born to them. Louise again associated with the nobility. Though she had a busy social and home life, Louise worked with an organization of women dedicated to helping the poor. Because of her experiences, Louise felt equally comfortable with the rich and with the poor.

After seven years of marriage, Antoine became ill. Worried, Louise became depressed. Then praying to know God's will, she had a vision of herself serving the poor as a member of a religious community. She had no idea how this would happen, but Louise believed that God's will would be done.

About the same time, Louise met Vincent de Paul, a priest who became her spiritual director. When her husband died two years later, Louise worked with Monsieur Vincent to direct his Confraternities of Charity. Unlike most cultured women, Louise went into poor homes to cook, clean, and tend the sick.

Four years later Louise started training young women in her home to serve the poor and to live as a community serving God. She was supported and guided by Vincent de Paul. This was the beginning of the Daughters of Charity. Over the next 10 years, many women joined Louise. They brought improved nursing practices to hospitals, treated soldiers on the battlefield, and ministered to galley slaves and prisoners. They ran soup kitchens, hospices, job training centers, and free schools.

When Louise was 51 years old, she and the first Daughters of Charity made vows. Up to that time, religious communities for women had been cloistered. The Daughters of Charity were the first order to take an active role outside convent walls. A year later her son married, and soon Louise was the grandmother of a baby girl. The next year Louise established the first mission of the Daughters of Charity outside of France in Warsaw, Poland.

In 1960 Pope John XXIII named Louise the patroness of social workers. Today there are 27,000 Daughters of Charity serving around the world.

REFLECT/RECORD *LUMIÈRES*

Louise said, "We must often think of what it is that God is asking of us." She called the vision she received in prayer a *lumière,* French for "light." Louise wrote her *lumière* on a piece of parchment and carried it with her to remind herself that even when life got hard, God was guiding her. Lead the children in prayerful reflection. First direct several deep breaths and slow exhalations to help the children focus. Dim the lights and burn a candle, or play soft music if you wish. Guide the children to ask God what he wants of them now. Then tell them to listen quietly for God's answer. Allow several seconds of silence. Pass out sheets of paper and pencils. Instruct the children to write down a few words or a sentence to remind them of any insight they received. Encourage them to carry their *lumière* in a pocket for a while.

PREPARE A GIVING TREE

Louise believed that love of God is best revealed in love of neighbor. Work with the St. Vincent de Paul Society or another charity such as Catholic Charities to find out the needs of the sick and poor in the parish or area in which you live. Write these out on individual slips of paper and attach them to a tree (or a large branch potted in sand) in the hall or church. Invite students, their families, and other parishioners to take the slips, supply the need, and return the slip with the items to be delivered to the needy. Names and addresses should not appear on these slips, but should be kept on a master sheet at the rectory, office, or Vincent de Paul center.

Catechist's Notes:

_____

_____

_____

_____

_____

_____

_____

_____

Saint Patrick

(c. 385–461)

March 17

Why are so many people wearing green today? You see shamrocks, parades, and parties to celebrate Saint Patrick. What do you know about him?

Patrick was the son of a Roman military officer stationed in Britain. Patrick grew up more interested in a career than in religion. At the age of 16, however, he was captured by Irish pirates and taken to Ireland. For six years he was put to work tending sheep. He suffered from cold and lack of food. Even more than these physical pains, Patrick suffered the loss of his family and freedom. All alone among the hills, he finally turned to God—his only hope as he looked for a way to return home. Eventually he escaped on a ship bound for Britain, paying his way by taking care of stolen dogs the crew planned to sell. His family was delighted when he returned home—but they were surprised to find a new Patrick. He now had a goal and a vision to serve God. Patrick began studying to become a priest.

When the Church called for missionaries to go to Ireland to teach the Christian faith, Patrick wanted to go, but he remembered his years of slavery. Then in a dream he heard the Irish people calling to him, "We beg you come and walk with us again." Now Church officials had to decide whether to send Patrick, for he was not well educated. However, Pope Celestine I saw in him the extraordinary qualities of a missionary. Patrick understood the people of Ireland because he had lived among them. He knew their language and already had spent 15 years in parish ministry. Most of all, Patrick believed in his vocation. At the age of 42, Patrick was ordained a bishop, and the pope sent him and several helpers to northern and western Ireland, where the Gospel had never been preached.

The people of Ireland lived in tribes and clans and worshipped pagan gods. Druids, who were like magicians or wizards, kept the people away from any other religion. Patrick knew he would have to convert the chief of a clan before he could win the people. Patrick courageously started with the most powerful clan at Tara. Immediately the chief respected Patrick, who was the son of a military official, who spoke the chief's language well, and who explained his beliefs with sincerity. The chief was converted, and Christianity began to take root in Ireland. Patrick often faced danger, for the Druids plotted to do away with him. But Patrick continued to preach the faith, ready for death at any time. He always remembered that he had been a slave, so he showed compassion for all classes of people. He set up monasteries and convents, established parishes, adapted Irish celebrations to Christian feasts, and worked to abolish paganism.

Patrick was a model missionary, and his methods of evangelization can be a guide for missionaries today. He helped the people of Ireland keep their beautiful history and culture and add to their heritage the richness of Christianity. Today Patrick is the patron saint of Ireland, but his feast is a worldwide day of celebration.

WITNESS TO THE GOSPEL

Patrick found his joy in serving God. Discuss with the children their own mission to witness the Gospel. For them at this time in their lives, this means witnessing in their classrooms, in their homes, on the way to and from school, and in the places they go with their friends.

PRAY AND MAKE SHAMROCKS

Give students copies of the morning prayer of praise called the Breastplate of St. Patrick or the Lorica. You may use the blackline master on page 451. The prayer was probably written down after Patrick died, but it does express Patrick's love and trust in God. After praying the prayer together, have each student make a shamrock out of light green paper, copy a line or two from the prayer onto it, and wear it for the rest of the day.

RESEARCH FOUNDING OF PARISH

The principal cathedral in New York City is dedicated to Saint Patrick. Because so many Irish immigrants had settled in that city, an Irish bishop was appointed and the cathedral dedicated appropriately. Have the students research the founding of their own parish church to discover why its name was selected.

SHARE CUSTOMS

St. Patrick's Day has inspired many colorful customs. Have the students share the ways their families and friends celebrate the day.

SHARE LEGENDS ABOUT PATRICK

The Irish had an oral culture. They passed on their history and heritage in poems and songs. Among their legends are many stories about Saint Patrick. Have the students find out about these stories and relate them to the class. A common story describes Patrick expelling all the poisonous snakes from Ireland. Many statues show Saint Patrick holding a shamrock. Ask the students to find out the story behind this representation.

LEARN ABOUT THE CELTIC CROSS

When Patrick came to Ireland, he did not find barbaric people. Though their culture was not as highly developed as that of the Romans, the people of Ireland were skilled craftsmen. When Christianity was adopted on the island, the people used their artistic talents to make chalices and religious articles. The Celtic (Irish) cross became very popular. Show the students an example of this art.

Celtic cross

PRAY FOR PEACE IN NORTHERN IRELAND

Patrick is said to have preached in the strife-torn city of Ulster in County Down. Help the students find out what is happening in Northern Ireland today. Discuss how religious division is far from the unity Patrick worked to build. As a group, pray for reconciliation and peace in Northern Ireland.

Saint Cyril of Jerusalem   March 18

(315–386)

Being well liked is not a requirement for being a saint. In fact Cyril's case was just the opposite. His brother bishops exiled him three times, he was accused of heresy, and another bishop sent to help Cyril administer his diocese left because the situation seemed hopeless.

Cyril was born and educated in Jerusalem and later became archbishop of that city. He was well acquainted with the Scriptures, and after he became a priest, his bishop put him in charge of the preparation of those to be baptized. The Church was facing a new situation. There were so many to be baptized that individual instruction was impossible. Cyril became well known for the clear, understandable catechesis he prepared for the baptismal candidates.

When Bishop Maximus was near death, he feared for the future of Jerusalem, "Mother of all the Churches." The heresy of Arianism, which denied the divinity of Christ, was spreading so fast and so far that even bishops and the emperor believed in it. Maximus wanted a successor who would be strong enough to stand up for the Church's teaching against heresy. No doubt Cyril was a good person for the position. Cyril was ordained a bishop in about 349 and began at once to bring law, order, and peace to Jerusalem. However, there was a staunch believer in Arianism in the neighboring diocese—a man named Acacius—who felt that the young bishop could be easily manipulated. When Acacius discovered he could not persuade Cyril to support Arianism, Acacius became angry. Now Cyril faced years of trouble. First Acacius and his friends accused Cyril of heresy. When Cyril remained firm in his faith, his enemies summoned him before a council of bishops, saying he had sold church property to feed the starving poor of the diocese. When Cyril refused to appear at the council, the group charged him with disobedience, and Cyril was exiled to Tarsus in southern Turkey. In exile he won the hearts of the people with his preaching.

When Cyril was finally allowed to return to Jerusalem, the Holy City was violent with heresy, schism, fighting, and crime. Even Gregory of Nyssa (later a saint himself), who was sent to help Cyril, left because conditions were so bad. Twice again before his death, Cyril was exiled over Arian disputes. He died at the age of 70. Fifteen hundred years later, in 1822, Cyril was completely vindicated and was declared a Doctor of the Church.

Ten years after Cyril's death, Lady Egeria made a pilgrimage to the Holy Land and wrote in her letters that she found a peaceful Christian community celebrating the liturgy and serving the poor. This period of peace was the result of the efforts of Bishop Cyril, who personally suffered to heal the wounds Arianism had inflicted on the Church. The example of Cyril teaches us to be like the Divine Healer, bringing peace where there is misunderstanding and disagreement.

LEARN FROM CYRIL OF JERUSALEM

Cyril of Jerusalem is remembered for the sermons he wrote instructing those preparing to be baptized. This section of Cyril's instruction to the catechumens emphasizes his deep reverence for Baptism. Read it to the class and thank God together for the gifts of Baptism.

> My brothers, this is truly a great occasion. Approach it with caution. You are standing in front of God and in the presence of the hosts of angels. The Holy Spirit is about to impress his seal on each of your souls. You are about to be pressed into the service of a great king.

DECORATE BAPTISMAL CANDLES

Have the students ask their parents the date of their Baptism and then mark it on their calendars. Let them each decorate a large white candle, using acrylic paints, to be lit on the anniversary of their Baptism.

DISCOVER DOCTRINES IN THE CREED

Cyril was influential at the Council of Constantinople, where the Nicene Creed was accepted. This council of bishops was especially strong in accepting and affirming the Holy Spirit as a divine Person in the Trinity and in opposing the Arians. Have the students read the Nicene Creed. Tell them that creeds were written to teach doctrine, and ask them to find the many doctrines included in this creed.

"TOUR" JERUSALEM

Jerusalem was called the Mother of Churches when Cyril was bishop. Have the students do group projects on Jerusalem. Some may collect pictures of the modern or ancient city, or search the Internet. Others may report on the importance of this city in salvation history or on historical events that occurred there.

BE PEACEMAKERS

Cyril was a peacemaker. Suggest that the students try to bring reconciliation to a situation involving their families or friends.

PRAY FOR THE BISHOP

Pray for the bishop of your diocese, that he will be strong in doing what is right.

Catechist's Notes:

_____

_____

_____

_____

_____

_____

_____

Saint Joseph, Husband of Mary

March 19

(first century)

If there were a photo album of Jesus' family, what pictures would be in it? Neither Mary nor Joseph appear much in Scripture, but some beautiful images are found there.

The Gospels of both Matthew and Luke show Joseph as the gentle but strong protector of Mary, the Mother of Jesus. When Matthew traces Jesus' human ancestry, Joseph's family is given (Matthew 1:16). Luke identifies Mary as the betrothed of Joseph, of the house and family of David (Luke 1:27). This "righteous man" does not know of the miracle worked in Mary, who is to be the Mother of God, and so he faces a terrible dilemma when he realizes that the woman he loves and to whom he is engaged is pregnant (Matthew 1:18–25). Through a dream Joseph is informed of what has occurred, and his loving protection of Mary increases. As the time for Jesus to be born draws near, Mary and Joseph must go to Bethlehem—not only to be enrolled among the members of the house of David, but also so that the Messiah will be born in the city of the great king, as prophecy foretold.

At Jesus' birth Joseph guards Jesus and Mary (Luke 2:4–20). Joseph is present also, protecting Mary as her legal husband, when the child is circumcised and when he is offered to his Father at the Presentation. With Mary, Joseph hears Simeon's prophecy about Mary's sufferings (Luke 2:21–35). When the child is in danger because of King Herod's hatred, Joseph guards and provides for his family in Egypt until he can safely take them back to Nazareth (Matthew 2:13–23). During one of her keenest sufferings, Mary has Joseph to rely upon. When Jesus is lost in Jerusalem, Joseph and Mary seek him and take him back to Nazareth (Luke 2:41–52). After this, Joseph slips out of the Scriptures, except for a few references to Jesus as the "carpenter's son." The word for "carpenter" used in Scripture means a worker in stone, metal, or wood. It is thought that Joseph died before Jesus began his public life.

These scriptural pictures of Joseph reveal him as a "just man," an obedient man, a good and loving husband and father.

Little attention was given to Joseph, but then people began to consider his role and his virtues. Public veneration of Saint Joseph existed in the Eastern Coptic church in the fourth century. The Western church began to celebrate his feast in the sixth century. Pope Pius IX proclaimed Saint Joseph the Patron of the Universal Church in 1870. Since then Saint Joseph has been named patron of different groups and countries. In 1955 Pius XII made May 1 the feast of St. Joseph the Worker. In 1961 Pope John XXIII proclaimed Joseph the protector of Vatican Council II and in 1962 included his name in Eucharistic Prayer I of the Mass.

WRITE THANK-YOU NOTES

Have the students make cards or write thank-you notes to their fathers, grandfathers, uncles, brothers, or other significant father figures in their lives. You may wish to schedule a similar activity later (perhaps in May) for writing to mothers, grandmothers, aunts, sisters, or significant mother figures.

LEARN FROM ART

Have the students examine the statue or picture of Joseph in the parish church. Talk about how he is represented and what characteristics the artist portrays. If possible, display paintings of the Holy Family or of Joseph alone. Discuss how representations of Saint Joseph have changed.

DISCUSS AGE OF JOSEPH

Sometimes Joseph is pictured as an old man. However, the custom of his time was that a man should marry between the ages of 13 and 19 and the girl should be between the ages of 12 and 16. Joseph would most likely have observed the customs of the day. Clarify this fact with the students.

WRITE ABOUT A JUST PERSON

Joseph is described in the Gospel as "just." The biblical notion of "just" is very broad and includes such ideas as law-abiding and holy—one transformed by God and open to his will. Have the students read the description of the just man given in Sirach (Ecclesiasticus) 35:1–6. Then ask them to write about any person they know who seems to fit this description. Tell them to explain why they chose the person they did.

WRITE PRAYERS TO SAINT JOSEPH

By papal documents Joseph has been made patron of prayer and the interior life, the poor, those in authority, priests and religious, travelers, and devotion to Mary. He is the patron of Mexico (1555), Canada (1624), Bohemia (1655), the Chinese missions (1678), Belgium (1689), and the Church's campaign against atheistic communism (1937). Joseph is also known as the patron of the fathers of families, bursars, artisans, manual workers, carpenters, and all those who desire a happy death (a widespread devotion since the 17th century). Acquaint the students with these titles. Have them each choose the title that means the most to them and write a short prayer to Joseph under that title.

Catechist's Notes:

_____

_____

_____

_____

Saint Toribio of Mogrovejo

March 23

(1538–1606)

Toribio, a member of a wealthy Spanish family had won scholarships to college; he was a brilliant professor of law at Salamanca University. He was a sharp judge at the court of the Inquisition, prudently dispensing justice. His responsibility and insight were praised by Philip II, King of Spain. Unexpectedly the pope appointed this layman archbishop of Lima, Peru. The news shocked Toribio. He frantically cited all the rules that forbade making laymen bishops. He was not a priest! He hadn't volunteered! But the pope, the king, and his friends knew that protestations were useless. Toribio's holiness and courage showed in every decision he made. God needed a man who would bring Christ's teachings and his peace and justice to the Church in South America. Greedy Spanish conquerors had taken over Peru. Those wealthy landlords were guilty of every type of oppression. In some cases priests had joined in neglect of the people. Toribio faced a critical situation when he rode into Lima, Peru, in 1581.

But Toribio was an energetic and zealous man who lived by strict principles. Immediately he began visiting every parish and mission in his diocese. This took seven years. He traveled thousands of miles without a companion through vast unknown areas plagued by wild animals and tropical diseases. Sometimes he went two or three days without food or a bed. The condition of the native people horrified Toribio. Thousands were poor and uneducated. Though baptized they had little idea of Christianity because there were no catechisms or Bibles in their language and no priests. The rich Spanish conquerors disregarded the poor. They lived in mansions and were interested only in making fortunes. Toribio resolved to make some changes.

Toribio gathered the bishops for the Third Council of Lima. They decided to print catechisms in the local Indian language, to set up classes for the poor, to regulate the administration of the sacraments, and to reform the priests. This last point was met with protests from priests who were content to serve only the rich. But Toribio was firm. He set an example by learning the native language. He spent himself in baptizing and confirming, in building hospitals, and in establishing the first seminary in the New World. He spoke out even to the King against the way the Spanish treated the poor. He was unusually effective because he loved Christ and did not work for his own interests.

Toribio was an old man, visiting a mission, when he felt sick. He dragged himself into a church and begged for the Sacrament of the Anointing of the Sick, and then died in that little mountain town. Toribio was the kind of witness a bishop should be.

COMPARE TWO HEROES

Efforts to bring justice, peace, and mercy continue into our times. Have the students compare the lives of Saint Toribio and Archbishop Oscar Romero (1917–1980).

TAKE A STAND FOR JUSTICE

Toribio had the courage to speak up for those who suffered, even though he became unpopular. Help students think of a situation where they can stand up for the right thing. Make plans to take a stand for justice.

HAVE A FIESTA

Enjoy the gifts of the Spanish and Latin Americans to world culture. Play music, show art, and eat food from these countries.

RESEARCH GEOGRAPHY AND HISTORY

Toribio of Mogrovejo was the bishop of the diocese of Lima, Peru. Have the students find Lima on a map. Point out that the majority of the population was Indian. Have the students look up information on Peru to find the answers to the following questions:

1. Who first brought Catholicism to the natives of Peru?

2. Why did the Spanish conquerors come to the New World?

3. If there were so many baptized Catholics, why were there no priests to care for all the missions?

4. Why was the poverty of these people not the same as the poverty of the spirit praised by Jesus in the Bible?

5. What changes did the Spanish conquerors make in their style of living after being made aware of the problems they caused?

Catechist's Notes:

_____

_____

_____

_____

_____

_____

_____

_____

Annunciation of the Lord

March 25

"I have some good news for you!" If someone gave you this message, what would be your response? Would you be cautious? Curious? Excited? You probably would want that person to tell you the news immediately. John's Gospel tells us the good news that "God so loved the world that he gave his only Son, so that everyone who believes in him . . . may have eternal life" (John 3:16).

At a moment in time that we now call the Annunciation, God revealed this good news to Mary. She was the first to hear the good news and to believe that God would do what he promised. Her faith assured her that nothing is impossible for God. Mary also heard God's invitation calling her to be the virgin mother of his Son. This call meant that her life in the future would be different from what she might have expected. This call meant that Jesus would be formed in her womb, and that she, as his mother, would nourish and care for him. This call meant that she had a special place in God's plan for salvation. She would be able to bring Christ to everyone she met.

Mary heard this word of God and responded, "I am the handmaid of the Lord. Let what you have said be done to me" (Luke 1:38). In her yes response, Mary agreed to God's plan because she wanted what God wanted. She was willing to accept all the joy and pain, all the unexpected events that would help her and guide her. She was willing to bring Christ to a waiting world.

In our lives let us, like Mary, listen to God's word and believe in God's promises. Like Mary, let us be ready to say yes to God's plan for our lives. Let us try by our words and actions to become so much like her Son, Jesus, that we bring him to everyone we meet.

DRAW ON SCRIPTURE

Slowly read Luke 1:26–38, the account of the Annunciation. Ask the students to jot down words or phrases that strike them during the reading. After the reading have them draw symbols that capture the meaning of the words or phrases they noted. Let students share their reflections and symbols with the class. Point out that a single Scripture passage can be very rich in meaning.

TALK ABOUT VOCATIONS

The call that Mary received from God was a call to a way of life. Have the class list the various calls, or vocations, a person might receive: married life, single life, priesthood, diaconate, consecrated life as a brother or sister. Have the students as a class compose a prayer, asking God to lead each one of them to know his or her vocation in life.

PRAY THE ANGELUS

Remind the students that the Angelus is a traditional prayer about the mystery of the Incarnation and is usually prayed each day in the morning, at noon, and in the evening. Have the students pray the Angelus at the end of the class.

STUDY ART OF THE ANNUNCIATION

Post various artistic representations of the Annunciation. Discuss with the students the way each artist portrays Mary. Have them choose the picture that best matches the way they understand her.

MATCH PROPHECIES OF JESUS

In the account of the Annunciation, the angel refers to some qualities that Mary's child will have. These qualities were first mentioned in the Old Testament. Have the students match the qualities and the Scripture references.

1. Isaiah 41:14   Son of the Most High
2. Daniel 6:28   great
3. Psalm 48:1   Holy One
4. Exodus 15:18   king
5. Genesis 14:19–20 savior (meaning of the name *Jesus*)

Answers:
1. Holy One
2. savior
3. great
4. king
5. Son of the Most High

PRAY A SCRIPTURAL DECADE OF THE ROSARY

Divide the Annunciation account of Luke 1:26–38 into 10 sections as follows: verses 26–27, verse 28, verses 29–30, verse 31, verses 32–33, verse 34, verse 35, verse 36, verse 37, verse 38. Then have the class pray the First Joyful Mystery of the Rosary, while volunteers read a section from the Gospel account before the recitation of each Hail Mary.

BRING CHRIST TO OTHERS

Mary brought Christ to others. Have the students plan ways to bring the story of the Annunciation to a younger class through coloring books, a play, or a puppet show.

RELATE FEAST TO SAINT JOSEPH

The feast of the Annunciation is celebrated as a Marian feast. However, in Matthew the angel of the Lord appears to Joseph rather than to Mary. Have the students read Matthew 1:18–25 and explain why the feast is also a feast of St. Joseph.

Saint Margaret Clitherow   March 26

(1556–1586)

Margaret was an upstanding citizen of York, a city in northern England. Her family lived in a comfortable house, and her husband, John, owned a butcher shop on the same street. John was a wealthy and well-known man who held various positions in city government. Margaret and John Clitherow had three children: Henry, William, Anne. Margaret was a loving wife and mother and a good neighbor. She kept a tidy home and helped out in her husband's shop. But there was one thing wrong.

On Sundays Margaret didn't attend church—the Church of England, that is. That was the official church in England, and Queen Elizabeth was the head of it. The law required everyone to attend Anglican services. Margaret did not go, though John did. This raised suspicions. And the suspicions were true! Raised a Protestant, Margaret had become Catholic about three years after her marriage. Practicing the Catholic faith was against the law. Harboring a priest, attending Mass, or teaching religion were punishable by death. Margaret committed all of those crimes. In fact Margaret was arrested and imprisoned several times over a period of seven years.

Margaret had risked her life—to become Catholic. A local doctor's wife supported other Catholics. Catholic women went to her house to deliver their babies and have them secretly baptized. When a priest was there, the doctor's wife would send a message to Margaret, saying that she needed help with a birth. Margaret would hurry over to "help," but actually to take instructions to become Catholic.

When the doctor's wife was arrested, Margaret invited the priests and people to gather in her own home to celebrate Mass. Margaret fixed in her home a secret room where a priest could hide, with a passageway for him to escape.

Margaret and John sent their oldest son to a seminary in France. (Eventually their other son also became a priest, and their daughter became a nun.) John was called in to explain to the authorities why his son had left the country. In the meantime two sheriffs went to search the Clitherow house. There they discovered a religion class. When they seized the teacher, a boy cried out that he was not the priest. A search revealed the passageway and the cupboard where Margaret kept the chalice, book, and vestments for Mass. Margaret was arrested.

Margaret did not want her family to testify at her trial because they would either have to lie or testify against her. To the judge she stated, "Having made no offense, I need no trial." She was sentenced to be pressed to death. She was laid on the ground, and a wooden slab was put on top of her. Weights adding up to 800 pounds were dropped until she was crushed. Her last words were "Jesus, have mercy on me."

ACTIVITIES

WRITE EPITAPHS

When John Clitherow heard his wife's sentence, he cried out, "Let them take all I have and save my wife, for she is the best wife in all England and the best Catholic also!" Ask the students to imagine what their families or friends would say about them. Then have them write on a sheet of paper a short description of themselves that they would like to be true when they die. Have them write on the other side of the paper what they will do now to make their words be true.

RESEARCH OTHER ENGLISH MARTYRS

Margaret was canonized in 1970, along with 39 other English martyrs. Encourage interested students to research the stories of the martyrs of England and Wales. Have the students compare and contrast the professions or careers, the various "crimes," and the means of death of these courageous men and women.

STUDY THE ISSUE OF ESTABLISHED RELIGION

Margaret's story shows the dangers of establishing a state religion. Ask the students if they think there are any advantages. Have them list pros and cons. Ask them to consider what would happen if Catholicism were the established religion. Then ask them to discuss in small groups the best way to lead people to worship God and live a moral life. Have the groups report their ideas to the class.

Catechist's Notes:

_____

_____

_____

_____

_____

_____

_____

_____

_____

_____

Saint Francis of Paola

April 2

(1416–1507)

Some saints are very young when they see what God is calling them to do. When Francis was only 13, he made a pilgrimage to Rome and Assisi with his parents. He was so impressed that he went home and did an unusual thing—he became a hermit in a cave overlooking the sea. By the time Francis was 20 years old, other men who had heard of his holiness had joined him. After still others entered the group, they took the name Hermits of St. Francis of Assisi, or the Franciscan Minim Friars. *Minim* meant they were "the least in the household of God." Like Francis, most of the friars were charitable, uneducated men who wanted to do penance for love of God. Francis felt that a person had to do heroic mortification in order to grow spiritually. To the vows of poverty, chastity, and obedience, Francis added a fourth vow: a perpetual Lenten fast. Interestingly this order attracted many candidates, and the whole countryside praised God for the gifts of prophecy and miracles that Francis possessed.

Though Francis loved the contemplative life of prayer and penance, he later felt God was calling him to an active life of defending the poor and the oppressed. Francis was fearless and did not hesitate to confront King Ferdinand of Naples and his sons for their wrongdoing. The fame of Francis spread far and wide. In 1482, when King Louis XI of France was dying after having suffered a stroke, he begged that Francis come to cure him, promising Francis money and favors. Francis at first refused, but Pope Sixtus IV ordered him to go to France, care for the king, and prepare him for death. When the king saw Francis, he fell on his knees, pleading for a miracle. Francis replied that the lives of kings are in the hands of God, and Louis ought to ask God, not Francis, to cure him. Francis did not settle into the ease and luxury of the court life; rather, he influenced the fate of nations, restoring peace between France and Great Britain by advising a marriage that united the families of the ruling parties. Francis also helped bring peace between France and Spain.

Francis died while he was at the French court. Though his miracles were numerous and well known, he was canonized for his humility and discernment in blending the contemplative life with the active one. He is a good example for busy people of today.

ACTIVITIES

MAKE PRAYER REMINDERS

Francis learned that both work and prayer are important. Remind the students that no matter how busy their days are, they should still remember the need for prayer. Suggest examples of morning and evening prayers. Have them make prayer reminders for their bedrooms.

DISCUSS THE PURPOSE OF PENANCE

Point out that Francis practiced penance as a help to spiritual growth. Be sure the students understand why Fridays are prescribed days of penance for Catholics. Tell the students they may abstain from meat on Friday or perform another penance, such as giving up snacks between meals or not watching TV. Talk about how small penances could help them grow closer to Jesus. (These penances help if you unite your penance with the suffering of Jesus, if you offer them in repentance for sin, and if you use them as a way to learn and strengthen self-discipline.)

PRAY FOR PEOPLE WHO WORK AT SEA

Because many of Francis's miracles were connected with the sea, he was named the patron of seafarers by Pope Pius XII. Encourage the students to pray for those whose occupations involve work on seas, lakes, and rivers.

DESIGN BOOKMARKS

Though Francis was an uneducated man, people said that his words were so wise that it was as if the Holy Spirit were speaking. Have the students use a concordance or the index of a study Bible to find passages where Jesus praises the simple and lowly. Let them design bookmarks using the quotations.

Catechist's Notes:

_____

_____

_____

_____

_____

_____

_____

_____

Blessed Laura Alvarado Cardozo

April 2

(1875–1967)

If you are looking for Mother María, you can find her in the chapel, or in the kitchen, or in the hospital.

In the kitchen she is making communion bread, hosts. Mother María prays as she works. She contemplates the wonder of it. Just bits of bread, yet Jesus Christ himself chooses to dwell within this host. What great love Jesus has for all. Mother María wants to share that great love. She distributes the hosts to nearby parishes free of charge.

Mother prays in the hospital and orphanage too. With great love and tenderness, she washes the children, brings broth and cool cloths for the feverish old ones. How small and unimportant they look, the poor, the weak, the elderly, the very young ones. Yet Jesus Christ chooses to dwell within them. He inhabits their pain, their misery, their loneliness. María often tells her spiritual daughters, "Those rejected by everyone are ours; those no one wants to take are ours."

In the chapel she contemplates the Lord of the universe who chooses to dwell in the tabernacle. She sees his humility and great love. And she reaffirms her great love for him. On the day she received her First Communion, when she was 13 years old, Laura Evangelista Alvarado Cardozo made a promise to Jesus. She vowed that she would be his forever, just as he was hers.

She would be humble and full of love. She would always be there for those who needed her most.

Laura was born in Choroní, Venezuela. When she was 17, she told her pastor, Father Vicente López Aveledo, about the promise she had made to Jesus. He allowed her to make a vow of perpetual virginity. Father Aveledo had founded a hospital in nearby Maracay, and Laura began to work there. During a smallpox epidemic, she devoted herself to the care of the sick. "Nothing frightens me," she said. She had given everything to Jesus.

When she was 26, Laura and Father Aveledo founded a religious congregation of women to care for the sick, the elderly, and the orphans. They were called the Augustinian Recollects of the Heart of Jesus, and Laura took the name María de San José, or María of Saint Joseph. In the following years, she opened 37 homes for the elderly and orphans in 11 cities in Venezuela.

She was buried in the chapel of the Immaculate Conception Home in Maracay, where thousands of pilgrims come to give thanks for the blessings they have received through her intercession.

The Augustinian Recollects of the Heart of Jesus continue María's work in Venezuela, and they made the hosts for the Mass of her beatification on May 7, 1995.

VISIT THE BLESSED SACRAMENT

Take the students to church to spend some time of prayer and quiet before the tabernacle. If your parish has regular exposition and adoration of the Blessed Sacrament, try to take them during those hours. Base the length of the visit on the age of the students.

OFFER GIFTS

Discuss with the class the significance of the bread and wine offered at the Eucharist. The gifts of bread and wine represent the work of creation and the work of human hands— their lives offered to God.

- Encourage the children to sign up with their families to present the gifts of bread and wine at Sunday Eucharist.

- Have the children make paper hosts. Direct them to write on their host something they will do to show love for another person, especially someone who is small or sick or old. Collect these offerings in an attractive basket or plate.

MAKE COMMUNION BREAD

Have the students find out where and by whom the hosts your parish uses are made. If your parish uses homemade bread for the Eucharist, find out if the students can help with this ministry.

SING THE MAGNIFICAT

Blessed Maria of St. Joseph had a deep devotion to Mary. She once said, "I would like to live and die singing the Magnificat." Briefly discuss with the students the kind of life that would be. Invite them to recite the Magnificat (Luke 1:46–55). You may use the blackline master on page 452 to make copies of it for the students. If your parish hymnal has a musical setting or if you have a recording, sing the Magnificat.

Catechist's Notes:

_____

_____

_____

_____

_____

_____

_____

_____

Saint Isidore of Seville

April 4

(c. 560–636)

People who knew Isidore as a boy may have wondered just how he would turn out in the future. After the death of their parents, Isidore was cared for by his elder brother Leander. Leander was a monk who later became the archbishop of Seville and was venerated as a saint. Leander wanted his younger brother to be an educated person, but Isidore did not like the hard studies in which his brother tutored him. He sometimes didn't do his homework and even skipped his studies. One day (when he should have been studying) Isidore found an old stone well. He noticed that there were grooves in the stone walls where thin wet ropes had worn the stone away. He was fascinated by the discovery that such thin rope could alter very hard stone. Isidore must have been pretty smart after all. He figured out that just as the rope could wear away the rock by consistently cutting a little bit at a time, so he could be successful at his studies if he tried consistently. Isidore made a resolution to persevere in his studies, and in later years he became known as the most learned man of his era. His influence was felt in politics, history, education, and religion.

Politics: Isidore presided over the council of Toledo in 633. This council helped settle the differences between the king and a rival for the throne. This council also decreed that Jews be given the freedom to keep their religion rather than being forced to become Christian.

History: Isidore wrote biographies and a history of the world from creation to his own times. This work is useful even today as a source book on Spanish history.

Education: Isidore worked to establish in each diocese a college to instruct seminarians. This action shows dramatically the change in attitude that Isidore had experienced since his youth. His principal work was a brand new idea in the seventh century. He wrote an encyclopedia that contained all the secular and religious knowledge available at his time: from astronomy to geography, from monsters to household utensils. What an undertaking!

Religion: Isidore worked hard to renew the Church in Spain. He greatly encouraged the reading of Sacred Scripture. Some of his theological works helped shape the spiritual outlook of the Middle Ages. Isidore was declared a Doctor of the Church in 1722.

At this point you may be wondering why this successful man was declared a saint. It was not because he wrote an encyclopedia, founded a college, or helped a king. Isidore is a saint because he worked hard at being open to God's love and grace. He was also outstanding in helping the poor. It was his love for God and others that gave Isidore the best success of all!

ACTIVITIES

TAKE A VOTE

Isidore of Seville has been unofficially called the patron of the Internet. Ask the students to debate whether this is a good title for him. Then let them hold a mock vote on the issue.

HOLD AN INFO EXPO

In honor of Isidore, hold an Information Exposition (Info Expo). Put a variety of subjects on slips of paper, enough for all the students. Gear the subjects for the grade level of the children. This can be very simple or more challenging. Let each child draw one slip, research that subject on the Internet or in an encyclopedia, and prepare a one-minute summary. Have the students share their findings with the class.

CHART PROGRESS TOWARD A GOAL

Isidore found that consistent effort made a big difference. Have the students think of one goal they have been trying to achieve, such as changing a personal habit or improving a family relationship. Have the students make a chart for a one-week plan, write in one thing they can do each day to achieve their goal, and record their progress and results.

BE HOMEWORK HELPERS

Isidore had difficulty with his homework.

- Suggest that the students make homework resolutions, such as "Keep trying" or "Take one step at a time."

- Organize a tutoring program. In religious education, older students may help younger children learn prayers or the Ten Commandments.

- Suggest that the students do all their homework this week in honor of Saint Isidore.

USE AN IMAGE FOR INSPIRATION

The thin, wet rope wearing away the thick stone wall was a metaphor that Isidore used for the way that he should work at his studies. Have the students think of an image that illustrates how they can work in school or at home. Have them write about the image or draw a picture of their own image.

Catechist's Notes:

_____

_____

_____

_____

_____

_____

Saint Vincent Ferrer

(1350–1419)

In the 1300s and 1400s, the Catholic world was in havoc. Three men claimed to be pope. Kings, princes, priests, and laypeople fought in support of the men who claimed the Chair of Peter. This chaos in the Church led to the Western Schism. During these years God raised up a Dominican priest, Vincent Ferrer, to heal the Catholic world by his preaching and to prepare the way for a Church under one head.

Vincent was a man with a fiery spirit; when he joined the Dominicans, he zealously practiced penance, study, and prayer. Vincent was gifted as a preacher, and he was well liked. What made his preaching effective was that he practiced what he preached. Many people joined or returned to the faith. He had to preach in the open air in France, Spain, and Italy because no church was big enough to hold the crowds.

But the schism in the Church distressed Vincent. He wanted to heal this division. Even the holiest of people can be misled. Pope Urban VI was the real pope, and he lived in Rome. But Vincent and many others thought that Clement VII and his successor Benedict XIII, who lived in Avignon in France, were the true popes. Using his eloquence and learning, Vincent convinced kings, princes, clergy, and almost all of the people of Spain to give their loyalty to Clement and Benedict. After Clement VII died, Vincent tried to get both Benedict and the pope in Rome to abdicate so that a new election could be held. It hurt Vincent to see that Benedict's stubbornness and pride refused peace.

Gradually Vincent came to see the error in Benedict's claim to the papacy. Discouraged and ill, Vincent begged Christ to show him the truth. In a vision he saw Jesus with Saints Dominic and Francis commanding him to "go through the world preaching Christ." For the next 20 years, Vincent spread the Good News throughout Europe. He rarely stayed in one place longer than a day. He fasted, preached, worked miracles, and by his enthusiasm for Christ, he drew many people to become faithful Christians. Again Vincent returned to Benedict in Avignon and asked him to resign. Benedict refused. Even though he was old and tired, Vincent knew what he had to do. While Benedict was presiding over a large assembly in a prominent church, Vincent, though close to death, mounted the pulpit and preached an unforgettable sermon. He denounced Benedict as the false pope and encouraged everyone to be faithful to the Catholic Church in Rome. Benedict fled, knowing his supporters had deserted him.

Later the Council of Constance met to end the Western Schism. Vincent refused any part in the Council, fearing more division. Fortunately the Council resolved the problem in the Church. Vincent died soon after. On his deathbed he asked for the account of the Passion to be read. Vincent models fidelity to the Church; despite confusion and tension, he always sought to defend the truth.

ACTIVITIES

DISCUSS SPIRITUAL GIFTS

Vincent was favored with the gift of tongues. It is said that when preaching in his own language, he was understood by Germans, Hungarians, Swedes, and others. Have the students read what Saint Paul has to say about spiritual gifts (1 Corinthians 12:1–11). Discuss the purpose of spiritual gifts.

MAKE QUOTATION PLAQUES

St. Vincent prepared all his homilies at the foot of the crucifix. He told others, "Never begin or end your study except by prayer" and "Consult God more than your books; ask God to help you understand what you read."

- Have each student choose one of these sayings. Provide supplies for everyone to make a plague of the quotation he or she chose.

- Post one or both of the quotations in the classroom to remind the students to ask God to guide their studies.

PREPARE FOR RECONCILIATION

The need for reconciliation was a theme of Vincent's preaching. Stress to the students the importance of the need for conversion. Read and discuss the two Eucharistic Prayers for Reconciliation. Encourage the students to make use of the Sacrament of Penance frequently.

PRAY FOR THE POPE

Remind the students to pray for the present pope, who bears responsibility for the Church.

Catechist's Notes:

_____

_____

_____

_____

_____

_____

_____

_____

_____

_____

Saint John Baptist de La Salle

April 7

(1651–1719)

Father John Baptist de La Salle disliked the awful smells and the sights of the slums. His good looks, polished manners, intelligence, and wealth set him apart from the poor. In 17th-century France, education was reserved for the rich.

By chance La Salle met a man who was establishing schools for poor boys. La Salle decided to help. He secured five teachers and rented a home for the boys. But when he checked on his school, he was shocked. The teachers were beating and insulting the boys. Some of the teachers could not read or write, and they spent their nights in taverns, drinking or playing cards.

Though he hated becoming further involved, La Salle decided he had to bring order to the school. He found teachers of better quality and trained them to be religious educators. La Salle discussed the problems of the school with his staff and worked to give the teachers a strong sense of self-respect. Gradually he saw that he must identify with his teachers, so he gave away his fortune and dedicated himself to education.

Some teachers thrived under La Salle's training in faith, prayer, and order. Soon he saw the possibility of a religious congregation of men to educate the poor. He founded the Brothers of Christian Schools, which was different from other orders of the time. In La Salle's community, no member would be a priest. The main purposes of the congregation were to train teachers and to provide religious education for the poor.

La Salle's leadership enabled him to influence education in four ways: the teachers taught in the language of the people, not in Latin; individual instruction was replaced by classroom teaching under well-prepared teachers; the students had to be silent during teaching; and the teachers kept the students occupied. The students attended daily Mass, learned the catechism and prayers, and had religion integrated into other subjects, as well as taught in separate classes.

By motivating the students to prepare for a career and to guide their lives by Christian principles, La Salle helped them become self-confident and strong Catholics. His schools attracted boys who could afford to pay for schooling. La Salle's teachers were in demand too. Other instructors became jealous, criticized his methods, and tried to bring lawsuits to ruin his work. But his efforts were praised by the people. King James II of England sent 50 young gentlemen from his court to be educated at La Salle's school. La Salle opened boarding schools for poor boys who learned practical skills. He founded schools for delinquents from wealthy families so the young men would not go to prison.

When La Salle died on Good Friday in 1719, he was praised as a man who lived and taught love, just as Christ, the Master Teacher, had.

ACTIVITIES

TRY TEACHING

Invite the boys in the class to help teach today.

EVALUATE YOUR PROGRAM

John Baptist de La Salle believed the main purpose of education was to help young people grow in becoming good Christians. Hold a class discussion on how your school or parish program achieves this purpose.

TREAT THE CATECHISTS

Discuss why religious education is the most important kind of education. Help students plan a special treat for the teachers of religion in your school or parish, or for your Director of Religious Education.

MAKE POSTERS

Help the students think about the elements they appreciate in their Catholic education: the Christian atmosphere, the encouragement of teachers, the good example of classmates, the emphasis on prayer and Scripture, and so on. Have them work together to make posters that highlight some of the projects and activities of their Catholic school or religious education program. Post these in the church entrance or parish gathering area.

INFLUENCE OTHERS

Brainstorm ways students can bring a more religious atmosphere into their school. List their ideas on a large sheet of paper. Choose one idea each week as a special project.

INVITE A SPEAKER

If there is a school nearby operated by the Christian Brothers, invite a speaker or arrange for students to visit the school.

Catechist's Notes:

_____

_____

_____

_____

_____

_____

_____

_____

Saint Julie Billiart

(1751–1816)

What is or was your favorite make-believe game? For Julie Billiart, it was playing school.

Julie lived in France where her father ran a small shop. When Julie was in her teens, her father's store was invaded by robbers, who took most of its stock. Later an enemy shot at her father in the room where Julie was also sitting. No one was hurt, but the event affected Julie's nervous system, and she was struck with paralysis.

The French Revolution was over, but the Church was still suppressed. Julie was firm in her faith. She gathered children to her bedside to speak to them about God and to tell them stories from the Bible. Julie was a delightful teacher, and the children loved her. Soon, however, it was reported to the government that Julie was teaching religion. To avoid arrest, Julie had to be smuggled from house to house, and each move was very painful for her. Finally a room was found for her at the home of a wealthy woman, Françoise Blin de Bourdon. It was to Françoise, who became a close friend, that Julie confided her dream of founding a community of women who would teach the faith to children. How could she accomplish such a dream? She was paralyzed and penniless. Julie and Françoise prayed.

One day, after a novena to the Sacred Heart, the priest who was Julie's confessor commanded her: "If you have any faith in the Sacred Heart of Jesus, walk." And Julie stepped forward! She was cured! Now at the age of 53, she began her active life. Together with Françoise, who gave her money to the project, Julie founded the Sisters of Notre Dame to care for orphans, to educate poor girls, and to train Christian teachers. What John Baptist de La Salle had done for poor boys about a hundred years earlier, Julie and Françoise now began to do for poor girls. Julie's energy, joy, and holiness were visible. The deepest lesson she had learned during her years of pain and sickness was "God is good." Soon other women joined Julie and Françoise in their work to spread the good news of the goodness of God. One day Julie had a vision of sisters in religious habits, standing around the cross of Christ. A voice said, "Here are the daughters I will give you in the institute marked by the cross." Indeed this was true. Julie's work was marked by the cross. The government had no use for Catholicism. Some of Julie's own sisters betrayed her, people withdrew financial support from her schools, and bishops were skeptical about her work. But through all this misunderstanding, Julie's confidence grew. With great hope she started schools, trained teachers, and performed countless works of charity. People called her "the walking love of God."

When she died Julie did not know that her sisters would one day be spreading the Good News of Christ around the world. Julie's story gives courage to all Christians. Through all her difficulties, Julie's motto was "How good is the good God!"

TRY TEACHING

Invite the girls in the class to help teach today.

SHARE A SMILE

Julie was cheerful and hopeful even when experiencing great pain or sorrow. Julie knew that everything God permitted could work toward the good. Challenge the students to greet everyone today with a smile, even when—especially when—they are not feeling happy themselves.

ENJOY A TREAT

As a teacher, Julie showed genuine love and concern for her students. Because she wanted the classroom to be a pleasant place, she gladly helped those who had difficulties. Plan to do something nice for the class today.

FIND OUT MORE

In the beginning of their apostolate, the Sisters of Notre Dame taught only girls, but now they teach both boys and girls. Invite a Sister of Notre Dame to speak about Saint Julie and the work her sisters do in the world today. Or have interested students use the Internet to find out more about the Sisters of Notre Dame and give a short report to the class.

MAKE A PLAQUE

Julie's motto was "How good is the good God." Have the children make and decorate plaques using these words and then display them in their homes.

MAKE BOOKLETS FOR YOUNG CHILDREN

Julie wanted all children to know about the life of Jesus and to practice their faith. Have the class make a book with stories and illustrations about the teaching and ministry of Jesus. Some of the students could share the book with students in a lower grade.

Catechist's Notes:

_____

_____

_____

_____

_____

_____

_____

_____

Saint Stanislaus

(c. 1030–1097)

April 11

Today everyone knows movie and TV stars, popular singers and musicians, and outstanding athletes.

Stanislaus was a legend in his day. In 1072 the people of Kraków, Poland, were without a bishop, and they begged Pope Alexander II to give them Stanislaus as their spiritual leader, which the pope did.

This well-loved Polish leader, who was so enthusiastically acclaimed, was generous to the poor and the needy. His courage proved itself when he opposed King Boleslaus II for unjust wars, violence, cheating the poor, and abducting a nobleman's wife. King Boleslaus pretended repentance, but his virtue was short-lived. Soon he returned to his old ways of corruption. And Stanislaus, in his outspoken way, tirelessly preached the ways of God to the monarch. Enraged by Stanislaus's reprimands, Boleslaus accused the bishop of various crimes.

One story reports that a man named Knight Peter had given an estate to the bishop. Later Peter died. Boleslaus accused Stanislaus of not paying for the property. Stanislaus fasted for three days, ordered the grave of Peter opened, raised him to life, and brought him to court. Peter upheld the good name of the bishop. Still Boleslaus behaved like a tyrant, and Stanislaus had no choice but to excommunicate him. Now Boleslaus was furious. The king entered the cathedral where Stanislaus was officiating, and services were suspended. Stanislaus, pursued by the king, fled to a chapel outside of town. The king ordered his guards to enter the church and kill the bishop. When they refused, the king boldly marched into the chapel and killed Stanislaus with his own sword.

Stanislaus, a brave witness for Christianity, is patron of Poland. He defended Christ and the Church and spoke the truth, even when it meant his death. Stanislaus was not a man who would lie just to please the authority, the king. Pray often to him that you may love your faith enough to witness it even to the point of sacrifice.

COMPARE TWO POLISH LEADERS

Centuries after the time of Stanislaus, the future Pope John Paul II served as the bishop of the diocese of Kraków. Have the students compare how Pope John Paul II and Saint Stanislaus witnessed to their faith.

LEARN ABOUT POLAND

Have the students locate Poland on the map. Ask them to find out how Poland is governed. Remind the students that in Poland the faith was tolerated under a Communist regime. Have them find out if the Church is thriving or struggling in Poland today.

READ ABOUT ANOTHER POLISH SAINT

Suggest that the students read about the life of Saint Maximilian Kolbe, a Polish saint who gave his life as a witness to Christian charity. See his biography on page 403, feast day August 14.

ASK FOR FORGIVENESS

Tell the students that Boleslaus finished his life as a penitent in a Benedictine abbey. Point out to the students how God always forgives even the greatest of sins. Encourage the students to seek forgiveness from those they may have hurt.

Catechist's Notes:

_____

_____

_____

_____

_____

_____

_____

_____

_____

_____

_____

Saint Marguerite d'Youville

April 11

(1701–1771)

Have you ever said, "I've done enough"? Most people have said that or thought it, but not Marguerite. Even when she had nothing herself, she found more to give others. Marguerite felt that she was simply doing what she, as the daughter of her provident Father, was meant to do. She used whatever God gave her to provide for his children, especially those who were poor or neglected.

Marguerite was born in Varennes, Canada, the oldest of six children. Her father died when Marguerite was seven years old, leaving the family destitute. Marguerite learned to rely on her eternal Father. She helped her mother care for the family. When she was 11, she went to school for two years, then came home to teach her younger brothers and sisters all she had learned.

At age 20 Marguerite married Francois d'Youville. She loved him, but he did not treat her well. He was gone for months at a time, involved in the illegal trade of liquor for furs. Marguerite lived with her domineering mother-in-law and bore six children, four of whom died as infants. When Francois became ill, Marguerite cared for him for two years until his death. Marguerite was left with no income and heavy debts. She opened a store in the house and sold clothing she sewed and household items.

Marguerite always saw people who had less than she. Marguerite visited the poor in the hospital and mended their clothes; she begged for money to bury hanged criminals. She took a blind woman into her home. In 1737 three women felt called to share Marguerite's mission. They consecrated themselves to God to serve the poor.

Ten years later Marguerite took charge of General Hospital of Montreal, which was deep in debt. It was home to many sick people, and Marguerite was determined to do what needed to be done. She opened the building to people with incurable or contagious diseases, abandoned children, and people who were mentally ill—people who were kept out of other hospitals. To care for everyone and repair the building, at night Marguerite made clothing for military troops. During the war between the French and English, Marguerite cared for wounded soldiers from both sides. In 1765 the hospital was destroyed by fire. The stone walls remained, so Marguerite rebuilt. Residents of Montreal contributed both labor and money; the restored hospital housed 170 people.

Today the Sisters of Charity of Montreal continue the work of their founder, Saint Marguerite d'Youville, in Canada, Ohio, New England, Brazil, and Colombia. They run hospitals, nursing homes, and homes for people with disablities. They minister to all kinds of needy people. Like Marguerite, they believe that God, the Father of all, is loving and provident.

PRAY TO THE FATHER

Marguerite relied on the goodness of her loving Father.

- Today pray the Lord's Prayer with the students for all people who are in most need of care.

- Have the children write prayers to their loving and provident Father.

PRAY THE TE DEUM

When the hospital was destroyed by fire, Marguerite and the sisters knelt in the ashes and prayed the Te Deum, a prayer of praise to God. This was their way of acknowledging that God always had and would continue to provide for their needs. Pray this prayer with the students today. You may make copies, using the blackline master on page 453.

LIVE THE ADVENTURE

Let the children act out some of the tragedies and triumphs of Marguerite's life.

HELP OTHERS

After reading about Saint Marguerite, have the students brainstorm how they could help others. Remind them that they don't need a lot of money. They also have time and energy to spend. After the class decides on a worthy project, support them, but let them do as much of the planning, organization, and work as possible.

DISCUSS RELIGIOUS HABITS

The Sisters of Charity of Montreal were commonly called the Grey Nuns because of their plain gray habit. They wore a simple gray dress of the times, a black head covering that resembled a widow's cap, and a cross with a heart on it. Discuss with the class the reasons for and against religious orders wearing a habit.

Catechist's Notes:

_____

_____

_____

_____

_____

_____

_____

_____

Saint Bernadette Soubirous April 16

(1844–1879)

Bernadette was an unlikely person to deliver a message from the Mother of God to the world. She was only four feet, eight inches tall, had asthma, and was not very intelligent. Her father was a miller who had six children, and the family lived in abject poverty.

February 11, 1858, was a cold day. Fourteen-year-old Bernadette Soubirous, her sister, and a friend had gone out to collect firewood. Being weak and sickly, Bernadette fell behind. She was preparing to cross a stream when she heard a strong wind. As she looked around, she saw a young woman, not much taller than herself, dressed in white, carrying a Rosary on her arm. Bernadette was frightened, but the smile and gentle manner of the Lady reassured her. Bernadette began to pray the Rosary, and the Lady joined her in each Glory Be. When the Rosary ended, Bernadette told the two girls what she had seen. At home Bernadette was questioned about her experience, and her parents were upset. But she was permitted to return to the spot, and the lovely Lady appeared to her 18 times from February 11 through July 16.

News of the vision spread, and crowds formed whenever Bernadette returned to the grotto where she had first seen the Lady. At one time nearly 20,000 people were present. No one saw or heard the Lady but Bernadette. The Lady told her many things. She assured Bernadette that although she would not find happiness in this life, she would have it in heaven. She told her to do penance and pray for sinners. She instructed Bernadette to tell the priests that a chapel was to be built at the site and processions held. When Bernadette asked the Lady's identity, she replied, "I am the Immaculate Conception." Bernadette repeated the words to the priest, not knowing what they meant. The Blessed Virgin had come to call sinners to a change of heart. She touched people deeply, inspiring them to care for the sick and the poor—and all those losing hope.

On February 25, 1858, the Lady told Bernadette to dig in the dirt and drink of the stream. Bernadette began to dig with her hands and, after several attempts, she found water to drink. The water continued to flow until it was producing over 32,000 gallons of water a day—as it still does. Three days later a mother with two paralyzed fingers was cured in those waters. Since that time there have been more than 5,000 cures recorded, but less than 100 of them have been declared miraculous by the Church.

To escape the fame and the crowds, Bernadette entered a convent. There she worked in the infirmary. When people tried to pay special attention to her, in all humility she said, "What does one do with a broom when one has finished sweeping? Why, put it away in the corner." She was not even present for the consecration of the basilica at Lourdes. Bernadette was misunderstood, and at times harshly treated. After suffering painfully, she died of tuberculosis at the age of 35. Bernadette was canonized on December 8, 1933. Her body lies incorrupt in a glass reliquary in her convent.

ACTIVITIES

DRAW INSPIRATION FROM BERNADETTE

There are many facets of Bernadette's life that could inspire young people. Point out some of these to the students:

- When the lovely Lady of the apparitions asked Bernadette to return each day for two weeks, Bernadette answered that she would if her parents would permit her to do so. She remained obedient to them.

- Bernadette was questioned, and at times threatened, by lawyers, doctors, police, civil authorities, priests, religious, her teachers, friends, relatives, and bishops. They were finally convinced of the truth of her story because of her honesty and her humility and straightforwardness. Honesty is its own reward.

- Bernadette was slow to learn to read and write, and she always had difficulty with her catechism questions. But she knew how to love and how to suffer. She knew the healing waters of the grotto would never help her, yet she did not let that stop her from showing kindness to everyone. Bernadette knew what was really important in life.

LOOK AT IMAGES OF MARY

When asked to describe the Lady, Bernadette said that she looked nothing like the images and statues she had seen in the church. The Lady was so much more beautiful and natural. Collect a variety of images of Mary and let each child select his or her favorite.

RESEARCH FATIMA

Have the students find out about Mary's appearances at Fatima and compare them with those at Lourdes. They might do this in a chart with two columns, one headed Similarities and the other Differences.

PRAY FOR SINNERS

Discuss how to carry out Mary's order to pray for sinners. When do the students do this? How else can they pray for sinners? What penance can they apply to their salvation?

Catechist's Notes:

_____

_____

_____

_____

_____

_____

_____

_____

Saint Anselm

(1033–1109)

April 21

Anselm took a detour on his way to greatness. As a boy in Italy, he thought of becoming a priest. His father, however, introduced him to court life. The lifestyle, with few responsibilities and many pleasures, made Anselm forget about his vocation. Then after his mother's death, Anselm became interested in Lanfranc, a popular spiritual leader of monasticism in Normandy, France. Lanfranc's monastery was said to be the best school, and when Anselm entered it to be a monk, he made friends with Lanfranc. Three years later Anselm became prior and began to publish his writings on God.

In the monastery Anselm was known for his virtue and his teaching. The monks praised his way of dealing with people. He was unanimously elected abbot in 1070, when Lanfranc was made archbishop of Canterbury in England. William the Conqueror had gained control of England in 1066 and was reorganizing the government and the Church under Norman lords. When Lanfranc died in 1089, the English clergy wanted Anselm as archbishop; however, Rufus, William's son, would not approve. For four years there was no archbishop of Canterbury.

Then suddenly Rufus became mortally ill. In fear of hell, Rufus appointed Anselm archbishop of Canterbury. Knowing he would come into conflict with Rufus, Anselm at first refused the appointment. The pope, however, ordered him to accept.

Rufus recovered and fell into his former sins, taking Church lands and attempting to appoint bishops. Anselm told the bishops that their obedience demanded they be loyal to the pope and ignore the king's interference in Church matters. Frightened by the conflict between the archbishop and the king, bishops and priests abandoned Anselm. The king then exiled him. In exile Anselm wrote papers in defense of the faith and took part in the Council of Bari, where he spoke eloquently on the Holy Spirit.

After Rufus was killed in a hunting accident, Anselm returned to England. Henry I, brother of Rufus, was now the king and continued to rule as his predecessor had. Henry also wanted to appoint bishops, and Anselm refused to accept his appointment from the king. Again Anselm was exiled to Rome. Pope Paschal worked out a compromise between the king and the bishop. He ruled that only the Church could invest a bishop with the ring and the crosier, but the king would have some power in the selection of bishops.

Until his death Anselm remained in England, defending the faith. His holiness, patience, and love of the Church were so well respected that Canterbury came to be recognized as the most important church in England. In 1720 Anselm was given the titles Doctor of the Church and Father of Scholasticism because he analyzed and taught the truths of the faith by the aid of reason. The Church encourages the faithful to live as Anselm did—loyal to God in every situation.

LOOK AT CROSSES

Anselm had great compassion for the sufferings of Christ on the cross. The Cistercians promoted this spirituality, and it was through them that we have the crucifix— the representation of Christ dying on the cross. Before this time Christ had been represented as crucified but glorified. Have the students look at a variety of crosses and crucifixes from religious goods catalogs. Speak to the students about reverence to the cross.

FOCUS ON SOCIAL JUSTICE

Anselm did not spend all his energies dealing with kings; he had great concern for the poor. Anselm was the first in the Church to oppose slave trade. It was through his efforts that the National Council at Westminster (1102) passed a law prohibiting the sale of human beings as though they were cattle. Guide the students in listing teachings of the bishops they are aware of that promote Christ's teachings through social justice.

WRITE A LETTER

Anselm's correspondence was phenomenal: 475 letters giving spiritual direction to popes, royalty, monks, nuns, and laity. This alone shows how much he cared about others. In his spirit have the students write a letter to a friend or relative they have not seen for a while.

WRITE ABOUT HAPPINESS

A biographer of Anselm records a famous speech he gave at the abbey of Cluny on the 14 happinesses of heaven. To Anselm the greatest happiness was to possess God. Have the students write about 14 happinesses they have or look forward to. Encourage them to write with a spiritual outlook.

SHARE A PERSONAL STORY

Anselm was an excellent teacher, and his students recalled that his oral method of teaching, based on parables drawn from life, showed the richness of his spiritual character. Share with the students today something from your life that has drawn you closer to God.

WRITE PRAYERS OF PRAISE

The 19 prayers and three meditations Anselm wrote show that he was an original and independent thinker. Have the students write an original prayer asking for God's help and praising God's goodness. Share a prayer at the end of each class until you have used them all.

Catechist's Notes:

_____

_____

_____

_____

_____

Saint George

(d. 303)

Everyone loves a superhero—and everyone loves stories about the bravery of their hero. Saint George is a Christian superhero. The real story of Saint George is heroic enough. George was probably a soldier in the fourth century who courageously and publicly defended the faith and encouraged his fellow Christians. For this action he suffered martyrdom under the Emperor Diocletian. For his heroism he was venerated as a popular saint in the East.

By the sixth century, the story of Saint George had been embellished. He had become the ideal Christian knight, and the story of his slaying the dragon had become immensely popular. In the seventh and eighth centuries, stained glass windows in the churches of Europe depicted this legend. George had become a popular saint in the West.

The story of Saint George, Superhero, tells of a dragon that terrorized the land and poisoned with its breath all who approached it. George slew the dragon and refused any reward; but he made the king promise he would build churches, honor priests, and show compassion to the poor. This act made George so popular he became the personification of all the ideals of Christian chivalry. He was named patron of soldiers, and when the English king Richard I led his soldiers in the Crusades, he placed his army under George's protection. In one famous battle, the opposition was so strong that the Christians were losing. Later the army leaders insisted that in the midst of the battle, Saint George rode forward and led the troops to victory. From then on, George became the patron of England. King Edward III founded an order of knights under George's patronage, and his feast was kept as a national festival.

Though the stories of Saint George seem extraordinarily courageous to us, no one can deny the fact that his real heroism was in dying for Christ.

ACT OUT THE STORY

Glorified stories of saints magnify their heroism, but also keep alive their love of Christ. Have the students dramatize the heroism of Saint George's life.

WRITE BALLADS

Poems have been written celebrating St. George's heroism, including *The Faerie Queene* by Edmund Spenser. Have the students write a ballad on George or on their own patron saints.

MAKE SHIELDS

Direct the students to read about Christian chivalry and the important part it played in the Middle Ages. Then let them make personal shields that show their loyalty to Christ.

POLL THE CLASS

Hold a class discussion on why legends of the saints are so popular. Poll the students on whether such popular tales can inspire people to lead better lives.

PRAY FOR SOLDIERS

Saint George is the patron of soldiers and all who work for the good of their country. Remind the class to pray for the armed forces of our country.

Catechist's Notes:

_____

_____

_____

_____

_____

_____

_____

_____

_____

_____

Saint Mark

(first century)

Have you ever been homesick? Mark was a traveling companion and assistant of Paul and Barnabas on the first missionary journey. Something happened to Mark on that journey—perhaps he became homesick—so he returned to Jerusalem. The incident caused a quarrel between Paul and Barnabas. Barnabas, Mark's cousin, was sympathetic to Mark's problems, but Paul would not hear of Mark accompanying them again. Later Paul and Mark must have been reconciled because when Paul wrote to Timothy during his final imprisonment, he asked for Mark's assistance (2 Timothy 4:11).

Little else is known of Mark, also called John Mark. Mark was not one of the twelve apostles, but he was a member of the first Christian community. It was probably Mark's mother who opened her house as a place of prayer for the apostles during Peter's imprisonment (Acts 12:12). Thus, Mark had firsthand experience of the early Church and apostolic life.

The Gospel of Mark was probably written around the year A.D. 70. Traditionally this Gospel was thought to have been written in Rome. Modern research indicates that it may have been written in Syria. It is the shortest and the oldest of the Gospels.

Papias, a contemporary writer, described Mark as Peter's interpreter. This may explain the influence of Peter on some of the material in the Gospel. But the author, who was probably a Greek Jewish Christian, included oral and written tradition—miracle stories, sayings, parables, and the Passion.

The Gospel was written to proclaim the Good News to a community that had as its members both Jewish and Gentile Christians. Its style is direct and simple to read. Jesus is presented as a savior who understands the difficulties and sufferings of the Christians and will one day bring them to share with him eternal joy and glory.

The Gospel of Mark shows Jesus as the suffering Son of God. To be a disciple of the risen Jesus meant to come to terms with the cross. But Mark also shows that the risen Jesus was glorified and his disciples can anticipate the assured victory of eternal life. Mark writes sincerely that anyone who wishes to follow Jesus must accept the cross.

ACTIVITIES

RESEARCH THE SYMBOL OF MARK'S GOSPEL

Let the students discover why artistic tradition uses the symbol of a winged lion to represent Saint Mark.

TAKE THE GOSPEL TO HEART

Write short verses from the Gospel of Mark on slips of paper. Let each child draw a slip of paper out of a box. Ask the children to pray and meditate on their passage.

STUDY SCRIPTURE

The spirit of Mark's Gospel is willingness to accept the destiny of Jesus as the suffering, dying, and rising Messiah. Have the students look up the following passages from Saint Mark and Saint Paul: Romans 8:17; 1 Corinthians 2:1–2; Mark 8:34–38; Mark 10:30; Mark 10:45. Discuss how these references fit Mark's theme.

PANTOMIME A PARABLE

Many of the passages of Saint Mark's Gospel are also found in Matthew and Luke. But Mark has some sections that are not repeated in the other Gospels. One parable on the Kingdom of God is unique to Mark. Read Mark 4:26–29 and let the students pantomime it.

REFLECT ON THE GOSPEL

The Gospel of Mark records many miracles that show Christ's power as the Son of God. Ask the students to define the word *gospel*. Then have them select a part of Saint Mark's Gospel to read quietly. Finally have them write in their journals one thought they had while reading this Gospel.

Catechist's Notes:

_____

_____

_____

_____

_____

_____

_____

_____

_____

Saint Pedro de San José Betancur

(1626–1667)

Pedro de San José Betancur was born in 1626 on the island of Tenerife in the Canary Islands. His family was poor, and Pedro worked as a shepherd. Pedro wanted to be a priest, but God had other plans.

When Pedro was 24 years old, he left home for what is now Guatemala in Central America. He hoped that a relative would help him get a government job there. But by the time he reached the city of Havana on the island of Cuba, he had no money. Pedro spent about a year working in Havana before he had saved enough money to continue his journey. Finally he arrived in Guatemala City, but there he had to depend on the free food that the Franciscans provided for those in need.

To follow his dream of becoming a priest, Pedro enrolled in a Jesuit college. But college was very hard for Pedro, and he couldn't pass the courses. Pedro left college without graduating.

A few years later in 1655 Pedro joined the Third Order of St. Francis. He was a janitor and gardener. In 1658 Pedro opened a hospital for poor people. He also soon founded a shelter for homeless people and a school for poor children. Pedro became known for his work with the poor, with children, and with prisoners. During the day he preached the Gospel to prisoners. At night Pedro walked the streets, ringing a bell, as he sought donations for orphans. Other men joined Pedro in his work, and together they founded the Bethlemite Congregation.

Pedro may have started the Christmas Eve event called *posada,* in which people playing Mary and Joseph seek a night's lodging from their neighbors. This lovely custom spread to other Central American countries and Mexico.

In 1980 Pope John Paul II beatified Pedro de San José Betancur along with four others. The pope said of them, "God lavished his kindness and his mercy on them, enriching them with his grace. He loved them with a fatherly, but demanding love, which promised only hardships and suffering. He invited and called them to heroic holiness. He tore them away from their countries of origin and sent them to other lands to proclaim the message of the Gospel, in the midst of inexpressible toil and difficulties."

In 2002 Pope John Paul II traveled to Guatemala to make Pedro the first Central American saint. More than 700,000 people attended the canonization Mass. During the Mass the bell that Pedro had rung when he was seeking donations for orphans was rung again.

Today a modern hospital built in Guatemala in Pedro's name serves more than 80,000 poor villagers every year. Also, Pedro's work caring for the sick and poor is continued by the Bethlemite Brothers and the Bethlemite Sisters.

TRACE A JOURNEY

On a world map or globe, have students trace Saint Pedro's journey from the island of Tenerife to Cuba and then to Guatemala. Ask: In what general direction did Saint Pedro travel? (*west*) Which ocean did he cross? (*the Atlantic*) What was probably his main form of transportation? (*boat or ship*)

HELP THE POOR

Have the whole class work together to make a list of ways it could help the poor and needy in your community. Have a volunteer write the list on the board. Hold a class discussion to select and implement one of the suggestions. Direct the discussion towards a suggestion that is actually achievable, given the time and financial resources of the students.

RESEARCH THE BETHLEMITES

Suggest that students use the Internet to find out more about the present-day good works of both the Bethlemite Brothers and the Bethlemite Sisters.

RESEARCH THE CHURCH OF SAN FRANCISCO

Tell children that pilgrims today can visit Saint Pedro's remains and altar at the Church of San Francisco in Antigua, Guatemala. Suggest that children consult resources such as the *New Catholic Encyclopedia* for additional information.

LEARN ABOUT GUATEMALA

Tell children that the nation of Guatemala suffered greatly in the closing decades of the 20th century. Suggest that interested students learn more about Guatemala's travails by researching the situation on the Internet.

Catechist's Notes:

Saint Peter Chanel

April 28

(1803–1841)

If not for his faith, Peter Chanel would be considered a failure rather than a saint. Peter belonged to a French peasant family. The parish priest noticed Peter's unusual intelligence and prayerful spirit, and he helped the young man into the local seminary. After ordination Peter's first assignment was to be pastor of a parish in a run-down district. Through endless patience and perseverance in showing kindness to the sick and all in need, he revived the parish. But Peter wanted to be a foreign missionary more than anything else, so after three years of parish work, he joined the new congregation of the Marist Fathers. He was already 28 years old at the time, but Peter was not sent to the missions immediately. Instead he was assigned to teach for five years in the seminary.

At last, Peter was sent with Bishop Pompallier and other missionaries to islands in the southern Pacific Ocean. The bishop left Peter and a brother on the island of Futuna, promising to return in six months. But it was five years before circumstances permitted the bishop to return. Peter and the brother were accepted by some of the natives, and their abilities to heal the sick were respected, but conditions were primitive and the work was difficult. Cannibalism still flourished on these islands, and the language seemed almost impossible to learn.

Peter Chanel was always cheerful in spite of hardship. The brother who worked with Peter described his life: "Because of his labors he was often burned by the heat of the sun, and famished with hunger, and he would return home wet with perspiration and completely exhausted. Yet he always returned in good spirits, courageous and energetic almost every day." Peter continued to work with faith, even though only a few natives came for instructions and Baptism. From every viewpoint the mission seemed a failure.

A turning point came, however, when the chief's son asked to be baptized. This conversion made the chief so angry that he sent a band of warriors to kill Peter. The warriors surrounded Peter's hut, clubbed him, and dragged his dead body out where others cut it up with knives and axes. Peter was the first martyr of Oceania. The chief had thought that the missionary's death would crush Catholicism on the island. But it had the opposite effect. Within a year the whole island was Catholic. Peter Chanel's life shows that we can never know how much good we do when we accept our sufferings with faith. Our example can be the source of another person's faith.

ACTIVITIES

LOCATE OCEANIA
Locate Oceania on the map and point out that Peter Chanel has been named patron of this territory.

RESEARCH THE MARIST ORDER
Ask for a small team of volunteers to do research on the Marist order and report to the class. Or invite a Marist priest or brother to explain the apostolic work of his congregation to the students.

COLLECT FOR THE MISSIONS
Have small groups of students decorate empty cereal boxes or coffee cans with pictures, words, and symbols of missionary activity. Let them place the collection boxes around the school or parish to collect money and prayers for the missions.

VISIT THE SICK
Peter Chanel showed great compassion toward the sick. Encourage the students to make a call or send a card to someone who is sick or needs their prayers.

OVERCOME MOODINESS
Peter Chanel was cheerful in spite of hardship. Ask the students what they believe was the source of Peter's optimism. Discuss how they can overcome their own occasional moodiness.

Catechist's Notes:

_____

_____

_____

_____

_____

_____

_____

_____

_____

_____

Saint Catherine of Siena   April 29

(1347–1380)

Catherine's mother had 23 children, 11 grandchildren, a small, overcrowded house—and now her youngest, Catherine, wanted a room of her own for prayer. Catherine was a lively, charming girl. Her mother could not understand why she did not want to marry or enter a convent. When her mother tried to interest Catherine in marriage, Catherine protested by cutting off her hair. Her mother gave in.

At 16 Catherine joined the Third Order of St. Dominic. Members of the Third Order wore the Dominican habit, spent a life of prayer and good works, but lived at home. For three years Catherine left her room only for Mass. Often after Communion Catherine experienced a prayer so deep that she could not see or hear because she was conversing with Jesus. Of course, her mystical experiences caused much curiosity and conversation. Even though Catherine was uncomfortable when others talked about her, she wanted only what Jesus asked of her.

After three years Jesus told Catherine to go out to serve him in her neighbor. She visited the prisons, encouraging the inmates to repent and receive the sacraments. During a plague Catherine was everywhere, bringing food and clothing, nursing the sick, and burying the dead. Her gifts of prophetic vision and spiritual guidance became apparent. Three Dominican friars had to hear the confessions of those who repented after talking to her. By the time she was 23, Catherine had attracted followers of all ages who accompanied her in her work. They were priests, religious, and laypeople. She was their spiritual guide, and Catherine called them her "family." Some addressed her as "Mama." There was criticism about her activities, but Catherine's honesty and charity eventually won the respect of all. A Dominican, Raymond of Capua, served as her confessor, secretary, and biographer. Catherine could barely read and write, but she dictated more than 400 letters and two books.

At this time Pope Gregory XI, a Frenchman, stayed in Avignon and took orders from the French king. This situation confused Christians, but Gregory lacked the courage to go back to the Vatican. Catherine went to Avignon to advise the pope to return to Rome. Over the protests of the French and his own father, Gregory did so.

But the crisis was not over. After Pope Gregory died, Pope Urban VI was elected. Pope Urban saw the Church's need for reform and often acted imprudently. His manner angered the French cardinals. They did not want Rome as the center of the Church. They rejected the Italian pope, went back to Avignon, and elected a rival pope. The Western Schism had begun. People blamed Catherine for having brought the pope back to Rome.

Now Catherine was broken by worry over the Church, in constant pain, and discouraged. She offered her life for the good of the Church. She died at the age of 33, one of the Church's greatest mystics and a Doctor of the Church.

DISCUSS LEADERSHIP ROLES

Catherine of Siena played an important role in restoring the spiritual power of the Church to Rome. Have the students report on how laymen and laywomen can influence the Church today.

PAINT OR WRITE

Catherine was a mystic. When she tried to describe her experience to people, one image she used was of swimming in the sea. She said that the Trinity is like a deep sea. When she prayed she was totally surrounded by the mystery of God. The deeper she went, the more she found; the more she found, the more she sought. Have the students paint their interpretation of this image or write their own image to describe their experience of prayer.

FIND OUT ABOUT DOCTORS OF THE CHURCH

In 1970 along with Saint Teresa of Ávila (feast, October 15), Catherine of Siena was declared a Doctor of the Church. Saint Thérèse of Lisieux (feast, October 1) was added in 1977. These are the only three women to bear this title. Have the students find out what it means to be a Doctor of the Church and why this honor has been given to Catherine of Siena.

MAKE A REMINDER CARD

What Catherine did in the Middle Ages was unheard of for a woman. Jesus had told her, "I am always with you in your heart, strengthening you." Point out to the students that Catherine shows us that the power of Christ working in us can do infinitely more than we can ask or imagine. Have them make a reminder card using Jesus' words to Catherine.

RESEARCH THE AVIGNON PAPACY

The papacy had been in France almost 75 years when Gregory XI returned to Rome. This time was called the Avignon Papacy. Have the students find out why this split in the Church occurred. Discuss with them how political problems were closely related to Church problems in the 14th century.

CELEBRATE RECONCILIATION

Catherine had a regular confessor to help guide her spiritual journey. Discuss with the students how going to the same priest for the Sacrament of Penance can help a person's spiritual life. Encourage the students to celebrate the Rite of Reconciliation regularly and to talk with a priest about their spiritual lives.

Catechist's Notes:

_____

_____

_____

_____

Saint Pius V
(1504–1572)

April 30

When Pope Pius V walked in processions through Rome barefoot, head uncovered, his long beard blowing in the wind, the people said there had never been a holier pope. This visibly saintly man had come from a poor Italian family and had entered the Dominican order at the age of 14. A teacher, a master of novices, a bishop, and finally a cardinal, he was known in all these roles as a strict and honest man, as well as a zealous reformer. He wept when the cardinals informed him in 1566 that he had been elected pope. The 18-year-long Council of Trent had ended just three years before, and he, as Holy Father, had the task of implementing its letter and spirit.

Pius V began his papal reign with immediate changes and surprised the Catholic world. The previous pope, Pius IV, had been easygoing. At first people did not like the new pope's changes. They complained that the atmosphere of Rome became like that of a monastery. But soon the integrity of the pope's character changed their minds. He ordered that the money given at his coronation be sent to hospitals and to those in need. Church finances were examined and accounted for, the army was reduced, and the lifestyles of the cardinals and bishops were simplified.

With the help of St. Charles Borromeo, seminaries were established, synods were held, dioceses were organized, and parish priests were called to regular meetings. A new catechism based on the decisions of the Council of Trent was completed, translated into many languages, and widely distributed. Parish priests were made responsible for the Catholic education of the young. The Roman Missal—both a restoration and a revision—was adopted as the official Mass book for the Western church (with a few minor exceptions). It was used for four centuries, until it was replaced by a Sacramentary (1970) and Lectionary (1969). (The Lectionary was revised again in 2002.) The Breviary, or Divine Office, was also revised. The lives of the saints were rewritten to emphasize their essential holiness and to delete exaggerated stories, and the sacred Scripture was given a more prominent place.

In international affairs Pius V had troubles. He was unsuccessful in restoring England to Catholic unity. Queen Elizabeth was determined to complete the separation of the Church from Rome begun by her father, Henry VIII. Pius V's excommunication of the queen opened new persecutions against the Catholics in England. The pope was more successful in checking the Turks, who threatened to overrun Europe. At the Battle of Lepanto in 1571, the Christian forces crushed the Turkish fleet in a spectacular battle.

After only six years as pope, Pius V died of a painful disease of which he had never complained. He was admired for his kindness to the poor and sick, for his self-discipline, his truthfulness, and his unfaltering efforts to make the Church effective in its mission to spread the Good News.

READ ABOUT ANOTHER SAINT

When Queen Elizabeth I was excommunicated, she forbade English Catholics to practice the faith. Anyone found participating in Mass was fined or sent to prison in the Tower of London. Priests were often condemned to die. Have the students read about Edmund Campion, a daring Jesuit who heroically worked to keep the faith alive.

DO HOMEWORK CAREFULLY

Pius V was a scholar, and he respected study. Encourage the students to resolve to do their homework this week neatly, carefully, and with pride.

SET UP A MARY SHRINE

The Battle of Lepanto was said to have been won through the intercession of our Blessed Mother. The feast of the Holy Rosary was established after the battle had been won. Pius V loved Mary and wanted devotion to her to be spread. Have the students set up a shrine to Mary in the classroom and ask for volunteers to bring flowers. Place a box and slips of paper near the shrine so the students can write prayer petitions to Our Lady.

MAKE SMALL SACRIFICES

Pius V prayed frequently, fasted, and denied himself many personal comforts because he wanted to show his love for Christ through sacrifice. Encourage the students to make small sacrifices to show their love: to sit up straight in class, to pay attention, to avoid distracting others, and so on.

BECOME FAMILIAR WITH THE LITURGY OF THE HOURS

Bring a Liturgy of the Hours book to show the students. Pray part of the Morning Prayer of the Church with them. Point out that priests, sisters, brothers, and an increasing number of laypeople pray parts or all of these prayers every day.

Catechist's Notes:

_____

_____

_____

_____

_____

_____

_____

Saint Joseph the Worker

(first century)

How do you feel about work? Have you ever wondered why people work? What if people didn't work?

Joseph, the carpenter of Nazareth, understood the importance of work. He was a worker himself, and he probably taught Jesus his trade. Perhaps they worked together, hour after hour, trying to make the world a better place in which to live. By the work of his hands, Joseph earned a fair wage and provided for his family, Mary and Jesus. His labor enabled them to live with dignity. And through his work, Joseph honored the Father in heaven and continued the act of creation.

Joseph was protector and provider for the Holy Family at Nazareth. Families often turn to him in prayer, for he understands the struggles of family life—the trials and heartaches—as well as the great joys. Over the years workers and people in need of work have also turned to Joseph.

In 1889 a group called the International Socialist Congress decided to celebrate May 1 as a day for workers, a holiday in their honor, a day to celebrate the importance of work. But these people and many Communists like them did not view work as a way to honor God, or as a reflection of human dignity, or as a way to share in God's work of creation. These people did not believe in God.

To give workers a patron, the Church turned to Joseph, who had been made the Patron of the Universal Church by Pope Pius IX in 1870 and the model for fathers of families 19 years later. Joseph was named protector of workers by Pope Benedict XV, and in 1955 the feast of St. Joseph the Worker was set on May 1 by Pope Pius XII.

You know how difficult work can be. Perhaps you also know how satisfying it can be. When you have worked hard at a job, you can stand back and admire it and praise God through it. Whether you build a cathedral or a sandcastle, it can bring you closer to God. Today pray to Saint Joseph for his help in all your work and for people who want and need jobs, but cannot find them.

ACTIVITIES

SPONSOR A CAREER DAY

Invite parents and parishioners to give short presentations on their jobs and careers. Ask them to point out in their talks how they are able to witness to Catholic Christian values through the work they do.

REGISTER AT A SKILLS BANK

A number of parishes and communities make use of a skills bank. People of all ages may register by listing services they are willing to provide free of cost to those who could not afford to pay for them. For example, a student might register with the bank to mow lawns and do yard work. When an elderly person or a parishioner with disabilities phones in and requests yard service, the student volunteer is contacted. Encourage the students to become a part of the local skills bank, if there is one, or set up such a group within the school itself. Jobs listed could include cleaning up the schoolyard or parish grounds, helping to set up and clean the classrooms, acting as student aides, providing babysitting service (particularly during Mass), and so on. In this way students can experience the dignity of labor and can witness to Christ through service to others.

DISPLAY BEST WORK

Display the students' best work in any subject area on May 1.

ENJOY AN ART PROJECT

We usually refer to Joseph as a carpenter, but the word used in Scripture concerning his trade can actually mean an artisan or craftsman, a worker in stone, metal, or wood.

Plan a special art or craft project to provide the students with an opportunity to be creative.

READ GENESIS

Read the Scripture account of creation and discuss with the students how human beings are made in God's image. Lead them to see that their gifts of thinking, loving, and choosing enable them to continue the work of creation.

HELP UNEMPLOYED WORKERS

Being out of work is a painful experience. Lead the students in prayer for unemployed workers and their families. Organize a food drive to stock the parish food pantry, or volunteer at a local food bank.

Catechist's Notes:

_____

_____

_____

_____

_____

_____

Saint Athanasius

(295–373)

May 2

Jesus said that his followers would have to suffer if they wished to live their lives according to his message. In every age since then, the Church has had to endure many hardships—either persecution from without or heresy and schism from within. To balance these evils, great champions have risen to defend Christ and the Church. Saint Athanasius is one of those champions.

Athanasius was born of Christian parents in Alexandria, Egypt. As a young man, he spent four years in prayer and solitude in the desert. It was here that he met Anthony the Hermit (see page 171), who had a powerful influence on him. Some years after he left the desert, Athanasius became a priest and was appointed secretary to Alexander, bishop of Alexandria.

Meanwhile, another talented young priest, Arius, had begun to preach that Jesus was not truly God, that he was only a good and holy man. To answer the false teachings of Arius, the Church held a council at Nicea in the year 325. Two important things happened at this council: Arius and his heretical ideas were condemned, and the bishops composed the Nicene Creed, a profession of faith in defense of Christ's divinity.

Athanasius, who had accompanied Bishop Alexander to the Council of Nicea, was deeply impressed by everything that he witnessed, and for the rest of his life, he defended the doctrines of the Church. When he became bishop of Alexandria in 328, it was the beginning of almost 50 years of persecution at the hands of the Arian heretics, who had become very popular with the clergy, the laypeople, and even the Emperor Constantine. During these long years, Athanasius was unjustly accused of various crimes and sins, was deliberately misunderstood and humiliated, and was exiled several times.

The last few years of his life were relatively peaceful. Unfortunately he did not live to see the Council of Constantinople affirm and expand the doctrines of the Nicene Creed in 381. It is this creed that we use as the profession of our faith in the Eucharist on all Sundays and other special days. Athanasius deserves the title of Saint because he defended the faith and also because of the meekness and charity with which he treated his enemies.

MAY

PRAY FOR THOSE WHO DEFEND THE CHURCH

Ask the students what they see as the greatest threat to the Church today. List their ideas on the board. Together offer prayers for the people who are defending the Church against these evils.

MAKE CHRIST CANDLES

Have the students make Christ candles as reminders of how Athanasius defended the divinity of Christ. They may use acrylic paints to decorate a candle with the Chi Rho or other symbols of Christ. Suggest that the students place their candles on their dining-room tables and light them during the evening meal.

MAKE SAND ART

Athanasius wrote a book about Saint Anthony, the founder of Christian monasticism, that inspired many men and women to follow the monastic life. Let the students work on a sand painting or sand sculpture as you discuss these questions: How might people today follow a monastic life? What in modern times could be the desert? How could silence be a part of our lives?

REVIEW THE CREED

Help the students review the Nicene Creed.

- Distribute copies of the creed with words missing and ask them to fill in the correct words.

- Write phrases or sentences of the creed on index cards; try to have one card for each student in the class. Ask the students to line up in proper order for the prayer, and then read their parts.

- Ask the students to write the creed from memory and then check their version with the one in the missalette, in their textbook, or on copies made from the blackline master on page 454.

Catechist's Notes:

_____

_____

_____

_____

_____

_____

_____

_____

Saints Philip and James

(first century)

Philip and James were both apostles, and both served Christ faithfully during the very early days of the Church.

Philip seems to have been an enthusiastic person. He was the one who brought his friend Nathanael to Jesus, insisting to Nathanael that he had found the person about whom Moses had written. Some years later it was Philip who made arrangements, with the help of Andrew, to have a group of Greek Gentiles brought to Jesus. Philip the apostle is not to be confused with the deacon Philip of Acts 8, who preached in Samaria and baptized the Ethiopian, although some writers say that they are the same person. Philip also had a practical, down-to-earth mind. He was the apostle who commented that it would take a considerable amount of money to feed a crowd of more than 5,000 hungry men, women, and children. It was

Philip who asked to see the Father when Jesus spoke about him at the Last Supper.

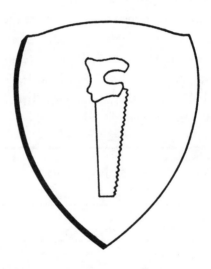

James was the son of Alphaeus and seems to have been born in Caesarea. He is mentioned less frequently in the New Testament than Philip is. Sometimes James is called the Less, which might be a hint that he was a short person or else that he was younger than the other apostle named James.

After Jesus' death James continued to preach the Gospel and is believed to have become the first bishop of Jerusalem. Assuming that James and the first bishop of Jerusalem are one and the same person, then he met his death as a martyr in that city about the year A.D. 62. Tradition identifies James as the author of the epistle associated with his name.

MAY

ACTIVITIES

MAKE SOMEONE HAPPY

One of the things that we can learn from Saints Philip and James is that external facts about our lives don't really matter too much. What does count is the way we fill our lives with the love of God and how we bring his love to others. Encourage each student to do one thing today to make a classmate or family member happy.

DRAMATIZE ACCOUNTS OF PHILIP

Philip is mentioned several times in the New Testament. Divide the class into three groups and assign one of the following references to each group: John 1:43–50; John 6:1–15; John 14:1–11. Have the groups read their stories and then act them out for the class.

LEARN THE APOSTLES

Have the students look up Matthew 10:2–4 to find the list of the twelve apostles. Let them work with a partner to memorize the names of the apostles.

ASSIGN PATRONS

Have the students suggest persons for whom Philip or James could be patron saints. For example, Saint James could be the patron saint of the person who toils quietly behind scenes to make a project a success; Saint Philip could be the patron saint of the friendly person who likes to share his or her friends with other people.

Catechist's Notes:

_____

_____

_____

_____

_____

_____

_____

_____

_____

_____

Blessed Damien of Molokai   May 10

(1840–1889)

The Gospels record that Jesus reached out to lepers with kindness and healing. Centuries later Father Damien heard the same cry and responded with mercy. He devoted his life to bringing the touch of Jesus to the outcasts of society.

Joseph de Veuster was born in Belgium, the son of well-to-do farmers. While at college, he decided God was calling him to be a priest. He joined the Congregation of the Sacred Hearts of Jesus and Mary, the same community his older brother had joined, and he took the name Damien. When illness prevented his brother from sailing to the missions in Hawaii, Damien offered to go in his place. He arrived in Hawaii and was ordained in Honolulu.

For nine years Damien served the people of Hawaii in different villages. But he was most interested in a settlement for people with leprosy (Hansen's disease) on the Hawaiian island of Molokai. The colony was very poor, and there was not a single doctor or priest on the island. Father Damien offered to go to Molokai and work with the lepers.

In 1873 all the lepers who could walk came to meet the boat to see the priest who wanted to work with them. They were sure he wouldn't stay very long. Lepers often have unpleasant sores, and some lose parts of their bodies. Those lepers who were not very ill sometimes lived a wild life because there were no laws and no police on the island.

Father Damien got busy cleaning up the huts, caring for the very sick, and trying new medicines. Those able to help were put to work building houses. Father Damien not only preached and offered Mass, but also built roads, water systems, orphanages, and churches and acted as sheriff, counselor, and undertaker. He even organized a choir and a band! He made the people feel they were important, so they began to take better care of themselves and their property. Through his efforts many people turned away from their immoral habits.

For 10 years Father Damien was the only priest on the island. He had permission to stay there permanently. Damien begged for money from the outside world to help his 800 lepers. Some people helped, but others attacked his reputation.

At Mass on Sundays Father Damien always began his homily with "My dear lepers." One day he said, "My fellow lepers." At first it was very quiet. Then people began to sob. They knew that their beloved Father Damien had contracted the disease. He carried on his work until a month before his death. Joseph Dutton, a layman from Vermont who was called Brother Joseph, joined Father Damien and stayed for 44 years. Franciscan Sisters from New York under the leadership of Mother Marianne Cope also came to help.

Father Damien worked with the lepers for 16 years before he died. He is sometimes called the Martyr of Molokai.

ACTIVITIES

IDENTIFY LEPERS OF TODAY

Inform the students that Hansen's disease is now a treatable disease. Then ask if they can think some groups of people today who are treated as lepers were. Have them find out what is being done to help these people.

DO YOUR PART

- Ask the students to propose ways they can help people who are suffering, such as volunteering at a soup kitchen or retirement home, or raising money for Food for the Poor or research in the fight against AIDS, cancer, or multiple sclerosis.

- Ask the students to think of someone they know who may feel left out or abandoned. Help them find ways to extend mercy and love to this person: prayer, cards, visits, and so on.

RESEARCH AND REPORT

Ask the students to choose a research topic and prepare a short oral or written report.

- Find out about a person today who is dedicated to helping a suffering group of people.

- Learn more about Brother Joseph Dutton or Mother Marianne Cope.

ACT OUT THE GOSPEL

Divide the class into four small groups and assign each group one of these Gospel accounts of Jesus' encounters with lepers: Matthew 8:1–4; Luke 17:11–19. Ask the groups to read and discuss their assigned accounts. Then ask two groups to act out their Gospel stories as they are written and the other two groups to act out their stories as they might happen today.

Catechist's Notes:

_____

_____

_____

_____

_____

_____

_____

_____

Saints Nereus and Achilleus

May 12

(first century)

Little is known about Saints Nereus and Achilleus, but what we know is engraved in stone. Damasus, one of the first popes and later a saint himself, wrote the epitaph for the tombstone of Saints Nereus and Achilleus. In this epitaph he proclaimed that it was love for Christ and a desire to witness to their new faith that inspired Nereus and Achilleus to "throw away their shields, their armor, and their bloody spears."

It seems that both men were Roman soldiers who obeyed orders in the persecution of Christians until they themselves were converted to Christianity. Because Christians were not allowed to bear arms, they resigned from the emperor's army and escaped from Rome. Eventually Nereus and Achilleus were captured and put to death for their beliefs. They were buried in the Catacomb of Domitilla. Some biographers place their martyrdom in the second century. They were among the first martyrs to be venerated as saints.

"O miracle of faith!" wrote Damasus. "Suddenly they cease from their fury, they become converted, they flee from the camp of their wicked leader. Professing the faith of Christ, they are happy to witness to its triumph. Learn now from the words of Damasus what great things the glory of Christ can accomplish."

ACTIVITIES

PRAY FOR SOLDIERS

Ask the students to work together to write petitions for soldiers involved in conflict and for the leaders of countries who make decisions about going to war.

TRY PEACEFUL ALTERNATIVES

Ask the students to suggest alternatives to conflict, consistent with their age and experience: decide not to fight, walk away, talk out problems, compromise, respect others, and so on.

LEARN ABOUT THE CATACOMBS

Nereus and Achilleus were buried in a catacomb. If possible, show the students pictures of the catacombs. Explain that these underground burial places near Rome were constructed in the first centuries of the Church. On the walls of these underground tunnels are drawings of scenes from the Old and New Testaments, the eucharistic banquet, and Baptism, as well as representations of early Christian martyrs. Discuss the importance of respect for the dead, which Christians have always had.

PRAY A PSALM SELECTION

Nereus and Achilleus died for Christ about 1,800 years ago, but Christians suffer and die for their faith in our time too. Direct the students to the Book of Psalms. Have them work in small groups to find a short prayer for modern-day martyrs from one of the psalms. Have each group copy a prayer and prepare to read it aloud together. Gather the class to offer a medley of psalm prayers.

MAKE A SACRIFICE OF LOVE

Encourage the students to think about the fact that the love of Christ was so strong that two Roman soldiers were able to sacrifice their lives for him. What might happen if each one of us were inspired by such love? Have the students write in their journals one sacrifice they could make out of love for Christ today.

Catechist's Notes:

_____

_____

_____

_____

_____

_____

_____

Saint Matthias

(first century)

People may have been surprised when Matthias was elected to take the place of Judas among the apostles after Jesus' death and resurrection. The New Testament mentions Matthias only once, and that is in the account of how he was chosen to become one of the apostles.

After the death of Judas, the apostles met to elect someone to replace him. Peter presided at this meeting and reminded the others of the qualification necessary for being an apostle: The candidate had to have been a follower of Jesus Christ from the time of Jesus' baptism by John until his Ascension into heaven. Soon the choice was narrowed to two men: Joseph, so good and holy that he was known as Joseph the

Just, and Matthias, also a very good and holy man. At this point it would seem as though Joseph had an edge over Matthias, but God's ways aren't the same as our ways. After the apostles prayed for divine guidance, they cast lots and Matthias was chosen to share in the ministry of the apostles.

So Matthias became an apostle and a witness with the others to the Resurrection of Christ. Tradition links Matthias with the country of Ethiopia, where he is believed to have met his martyrdom. The known facts about the missionary work and martyrdom of Matthias are not many. What is known is that he loved Christ and that he lived and died to spread the Good News as far as possible.

PRAY FOR VOTERS

Every year voters elect leaders and officials to run the government. Suggest that the class say a prayer for voters the world over, that these citizens will pray and study about candidates for public office and then have the insight to vote for the best-qualified persons. Ask the class if they themselves voted for the best-qualified students when they last participated in school or classroom elections.

DRAW LOTS—JUST FOR FUN

Draw lots for games, prayer leaders, roles in skits, and so on during class today. Keep it simple: draw bits of colored paper from a basket; the person who draws the one marked piece is selected.

WRITE AN AD FOR CHRISTIAN LEADERS

Review the qualification needed to be chosen to succeed Judas as an apostle and the reason for it. Then ask the students to consider qualifications they think a Christian leader should have today. Have them write a "help wanted" ad describing qualities needed to be a Christian leader.

READ MORE ABOUT IT

Have the students read Acts 1:15–26 to find out more about how Matthias was chosen to take the place of Judas. Then ask the following questions and draw lots to decide who will answer:

1. Why did the apostles need to choose a replacement for Judas? *(To fulfill the prophecy that said, "May another take his office." Judas had died and they needed another to take his place in the apostolic ministry. The number of apostles also symbolized the 12 tribes of Israel.)*

2. Where were the apostles gathered on this occasion? *(An upper room in Jerusalem.)*

3. What qualification did the new apostle have to have? *(He had to have been a follower of Jesus from the time of Jesus' baptism until his Ascension.)*

4. Why did he have to have this qualification? *(So he could witness to the Resurrection of Jesus with authority.)*

5. How did the apostles learn which candidate God wished to take Judas's place? *(They prayed for inspiration and then drew lots.)*

PRAY FOR BISHOPS AND RELIGIOUS SUPERIORS

Becoming a priest, a deacon, a brother, or a sister is not a decision made by the candidate alone. The bishops, heads of seminaries, and superiors of religious institutions must also decide whether the candidate is suited for that type of life. Have the class say a prayer today for all those persons who must make difficult decisions concerning the candidates in their charge.

Saint Isidore the Farmer   May 15

(1070–1130)

On Ash Wednesday every year, we are powerfully reminded of our strong link to the earth. The ashes placed on our foreheads are a visible reminder that each of us comes from the earth, is nourished by it during life, and will someday return to it. Isidore understood his connection with the earth.

Isidore was born in Madrid, Spain, and farming was to be his labor, working for the same landowner his whole life. While he walked the fields, plowing, planting, and harvesting, he also prayed. As a hardworking man, Isidore had three great loves: God, his family, and the soil. He and his wife María, who is also honored as a saint, proved to all their neighbors that poverty, hard work, and sorrow (their only child died as a little boy) cannot destroy human happiness if we accept them with faith and in union with Christ. Isidore understood clearly that, without soil, the human race simply cannot exist too long. This insight may explain why he always had such a reverent attitude toward his work as a farmer.

Isidore and María were known for their love of the poor. Often they brought food to poor, hungry persons and prayed with them.

During his lifetime Isidore had the gift of miracles. If he was late for work because he went to Mass, an angel was seen plowing for him. More than once he fed hungry people with food that seemed to multiply miraculously. He died after a peaceful life of hard manual labor and charity.

Isidore's goodness continued. In 1211 he helped the King of Castile in Spain during a war. He appeared to the king and showed him a path by which the king surprised and defeated the enemy. In the 1600s when King Philip of Spain was near death, people processed to his room, carrying Isidore's incorrupt body. By the time they reached the room, the king had recovered.

Today Isidore is honored in Spain as one of that country's greatest saints, and he is also honored especially in the rural United States. Not surprisingly, he is the patron of farmers and of Madrid, the capital of Spain.

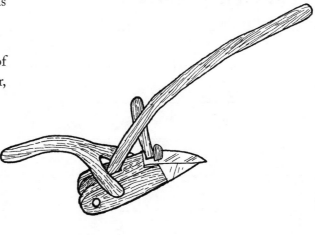

ACTIVITIES

DECORATE NATURALLY

In honor of Saint Isidore, decorate your prayer table today with gifts of nature: grain, fruits, flowers, and so on. Offer the Prayer over the Gifts (from the Mass) as an opening prayer for class today.

USE YOUR IMAGINATION

Play a pretend game. Ask the children: If Saint Isidore were to take a walk through our city, town, or rural areas today, what would he see? Would he be disturbed by the litter? Would he see gardens and fields? What could we do to make him feel at home?

TAKE A WALK OUTDOORS

Take the class out to plant some flowers or to tend a flower bed on church or school grounds. Or pick up litter on the grounds and in the neighborhood.

PRAY FOR FARMERS

In the United States Saint Isidore is patron of the National Rural Life Conference. In the state of New Mexico, his statue is brought into the fields on his feast day and also when there is a shortage of rain. Have the students pray for all farmers today, that they may be blessed with good weather, healthy crops, and a generous harvest through the intercession of Saint Isidore.

SHARE HEALTHFUL SNACKS

Invite the children to bring in healthful snack items (wrapped and with good shelf life, such as breakfast or granola bars or juice boxes) to fill an emergency ration box. If a classmate misses breakfast, forgets his or her lunch, or needs an after-school snack, the child may take an item from the ration box. If food is left at the end of the year, use it for game prizes.

ENJOY FRESH PRODUCE

- Bring in a tray of fruits and vegetables to share with the children. As they eat, ask how many of the students' families plant a garden or even an outdoor container of strawberries or cherry tomatoes. Talk about which fresh fruits and vegetables the children like most. Suggest that they help in the garden.

- Attend a farmers' market and thank the farmers who bring their produce to market. Buy a melon or other treat to share when you return to the classroom.

Catechist's Notes:

_____

_____

_____

_____

_____

Saint Bernardine of Siena   May 20

(1380–1444)

What connection can there be between decks of playing cards and a religious symbol for Jesus? The answer to this question is found in the life of Saint Bernardine of Siena.

Bernardine lived in Siena, Italy. As a little boy, he lost both parents and was cared for by his aunt. He had a brilliant mind, but when he became ill with the plague at the age of 20, it looked as though he would never have a chance to use his talents for God and the Church. Bernardine did recover, however, and entered the Franciscan order two years later. The young seminarian was ordained a priest in 1404, and the first few years of his priestly life passed quietly and unnoticed. In time, however, he began to gain fame as a remarkable preacher. Soon he was known throughout all Italy. He could hardly keep up with the many requests for his sermons. Bernardine was a fascinating speaker who had the rare ability to move his listeners to tears and to laughter in the same homily. He had a great devotion to the Holy Name of Jesus and became famous for creating the symbol IHS, which he devised from some of the Greek letters in the name of Jesus.

One of the things that Father Bernardine successfully preached against was gambling. Once he was approached by an angry man whose card making business had suffered as a result of the priest's sermons. Bernardine suggested that the man start making religious cards, instead of playing cards. The merchant's first reaction was one of disgust, but he later took Bernardine's advice and became a very wealthy man.

Throughout his life Bernardine worked humbly and patiently to spread the Good News of Jesus. Three times he refused the offer to become a bishop. He received the power to work miracles and used this gift only to help others.

MAY

LOOK FOR RELIGIOUS SYMBOLS

St. Bernardine had a great devotion to the Holy Name of Jesus and widely used the IHS symbol. Take a tour of the parish church and discover religious symbols used in the church building or furnishings.

USE STICKERS

Give each child a Jesus sticker to put on an activity page or worksheet today.

REVIEW THE SECOND COMMANDMENT

Review the second commandment: You shall not take the name of the Lord, your God, in vain. Talk about how people today use the name of Jesus. Give each child a card (playing card size). Have the students write the name *Jesus* and decorate it.

PLAY A CARD GAME

In honor of Saint Bernardine, play a card game. Using ordinary decks of cards, place a Jesus sticker on a joker. Play the game like "Old Maid," except that the person who is left with the Jesus card wins.

PRAY THE DIVINE PRAISES

Give the students a copy of the Divine Praises and lead this prayer with them. You may use the blackline master on page 455 to make copies. Call attention to the second and fourth invocations. Have the students select one of these short prayers and encourage them to say it silently during the day, especially when they meet difficulties or temptations.

LEARN ABOUT THE HOLY NAME SOCIETY

Some parishes have an organization called the Holy Name Society to promote love and respect for the name of Jesus Christ. Invite a member of this organization to speak to the class about how the society carries out its mission.

Catechist's Notes:

_____

_____

_____

_____

_____

_____

_____

_____

Saint Gregory VII

(c. 1028–1085)

Do you have the courage to tell someone that he or she is doing wrong? What if that person is the most popular kid in the class?

It takes courage to tell someone that he or she is doing wrong, but it takes heroic courage to do this when the wrongdoer is a powerful person. Pope Gregory VIII had that kind of courage. Gregory lived at a time when the Church had to battle several kinds of wrongdoing. One of the worst of these was lay investiture. This was the custom by which a layperson, usually a king or an emperor, had the right to appoint churchmen to the high office of bishop, archbishop, or abbot. This, of course, created many problems for the Church and caused much conflict among the rulers of various Christian nations.

When Gregory became pope, he began to preach against lay investiture. His chief enemy in this battle was Henry IV, emperor of Germany. The pope asked the Norman rulers of Southern Italy to help him in his fight against Henry. With their assistance the pope succeeded in having the emperor apologize for his wrongdoing, but this was not a sincere act on Henry's part. In a short time, he again attacked Pope Gregory, who was forced to leave Rome and go into exile at Salerno, Italy. Pope Gregory died in exile, after having been pope for approximately 12 years. Although he had not been totally successful in his battle against lay investiture, Pope Gregory VII was responsible for beginning the long fight that eventually managed to do away with this misuse of power.

289

LEARN ABOUT CHURCH APPOINTMENTS AND ELECTIONS

In some countries civil authorities still try to interfere with Church appointments and elections. Invite one of the parish priests to the class to explain how a bishop is appointed today or how a pope is elected. Or have small groups of volunteers research these subjects and give short reports to the class.

PRAY FOR COURAGEOUS PEOPLE

In various parts of the globe today, there are men and women who are courageously speaking out against the abuse of power by civil authorities. Encourage the students to remember these men and women in their prayers today.

PRAY FOR THE POPE

Gregory VII was the advisor to eight popes before he himself became pope. Ask the students what advice they would give the pope today. Together pray for the pope, especially that he will always have the courage to do what is right.

LOOK UP FACTS ABOUT POPES

The Church has had a long, unbroken line of popes. Direct the class to look up (in the *Catholic Almanac* or *New Catholic Encyclopedia* or on the Internet) the list of the popes and answer the following questions:

1. Who was the first pope?

2. Who is pope today?

3. How many popes has the Church had?

4. How many popes are honored with the title of saint, blessed, or venerable?

5. Who was pope the longest? the shortest?

6. Which three names have been chosen most frequently by popes?

Catechist's Notes:

_____

_____

_____

_____

_____

_____

_____

_____

Saint Mary Magdalene de Pazzi

May 25

(1566–1607)

Have you ever said, "There's something on my mind, and I'd like to talk it over with you"? If you had been acquainted with Sister Mary Magdalene de Pazzi, you would never have had to tell her what you were thinking because God gave her the ability to read minds!

Catherine de Pazzi lived in Florence, Italy. Her family was quite wealthy, and Catherine was raised to become a woman of high society. But she surprised everyone by becoming a Carmelite nun at the age of 16. She took the name Mary Magdalene and led a life of deep prayer, humility, and penance. After a number of years, she was appointed mistress of novices and then superior. It was at this time that she was given the ability to read others' thoughts, a gift that she used only for the good of the nuns.

Mary Magdalene de Pazzi suffered for three years from a severe illness that finally caused her death. During this painful period, she was heroically cheerful and kind to everyone around her. It is her deep prayer, her humble use of her God-given talents, and her practice of great charity toward others that make this quiet nun such a wonderful saint.

PLAY A REVIEW GAME

In honor of Saint Mary Magdalene de Pazzi, play a review game called Mind Reader. Print religion vocabulary review words on index cards. Give a card to a volunteer, who is NOT to look at, but to hold up to his or her forehead so others can see it. Other students give clues about the word on the card until the child guesses the correct word. If you have a large class, let them play the game in groups of four. Give each child a card to keep face down on the table and have them take turns.

TALK ABOUT CONTEMPLATIVE NUNS

Saint Mary Magdalene de Pazzi was a contemplative nun, a woman who spends her entire life in quiet prayer and hidden penance. Find out if there is a convent of contemplative nuns in your area. If so, tell the children a little bit about it. Talk about how the prayers and penances of the nuns help the whole Church.

PRAY FOR NUNS AND MONKS

Contemplative nuns and monks spend their whole lives praying for the needs of the world and doing penance for the sins of others, but they also need our prayers because they are human beings. With the students say a prayer today for all contemplative nuns and monks, and for those young men and women who may be considering serving God in such a challenging way.

MAKE A CHARITABLE RESOLUTION

To honor Saint Mary Magdalene on her feast day, encourage the students to imitate her great charity by making a resolution to think or say nothing mean about anyone, either at home or at school, and to say something kind to someone instead.

TAKE INVENTORY

Prayer was very important to Saint Mary Magdalene. She loved to pray because she loved God so much. Have the students take a personal inventory of their prayer life. You read the following; they are to write yes or no on a sheet of paper depending on whether the attitudes and actions are part of their daily life.

1. Spend some time in personal prayer.

2. Offer the day to God each morning.

3. Concentrate on class prayers.

4. Read the Bible.

5. Speak the name of Jesus reverently.

6. Pray to the Holy Spirit for guidance.

7. Join in mealtime prayers.

8. At bedtime, talk over the day with God.

Catechist's Notes:

_____

_____

_____

_____

Saint Bede

(673–735)

May 25

Saint Bede worked no miracles, saw no visions, and found no new way to God. He won heaven by living an ordinary Christian life, by doing the will of God moment by moment. He said of his life, "I have spent the whole of my life . . . devoting all of my pains to the study of the Scriptures, and amid the observances of monastic discipline and the daily task of singing in church, it has ever been my delight to learn or teach or write." Bede's life was as undramatic as that.

Bede lived in England, and by the age of seven was already in the monastery school. At 29 he was ordained a priest. His gifts for writing and teaching were noticed immediately, and he devoted his life to these two tasks. He composed 45 books. Thirty were commentaries on the Scriptures, others were on the lives of the saints and secular subjects. But his most widely recognized work was the *Ecclesiastical History of the English People*. This book has given us a clear picture of the history of the Church of early England and Ireland. It is objective, historic, and documented from trustworthy sources. Bede's whole life was dedicated to faith and learning. He died as simply as he had lived. When he felt close to death, he summoned the monks to his bed, gave them each homemade gifts, dictated the last line of his book to his secretary, and died singing the Glory Be, his favorite hymn. He is often referred to as Venerable Bede, a title of esteem.

You can learn from Bede the importance of being faithful to God in every ordinary task. Call on him for help with your present task—your studies.

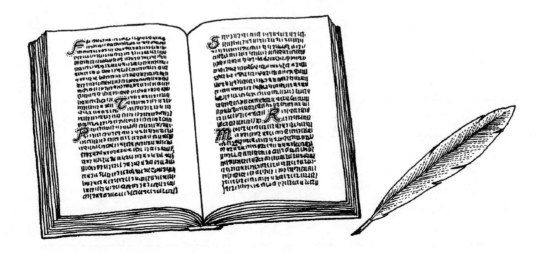

PRAY TO BEDE

Before history class today, pray to Saint Bede, a patron of historians. Or encourage the children to pray to Saint Bede before doing history homework.

LEARN ABOUT THE BENEDICTINES

Bede, a Benedictine, was educated by monks. In the Middle Ages, it was monasticism that zealously kept alive the truths of the faith and carried on the teaching of secular subjects. The monks preached, healed, labored, and continued to serve through the works of mercy. Invite a Benedictine monk or nun to the class to share some of the history of the order.

VISIT THE LIBRARY

Bede respected the resources of libraries. Today have the class visit the library, select a good book, and thank the librarian for the services he or she offers. If possible, have the children volunteer their help in the library. Or write thank-you notes to the parish or school librarian.

BE GOOD STUDENTS

Bede was an excellent student, as well as an excellent teacher. Suggest that the students imitate Saint Bede by paying close attention in class today and trying to do their work carefully and neatly.

Catechist's Notes:

Saint Philip Neri

May 26

(1515–1595)

Do you like jokes and riddles? So did Philip Neri. His two favorite books were the New Testament and a book of jokes and riddles. He is especially remembered for his great sense of humor, his cheerfulness, and his ability to bring out the best in people. "Pippi buono" (good little Phil) as his family called him, was born in Florence, Italy. The family was poor, but his parents had planned an ambitious future for Philip. When he reached 18, they sent him to be trained as a businessman with his uncle in the city. After several months, Philip wrote a thank-you note to his uncle, packed his bags, and headed for Rome. There he tutored two boys, attended the university, and lived in a small attic with only a bed, books, and a line to hang clothes. Philip achieved brilliant grades at the university. During his free time, he enjoyed Rome and visited the churches and catacombs to pray.

Once, while praying at the catacombs, Philip had a mystical experience that transformed his life. He sold his books, and for the next 13 years ministered to the young men of Rome. Philip wanted them to love their faith and to practice it. His personality helped him make friends. He encouraged young men to pray and do good works. Soon young men, rich and poor, were flocking to be with him. They went to the hospitals, made the beds, cleaned the filth, and brought food and gifts. Philip was always with them, full of jokes and ready for fun. Philip and his men gathered in the afternoons for spiritual talks, discussions, prayer, and music. Philip loved singing. Later he formed these men into a community called the Oratorians.

People noticed Philip's appealing personality, his gift of reading hearts, and his ability to direct people spiritually. They persuaded him to be ordained. His advice was welcomed by all. Ignatius Loyola, Francis de Sales, Charles Borromeo, and Camillus de Lellis are all saints who had Philip as their spiritual director. Even popes, cardinals, and bishops looked to Philip for guidance.

People enjoyed Philip's good humor and appreciated his humble and simple ways. Philip was opposed to anything that was pretentious or snobbish. He went about in old clothes and big white shoes, with his hat cocked to the side. When the pope wanted to make Philip a cardinal, he left a cardinal's hat outside Philip's door. Philip used it to play catch. Another time when people were following him around saying he was a saint, Philip shaved off half of his beard.

After hearing about the great conversions of Francis Xavier, Philip wanted to go to the Indies. But a friend of his persuaded him to continue his good works in Rome.

Philip teaches us that being holy does not mean being sad. One can be joyful and spontaneous in loving God. God's love impels us to go out and spread the Gospel in charity and service. And when we serve God, people should see smiles on our faces!

SING A SCRIPTURAL SONG

Philip Neri loved music and singing. He felt that the best musicians were those who composed songs based on Scripture and who wrote them in the people's native language. To celebrate Philip's feast, sing a scriptural song the children enjoy, for example, "This Little Light of Mine," or a joyous psalm from the parish hymnal.

USE HUMOR

Philip felt that it was a great grace to be able to laugh at oneself. Discuss this idea with the students. Then ask each of them to choose one of the following ways to use their own sense of humor:

- laughing rather than pouting when things don't go your way.

- cheerfully accepting difficulties.

- acting enthusiastic rather than indifferent or bored when the class has a project.

USE GIFTS FOR GOOD

Philip used his natural gifts—his personality, his humor, his spirit of fun—to influence people to be good. Give each child a paper on which you have written a natural gift you see in him or her. Ask the children to write about or draw one way they will use this gift to help others or do some good.

TELL JOKES OR RIDDLES

Have a couple of jokes and riddles ready to share with the students. Invite them to share their favorite jokes or to perform comedy skits.

Catechist's Notes:

_____

_____

_____

_____

_____

_____

_____

_____

_____

_____

Saint Augustine of Canterbury

(c. 605)

May 27

Do you think it would be exciting to go to a strange and unknown place? Or would it be scary? Or both? Today's saint—Augustine of Canterbury—shows us that it's OK to be a little bit afraid.

Augustine was a monk and a friend of Pope Gregory the Great's. The pope respected Augustine's virtues of loyalty and perseverance, and appointed him to lead a group of 30 missionaries to evangelize England. The men started out in fine spirits, but as they traveled on, they heard stories about the treacherous channel of water they had to cross and about the tribes of fierce warriors in England. The missionaries became so afraid that they persuaded Augustine to return to Rome to ask the pope if they could give up the journey. But Gregory encouraged the fearful Augustine and sent him back to lead the missionaries on to England.

The terrified missionaries, who could not speak English, were met by Ethelbert, overlord of Kent. Fortunately the king was married to a Christian princess from Paris, so he gave them a house and allowed them to preach. But he was hesitant to give up his own pagan beliefs. During his stay in England, Augustine wrote many letters to Pope Gregory, asking for advice about his missionary work. It was through the wisdom and direction of Gregory that the missionary efforts in England were profitable. Pope Gregory instructed the men to respect local customs, to leave pagan temples standing and destroy only the idols, and most of all to give witness by their lives of Christianity. The monks did just that. They preached, cared for the poor, endured hardships patiently, lived simply, and prayed much. By 601 Ethelbert and many others were baptized. Augustine wrote to Gregory, pleading for more missionaries. Gregory responded by sending more men, sacred books and vessels, and relics. Augustine built the first cathedral in Canterbury.

Augustine died after only seven years of work in England, so he was never able to see the faith take root. Like Augustine, we must have faith and proceed slowly, even if we meet with what we think is limited success in doing God's work. The advice of Gregory to Augustine still holds true today. "He who would climb to a lofty height must go by steps, not leaps."

ACTIVITIES

GO ON A MISSION TRIP

If the weather is nice, lead the children on a little mission trip. Give them some sidewalk chalk and let them draw and write the Good News of Jesus on the playground, parking lot, or church sidewalk.

WORK FOR RECONCILIATION

When Augustine met with the leaders of the Irish church, he forgot to stand when they came into the room. They were hurt and refused to listen to him, speak to him, or acknowledge him as archbishop. Augustine continued to work patiently for reconciliation with them. Ask the students to follow Saint Augustine's good example and ask forgiveness today of anyone whom they have hurt.

TALK ABOUT MISSION WORK

Pope Gregory the Great supported mission work. He brought the faith to different countries by sending groups of missionaries and encouraging their efforts. Discuss with the students how the present pope encourages mission work by his letters, his visits, and his prayers. How does this help the faith of people in mission lands? In what ways is our country a mission land?

BE SCHOOL MISSIONARIES

Augustine has been called "Apostle of England" because of his missionary efforts. Yet he had normal, human struggles. Tell the students that today they should see who can be an "Apostle of (name of your school)" by being neat in the cafeteria, by listening and participating during class, or by helping other students. Stress that good example is a powerful way to spread the faith.

READ AND WRITE LETTERS

Have the class read Saint Paul's letters to Timothy and compare the advice given by Paul to the advice given by Pope Gregory to Augustine. Then have the students imagine that they are Augustine and have them each write a letter to Gregory.

Catechist's Notes:

Saint Bernard of Montjoux   May 28

(c. 996–c. 1081)

Yuu probably know that cities are sometimes named after saints: think of St. Louis, Missouri, and St. Paul, Minnesota. And how about San Francisco and San Antonio (Spanish for Saint Francis and Saint Anthony) or St. Petersburg, Florida? You know that people and parishes are given the names of patron saints. But did you know that Saint Bernard dogs are named for a real saint?

Bernard was a priest in the Northern Italian region of Aosta. This is a mountainous area where the Alps, a very high mountain range, cross through Italy, France, and Switzerland. Bernard knew these mountains. For more than 40 years, he traveled throughout his diocese, visiting every mountainside village and valley. He celebrated Eucharist and Reconciliation with the people, gave instructions in the faith, built churches, and started schools. Everywhere he went he heard stories of travelers who had been lost in the mountains and frozen to death or been ambushed by robbers. Perhaps he himself experienced the threat of a sudden snowstorm or avalanche. Perhaps a family he knew took him in until he could continue on his way.

Today you can fly over the Alps or travel smoothly by rail or car. But back in the 11th century, people traveled on foot, on horseback, or in carts. You may wonder why people would try to cross the Alps if it was so treacherous. Well, some were soldiers and some were businessmen, but many of the travelers were pilgrims on their way to Rome, the center of the Church. Remember, these mountains cut Italy off from the western part of Europe.

Bernard saw a need, and he decided to do something about it. Bernard built two hospices (something like motels) for travelers where they could find not only shelter from the weather and safety from robbers, but also a place to rest and eat. These hospices were located along two of the most frequently used routes, which eventually were also named for Bernard—the Great St. Bernard Pass and the Little St. Bernard Pass. He brought Augustinian monks to run the hospices, and they built a monastery in the mountains. The monks welcomed all travelers—day and night—without asking if they had money to pay or what their religion was. Every morning a patrol went out to look for travelers who were lost or injured and brought them back to the hospice. It was the monks who eventually bred the large, furry dogs—now called Saint Bernards—to help them find and rescue lost travelers.

In 1923 Pope Pius XI named Saint Bernard the patron of Alpinists and mountain climbers, and he is also claimed by skiers.

ACTIVITIES

ILLUSTRATE A PSALM

Have the students copy Psalm 147:15–18 on a sheet of drawing paper and illustrate these verses.

FIND IT ON A MAP

Locate Valle d'Aosta and the Alps on a map. Look for the Great St. Bernard Pass and Little St. Bernard Pass. Have students find the altitudes of the Alps and these passes and compare these figures to the altitude where they live.

PRACTICE HOSPITALITY

Have the children find out about hospitality in their parish. What is being done to help travelers feel welcome in the parish? Is there a Web site, a list of Sunday Masses, a sign outside church, a sign at the edge of town, information at motels in the area? Let the students undertake one of these projects if they find a need.

PRAY FOR TRAVELERS

Invite the students to pray for all travelers today. Let individuals mention names of people they know who are traveling.

Catechist's Notes:

_____

_____

_____

_____

_____

_____

_____

_____

_____

_____

_____

_____

Saint Joan of Arc May 30

(1412–1431)

Safe on the farm at Domremy, herding her father's sheep, Joan was unaware of the troubles France was having. The Hundred Years War was raging, and France was surrendering town after town to the English.

When she was 14 years old, Joan was working in the garden. A bright light descended and she saw three heavenly visitors, whom she identified as Saint Michael the Archangel and the virgin martyrs, Saint Catherine of Alexandria and Saint Margaret of Antioch. Over time they revealed to Joan her mission: to save the city of Orleans from the English, make sure the prince was crowned king of France, and drive the English out of France. The voices also helped her pray.

Two years later the voices insisted that she tell the general of the forces near her town of her mission to save France. Her visit to the general proved fruitless. He laughed at the thought of soldiers being commanded by a young girl and sent her home. When Joan pleaded with her voices that she could not do the task they asked because she could not read, write, or fight, and because the general had refused her assistance, the voices told her, "It is God who will command the army."

Joan returned to the general. This time he gained her an audience with the crown prince. He sent Joan to theologians to be questioned. They declared she sounded authentic, and Joan was given the leadership of the French forces. Joan's positive attitude lifted the soldiers' morale.

The sight of Joan in white armor, holding the flag with the symbol of France, the fleur-de-lis, and the words *Jesus* and *Mary* on it, rallied the men. They marched to Orleans. Joan had every soldier go to confession and prepare spiritually. The fighting began, but after 12 hours, the French were still not successful. Joan had been wounded by an arrow, but after treatment, she re-entered the battle and urged the army on to victory. The French credited Joan and the power of God with the victory. It was the feast of St. Michael.

The crown prince was made king after many difficulties. Finally Joan's army occupied nine towns, and she was winning France back from England. But some were jealous of her, and she was captured and sold to the English. Not one person in France came to her aid. No soldiers. Not the King. The English put her on trial. They tried to get her to deny that her voices were from God. They tortured her. Finally, afraid and exhausted, she signed a paper denying her voices. But immediately she refuted the document and declared the holiness and truth of her mission. For this the court condemned her to be burned at the stake. As she was led to the stake, an English soldier made her a cross of twigs. She died crying, "Jesus, Jesus."

Twenty-five years later, the Church examined Joan's trial and declared her innocent. She was beatified in 1910 and canonized in 1920. We learn from Joan that when we allow God to work in our lives, we can do impossible things.

ENJOY A DRAMATIZATION OR VIDEO

The life of Saint Joan of Arc has often been depicted in plays and novels. Have the students choose portions of her life to dramatize, or show a video of her story.

OBEY PARENTS AND TEACHERS

Ask the children to think about who guides them and tells them what God wants them to do (parents, teachers, grandparents, older brothers or sisters, friends, pastor, and so on). Encourage students to obey these guides who help them do what is good.

LEAD CHEERS

Joan placed her confidence in God. Suggest that the students try to face difficult situations in their lives in the spirit of Joan of Arc. Talk about how an enthusiastic, uplifting spirit can make a home, a playground, a classroom, or a gym a happier place. Divide the class into groups and let the members of each group come up with a cheer in which they can lead the class.

MAKE BANNERS

Show the class a fleur-de-lis, a stylized lily that is the symbol of France and of Our Lady, a symbol of purity. Compare it to the Irish shamrock, which is also a national and religious symbol. Then have the students make banners like the one Joan carried into battle, but using their own symbols for faith and for their class. Decorate the classroom with their banners.

IDENTIFY THE SAINTS

Have the students find out about the three saints who spoke to Joan: Saint Michael the Archangel, Saint Catherine of Alexandria, Saint Margaret of Antioch. Then ask them to tell why they think these saints were good helpers to Joan and France.

Catechist's Notes:

_____

_____

_____

_____

_____

_____

_____

_____

Visitation

Have you ever waited for a friend or special relative to arrive? You watch at the window, you listen for the car. And you know the joy you feel when you see your friend or loved one at the door.

Perhaps the greatest visit ever made was the one Mary made to her relative Elizabeth. This event is called the Visitation. The Gospel of Luke records that after the angel announced to Mary that she was to be the Mother of God, she left at once to visit Elizabeth, who in her old age was to give birth to a son. Elizabeth was already six months pregnant. Mary went to help her and also to enjoy the support of this older, holy woman.

The four-day journey over rocky roads in the heat was not an easy one, especially considering that Mary was pregnant. Mary most likely traveled with a caravan.

What a wonderful visit it must have been. As soon as Elizabeth saw Mary, her baby leaped for joy within her. She greeted Mary as the Mother of the Lord. And Mary's response was a hymn of praise to God, the Magnificat. Mary stayed with Elizabeth three months, probably until her son, John, was born.

Mary's whole life was filled with the good news that Jesus was coming. The Church has always praised Mary as the Christ-bearer for two reasons. First by the power of the Spirit, Mary physically brought Christ to the world. Second she brings Christ spiritually to everyone by the holiness of her words and example.

We can love and imitate Mary by bringing Christ to others too. We can reach out, visit others, and share the Good News of Jesus Christ by our love and concern for them. The more we think about Mary and the message of the Gospel, the more we will be like her in our own lives.

MAY

Blessed are you among women

BRING SCRIPTURE TO LIFE
Read the account of the Visitation directly from the Bible, Luke 1:39–56. Have the children act out the story or write a news story as if the event is taking place today.

PRAY THE SECOND JOYFUL MYSTERY
Pray the Second Joyful Mystery, the Visitation, with the class today. You may wish to divide the Scripture account (Luke 1:39–56) into 10 parts to read as short meditations before each Hail Mary of the decade.

PRAY THE SONG OF MARY
Use the blackline master on page 452 to make copies of the Magnificat for the students. Divide the class into two groups to alternate the verses of the prayer.

VISIT OR WRITE TO RELATIVES
Tell the students that Mary visited the elderly Elizabeth because Mary was concerned about her relative. Encourage them to visit an elderly neighbor or relative, or write to their grandparents on this feast day.

SCRIPTURE STUDY
Explain to the students that the message of Mary's Magnificat, Luke 1:46–55, has special importance for our times. Mary rejoices because the good news about Jesus means that God has exalted the lowly. The Gospel of Jesus is for those who are poor in spirit. Salvation is for those who trust only in Jesus. Have the students compare the words of the Magnificat to Luke 6:20–26. How are the words of Jesus in this passage saying the same thing? Conclude by praying the Magnificat. You may use the blackline master on page 452 to make copies for the students.

HELP MOTHERS
Mary is the example of bringing Christ to others through charity and the spirit of service. Suggest that the students assist their mothers in some service this evening in imitation of Mary.

Catechist's Notes:

Immaculate Heart of Mary

Ordinary Time

(Saturday following the Second Sunday after Pentecost)

"Conquests and empires not founded on justice cannot be blessed by God. . . . Nothing is lost by peace, but everything may be lost by war," wrote Pope Pius XII on August 24, 1939. A week later Adolph Hitler unleashed his army and opened fire on Poland. The Second World War had begun. On the radio, by letter, and in person, the pope pleaded for peace. Nation after nation entered the war, and thousands were killed in battle daily.

It seemed the world needed someone whose heart could bear the sorrow of the Church and the world and bring comfort. Who other than Mary? The Mother of God possesses such a heart of charity that she wishes all people to love her Son and be saved. It was at this time in 1942 that Pope Pius XII consecrated the world to the Immaculate Heart of Mary and recommended this devotion. But this devotion is not just for times of war; it is for all times.

Mary's heart is a symbol of her love and her holiness. By honoring the heart of Mary, we honor her and ultimately God.

Mary loves each person, and when we dedicate ourselves to her Immaculate Heart, she will help each of us deepen our friendship with God. By coming to know the love of Mary, we will come to know better the overwhelming love of God. Today let us dedicate ourselves to the Immaculate Heart of Mary and confide to her all those intentions we have that most need her love and care.

ACTIVITIES

ENTRUST LOVED ONES TO MARY

The heart of Mary is mentioned in the Gospel of Luke 2:52. Read the reference and ask the children what Mary was "storing in her heart." Have the students cut out hearts of different sizes, decorate them, and make a design of them. In the middle of each heart, have them write the name of someone they would like Mary to protect and help. Above the hearts, print "Immaculate Heart of Mary, pray for us."

PRAY OR SING TO MARY

Have the class pray to the Immaculate Heart of Mary or sing a Marian hymn to ask Mary to intercede for world peace.

READ ABOUT FATIMA

Tell or have the children read the story of Our Lady of Fatima. You may use the story of Francisco and Jacinta Marto in this book (feast February 20, page 211). Tell the class that this appearance of Mary reawakened devotion to the Immaculate Heart of Mary.

Catechist's Notes:

_____

_____

_____

_____

_____

_____

_____

_____

_____

_____

_____

Saint Justin

(c. 165)

"Nobody in his senses gives up truth for falsehood." Would you be willing to say this if a powerful judge ordered you to deny your faith in Jesus Christ or lose your life?

Justin was not afraid to be loyal to his Christian faith. As a young man, he searched everywhere for truth. He traveled to many big cities, where he talked and studied with wise teachers. One day a stranger told Justin to read the books of the Old Testament prophets, who had foretold the coming of Christ. He did this, and it eventually led him to the recognition that the Christian religion taught the truth—that Jesus had brought the truth into the world. He accepted the newfound faith and was baptized.

Justin began to speak and write in defense of Christianity, since some people of the time were attacking what Christians believed and practiced. His books gave us some insight into what the early Church was like. In one of them he described the ceremony of Baptism in the Church around the year 160. It was very similar to the ceremony today. In another place he wrote that the Sunday meetings of the Christian community included readings from Scriptures, a homily, offering of bread and wine, and giving Communion to the assembled people. Doesn't this remind you of the eucharistic celebration today?

In about 165, Justin was arrested for being a Christian, but he refused to give up his faith in Jesus. The judge asked him, "Do you have an idea that you will go up to heaven and receive some suitable rewards?" Justin answered, "It is not an idea that I have; it is something that I know well and hold to be most certain." The judge ordered him to be killed. Justin was a strong and courageous martyr.

JUNE

ACTIVITIES

COMPLETE A CHECKLIST

Justin was the first to record the beliefs and actions of eucharistic worship. He loved to participate in the Eucharist because he gained peace and strength from its nourishment. Discuss ways students might participate in the eucharistic liturgy and give each of them a copy of the list on the blackline master on page 456.

Check the ways you can participate in the eucharistic liturgy.

_____ planning the liturgy

_____ playing an instrument

_____ presentation of gifts

_____ giving to the collection

_____ singing and giving responses at Mass

_____ being a lector

_____ reading the general intercessions

_____ designing a banner for the liturgy

REVIEW ACTIONS AND RESPONSES

Review and practice gestures and responses for the Mass with the children, for example, making the Sign of the Cross with holy water, receiving Communion, genuflecting, standing tall for the Gospel reading, and so on.

PLAN LITURGY

Have the class prepare a liturgy for the feast of Saint Justin. Allow the students to study and discuss the life of the saint and the readings chosen for the Mass. Have them suggest appropriate songs for the liturgy, compose petitions, and choose lectors, servers, and gift bearers. Let the whole class participate in the entrance procession—a sign of unity of priest and people and of our journey to the promised land of heaven.

LEARN TERMS

Help students become more familiar with the following terms used in the celebration of the liturgy:

altar of sacrifice	paten
bread (host)	pew
candle	priest/presider
chalice (cup)	presider's chair
cross	sacramentary
crucifix	tabernacle
incense	vestments
lectionary	wine
lector	

Children may draw pictures or cut pictures out of old religion textbooks or religious goods catalogs in order to do one of the following:

- Using the words, make an illustrated dictionary.

- Make and play a matching game. Write the illustrated words and definitions or words and pictures on separate index cards.

- Make and use illustrated flash cards.

LEARN THE TRUTH

Justin spent many years searching for the meaning of life. He found his answer when he discovered Jesus. Remind the students they have rich opportunities every day or week to study their faith. Encourage them to participate enthusiastically in religion class and to share faith experiences so that they can help one another to know and love the faith.

Saints Marcellinus and Peter

June 2

(d. c.300)

Long ago, people hardly ever wrote down the story of a person's life. Of course, there were no computers or printing presses in those days. But Pope Damasus I (366–384) was devoted to the martyrs of the Church. He restored and decorated their tombs in the catacombs and wrote verses about them. It is through him that we know about the martyrdom of Marcellinus and Peter, which took place during the persecution by Diocletian (284–305). Pope Damasus obtained the information from the executioner himself.

Marcellinus was a good, holy priest who lived about the year 300 in Rome. One day a Christian named Peter, who was in prison because of his faith in Jesus, asked Marcellinus to baptize the jailer and his family. Peter had converted this family while he was serving his prison sentence. When the governor learned that Peter had been spreading the Christian faith and that Marcellinus had baptized Peter's converts, he called both men into court. He ordered them to offer incense to the false gods. When they refused, the governor commanded his soldiers to kill them. They were taken out to a grove of trees and beheaded. A few years later, Constantine, the first Christian emperor, had a large church built over the place where these two martyrs were buried.

If it sometimes seems hard to admit that you believe in Jesus and the faith of the Church, remember how brave Marcellinus and Peter were long ago.

JUNE

DRAMATIZE STORY FROM ACTS

Tradition holds that Marcellinus and Peter converted the jailer and his family. Have the students read a similar story in Acts 16:25–34. Then let them dramatize the story.

REPORT ON MARTYRS

Marcellinus and Peter are included (optional) in Eucharistic Prayer I. Equip the students with missalettes and have them find the saints mentioned in this prayer. Recall the saints you have already learned about this year. Or assign the ones who are in this book to various students for short reports.

LEARN ABOUT THE CATACOMBS

Both Marcellinus and Peter were buried in the catacombs. See what the students remember about the catacombs. Refer to the activity for May 12, the feast of Saints Nereus and Achilleus, on page 282.

WRITE A STATEMENT OF FAITH

Read aloud the following epitaph Pope Damasus wrote for his own grave. Then invite the students to write a statement that expresses their own faith in the risen Christ.

> He who walking on the sea could calm
> the bitter waves, who gives life to the
> dying seeds of the earth; he who was able
> to loose the mortal chains of death, and
> after three days' darkness could bring
> again to the upper world the brother for
> sister Martha: he, I believe, will make
> Damasus rise again from the dust.

DESCRIBE CHRISTIAN COURAGE

Have the students print the word *courage* vertically on their papers. For each letter have them write a word or phrase that describes Christian courage.

C _____

O _____

U _____

R _____

A _____

G _____

E _____

Catechist's Notes:

_____

_____

_____

_____

_____

_____

_____

Saint Charles Lwanga and Companions

June 3

(d. 1886)

Yesterday the Church honored two martyrs who were beheaded in Rome early in the fourth century. Today we remember and celebrate a group of martyrs from the 19th century.

Charles Lwanga lived in the kingdom of Buganda, now the country of Uganda in central Africa. Charles was assistant to Joseph Mkasa, the chief of the pages of Mwanga's court, who was secretly a catechist. Mwanga, a cruel tyrant, had forbidden the practice of Christianity because the Christians put loyalty to Christ above loyalty to the king. On November 13, 1885, he had Mkasa beheaded for his faith. Charles requested and received Baptism that same night.

Charles was then made head of the page boys and did his best to protect them from Mwanga's immoral sexual demands. A few months later when Mwanga called for one of the pages and he couldn't be found, he learned that the boy had been receiving religious instruction. Mwanga was enraged. He ordered that the compound be closed so no one could escape and summoned the royal executioners. That night Charles baptized four boys who had been preparing for Baptism. One of them was a 13-year-old named Kizito.

In the morning Mwanga gathered all the members of his court. He demanded that "those who pray" (the Christians) stand aside. Fifteen young men, all under 25 years old, identified themselves as Christians, and though Mwanga threatened them with death, they stood firm. At least two Christian soldiers joined them.

Mwanga ordered that the Christians be taken to Namugongo, 37 miles away. Witnesses reported that they went joyfully, singing hymns and praying loudly. Several died on the long walk. When they arrived Mbasa, the son of the chief executioner, was struck down first. Charles Lwanga and the others were wrapped in reed mats, placed on a pile of wood, and burned.

Thirty-two Christians—both Catholics and Anglicans—were martyred during a two-year period. The missionaries who had brought the faith were expelled. Mwanga thought that this would be the end of the Christians. But the African Christians took courage from the martyrs. They translated the catechism into their native language and continued to secretly instruct others in the faith. When missionary priests returned after Mwanga's death, 500 Christians and 1,000 catechumens were waiting for them.

COMPOSE A SONG

Invite the children to compose a song that Charles Lwanga and his companions could sing, or choose a song from your parish hymnal. If possible, accompany the singing with drums and rhythm instruments.

CITE EXAMPLES OF GROUP STRENGTH

Ask the students to give examples of groups whose members have stood firm when faced with evil, sin, or social pressure. Have the students use examples from the news, from their reading, or from their personal experience. To begin the discussion, share some examples from your own experience.

RESEARCH MISSIONARY WORK IN AFRICA

Have the students locate Uganda on a map or globe. Have them research on line the status of the Church in Uganda today and missionary work in Africa of groups such as Holy Childhood Association and the Society for the Propagation of the Faith. Work together to write a prayer for the Catholics of Uganda and for missionaries who serve in Africa.

CELEBRATE THE LITURGY

The martyrs of Uganda joyfully accepted death rather than betray their Christian faith. Encourage the students to proclaim their own faith by participating wholeheartedly in the celebration of the liturgy. Have the students pray today to Saint Charles to help them be strong in their faith.

LEARN MORE ABOUT CATECHUMENS

Ask the students to look up the meaning of *catechumen* and to find out what catechumens do in preparation for Baptism.

Catechist's Notes:

_____

_____

_____

_____

_____

_____

_____

_____

_____

Saint Boniface

(675–754)

Let's move back in time and pretend. The date is about 723. The place is Mount Gundenberg in Hesse, a region that is in Germany today. The characters are Bishop Boniface and a crowd of pagan tree-worshipers.

Pagan 1: Who is that?

Pagan 2: He is Bishop Boniface.

Pagan 3: What is he going to do with that ax?

Pagan 1: Maybe he is going to offer a sacrifice to Thor.

Pagan 2: No, he is a Christian. He will never offer a sacrifice to our gods.

Pagan 1: Look! He is going to chop down Thor's sacred tree!

Several Pagans: He can't do that! The gods will strike him dead!

Boniface continues to chop steadily and firmly. The pagans watch him, terrified. Finally, the tree falls to the earth with a crash like thunder.

Pagan 3: Watch out! The thunder god will punish him—and us! Look out everyone!

Boniface: My friends, I have only destroyed this tree. There is no lightning to strike you, no thunder. See how the tree has fallen. It looks like a cross. Listen to what I want to tell you about the one true God and his wonderful Son. His Son came to earth to tell us how to live in order to earn heaven, his home, forever and ever. Just listen.

Before he became a bishop, Boniface, who was baptized Winfrid, was a brilliant and talented monk in a Benedictine monastery in England. He was the head of a monastery school, but he thought God wanted him to be a missionary in a pagan land. He went to Frisia, a region that is now in Holland, to begin his work. A war in that country forced him to return to England for a few years.

But he did not give up. Next he journeyed to Rome to ask the pope to tell him where to serve. Pope Gregory II changed his name to Boniface and sent him to eastern Germany. For nearly 35 years, Boniface traveled all over Germany, preaching, teaching, and building schools, monasteries, and convents. He made another trip back to Rome to report to the pope about his work. While he was there, the pope ordained him a bishop and sent him back to Germany to continue his missionary work. He invited monks and nuns—including his cousin Lioba—from England to come and help him. The Benedictine monastery at Fulda is probably the most famous one Boniface started.

As an old man, Boniface returned to Frisia to work there among the pagans. Early one morning he was waiting to confirm about 20 converts. A band of angry natives ambushed and murdered Boniface and his companions. Today Saint Boniface is called the Apostle of Germany.

WRITE ABOUT THEIR WORK AS APOSTLES

Boniface is called the Apostle of Germany. An apostle is one who is sent to bring the Good News of Jesus. Ask the students to think of where Christ is sending them as apostles. Have them write a paragraph with one of the following titles:

> (Their name): An Apostle to the _____ Family

> (Their name): An Apostle at _____ School

> (Their name): An Apostle to _____ Parish

RESEARCH THE MEANING OF NAMES

Pope Gregory II gave Boniface his name, which means "a man who does good deeds."

- Encourage the students to find out the roots of their Christian names. Two books that may help are *A Saint for Your Name: Saints for Girls* and *A Saint for Your Name: Saints for Boys* by Albert J. Nevins, M.M., revised and updated by Ann Ball (Our Sunday Visitor, Inc., 200 Noll Plaza, Huntington, Indiana 46750).

- Remind students that they will have an opportunity at Confirmation either to chose a new name or to keep their baptismal name.

REFLECT ON FRIENDS AND FRIENDSHIP

St. Boniface is remembered for the great strength of his friendships. He cared for his friends deeply and led them to live holy lives. Ask the students to reflect on the importance of friends and the friendships they have now. Have them write in their journals how they have led their friends to Jesus or how their friends have led them to Jesus.

CELEBRATE GERMAN HERITAGE

Boniface's work planted the seeds of the Catholic Church in Germany. This later became a strong Catholic country, whose patron is Saint Boniface. Have the students discover some of the rich religious customs that have come from Germany and present them to the class on a special day. Perhaps some students could bake German cookies and serve them to make the day festive.

LEARN ABOUT SAINT LIOBA

The missionary success Boniface achieved for the Church could not have been possible if it had not been for his cousin Lioba and her sisters, who helped him in his preaching and teaching. Tell the students the following story of Lioba, who was loved for her kindness and wisdom.

> Lioba was educated in an English convent. When Boniface was sent to convert the Germanic tribes, she wrote him letters promising prayers and asked Boniface to pray for her studies. Boniface wrote to Tetta, who was superior of Lioba's convent, asking for help in his work. Tetta sent Lioba and 30 sisters to act as assistants to Boniface. The holiness and gentleness of Lioba encouraged many girls to become nuns also.

REPORT ON SAINTLY TEAMS

Lioba worked closely with Boniface in Christianizing central Europe. Have the students find out about other saintly "teams" in Church history and report on them. A few of them are Saints Francis de Sales and Jane de Chantal, Saints Francis of Assisi and Clare, Saints Vincent de Paul and Louise de Marillac, Saints Jerome and Paula, and Saints Teresa of Ávila and John of the Cross.

Saint Norbert

(1080–1134)

June 6

Do you remember how Saint Paul was changed from an enemy of Jesus into a strong, loyal Christian? Norbert had a similar experience when he was a young man.

Norbert was born in Germany, a cousin to the emperor, so he had nearly everything he wanted in life: money, popularity, success. But his carefree life did not make him happy. One day he went horseback riding through the woods. Unexpectedly a heavy storm broke. A sudden bolt of lightning frightened his horse. As the horse reared up, Norbert fell to the ground. When he regained consciousness, he considered the accident a warning from God. Like Saint Paul, he wondered. "Lord, what do you want me to do?" Norbert seemed to hear a voice deep within him say, "Give up the foolish, empty life you are leading. Begin to do good to those around you." Norbert took these words very seriously. He sold all his property and prepared to be ordained a priest.

Once he was a priest, Norbert preached to everyone about the danger of living the way he had lived a few years before. Over the years so many young men wanted to live the way Norbert did that he had to start several monasteries. He tried to build these monasteries in out-of-the-way places, where people did not hear the word of God very often. Near each monastery, Norbert usually opened a hospice. Here sick people, travelers, and pilgrims could find rest and help.

By the time he died, Norbert was an archbishop. He had worked very hard to stop heresies and to encourage loyalty to the pope. He had preached with great success to the rich and the poor, to the wise and the uneducated, and to believers and nonbelievers. Norbert was a man of faith, goodness, and loyalty.

JUNE

POST A CLASS MOTTO

Norbert wrote a rule for his priests to follow. The first sentence begins, "Be of one mind and heart in God." Tell the class this is a good rule to have in the classroom. Have volunteers print this quote and decorate it. Then hang it in the room as a class motto.

WRITE NOTES TO PARISH PRIESTS

Norbert saw the value of the priestly ministry and tried to help priests in any way he could. Encourage the students to get to know the names of their parish priests and how to spell them. Perhaps they could write letters to the priests, telling them how much the students appreciate the service the priests give to Christ and the Church.

LIST WAYS TO LIVE LIKE THE FIRST CHRISTIANS

Norbert loved to teach about the faith and generosity of the early Christians who had been empowered by the Holy Spirit. Have the students read Acts 4:32–35. Brainstorm and list the things they could do to live in the spirit of the early Christians.

REVIEW REVERENCE FOR THE EUCHARIST

Respect and reverence for the Holy Eucharist meant much to Saint Norbert. Review with the students the importance of being reverent when they receive this sacrament. Remind them not to chew gum or talk when they are attending the celebration of the Mass. Have them recall what the eucharistic fast is.

MAKE A LIST OF SPENDING

Before Norbert reformed, he led a carefree and worldly life. He wastefully spent money on luxuries he did not need. Discuss with the students the importance of sharing their own wealth with the needy. Have them make a list of how they use their personal funds. Suggest they add to the list "Give to the needy" if it isn't already there.

Catechist's Notes:

_____

_____

_____

_____

_____

_____

_____

_____

Saint Ephrem

(306–373)

Have you ever thought of being a writer? Authors are an interesting group of people. Some of them write history or science fiction; others write westerns or travel stories. Ephrem was a different sort of author. He wrote poems, hymns, and homilies.

He was born in the country that today is Turkey. As a young man, Ephrem had outbursts of temper. Gradually he gained control of his anger by relying on God's help. Ephrem was ordained a deacon and became a well-known teacher. Years later the bishop suggested that Ephrem be ordained a priest. Ephrem begged the bishop to allow him to stay a deacon because he thought he was not good enough to be a priest.

Although Ephrem never became a priest, he did become a monk. When the Persian army conquered his homeland, Ephrem had to seek refuge. He escaped to the mountains and lived alone in a cave. Once people in the nearby city discovered him, many came to listen to him and ask for help with their problems.

At this time Ephrem did a lot of writing. His homilies were very popular and so were his religious poems. He also took the songs that heretics were teaching and changed the words. He used these same popular melodies to teach the truths of the Catholic faith. Ephrem was one of the first to write songs for the liturgy of the Church. He wrote so many beautiful and original hymns that he has been called "Harp of the Holy Spirit." Quite a few of his homilies and hymns were devoted to Mary, the Mother of God.

A long time after Ephrem died he was named a Doctor of the Church.

PRAY FOR SELF-CONTROL

Discuss with the students the importance of having self-control in daily life. Lead them to decide on an area in their lives in which they could improve their self-control. Take time to pray silently for God's help in this.

COMPOSE PETITIONS TO PRAY FOR REFUGEES

Recall that Ephrem was a refugee at one point in his life. Raise the class's awareness of the sufferings of present-day refugees by having the students list the painful situations that refugees might have to face in leaving their homeland. Then have each student compose a petition for refugees. Lead the class in a litany of petitions. The response to each petition could be "Lord, guide your people."

WRITE SONGS FOR REVIEW

Have the students work together in small groups to write new words to a familiar melody about a topic the class is studying. Let groups sing their songs for the class.

ILLUSTRATE A FAVORITE HYMN

Provide music books and direct students to choose one of their favorite hymns. Have them print the words of one stanza on a sheet of paper. Then have them write a few sentences on the paper, explaining the meaning of those words. Finally have them illustrate the song or create a border design on the paper.

WRITE ALPHABET PRAYERS

Encourage the students to compose a religious song or prayer. To give them some structure for this, suggest an alphabet prayer. Tell the students to print a sequence of letters from the alphabet on the left side of the paper and use each letter as the first letter of a line of the prayer. Here is one example.

> **A**lways I praise you, my Creator and Father.
> **B**ecause you give me life and faith and friends.
> **C**an I ever thank you enough?

SING A NEW SONG

In honor of Saint Ephrem, teach the students a new song that could be used in the eucharistic liturgy. Encourage the students to sing with conviction and joy.

Catechist's Notes:

_____

_____

_____

_____

_____

_____

Saint Barnabas

(first century)

He was called Joseph at first. When he left his native island of Cyprus, he may have had no idea what life held for him. Soon he became a Christian, perhaps on the day of Pentecost.

The apostles welcomed Joseph into the Christian community and changed his name to Barnabas, which means "son of encouragement." Barnabas sold his property and gave the money to the community in Jerusalem. Gradually other Christians came to see that Barnabas was a man of deep faith, filled with the Holy Spirit.

After Paul's conversion, it was Barnabas who introduced Paul to the apostles and encouraged everyone to accept him. Barnabas trusted Paul and took the risk of defending him.

For a while Barnabas and Paul were leaders in the Church at Antioch. There for the first time, followers of Christ were called "Christians." This name shows that others began to think of Jesus' followers as a religious group separate from Jews and pagans.

When Barnabas and Paul returned to Jerusalem, the Holy Spirit had other plans for them. One day as a few Church leaders were fasting and praying together, they came to see that Barnabas and Paul were to be set apart by the Holy Spirit for special missionary work. Their mission first took them to Cyprus, where they welcomed many Jewish and Gentile converts into the Church. Then they sailed north to the city of Lystra in Asia Minor. There Paul cured a crippled man by telling him to stand up, and the people were astonished. In their native language, they enthusiastically declared Barnabas and Paul to be gods in disguise. Once Barnabas and Paul realized the misunderstanding, they tried to explain that they were only men who came to teach about the living God who created the world. But the crowds turned against them, so the next day Barnabas and Paul left Lystra and traveled on to other cities to preach the Good News.

In every place where they established a Christian community, Paul and Barnabas appointed leaders to guide the local church. Eventually the two of them separated. Barnabas took the disciple John Mark to Cyprus, while Paul set out on another missionary journey.

Christian tradition says that Barnabas was martyred, and a handwritten copy of Matthew's Gospel was found clasped to his heart. Why is Barnabas called an apostle? He was not one of the first twelve chosen by Jesus, but he played an important part in the early Christian Church.

JUNE

ACTIVITIES

ILLUSTRATE THE MISSION OF BARNABAS

Have the students read about Barnabas in one of the following passages from the Acts of the Apostles:

Acts	3:36–37	Acts	13:27–30
	9:26–29		13:44–52
	11:27–30		14:1–7
	12:23–25		14:8–14
	13:1–3		14:21–23
	13:3–12		14:36–40

Then ask them to choose a selection to illustrate and print a title and the Scripture reference on their picture. Have the students post the pictures in sequence.

CHART WAYS OF HANDLING DISAGREEMENTS

To settle a serious problem, Barnabas and Paul met with Church leaders at the Council of Jerusalem. Through prayer and discussion, they came to a decision. Have the students make a chart to show how they deal with disagreements. Tell them to draw three columns. In the first column, have them list some recent disagreements they have had. In the second column, have them explain how they handled each disagreement. In the third column, have them write the results of their actions. Then have them put a check next to each disagreement that they handled in a Christian manner. Finally have the students discuss ways to handle disagreements as Jesus would.

GIVE HELP AND SUPPORT

Barnabas, an important member of the Jerusalem Christian community, took Paul's part when no one else would take the risk. Ask the students to think of someone they know who needs support or a friend. Challenge them to help that person in some way in the coming week.

FEED THE HUNGRY

Barnabas and Paul were once sent to bring relief from Antioch to Christians in Jerusalem who were suffering from famine. Bring in brochures or have the students check the Internet for information on Christian organizations that help to feed hungry people, such as Catholic Relief Services, Rice Bowl, Food for the Poor, and The Heifer Project. Then have the class choose an organization and decide on a way of helping that group.

Catechist's Notes:

_____

_____

_____

_____

_____

Saint Anthony of Padua   June 13

(1195–1231)

Do you dream of doing great things? Have you ever longed to follow in the path of your hero?

In Lisbon, Portugal, a young man named Fernando, who was from a noble family, witnessed the burial of several Franciscan missionary priests. These priests had been tortured and martyred in Morocco, Africa. Listening to the heroic adventures of these men lit a bright flame in Fernando's heart. He decided to become a Franciscan and go to Morocco to be a missionary. He took the name Anthony.

Soon after he arrived in Africa, Anthony became very ill. Reluctantly he boarded a ship to return to Portugal. God had a very different plan for him, however. His ship was driven off course by a strong wind, and he landed in Sicily. After a few months, he made his way to Italy, where the Franciscan brothers were holding an important meeting. Anthony attended that meeting and met Francis of Assisi.

While Anthony was in Italy, it was discovered that he was an expert on the Scriptures. A story is told that at an ordination Mass, the priest who was to give the homily did not arrive on time. At the last minute, Anthony was asked to give the homily. He did, and from that day on, his reputation as an inspired preacher spread through Italy and France. Anthony brought so many back to the Church through his preaching that he was called the "Hammer of the Heretics."

The very fast pace of Anthony's preaching and teaching weakened his health, which had never been good. Anthony died at the age of 36 and was buried in Padua, Italy. His fame spread throughout the world. According to tradition, Anthony had experienced a vision of the Child Jesus. That is why many statues of Anthony show him holding a Bible with the Child Jesus standing on it. Today Anthony is well known as the saint who helps in finding lost objects.

JUNE

ACTIVITIES

SHARE CUSTOMS RELATED TO SAINT ANTHONY

As a Franciscan friar, Anthony was very poor, and he had a great love for the poor. In Italy there is a fund called St. Anthony's Bread, which is used for the poor.

- Have students share other customs or devotions about Saint Anthony with which they are familiar.

- Have the students evaluate how they have shown love for the poor, the lonely, and the elderly in the last few months. Encourage them to give examples of their own experiences or examples in which the whole class has participated.

MEDITATE ON GOD'S CALL TODAY

Early in his life, Anthony learned that what he wanted was not always what God wanted. Through various circumstances, Anthony found God's will for him. Lead the students in a short meditation: Where is God sending me today? Vary the time of silence: grades K–2, 10 seconds; grades 3–5, 30 seconds; grades 6–8, 60 seconds. Then offer a prayer for openness to whatever God wants for the students in their everyday lives.

LIST QUALITIES OF EFFECTIVE PREACHERS

Anthony was a Scripture scholar and an outstanding preacher. Have the students form groups and list the qualities needed to be an effective preacher of the Good News. Be sure that students include in their lists "being open to the guidance of the Holy Spirit." Then have them think of someone they know who has each of the qualities on the list.

WRITE A VERY SHORT HOMILY

Have the students write one-minute homilies and deliver them to the class, following these steps:

1. Choose a Scripture passage.

2. Think of an opening that is related to the Scripture passage and is interesting to the people.

3. Decide on one way that Christians could live out this passage.

4. Think of a closing that will inspire listeners to follow Jesus more closely.

5. Practice giving the homily.

Catechist's Notes:

_____

_____

_____

_____

_____

_____

Saint Aloysius Gonzaga

June 21

(1568–1591)

Do your parents have plans for you? As soon as Aloysius was born, his parents began planning for his future. His mother wanted him to be a priest. His father was determined to have his oldest son become a military leader or famous political figure—anything but a priest.

At the age of five, Aloysius was sent to a military camp to get started on his career. His father must have been very pleased to see his son marching at the head of the platoon of soldiers around the campgrounds. His mother and his tutor were extremely displeased, however, when Aloysius came home using the rough, coarse language of the camp. At the age of seven, Aloysius received a special insight from God. While other boys were dreaming about being military heroes or heads of wealthy estates, Aloysius thought of other matters. He decided to become a saint, and he began acting on that decision. He prayed long hours at night and fasted several times a week.

While he was on a visit to Spain with his parents, Aloysius read the lives of saintly Jesuit missionaries, and he decided to become a Jesuit.

His father and some other relatives tried hard to change his mind. It was a fierce battle of wills, but after several years, Aloysius won. With his father's permission, Aloysius gave his large inheritance to his brother and joined the Jesuit order at 17 years of age. The novice director, who was in charge of training Aloysius, told him to cut down on his long hours of prayer and to give up some of his fasting and other penances. Aloysius obeyed willingly. He understood that obedience was better than "doing his own thing."

When Aloysius was 23, a serious epidemic broke out in Rome. Aloysius volunteered at once to help in the hospital. At that time hospitals were not the clean, orderly places with which we are familiar today. It was very easy to catch an illness. That is what happened; Aloysius became very ill. No medicine could help him. Aloysius was not afraid to die.

Aloysius shows that young people are not too young to become saints. During his life he had focused on doing what God wanted—serving and loving God and his neighbor.

ACTIVITIES

CHOOSE ONE WAY TO GROW IN HOLINESS

Have the students list on the board the various actions Aloysius chose in order to become holy, which is to become like Jesus: he prayed daily, overcame bad habits, read lives of the saints, practiced self-control, obeyed his father, took advice from a priest, and cared for the sick. Ask the students to choose one thing they will do today to grow in holiness.

RESPOND TO NEEDS OF SOCIETY

When Aloysius was growing up, society was filled with brutality, dishonesty, and immoral behavior. Today's society, too, needs Christians who rely on God's power to live saintly lives. Direct the students to find three newspaper headlines that reflect needs in our society, then cut them out and glue them to a sheet of paper. Then have the students write something they can do to respond to these needs with Christian attitudes.

MAKE AN EXAMINATION OF CONSCIENCE

Aloysius came from a wealthy and famous family, but he never used the power that his family had or boasted of his wealth. He would sign his name "Aluigi" or "Luigi" instead of using his formal name. Have the students listen to the following questions and answer them silently:

Do I volunteer for unpleasant jobs?

Do I avoid boasting of my talents?

Do I want people to always notice the good things that I do?

Do I try to be first in line?

Do I use money to get people to like me and do what I want?

Do I avoid being with unpopular people because I think they will ruin my "image"?

Do I put other people down so that I can look good?

Then have the students listen prayerfully as you play a song that reflects the love Christians have for one another.

DO A WORD SEARCH

Aloysius had to overcome the habit that he had acquired at military camp of using offensive language. Recall with the students the second commandment: "You shall not take the name of the Lord, your God, in vain." Then distribute copies of the word search. Use the blackline master on page 457. Instruct the students to cross out the words when they find them in the puzzle, as a sign that they want to eliminate these sins in their lives.

Find and cross out these terms:
perjury
cursing
blasphemy
profanity
obscene language

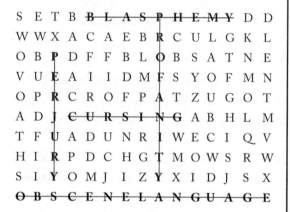

When the students have finished the word search, lead a brief discussion about how a person could break the habit of using offensive language.

Saint Paulinus of Nola

June 22

(355–431)

Do you know someone who collects letters and autographs of famous people? Paulinus of Nola, Spain, who lived in the fourth century, wrote letters to and received replies from the following, all of whom became saints: Ambrose, Jerome, Gregory, Martin, Augustine. Paulinus was not only a good letter writer, but also a successful lawyer, a wealthy governor, and a talented poet.

Paulinus married a rich Spanish noblewoman named Therasia. For some years the two of them enjoyed the comfortable life of the very rich. Then in 389 both of them decided to become Christians, and they were baptized. Later they had a son, Celsus, who died after only eight days. This event could have led Paulinus and Therasia to turn away from God or to feel sorry for themselves. Instead they decided to give their wealth to the poor, as Jesus had taught, and to live a very simple, plain life.

Paulinus and Therasia lived in a large two-story home. They made the first floor into a place where debtors, wanderers, and the very poor could find shelter. On the second floor of the house, Paulinus and a few other men lived as monks. And holy Therasia took care of the whole household. The people in the city admired and loved Paulinus so much for his Christian witness that they wanted him to become a priest. Eventually he did become a priest and even a bishop.

Just before he died, Paulinus gave to the poor 50 silver pieces that he had just received as a donation. To the last day of his life, Paulinus followed these words of Jesus: "Sell your possessions, and give alms. Make purses for yourselves that do not wear out, an unfailing treasure in heaven, where no thief comes near and no moth destroys. For where your treasure is, there your heart will be also" (Luke 12:33–34).

WRITE THANK-YOU NOTES TO STAFF

At least 50 letters written by Paulinus have been preserved. He wrote often in poetry and used many Scripture quotations. Have the students find a Scripture quote and use it in a thank-you note. Direct them to write the note to someone who works in the school or parish program: maintenance personnel, cafeteria workers, office staff, crossing guards, bus drivers, teacher aides, tutors, and so on.

WRITE A POEM TO HONOR YOUR PATRON SAINT

Early in life Paulinus was placed under the protection of Saint Felix, a saint of the third century. Every year Paulinus wrote a poem in honor of Saint Felix on his feast day. Have each student write a short poem about his or her patron or favorite saint. A cinquain would be an easy pattern to use:

line 1: name of saint
line 2: two adjectives describing the saint
line 3: three verbs telling what the saint did
line 4: phrase or sentence about the saint
line 5: one noun; another name to describe the saint

Example:

> Paulinus
> wealthy, generous
> cared, shared, loved the poor
> sheltered the homeless
> Christian

PRAY FOR PEOPLE WHO EXPERIENCE TRAGEDY

After their infant son died, Paulinus and Therasia began to reach out to others. Lead the class in a prayer of petition for people who are suffering from a tragedy. The response could be "Lord, help them." For example:

> For those who are starving,
>   let us pray to the Lord.
> For parents whose children are ill,
>   let us pray to the Lord.

FIND WAYS TO SIMPLIFY THEIR LIFESTYLES

Paulinus and Therasia gave away their money and shared their home so they could be one with the poor and help the poor. Encourage the students to reflect on how they can simplify their lifestyles. To help them, ask questions similar to the following:

- Do you borrow and lend CDs, games, videos, and books or must you own every book, CD, game, and video yourself?

- Do you have clothes in your closet that you don't wear, even though they still fit?

- Are you careful to turn off lights and water when they are not needed?

- Do you ask your parents to buy expensive food or games, or to take you to expensive places?

- Do you enjoy activities that don't cost money?

- Are you satisfied with what you have, or do you always want more things?

After the reflection have the students compile a master list of ways to simplify their lifestyles. Ask each student to make a specific resolution on one way to live more simply.

Saints John Fisher and Thomas More

June 22

(1469–1535; 1477–1535)

There are two saints listed for today. They share the same day because they were beheaded just two weeks apart for the same "crime" against the King of England. They died rather than betray their consciences.

John Fisher was educated at the best schools in England and was ordained a priest. A holy and learned man, he was appointed tutor for the young Prince Henry, later King Henry VIII. In 1504 Fisher became Bishop of Rochester and Chancellor of Cambridge University. Fisher wrote eight books against heresy, and Henry, now king, was proud to be his friend.

Thomas More was the son of a successful lawyer in London. In his teens he studied Greek, French, Latin, and math. At first he planned to become a priest, but instead he entered law school, married, and had four children. Besides being a keen lawyer, Thomas More was a charming, witty man who won the king's friendship. Soon Thomas became Chancellor of England—the position next to the king in importance.

Henry VIII began his rule of England as a devout and sincere king. He even wrote a book in defense of the Catholic Church. But all this changed when King Henry wanted to divorce his wife and marry another woman. Henry asked the pope to approve a divorce on the grounds that his marriage was not valid, but the pope refused. King Henry had a document of support written, and all the others bishops of England signed it. Both John Fisher and Thomas More foresaw the serious danger they would be in, but they refused to sign the document in support of the king. The king became furious, especially with Thomas More, whose opinion was highly respected.

Henry went even further. He had the Parliament—his Congress—write a decree stating that the king would be the head of the Catholic Church in England. Many important people in the Church and the government signed the Oath of Supremacy.

Again John Fisher and Thomas More refused to sign this decree although all the other bishops in England had. Thomas More knew his stand would mean certain death for him and disgrace for his family, but he followed his conscience. John Fisher and Thomas More were imprisoned in the Tower of London on the charge of high treason. Despite hunger, cold, and loneliness, both men stood firm.

After 14 months in prison, John Fisher was beheaded on June 22. Two weeks later, on July 6, Thomas More was led out to his death. He saw that the masked swordsman was quite nervous. So Thomas said calmly, "Be not afraid, for you send me to God." Then he told the crowd of people, "I die the king's good servant, but God's first."

JUNE

DISCUSS TRUE FRIENDSHIP

John Fisher and Thomas More were both friends of King Henry VIII. Ask the students how these men could call themselves friends of the king and still not approve his actions. Lead them to see that helping our friends to choose good and avoid evil is a sign of sincere, unselfish love. Have the students discuss ways they could actually help their friends make good choices. Give them two good rules to follow:

- Pray for the courage and the right moment to speak.

- Advise their friends in an honest, respectful way.

PUT ON SKITS

Both John Fisher and Thomas More were loyal to God and to themselves in doing what they believed was right. Have the students get into small groups and make up a short skit to illustrate one of these statements:

- Honesty is the heart of friendship.

- Honesty is the best policy.

- Some people are honest or dishonest because _____.

SHARE PERSONAL STORIES

Thomas More was known and loved for his sense of humor. Even when he was in prison, he would joke with his daughter and other visitors. Have the students tell about people they know who bring joy to others, even when they themselves are suffering. Share with the class the story of someone you know who does this.

LIST PRESSURES KIDS FEEL

Although they were under enormous outside pressure, John Fisher and Thomas More did not change their minds. Engage the class in making a list of pressures that keep kids their age from being honest or following their conscience. Talk about ways they can do what is right in the face of outside pressure. Then pray for God's help in the future.

> Father,
> you confirm the true faith
> with the crown of martyrdom.
> May the prayers of Saints John Fisher and
>   Thomas More
> give us the courage to proclaim our faith
> by the witness of our lives.
> *(from the prayer for the feast of*
> *Saints John Fisher and Thomas More)*

WRITE A PSALM

John Fisher once wrote a book on the penitential psalms in the Bible. Read aloud or have a student read aloud Psalm 28 or 86. Describe the pattern the psalmist used for these psalms:

- Address God

- Explain the situation

- Express trust in God

- Praise God

Then have the students choose a situation in their own lives and write a psalm that has the same pattern.

Birth of John the Baptist   June 24

Some athletes who have won Olympic gold medals began their training as early as the age of two. They spent their childhoods preparing to achieve their goal of being the best in their sport. John the Baptist seems to have had an even earlier start in preparing for his goal.

According to Luke's Gospel, Zechariah, John's father, was the first to be prepared for John's birth. While he was offering incense in the Temple, the angel Gabriel came with the announcement. The angel said that the baby's name would be John, that he would be his father's joy and delight, that he would be filled

with the Holy Spirit, and that he would bring people back to God. Because of his momentary lack of faith, Zechariah lost the power to speak and hear until John was born.

The same Gospel also tells of the visit between Mary and Elizabeth, John's mother, before both John and Jesus were born. Elizabeth revealed that at the sound of Mary's greeting, John leaped for joy. Tradition holds that at this moment John was freed from original sin.

Luke also tells of the joyful reaction of relatives and neighbors at John's birth. Eight days later these same people wanted to name the baby Zechariah. However, his father indicated in writing that he wanted his son to be named John. With this action, Zechariah recovered his ability to speak, and the people were amazed. They began to ask the question, "What then will this child become?" (Luke 1:66). Some years after this event of the naming, Luke's Gospel records that John spent his youth in the wilderness, preparing for his mission. What was his mission? His father gave a prophecy on the day that John was named:

And you, child, will be called the prophet of the Most High; for you will go before the Lord to prepare his ways.

(Luke 1:76)

ACTIVITIES

READ THE BENEDICTUS

Zechariah foresaw that his son would some day prepare the way for the Messiah, the Savior. At John's naming Zechariah spoke a canticle recorded in Luke 1:68–79. Tell the students that this prayer is called the Benedictus, which is the first word of the canticle in Latin. Make copies of the blackline master on page 458 and have students read the canticle aloud. Then have them do one of the following activities:

- Paraphrase the canticle, print it on onionskin or other fine paper, and decorate the edges.

- Make transparencies for various parts of the canticle.

- Recite the canticle in sections for a choral speech presentation.

WRITE A NEWS REPORT

Have the students read Luke 1:5–25 and write a news report of the events recounted there. Have them print the report on unlined paper and draw an appropriate illustration to accompany it. Display the finished reports.

RESEARCH THE NAME *JOHN*

Show students how the name *John* is written in Hebrew, which may be the language in which his name was originally written.

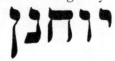

The name *John* written out in square Hebrew letters, as Zechariah must have written it. This name means "Yahweh is gracious."

Then have the students research the name *John* in different languages. Some forms of the name are given here.

Johannes (Norwegian)   Ian (Scottish)
Joao (Portuguese)   Sean (Gaelic)
Janos (Hungarian)   Giovanni (Italian)
Evan (Welsh)   Juan (Spanish)

LOOK AT THE ADVENT PROPHECY

Read to the students the prophecy in Isaiah 40:3–5. Then in honor of John the Baptist's birthday, have the students listen to an Advent song that mentions the role of John or the Isaian prophecies.

Catechist's Notes:

_____

_____

_____

_____

_____

_____

_____

Saint Cyril of Alexandria   June 27

(370–444)

This saint lived in the land of camels, pyramids, and the Great Sphinx. Cyril was born in Alexandria, a famous Egyptian center of learning. He received an excellent education.

Very little is known about Cyril's early life, but we do know that later on he became archbishop of Alexandria when his uncle, the former archbishop, died. During his first years in this position, Cyril was quite strict, sometimes even severe, with heretics and other people who caused trouble for the Christians of his diocese. He played a role in deposing Saint John Chrysostom, the bishop of Constantinople, and expelled the Jews from Alexandria. As he grew older and had more experience, Cyril learned to reflect the compassion and forgiveness of Jesus.

Cyril is most famous for his action at the Council of Ephesus, over which he presided. Through letters Cyril tried very hard to make the heretic Nestorius, Patriarch of Constantinople, understand that Christ was truly God and man united as one Person. He defended the teaching that Mary is the Mother of God and insisted on calling her *Theotokos,* a Greek name meaning "God-bearer" or "Mother of God."

Several bishops who sided with Nestorius succeeded in having Cyril imprisoned for three months. They called him the heretic. Three representatives from the pope arrived in Ephesus in time to save Cyril from further trouble. Because of his long, hard struggle with heretics and his forceful writing about doctrine, Cyril was named a Doctor of the Church.

JUNE

HONOR MARY

Sing a hymn to honor Mary as the Mother of God.

DISCUSS CASE STUDIES

As archbishop of Alexandria, Cyril had to make important decisions and be responsible for his actions. Every Christian is responsible for making decisions based on Gospel values. Read the following situations to the students. Have them write down the decision they think each person should make. Then discuss their answers.

1. Miguel must give a speech in class tomorrow. He is very afraid that he'll forget his lines. The last time he gave a speech, he was so fearful that he froze and could not continue. What should Miguel do?

2. Sarah was chosen for the lead in the play. Julia, one of her good friends, really wanted the part. What should Julia do?

3. Matt overheard some boys and girls saying that his friend had offered them marijuana. What should Matt do?

MEDITATE ON THE GOSPEL

Cyril's writings show that he reflected deeply on the Bible. Teach the students the steps for a prayerful reflection on a Gospel story:

1. **See:** visualize the persons, place, setting (circumstances: who, what, where, when, why, and how).

2. **Catch:** look for the message.

3. **Apply:** apply the message to your own life.

Have the students choose a Gospel story and prayerfully follow the steps. Finally have the students write their thoughts in their journals.

MAKE ACROSTICS ABOUT MARY

Have the students work in groups to create acrostics, using either the title *Theotokos* or "Mother of God." Direct them to use other titles of Mary in the acrostic.

Example:

Mother of the Church
Our mother too
Mo**T**her of Mercy
Queen of **H**eaven and Earth
Immaculat**E** Conception
Our Lady of the **R**osary
Queen **O**f Peace
First Disciple
Refu**G**e of Sinners
Mary Most H**O**ly
Our La**D**y of Sorrow

Catechist's Notes:

_____

_____

_____

_____

Saint Irenaeus

(130–200)

Irenaeus was one of the very strong links in the chain that joins the Church at the time of the twelve apostles and the Church of the second century. He was a link because he wrote and taught the faith handed on by the apostles, and he preserved the faith when it was attacked. His chief concern was unity among the churches.

We do not know very much about Saint Irenaeus. He was born in Smyrna, a port town in western Turkey and became a disciple of Polycarp, who was bishop there. For some reason Irenaeus traveled to France, where he was ordained a priest. Eventually he became the bishop of Lyons, a growing commercial city.

Irenaeus was very much concerned about heretics who were attacking the teaching of the young Christian Church. Irenaeus realized the importance of guarding the teaching of the twelve apostles from false doctrine. Especially strong was his battle against Gnosticism, one of the worst dangers ever faced by Christianity. This heresy claimed that eternal life could be gained only by receiving special knowledge about God, knowledge that was available just to a few chosen people. Irenaeus taught that, according to Scripture, God wished all persons to be saved and to come to know the truth. Irenaeus and other Christian writers insisted that knowing God, obeying his commandments, and having a close relationship with him were the important things.

At one time a group of Christians in Asia Minor, which was Irenaeus's homeland, did not want to celebrate Easter at the time the Church in Rome did so. Irenaeus explained to Pope Victor I that this was not a matter of faith. The date for celebrating Easter was an old tradition for these people. His pleading for them "saved the day." Some years later the matter was cleared up, and the date of Easter was settled.

Irenaeus was one of the important writers in the early Church. He was a strong witness to the teaching of the Church as it came from Peter and the other apostles. Irenaeus died a martyr for his faith.

JUNE

MAKE A TRUTH CHAIN

Irenaeus spent much of his life defending the truth. Direct the students to make a "truth" chain by following these directions:

- Distribute one slip of light-colored construction paper ($8\frac{1}{2}$" $\times$ $1\frac{1}{2}$") to each student.

- Have each student choose one of the following Scripture references and write the quotation on his or her link:

Romans 2:20	Galatians 2:14
Romans 3:7	Ephesians 1:13
Romans 9:1	Ephesians 4:21
1 Corinthians 13:6	2 Thessalonians 2:13
2 Corinthians 4:2	1 John 3:19
2 Corinthians 6:7	1 John 4:6
2 Corinthians 13:8	1 John 4:16
Galatians 2:5	1 John 5:6

- Have the students assemble the chain with staples or glue. Tell them to be careful to keep the quotations on the outside of the chain as they assemble the links.

- Display the chain.

PREPARE A MOCK DEBATE

Have the students research the controversy over the date of Easter in the early centuries. Direct them to discover what role each of the following saints played: Cyril of Alexandria, Hippolytus, Pope Leo, Augustine of Canterbury. Then conduct a mock debate over the date celebrating Easter.

MAKE PEACE POSTERS

The name *Irenaeus* means "peace," and this saint was true to his name. Irenaeus worked for peace and promoted respect among Christians.

- Have the students make posters promoting peace.

- Or have them choose a name they will try to live up to and then make nametags to wear for the day.

PRAY FOR THE CHURCH

Irenaeus safeguarded the truth that had been handed down by the apostles. With the class pray the following prayer to Saint Joseph, the protector of the Church.

> Saint Joseph, watchful guardian of the Holy Family, defend the Church. Keep it from all error and sin. Once you rescued the Child Jesus from danger. Now protect God's holy Church from all harm. Help us to imitate your example in life and to die a happy death. Amen.

REVIEW THE TEN COMMANDMENTS

Irenaeus and other Christian writers insisted that obeying God's commandments was very important for the Christian life. Put the numbers 1 through 10 on separate slips of paper and place the slips in a box. Have the students draw a slip, recite the commandment that has that number, and give an example of a person keeping the commandment.

Catechist's Notes:

_____

_____

_____

Saints Peter and Paul

June 29

(d. 64 or 65; d. 67)

These two men are the giants of the early Church. Besides this shared feast, they each have another: Chair of Peter, February 22 and Conversion of Paul, January 25.

Peter was very likely a middle-aged man when Jesus called him. He was a fisherman from Bethsaida, a village near the Lake of Galilee. His brother Andrew introduced Peter to Jesus. Jesus looked at Peter and said, "You are Simon son of John; you are to be called Cephas" (which is translated Peter) (John 1:42).

During the three years the apostles lived with Jesus, Peter showed leadership. He was often the spokesman. He answered for all when Jesus asked, "Who do you say I am?" Simon Peter spoke up, "You are the Christ, the Son of the living God" (Matthew 16:16–17). It was Peter who objected very strongly to Jesus' stating that he was on his way to Jerusalem to suffer and die. This time Jesus scolded him. Peter is mentioned 195 times in the New Testament. He appears lovable, impetuous, practical—and sometimes weak under pressure. But Jesus loved him dearly.

Peter became the leader in the early Church. According to the Acts of the Apostles, he was the first to preach on Pentecost. He arranged for the selection of Matthias to replace Judas. He worked the first public miracle—curing a lame man at the Temple gate. He welcomed the first non-Jewish person into the Church. His reputation became so great that people thought just his shadow passing by would cure people.

Peter was put into prison three or four times. Just as soon as he was released, he began preaching again about Jesus Christ. Finally in Rome, he was sentenced to death by crucifixion. Out of deep respect for his Master, Jesus, Peter asked the guards to fasten him to the cross upside down. Peter was buried in an old Roman cemetery where the huge basilica of St. Peter is today.

Paul received the very best education as a young boy. Because he was a strict Jew, he thought it was his duty to persecute the Christians. He was converted one day while traveling to Damascus and became the greatest missionary. In the beginning Paul had great difficulty convincing the Jews that the Old Law of Moses did not apply strictly anymore. Jesus came to teach a way of love and service freely given. The Jews who were part of the early Church were unwilling to baptize anyone who was not Jewish. But Paul argued so skillfully, under the guidance of the Holy Spirit, that he won this battle.

Paul worked very hard for about 30 years, traveling around the Roman Empire and preaching Christ. From his letters and from the Acts, he seems to have been an affectionate, loyal, courageous, and dedicated man. He was the right man to build the bridge between the Jewish religion of the Old Testament and the Christianity of the New Testament. Paul was imprisoned at Rome and beheaded in a prison outside the old city walls.

CREATE FLANNEL-BOARD STORIES

Divide the class into pairs. Direct each pair to choose an incident about Peter or Paul from the Acts of the Apostles. Then have the students draw figures and scenery for the story on heavy paper, cut out each piece, and glue a piece of flannel to the back of it. Give each pair a chance to practice telling their story and moving the figures on the flannel board. Then let the students present their stories for younger children.

MAKE TRIPTYCHS

Have the students design triptychs showing Jesus, Peter, and Paul. First have them fold a piece of construction paper into three equal parts. While the paper is folded, have them cut the top of the paper into the shape of an arch.

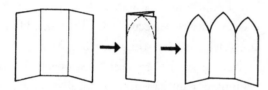

Discuss with the students appropriate symbols for Jesus, Peter, and Paul. On another sheet of paper, have them draw pictures and symbols that represent the three figures. Peter is often represented in art with a set of keys, with a ship or fish, with a rooster (representing his denial of Christ), or as being crucified upside down. Paul is shown writing on a parchment scroll or with a sword.

Finally have them glue their drawings on the background, putting Jesus in the center and Peter and Paul on either side.

ANSWER FAQS

Have the students write questions about Peter and Paul on slips of paper. Put the slips in a box and have each student draw a question and answer it. You might wish to include the following questions:

- What is a quality of Peter's character?

- How did Peter receive the call to follow Christ?

- The names *Cephas* and *Peter* both mean "rock." In what way did Jesus mean that Peter was like a rock?

- How did Paul die?

- Why are the names of Paul and Barnabas often associated?

MEMORIZE THE LETTERS

Encourage students to memorize the following jingle for the names of the first 14 epistles of the New Testament in order. This device is helpful when doing Scripture research or looking up a citation.

Ro–Co–Co

Gal–Eph–Phi

Col–Thess–Thess

Tim–Tim–Ti

Phil–Heb

Catechist's Notes:

_____

_____

_____

Blessed Junípero Serra   July 1

(1713–1784)

San Francisco, Santa Barbara, and San Diego began with the efforts of a five-foot-two-inch Franciscan friar named Junípero Serra. This "Father of California" is proof that in weakness God's power is shown.

José Miguel Serra was the son of a farmer in Spain. When he applied to the Franciscans, they rejected him because he looked frail. He joined later at age 17. He took the name Junípero for Juniper, the beloved companion of Saint Francis. Junípero taught philosophy, got a doctorate in theology, and taught theology at a university. Then this popular preacher asked to be a missionary. He wrote, "All my life I have wanted to be a missioner. I have wanted to carry the Gospel teachings to those who have never heard of God and the Kingdom he has prepared for them."

In 1749 Father Serra sailed for Mexico with other Franciscans, including Father Palou, a former student, who became his confessor and biographer. On the 98-day journey, there was not enough fresh food and water, and the thirst was almost unbearable. A storm drove the ship off course and almost wrecked it.

After landing in Mexico, Father Serra and another friar walked the 300 miles to Mexico City. On the way Father Serra was bitten on the left leg by a poisonous insect. For the rest of his life, this leg caused him pain and made him lame. The travelers stopped at the shrine of Our Lady of Guadalupe. There Father Serra dedicated to her his work among the Indians.

Father Serra worked with the Pamé Indians for eight years. Then he worked as a traveling missioner in many cities. In 1767 the viceroy of Mexico forced all Franciscans to leave, and Junípero was made president of their 14 missions in Lower California. Then when the Spaniards took over Upper California in 1769, Junípero went with them. At the age of 56 and with his leg and foot swollen, he traveled 900 miles by mule to San Diego, where he founded the first of the 19 missions he had planned. Junípero established nine of the 21 Franciscan missions along the Pacific Coast: San Diego, San Carlos Borromeo, San Antonio de Padua, San Gabriel, San Luis Obispo, San Francisco, San Juan Capistrano, Santa Clara, San Buenaventura.

In the missions everything was held in common. The Native Americans who made up these communities were taught how to grow crops and raise livestock. They learned to read and write, to sing, and to paint. Most exciting for Father Serra, they learned about the faith and asked to become Catholics. He baptized about 6,000 Native Americans.

When Father Serra was dying, he insisted on walking to chapel for Holy Communion. Father Palou and some Indian converts were with him when he died. Indians stayed with the body through the night. Father Palou recorded that at the funeral the weeping drowned out the singing. Father Serra is buried at the Carmel mission. He was beatified in 1988.

TAKE A VIRTUAL TOUR

Have the students go on line to learn more about the California missions Junípero Serra founded. They can "tour" San Juan Capistrano at http://library.thinkquest.org/3615/tour.html or www.missionsjc.com/tour.

MODERN MISSIONS

The California missions now house museums as well as vibrant parish communities. Have the students find out where the Church operates missions to Native Americans today. Explore ways they can support these missions.

HONOR FOUNDERS

Father Serra has not only been recognized by the Church, but also by the state of California and the country. Father Serra's statue stands in the Hall of Fame at the Capitol in Washington, D.C. When this tribute to the founders of the United States was planned, Father Serra was nominated by the state of California. Have the students find out about Catholic pioneers or missionaries who were influential in your parish, city, or state. Ask the students to design statues or other memorials to these founders of your church.

WRITE ABOUT THEIR VOCATION

Ask the students how old they think Father Serra was when he went to Mexico. Have them figure it out (he was 36). Point out that he had a long-time desire to be a missionary. Ask the students to give some thought to their vocation in life. Have them each write a short paragraph or journal entry about what is in their hearts.

INVITE A SERRA CLUB SPEAKER

In 1935 the Serra Club was founded to foster vocations and promote Catholicism in the United States. Invite a member of the Serra Club to speak to the class about the club's goals and what the members do.

DESIGN A STAMP

A United States airmail stamp issued in 1988 bears the picture of Junípero Serra. Have each student design a postage stamp to honor an achievement he or she would like to make in the world.

Catechist's Notes:

_____

_____

_____

_____

_____

_____

Saint Thomas

(first century)

Surprisingly the expression "a Doubting Thomas" refers to an apostle who made one of the clearest professions of faith in Jesus in the whole Gospel.

Thomas was most likely a Galilean fisherman, like Peter, James, and John. Jesus called him, and he followed loyally. One day a messenger came to tell Jesus that his friend Lazarus was quite sick. Mary and Martha, the sisters of Lazarus, asked Jesus to come and cure their brother. The apostles knew this would be a dangerous trip for Jesus because he had many enemies in the area around Jerusalem. But Thomas said he would be very glad to go with Jesus and even to die with him.

On Easter Sunday evening, when the apostles reported that the risen Lord Jesus had appeared to them, Thomas could hardly believe them. He loved Jesus and wanted to see him again; he insisted that he would believe when he could put his finger into the wound in Jesus' side. He was referring to the wound that resulted when a soldier pierced Jesus' side with a spear while he hung on the cross.

A week later Jesus appeared again to the apostles. This time Thomas was there. Jesus called him over and told him to put his finger into the wound. Thomas fell to his knees and said, "My Lord and my God!" Then Jesus said something that should give us great courage and trust. He said to Thomas, "Have you believed because you have seen me? Blessed are those who have not seen and yet have come to believe" (John 20:29).

We do not know for sure what happened to Thomas later on. Tradition says that he went to India and preached there. Perhaps he was martyred there too. The Catholic people of India believe firmly that he is their special apostle and patron.

Many Catholics repeat Thomas's profession of faith, "My Lord and my God," during the eucharistic prayer when the priest holds up the consecrated bread.

ACTIVITIES

MAKE A PROFESSION OF FAITH

Invite the students to imagine that they are Thomas. Read John 20:24–29 aloud slowly. Pause for a minute of silent reflection. Remind the students they are always in God's presence and they can turn to God anytime. Encourage them today to use the prayer of Thomas: "My Lord and my God." End with the Sign of the Cross.

MAKE AN ACT OF FAITH

Faith is a free gift from God. Faith can be nourished and should be treasured. Have the students compose an act of faith and print it on a card. Ask them to listen to a song about faith and then to sign their cards. Post the cards or encourage the students to use them as prayer reminders.

HEAR FROM TWINS

According to the Gospel, Thomas was a twin. If there are any twins in the class, have them tell about the advantages of being a twin. Pray a special prayer in class today for all twins.

STUDY CHURCH ARCHITECTURE

Thomas is the patron of architects. Have the students study the architecture of their parish church. Then have them make sketches of the exterior of their church. Discuss briefly: What in the building's design inspires prayer or reflection? How does the architecture speak of the presence of God?

Catechist's Notes:

_____

_____

_____

_____

_____

_____

_____

_____

_____

Saint Elizabeth of Portugal   July 4

(1271–1336)

Elizabeth, or Isabella, was a Spanish princess named for her great-aunt, Saint Elizabeth of Hungary. She married Denis, King of Portugal, in 1255 when she was only 12.

Elizabeth knew that peace in the world begins with peace in the family. As a young girl she was known for her spirit of prayer and kindness. She had come from a long line of nobility, and so she was very familiar with the politics, weaknesses, and wastefulness that often went along with royal living. She could see that none of this could bring her peace and happiness. Elizabeth had a special love and concern for the poor and needy. Very early in her life as queen, she began to help the poor and devoted much of her time to them. She built a hospital, an orphange, and a shelter for poor travelers.

Besides these good deeds, Elizabeth devoted a great deal of time and effort to trying to make peace between the fighting members of her family. King Denis was a good ruler but not a very good husband and father. In fact Elizabeth finally wore herself out trying to make peace between the king and their only son, who was warring against his father. She reconciled her husband and son after a serious disagreement. She even rode into battle to force the rulers to stop fighting and make peace. The political situation in Europe at that time was very complicated, and often the fights were between kings who were relatives. Family feuds became national wars. Elizabeth worked for peace until her death. One of her last acts was to settle a dispute between her son, the king of Portugal, and his son-in-law, the king of Castile. Statues and pictures of Elizabeth often show her holding an olive branch or a dove.

After her husband died, Elizabeth moved to the monastery of the Poor Clares and became a member of the Third Order of Saint Francis.

JULY

COMPARE SAINTS WHO WERE RELATIVES

The sister of Elizabeth's grandmother was Elizabeth of Hungary. Have the students compare the lives of these two saints.

SHARE PERSONAL STORIES

Share the story of a time when you tried to be a reconciler. Invite the students to share their experiences also. Then discuss the risks involved in trying to reconcile two people and the words and actions that might help. Close by praying the Prayer of St. Francis or an original prayer for peace.

RECITE THE WORKS OF MERCY

Elizabeth was well known for giving shelter to the homeless and feeding the hungry. Divide the students into pairs and have them quiz each other on the spiritual and corporal works of mercy.

WORK AND PRAY FOR JUSTICE

As queen, Elizabeth respected and protected the rights of those who were powerless and poor. Through such actions she promoted justice in the world.

- Have the students give examples of ways to provide equal opportunities for people who are mentally, emotionally, or physically disabled.

- Pray for justice, using a prayer from the Mass for the Progress of Peoples. Encourage the students to pray it often. You may use the blackline master on page 459 to make copies for the students.

Father,
you have given all peoples one common origin,
and your will is to gather them as one family in yourself.
Fill the hearts of all men with the fire of your love
and the desire to ensure justice for all their brothers and sisters.
By sharing the good things you give us
may we secure justice and equality for every human being,
an end to all division,
and a human society built on love and peace.

We ask this through our Lord Jesus Christ, your Son,
who lives and reigns with you and the Holy Spirit,
one God, for ever and ever.
Amen.

Catechist's Notes:

_____

_____

_____

_____

_____

_____

_____

Saint Anthony Zaccaria

July 5

(1502–1539)

Anthony Zaccaria is one of those saints who lived a short life full of service to others. He was born in Cremona, Italy. His mother, widowed at 18, saw that Anthony got a good education. He studied medicine and became a doctor. While he was busy healing the bodies of the poor in Cremona, he kept wishing he could be a priest in order to heal souls. He renounced his inheritance and began teaching catechism.

After a few years, he entered the seminary and was ordained a priest at the age of 26. Anthony took the great Saint Paul for his model and patron. His days were filled with preaching in churches and on street corners. Because several men wanted to join him in his work, Anthony founded a religious order. He called his group Barnabites in honor of Barnabas, the companion of Paul. With the help of a countess for whom he served as chaplain, he also founded a community for women, the Angelicals of St. Paul.

At the very time that Luther was dividing the Church in Germany, Anthony and his followers were drawing half-hearted Catholics back to their faith. He began with the clergy and included monasteries. He encouraged Catholics to receive Holy Communion often, even every day, and promoted exposition of the Blessed Sacrament. He had his priests conduct missions in the local parishes. He tried hard to stir up the faith of the Catholic people—even preaching in the streets and performing public penance.

When Anthony was only 36 years old, he paid a last visit to his mother and then died, exhausted from his hard work of preaching, teaching, and traveling. He is usually pictured with a symbol of the Eucharist, a crucifix, or with his first two companions or Saint Paul.

PRAY FOR HEALTH PROFESSIONALS

Anthony studied medicine before he became a priest. Have the students think of the ways doctors have helped them. Invite the students to write prayer petitions for a doctor, nurse, or other health-care professional they know. Offer the prayers with the response "Saint Anthony, pray for us."

PRESERVE LIFE

Doctors take the Hippocratic Oath, promising to preserve life. Every Christian should be dedicated to preserving life, which is created by God. Have the students find this oath in an encyclopedia or on the Internet and explain the name *Hippocratic.* Read them the following list and have them answer yes privately to the ways they help to protect life.

1. I make every human being feel important and welcome.

2. I give money so that others may have a decent life.

3. I compliment younger brothers and sisters honestly and often.

4. I volunteer to help others who seem in need.

Ask the students to add items to the list.

FIND HEALING IN THE EUCHARIST

Anthony encouraged Catholics to receive Holy Communion often. Remind the students that in the Eucharist, Jesus is the Bread of Life. Lead the students in a discussion on how the Bread of Life heals those who receive it (venial sins are forgiven, the presence of Jesus fills spiritual needs for peace and love). Have them examine the words of eucharistic hymns to see how this belief is expressed in the liturgy. Hymns in praise of the Eucharist can be found in the missalette or your parish hymnal.

COMPARE SAINTS

Anthony took Saint Paul as a model for his life. Have the students make a chart comparing the two saints. Refer to the Acts of the Apostles, chapters 13–28, for more information on Saint Paul.

BRAINSTORM WAYS TO REACH OUT

Anthony was keenly aware of the many halfhearted Catholics who were not experiencing the joy and peace of God's love. Have the students list the ways in which Anthony tried to help these Catholics. Then have them think about the people in their own parish who may feel lonely or are uninvolved. Brainstorm ways students can reach out to such people. Help students decide on one thing they can do to welcome or encourage these people. Tell the students that their efforts to help others will build real community in their parishes.

Catechist's Notes:

_____

_____

_____

Saint Maria Goretti

(1890–1902)

If you lived in Italy or visited there, you could go to the house where Maria lived. You could see the spot on the riverbank where she washed clothes and the fountain where she went for water. You could see the stone step where she sat to mend Alessandro's shirt, and you could see the place in the kitchen where she lay wounded.

When Maria was 10 years old, her family moved to a farm near Nettuno, not far from Rome. Her family was so poor that they shared a home and the work on the farm with the Serenelli family. Just two years later, Maria's father died, leaving his wife with several small children.

Maria's mother had to take over the farm work in order to support her family. Managing the home became Maria's job—cooking, cleaning, mending, and caring for her baby sister, Theresa.

Nineteen-year-old Alessandro Serenelli was attracted to Maria, who was 12 at the time. He saw her beauty and innocence and loving personality. One day he came in from the fields and tried to persuade Maria to have sex with him. Maria told him that what he wanted to do was a serious sin. Alessandro dragged her inside the house, but Maria resisted with great firmness. Alessandro was so terribly angry about her refusal that he stabbed Maria 14 times.

Maria lived until the next day. Before she died she forgave Alessandro. He was arrested and sentenced to prison for 30 years. At first he was very angry and resentful. After six years of prison life, Alessandro said Maria appeared to him in a dream and gave him a bouquet of lilies. This impressed him so deeply that he spent the rest of his imprisonment in prayer and repentance for the attack he had made on Maria.

When he was released from prison, Alessandro visited Maria's mother to ask for her forgiveness, which she gave him. Alessandro worked as a gardener at a monastery for the rest of his life. During the inquiries for Maria's beatification, Alessandro testified to her holiness. When Maria was canonized in 1950, her mother, brothers, and sister attended the ceremonies.

JULY

ACTIVITIES

Saint Maria Goretti / July 6

PRAY THE HAIL MARY

Have the students pray silently for all young people who are sexually assaulted and abused. Pray also for people who are struggling with temptations against chastity or who feel trapped in sinful circumstances. Because the Blessed Virgin wants to help all Christians be chaste, end by having all pray the Hail Mary.

DISCUSS THINGS THAT ENCOURAGE CHASTITY

Write this question on the board: "What can help a person to be chaste?" Have the students list their ideas on the board. Use the following ideas to help round out the list:

- Good reading material
- Friendship with Jesus through the sacraments
- Good choice of friends
- Correct information (especially from parents)
- Daily prayer
- Respect for oneself
- Awareness that sex is a sacred gift and not a "toy" to be played with
- Decent jokes
- Right conscience

REFLECT ON THE POWER OF FORGIVENESS

Explain to the students that forgiveness was the key to Alessandro's conversion. Review with them the importance of Jesus' death to make up for our sins. Discuss our belief that God will forgive every sin and help each person to make a fresh start. Then have the students read silently and think about Colossians 3:5–11.

REVIEW THE SIXTH COMMANDMENT

Discuss with the students modern society's general acceptance of premarital sex. Then clarify for them the Church's stand on premarital sex and faithfulness in marriage, and the reason behind that teaching. Ask the students how to avoid temptations against this commandment and how to overcome them.

RECOGNIZE WHOLESOME ENTERTAINMENT

Have the class compile a list of current television and radio shows, movies, videos, songs, and books that are wholesome entertainment and promote Christian values.

Catechist's Notes:

_____

_____

_____

_____

_____

Blessed Peter To Rot   July 7
(1912–1945)

Peter To Rot lived on a tropical island in the Coral Sea, just north of Australia, in what is now Papua New Guinea. He was born in the village of Rakunai, where his father was the tribal chief. Peter's parents, like many other villagers, were catechized and later baptized by Missionaries of the Sacred Heart.

Peter grew up Catholic and thought of becoming a priest, but his father said it was too soon. So Peter studied to become a catechist who could work with the missionaries to spread the faith. He went to school for three years, and in 1933 he received his diploma. Then Peter was assigned to work as a catechist in his own village. As a teacher he was direct and dynamic. He often quoted from the Scriptures to make his point. And he genuinely cared about the people. In 1936 Peter married Paula la Varpit, who was also Catholic. They joyfully celebrated the Church's sacraments as well as local traditions. Peter and Paula were the parents of three children; one daughter, Rufina, is still alive.

Then in 1942, the world was at war, and Japan occupied Peter's island. The missionary priests were imprisoned. Peter, a layman, remained free. Peter worked even harder then. He and the catechists who worked under him continued the prayers and religious instruction. He baptized babies and converts, visited the sick, assisted with charity, conducted Sunday services, and distributed the Eucharist that had been consecrated by the priests in prison.

Then the military police cracked down. They banned Christian worship and religious gatherings. They decided that the islanders should return to their former practice of polygamy, in which a man had many wives. Peter publicly objected to this.

Peter was arrested in the spring of 1945 and confined to a cave. When his wife and mother came to visit, he informed them that a Japanese doctor was coming to see him, but he was not sick. He suspected a trick. He asked Paula to bring his good clothes—he wanted to be ready to meet God.

Another prisoner saw what happened to Peter. The doctor arrived, gave Peter an injection and something to drink, and plugged his nose and ears. When Peter began to convulse, the doctor covered his mouth, and the soldiers held him down until he suffocated. Soon the rest of the prison camp knew what had happened to Peter.

The next morning the Japanese guards acted surprised to find Peter dead. They said he had died of an infection, and they sent his body to his family for burial. The crowd that attended Peter's funeral knew the truth. They knew that Peter was a martyr for the faith.

Peter To Rot was beatified by Pope John Paul II in 1995. The ceremony took place in Papua New Guinea.

ACTIVITIES

BUILD UP THE CHURCH

After the village church was destroyed by soldiers, Peter built a small church out of branches. Ask the students to tell how Peter built up the Church. Then have each child cut a "branch" out of construction paper. Ask the children to write on their branch one thing they do to build up the Church in their parish. Invite them to use their branches to "build" a church on a bulletin board or posterboard you have prepared.

LEARN THE GEOGRAPHY

Have the students find Papua New Guinea on a map. Let them go on line or use reference books to find pictures of the island and the native people.

RECOGNIZE PARISH CATECHISTS

Peter was a dedicated catechist who had great zeal for his work. Have the students work on a project to give recognition to the catechists in your school or program. Divide the class into three crews. Have the photo crew take pictures of each catechist. Have the news crew interview each catechist and write a short summary of his or her background. Finally have the publicity crew make a display of the photos and summaries to display in the parish gathering area.

Catechist's Notes:

_____

_____

_____

_____

_____

_____

_____

_____

_____

_____

_____

Saint Benedict

July 11

(c. 480–547)

Benedict was a young man who followed his heart. He found something so wonderful that men and women have been following his example ever since—even today!

Benedict was born in Nursia, Italy. His parents were fairly rich, so they sent him to Rome to be educated. After a few years, when he was about 17 years old, he became disgusted with the lack of morality he saw all around him. Benedict decided to leave Rome and become a hermit. With the help of an old monk, Benedict found a lonely cave on Mount Subiaco, about 50 miles south of Rome. For three years he lived there as a hermit, garbed in a habit. Gradually other men recognized his holiness and wanted to live the way he did. Benedict set up 12 monastic communities, each with 12 monks.

Sometime around 529 Benedict led a group of monks still further south, and he built Monte Cassino. This monastery was destroyed and rebuilt three times over the centuries and has become the best known of all Benedictine abbeys. At Monte Cassino Benedict wrote his famous Rule. This rule of life, based on Scriptures, was written to help all the monks live in community. It is full of common sense. Benedict's monks followed the motto *Ora et labora,* which means "Pray and work." The first duty of the monks was liturgical prayer.

Benedict's twin sister, Scholastica, became a nun and she, too, was later canonized. Both were buried at Monte Cassino.

The Benedictine monasteries that spread over much of Europe became centers of learning, agriculture, hospitality, and medicine. Benedict's monks helped repair the damage caused by the barbarian invaders. It was Pope Gregory the Great who encouraged the Benedictines to move north past the Alps.

Benedict, whose name means "blessed," was a blessing to the world. In pictures and church windows, Benedict is usually shown with a copy of his Rule, which became the basis of all western monasticism. In 1964 Pope Paul VI named him the patron of all Europe.

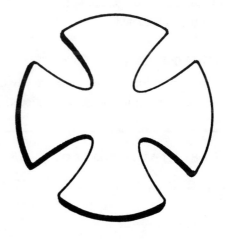

DISCUSS NEED FOR RULES

Benedict wrote a rule of life that all Benedictine monks and nuns have followed. Have the children list rules they follow each day at home, at school, in the car or bus, on the playground, with friends, and so on. Talk about why they need these rules.

EXTEND HOSPITALITY

Hospitality is part of the Benedictine rule of life.

- Have the students design a bulletin board with the theme of hospitality.

- **Grades K–2:** Have children act out ways to be welcoming to people in their homes, their play groups, and their classroom.

- **Grades 3–5:** Invite guests, such as the school maintenance personnel or people in the neighborhood, to come to class for a short program. Let the class plan the program and supply refreshments.

TREAT SISTERS WELL

Have the students read about Benedict's sister, Scholastica (feast day February 10, page 205). Suggest that if students have a sister, they do something kind or generous for her today in honor of Saint Benedict.

PRACTICE OBEDIENCE

Benedict recognized the value of having a responsible leader in charge. He believed that God's will came through the person in authority, who made decisions according to the Gospels and the rule of life. Benedict encouraged his monks to obey without delay. Challenge the students to obey promptly when their parents or teachers ask them to do things that are right.

PRAY THE PSALMS

Benedict had the monks memorize the psalms. He and his monks would meet seven times a day to pray certain psalms: "Seven times a day I praise you" (Psalm 119:164). Write one line from a psalm on the board each day and encourage the students to pray that psalm prayer during the day. After some time they will have many short prayers that they can pray from memory. The following are some verses with which you might begin:

- *Send out your light and your truth; let them lead me* (Psalm 43:3).

- *Hope in God; for I shall again praise him, my help and my God* (Psalm 42:11).

- *The Lord has become my stronghold, and my God the rock of my refuge* (Psalm 94:22).

- *As a deer longs for flowing streams, so my soul longs for you, O God* (Psalm 42:1).

- *My help comes from the Lord, who made heaven and earth* (Psalm 121:2).

Catechist's Notes:

_____

_____

_____

Saint Henry

(973–1024)

July 13

You know that the president of the United States is elected by the people. If he doesn't do a good job or doesn't take care of the needs of the people, they will elect someone else the next time. In the 10th century, leaders were not elected, and so they did not have to worry about pleasing their subjects in order to stay in power. Because of this, many emperors and kings took advantage of the power, luxury, and honor of their position without responsibly working for the good of their people. Kings often chose to ignore or to squelch conflict rather than to resolve it justly. In the midst of these circumstances, Henry, the son of the Duke of Bavaria, set the example of a Christlike leader. Jesus said that a leader is one who serves. And that is what Henry did.

Henry was married to Cunegunda of Luxembourg, but they had no children. When he was 34 years old, Henry became king of Germany. As a ruler, Henry concentrated on the good of his people. He built monasteries, helped the poor, fought against unjust seizure of power, and relieved all kinds of oppression.

Once his brother-in-law and some other relatives complained that Henry was wasting the family fortune on the poor. They actually got an army together to challenge Henry's rule. Henry met them on the battlefield and put down the uprising, then pardoned them out of Christian charity.

In 1014 Henry was crowned emperor of the Holy Roman Empire. That title made him ruler of Germany, Austria, Switzerland, Belgium, Holland, and northern Italy, as we know these countries today. Henry was well known for his missionary spirit and for his protection of the pope in times of trouble.

Henry ruled with a spirit of great humility and always sought to give the glory to God. He used his position to promote the work of the Church and the peace and happiness of the people. Henry is buried in the Cathedral of Bamberg beside his wife Cunegunda; he was canonized in 1146, and she was canonized in 1200.

JULY

ACTIVITIES

Saint Henry / July 13

PRAY FOR LEADERS

Ask the students to find out who the current leaders are in their city, county, state, and country. Then have them compose prayer petitions for these leaders, asking that they may have qualities like those of Jesus. During a class prayer time, ask each student to read his or her petition. For each petition, have the class respond, "Lord, guide our leaders."

DISCUSS THE NEED FOR GOOD LEADERS

Henry was a Christian emperor who acted justly. Lead the students in a discussion on the importance of having Christian leaders in government. Discuss the danger of having leaders who do not value the God-given dignity and rights of every human being.

DISCUSS CITIZENS' RIGHTS AND RESPONSIBILITIES

List on the board some of the basic rights that God has given to all people. You might include the right

to life and a worthy standard of living

to a good reputation

to be informed truthfully about public events

to a basic education

to honor God according to a person's conscience and to worship freely

to take part in public affairs and to contribute to the good of the country.

Explain to the students that government leaders have a responsibility to protect these basic human rights for every person. Then point out that these rights also entail responsibilities, and have the students list the corresponding duty that accompanies each right. For example, the right to a good reputation implies that each person must safeguard the reputation of all other people.

SET A GOOD EXAMPLE

As a Christian leader, Henry realized that people looked to him for a good model, or example, to follow.

- Have the class role-play situations in which they can set a good example for others.

- Have the students write the names of two or three people who look to them for a good example. Then have them write a short paragraph explaining how they can set a good example for these people.

Catechist's Notes:

_____

_____

_____

_____

_____

352

Blessed Kateri Tekakwitha   July 14
(1656–1680)

The name *Tekakwitha* means "moving all things before her" or "she who puts things in order." This young woman moved away the obstacles to her Christian faith and put her life in order in a short time.

Tekakwitha belonged to the Turtle Clan of the Mohawks, an Iroquois nation. She was born in the village of Ossernenon, near what is now Auriesville, New York, 10 years after Isaac Jogues and his companions were martyred there. Her mother was a Christian Algonquin, and her father was a non-Christian Mohawk chief. When Tekakwitha was four, smallpox devastated the village. Her parents and baby brother died, and the disease left her eyes weak and her face scarred.

Anastasia, a Christian friend of Tekakwitha's mother, took care of Tekakwitha and told her about God. When Anastasia went to Canada to be with Christians, Tekakwitha's uncle, a Mohawk chief, took her as his daughter.

Tekakwitha obeyed and worked hard. She was indoors a lot because light hurt her eyes. She excelled at cooking, beadwork, and repairing canoes. But when her relatives wanted to arrange her marriage, she refused. She felt that the Great Spirit was the only one she could love. This angered her uncle.

Tekakwitha learned more about God from a missionary. She was baptized on Easter Sunday when she was 20 and received the Christian name Katherine or Kateri. The following Christmas, she received her First Communion.

It was hard for Kateri to live as a Christian. Her people expected her to work in the fields on Sunday, the Lord's Day. Sometimes they didn't feed her. Children made fun of her and threw stones at her. Kateri endured this for two years.

Father de Lamberville, a Jesuit missionary, advised Kateri to go to an Iroquois village in Canada, where other Christians lived. One day when her uncle was away, Kateri escaped with a Christian named Hot Ashes. When Kateri's uncle discovered she was missing, he followed but did not catch her. After an exhausting journey, Kateri arrived at Kahnawake, near modern-day Montreal. She gave the priest there a note from Father de Lamberville. It said, "I send you a treasure, Katherine Tekakwitha. Guard her well." Kateri was an outstanding Christian. She went to Mass daily, made frequent visits to the Blessed Sacrament, and prayed the Rosary often. She cared for the sick and the old, and she taught children. She was known for her gentleness, kindness, and joyful spirit.

Kateri endured severe headaches. She was not strong and could eat very little, but she offered her suffering to God. When she was 24, Kateri contracted a disease and died. Her last words were "Jesus, I love you." The scars on her face suddenly disappeared. Kateri Tekakwitha was beatified in 1980 and is called the "Lily of the Mohawks."

MAKE SMALL CROSSES

One of Kateri's favorite devotions was making small crosses out of sticks and placing them in the forest. Then she used the crosses as stations, places to stop for a moment of prayer. Have the students make crosses from twigs and rawhide laces. Suggest that they put the crosses in their lockers at school or their rooms at home as prayer reminders.

DISCUSS EXCLUSION OF OTHERS

Kateri was mocked for being different. Kateri's face was pockmarked and her vision was poor, but that was not the reason for her rejection. What her people could not accept was her Christianity. Discuss with the class why some students are made fun of or shunned. What are the most important qualities for a person to have? What makes a good friend? a good classmate?

MAKE A PILGRIMAGE

If you live nearby, plan a day pilgrimage to the St. Francis Xavier Mission Church in Kahnawake, Quebec (near Montreal), where Blessed Kateri is buried; to the National Kateri Shrine at Fonda, New York; or to the North American Martyrs Shrine in Auriesville, New York. Or, have the students do an on-line search for pictures and information about these sites associated with Blessed Kateri. They may also find the trail she traveled to the mission in Canada.

RESEARCH AND MAKE A COLLAGE

Have the students do some online research on Catholic Native Americans today. Have them work together on a collage about a Native American parish or on ways Native Americans adapt liturgy to their culture.

ILLUSTRATE THE STORY

After listening to her story, have the children draw a picture of a scene from Kateri's life.

PRAY IN YOUR OWN WORDS

Kateri's last words were "Jesus, I love you." Invite the children to think of their very own way to tell Jesus about their love for him. Give them a short silence in which to pray in their own words. Suggest that they think of a difficult thing to do today as a way to show their love.

Catechist's Notes:

_____

_____

_____

_____

_____

_____

Saint Camillus of Lellis   July 14

(1550–1614)

Camillus was a gambler. When he gambled for money, he nearly lost his life. When he gambled on God, he found his life.

Camillus, who was born in southern Italy, was the son of a professional soldier. Camillus trained to be a military man like his father. As a young man, he joined the army of Venice to fight the Turks. He was in rough company, and by the time Camillus was 25 years old, he was a reckless and compulsive gambler. Then a serious wound in his leg forced him to go to St. James Hospital in Rome.

There Camillus saw the sad condition of the patients. He wanted to help them, but he was dismissed from the hospital because he began to gamble again. Camillus tried to join a monastery, but he could not adjust to the lifestyle. Finally he returned to St. James Hospital in Rome.

For the rest of his life, Camillus gambled on God. Camillus became a priest and devoted himself to his priestly duties and to caring for the sick. Other young men in the hospital were inspired by his change of behavior. They joined him, and together they formed a religious order called the Servants of the Sick.

Camillus became a pioneer in setting up proper diets and providing fresh air for patients, and in separating those with contagious diseases. During a war in Hungary, he and his brothers formed the first recorded military field ambulance corps. Right up until his death, Camillus worked hard for sick people—especially the poor. Today he is the patron of nurses and hospitals, and one of the patron saints of gamblers.

FIND ARTICLES ABOUT HAPPINESS

For many years Camillus lived without a purpose in life. He pursued only pleasure. Have the students find two articles in the newspaper: one an example of a person seeking passing happiness, the other an example of a person seeking lasting happiness. Have the students contrast the two situations on a chart.

IDENTIFY CRUTCHES TEENS USE

Camillus used gambling as a crutch to get through each day and to escape from the important things in life. Have the students list crutches that some teens rely on to help them escape from life's problems. The following might be included: withdrawal, over-conformity, sexual experimenting, frequent fighting, drugs, alcohol, refusal to eat. Discuss what these teens are missing in life and how they can be helped.

DISCOVER THE SECRET OF HAPPINESS

Camillus of Lellis was a troubled person who reached out to help others. Ask students to try an experiment: Every day for two weeks, do something to make someone else happy. Tell them to keep a record of what they do. After two weeks, ask them to report. Do they think they made others happy? Do they feel happier? Point out that they may have discovered the secret of holiness/happiness.

REVIEW THE SACRAMENT OF ANOINTING

Camillus was very devoted to the sick and the dying. Review with the students the Sacrament of the Anointing of the Sick. Then direct them to number a paper from 1 to 8 and take a short quiz on this sacrament, answering true or false. Then read aloud the following items:

The Sacrament of the Anointing of the Sick

1. may be celebrated at home, in a hospital, or in a church. *(T)*
2. brings peace and courage to a person who may be faced with continued suffering. *(T)*
3. may be given to a sick person before surgery for a serious illness. *(T)*
4. is another name for the Sacrament of Penance. *(F)*
5. assists in restoring the physical health of a person if this is God's will. *(T)*
6. is given only to the dying. *(F)*
7. uses olive oil for the anointing and as a sign of the rite. *(T)*
8. is sometimes celebrated within Mass. *(T)*

VISIT THE SICK OR ELDERLY

Camillus was well known for repeating these words adapted from Matthew's Gospel: "I was sick and you visited me." He really sensed the presence of Christ in those who were sick and dying. Prepare the students for a visit to a home for the elderly. Help them imagine themselves in the position of the individuals in that home. Guide them to think of what they can say and do to make their visit uplifting. Help them to be understanding and patient with the elderly by explaining some of the physical problems older people might have. After the visit, allow the students to share their feelings and insights. Ask what they have gained from the experience.

WRITE CHEERY LETTERS

Have the students write a letter to someone they know who is in the military or who is hospitalized. Encourage them to share with the person some interesting, upbeat things that are happening in their own lives.

Saint Bonaventure

(1218–1274)

July 15

Shortly after Bonaventure's death, it was written, "At the funeral there was much sorrow and tears; for the Lord had given him this grace, that all who saw him were filled with an immense love for him." What do you think made everyone love Bonaventure?

Bonaventure was born in Italy, not far from Naples, and was baptized John. The story is told that when he was about four years old, he was deathly sick. His mother begged Francis of Assisi to cure her child, and the little boy recovered. John went to Paris, where he met the great Thomas Aquinas. They both studied at the famous University of Paris, where John later became a professor. Attracted by the holiness of Saint Francis and the Paris friars, he entered the Franciscan Order and received the name Bonaventure. After some years Bonaventure became the Father General, the person in charge of the Franciscan Order, which he soon renewed. He was renowned as a guide and teacher of spiritual life. Once when Thomas Aquinas asked him where he gained his great knowledge, Bonaventure pointed to a crucifix and said, "I study only the crucified one, Jesus Christ." He was appointed cardinal bishop of Albano shortly before his death. He died unexpectedly at the Second Council of Lyons, which he had helped the pope prepare.

Bonaventure wrote many books about theology because he wanted to teach everyone how to live closely with God. For this, he was named a Doctor of the Church. Bonaventure's motto was "To God alone be honor and glory."

JULY

ACTIVITIES

DISPLAY A CRUCIFIX

Bonaventure kept a crucifix in his room to remind himself to imitate Jesus as completely as possible. Distribute pictures of Jesus crucified or small crucifixes to the students to keep on their desks or in their prayer place at home. Tell them the religious object is a reminder to imitate Jesus by loving others.

FIND WAYS TO PRACTICE POVERTY

As head of the Franciscan Order, Bonaventure guided the friars to a better understanding of the poverty in which they were called to live. Have the students give practical examples of how people their age could live these aspects of the virtue of poverty:

- Spending money wisely

- Not bragging about what they own

- Depending on God for help

- Sharing what they have with the poor

GO ON A FACT-FINDING TRIP

Bonaventure traveled a great deal, visiting the various groups in his order so that he could better understand the needs and problems of the Franciscans in his care. Organize a field trip to discover the needs of people at a retirement home, hospital, family shelter, hospice, or daycare center. Discuss and decide how your class can help. Then put your plan into action.

USE A QUESTION BOX

Bonaventure spent much of his life contemplating various doctrines about God. He always wanted to learn more about the mysteries of his faith. Decorate a question box and invite the students to submit any questions they have about the Catholic faith.

Preview the questions, removing any that are not appropriate, and adding others so that you have an interesting variety. Divide the class into groups, and have each group draw one or more questions. Have the students in each group pool their knowledge and try to come up with an answer or list all they know about their topic. Then have each group read the list to the whole class.

WRITE SHORT BIOGRAPHIES

Bonaventure wrote an excellent biography of Saint Francis of Assisi, the founder of the Franciscans. Using a marker, draw a picture of a shelf of books across the top of a large sheet of poster paper. There should be one book for every person in the class and one for yourself, and there should be enough room left at the bottom of the paper for the students' summaries of the books.

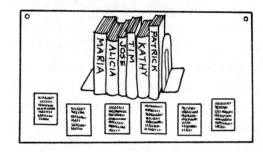

Distribute small sheets of light-colored paper, and have the students write a short synopsis of the life of a saint whose biography they have read. They should put the title and author of the book at the top of the paper. Then direct each student to write the title and author of the book he or she has read on the spine of a book in the picture. Add a title and author from your own reading. Arrange the synopses underneath in an attractive way, and ask the class to think of a good caption for the chart. Post the completed project in the hall.

Our Lady of Mount Carmel

O n one side of the mountaintop, the priests of Baal stood next to the stone altar dedicated to their false god. They had been praying aloud all day, but no god had answered them. On the other side, the prophet Elijah stood alone next to a stone altar dedicated to the Lord God, Yahweh. That day Yahweh sent fire from heaven onto the altar, proving that he, Yahweh, was the one true God. The Old Testament records this showdown on Mount Carmel in northern Palestine (1 Kings 18:16–39).

During the many centuries between that event and the year 1156, people who wanted a quiet place to pray and to live close to God began to come together on Mount Carmel. A large monastery was built there to honor the Mother of God. The members of the monastery were called Carmelites.

In 1251, according to the tradition of the Carmelites, the Blessed Virgin Mary appeared to Simon Stock, the sixth general, or person in charge of the Carmelite Order, and gave him a scapular. The scapular was a long piece of cloth worn over the shoulders and hanging, in front and in back, down to the ankles. After that, all the members of that Carmelite community wore scapulars. Today some religious men and women still wear the full scapular. Some people wear a small scapular made of two small pieces of cloth connected by narrow cord or braid. It, too, is worn over the shoulders. Wearing a scapular medal or the shortened scapular is a way of honoring the Blessed Mother. July 16 is a major feast for all Carmelite priests and sisters.

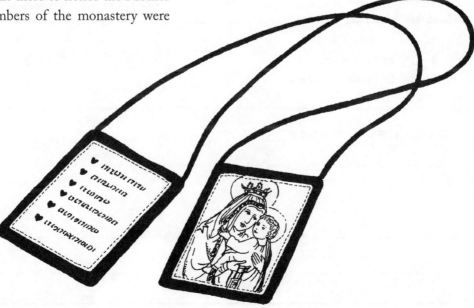

JULY

DISPLAY IMAGE OF OUR LADY OF MOUNT CARMEL

Show the students a picture of Our Lady of Mount Carmel. Invite them to tell about other images of Mary they cherish—pictures, statues, or stained glass windows.

CREATE A TITLE FOR MARY

We honor Mary by giving her special titles. Some titles, such as Our Lady of Mount Carmel, refer to a place. Others, such as Our Lady of the Snows, refer to a symbol. Make a group list as the students name as many titles of Mary as they can. If you have time, let them do some research to find more titles to add to the list. Finally let the students make up their own title for Mary, based on their own experiences. Have them share their titles with the class and then add them to the list.

MOUNTAIN MATCHING

Mountains are frequently referred to in both the Old and New Testaments as places to meet God, places to pray, and places to seek refuge. Make copies of a biblical matching exercise, using the blackline master on page 460. Have students work on it in pairs.

Mountain Matching answers are
1. (e) Mount of Olives
2. (d) Temptation of Jesus
3. (h) Call of the disciples
4. (c) Transfiguration of Jesus
5. (f) Sermon on the Mount
6. (b) Jesus prays
7. (g) Jesus is almost killed
8. (a) Mount Zion

REVIEW SACRAMENTALS

Review with the class sacramentals—things or actions that are reminders of Christ, Mary, and the saints. A scapular is one example. Some other sacramentals would be the cross, medals, statues, blessed palms, blessed candles, holy water, the Sign of the Cross, the Stations of the Cross, and the Rosary. Guide the children to see that these sacramentals are to help us remember that God is present and that he loves us.

SCRIPTURE STUDY

*   Tell the story of Elijah on Mount Carmel (1 Kings 18:16–39), or have students volunteer to read parts of it. Then discuss with the class the courage, the faith, and the perseverance of Elijah. Finally have the students select the single most important lesson that can be learned from this event.

*   Tell the story of Elijah on Mount Horeb (1 Kings 19:11–13), or have a student volunteer to read it. Discuss with the class the meaning of this mountaintop experience.

Catechist's Notes:

_____

_____

_____

_____

Saint Lawrence of Brindisi

July 21

(1559–1619)

Do you know anyone who can speak eight different languages? No? Then meet Lawrence of Brindisi.

He was born to a devout middle-class family in Brindisi, Italy, and named Julius Caesar. He studied in Venice, where he became a Franciscan priest. Because he was able to speak in many languages, including Hebrew, he became a popular and powerful preacher in several different countries. His sermons were woven with Scripture. Many of them were published in 15 large books. Lawrence devoted his life to preaching the truths of our faith and especially to correcting the errors that many Reformation preachers were spreading. Numerous Protestants returned to the Church because of him.

In Hungary as chaplain to the Christian army, Lawrence rode before it, holding up a cross and leading the soldiers to victory over the Muslims. Lawrence became known for his goodness, his simplicity, and his prudence as a teacher. He had a great devotion to the Blessed Virgin. Her feasts of the Immaculate Conception and the Assumption were two of his favorites.

After holding several positions of leadership in his community, Lawrence became the superior general. On foot he visited most of the 9,000 Capuchin friars in Italy, France, Belgium, Spain, and Switzerland, preaching along the way!

Lawrence also had a splendid reputation as a missionary and as a diplomat. He forged the Catholic League and made peace between Spain and Savoy. On the way home from a mission to Spain on behalf of the people of Naples, Lawrence died in Lisbon, Portugal. In 1959 Pope John XXIII declared that Lawrence should be considered a Doctor of the Church.

ACTIVITIES

LEARN A LANGUAGE

Teach the students a prayer or the name of God in various languages. Point out that Jesus sent his disciples to teach and baptize the people of every nation.

LEARN ABOUT SAINTS WHO LOVED MARY

Have the students find other saints whose devotion to Mary brought them closer to Jesus. Make a chart with the name of each saint and a small paragraph on the saint's devotion to Mary. You may wish to give each student a prayer card with a picture of or prayer to Mary.

WRITE TO A FAVORITE TEACHER

As a teacher Lawrence showed qualities of simplicity, goodness, and prudence. Have the students list the positive qualities of a favorite teacher they have had. Then have them write a note to that teacher, explaining how much they appreciated these positive qualities. Be sure to send the notes.

DISCUSS THE USE OF THE INTERNET

One of Lawrence's gifts was the ability to communicate. He used his talent in languages to show God's love and truth to others. Have the students consider a modern means of communication—the Internet. Lead them in a discussion of ways the Internet could be used to help or hinder the spread of truth and love.

DESCRIBE FUTURE SERVICE

Have the students list the various roles of service that Lawrence fulfilled in spreading the Good News: priest, preacher, teacher, superior general, missionary, diplomat. Then have them list as many roles of service in the Church today as they can. Finally have them choose three roles that they could fulfill 10 years from now, and have them write a sentence on each role, explaining their choices.

Catechist's Notes:

_____

_____

_____

_____

_____

_____

_____

Saint Mary Magdalene

July 22

(first century)

A number of women named Mary are in the Gospels: Mary, the sister of Martha and Lazarus; Mary, one of the women who cared for Jesus and his apostles on their journeys; Mary, present on Calvary; Mary, visiting the tomb very early on Easter morning. Although Mary Magdalene has traditionally been identified as the sinner who washed Jesus' feet with her tears, there is some uncertainty about whether Mary Magdalene can be identified with all of these Marys.

Mary came from the fishing village of Magdala on the west shore of the Sea of Galilee. In Luke's Gospel, Jesus frees Mary of Magdala from possession by seven devils. This possession is probably a violent nervous disorder, not the state of sin. Afterward Mary joins other women in providing for the material needs of Jesus and his apostles.

Matthew, Mark, and John record that Mary of Magdala was present at the crucifixion of Jesus and that she was among the women who visited the tomb on Easter morning. Luke mentions only the Easter incident.

According to John, Mary was the first to see the risen Lord in the garden. Through her tears over his missing body, she sees him in the garden and mistakes him for the gardener. Jesus speaks only her name, and immediately she knows him. He sends her to tell the apostles that he is risen. That is why she is called the apostle to the apostles.

What we know for sure is that Mary Magdalene was near Jesus in his darkest hour and again in his most glorious hour. For centuries Mary has been considered a model of complete generosity and of sincere sorrow for sin.

In art, because she's been identified with the repentant woman, Mary is shown with long hair, weeping at Jesus' feet. Earlier art depicts her at the Resurrection.

DRAMATIZE MARY'S POINT OF VIEW

Read a Gospel account of Mary of Magdala with the class (John 20:11-18). Then have them act out the story from Mary's point of view.

DRAW BEFORE-AND-AFTER PICTURES

Talk with the students about how Mary Magdalene might have felt when she stood at the foot of the cross. Invite the students to put themselves in Mary Magdalene's place as you read aloud John 20:25–42. Then talk about the scene of the empty tomb and Mary's encounter with Jesus in the garden. Again invite children to put themselves in Mary Magdalene's place as you read aloud John 20:1–18. Then have students make before-and-after pictures to express these feelings in art.

Directions: Fold a piece of drawing paper in half. Use either dark and light crayons or dark and light construction paper. On the left side of the paper, create a picture showing how Mary Magdalene felt at the death of Jesus. On the right side of the paper, create a picture showing how Mary felt at the Resurrection of Jesus. Note: These pictures may be abstract. They do not have to depict the actual scenes, but the emotions.

GIVE WITNESS TO THE RESURRECTION

Mary was the first to proclaim the Good News of the Resurrection. Have the students think of a way that they can proclaim the Good News today. Complete the activity with the prayer for the feast of Mary Magdalene from the Liturgy of the Hours. This prayer can be found on the blackline master on page 461.

USE THE PENITENTIAL RITE FOR PRAYER

Mary Magdalene has been considered by many artists and devout Christians as a person who admitted her sins and was very sorry for them. Review the options for the Penitential Rite of the Mass. Use one option as prayer in class today.

COMPOSE AND PRAY BERAKAHS

One of the Jewish prayer forms that Mary might have used is called the berakah, or thanksgiving prayer. This prayer contains both praise and petition. Have the students write original berakahs using the following pattern:

First sentence: "Blessed be the Lord, for he . . . ." (*Add what God has done for you.*)

Second sentence: "May he . . . ." (*Write your petition.*)

When the students are finished, light a prayer candle (if fire regulations permit) and have a short prayer service in which the students pray their berakahs. They might also print their prayers neatly on colored construction paper for display.

Saint Bridget of Sweden

July 23

(1303–1373)

You could say that Saint Bridget had her head in the clouds and her feet on the ground. Bridget was given the gift of visions, particularly visions of Christ's passion. At the same time, she was very practical and down-to-earth in living out the Gospel of Jesus.

Bridget was the daughter of a wealthy landowner in Sweden. When she was 14, she married Ulf, a young man of 18 who also wanted to serve God. Together they had eight children, one of whom, Catherine, became a saint. Together they made a pilgrimage to Compostela in Spain.

Once Bridget was invited to become the chief lady-in-waiting to the queen. She and Ulf served at the court for two years. While she was there, Bridget tried to encourage the queen and king to live holy lives.

After Ulf's death, Bridget exchanged her rich clothing for the plain habit of a nun. She started the religious order of the Most Holy Savior, commonly known as the Bridgettines, who made

great contributions to the culture of Scandinavia. She showed a loving concern for the poor and the sick, and many people came to her for help.

Bridget continued to receive visions and messages from God. With great humility she carried these messages to rulers and Church leaders as God directed her. Like Saint Catherine of Siena, she urged the pope to leave Avignon in France and return to Rome, the center of Christianity. She made many pilgrimages around Italy, and shortly before she died she went to the Holy Land. Bridget spent her last years in Rome. Her revelations of the Passion of Jesus and fifteen prayers given to her were published after her death.

ACTIVITIES

DISCUSS ROLES OF WOMEN

Bridget had many vocations. She was a wife, mother, mystic, founder, and advisor to the pope. Talk about the roles that many women today have: wife, mother, wage earner or professional, volunteer at church and school, and so on. Talk about how a woman can be a Christian and a saint in each of these roles.

CHOOSE A PENANCE

Bridget meditated on the Passion of Christ. The crucifix showed her the sufferings that Jesus accepted out of love for the sins of all people. In response Bridget offered her suffering to Jesus out of love. Remind the students that they can offer their sufferings to Jesus out of love too. Sometimes very small acts can be very difficult. Have the students consider the penance and charity of small things, such as not interrupting others in conversation and being punctual for class, meals, carpools, and curfews. Encourage the students to choose for a day a penance that would show their love and care for others.

LEARN MORE ABOUT IT

- Let interested students research and report to the class on the life of Bridget's daughter, Catherine of Sweden, and on the Bridgettines, also known as the Order of the Most Holy Savior.

- Tell the students that some other Christian mystics are Hildegard of Bingen, Teresa of Ávila, John of the Cross, Catherine of Genoa, Catherine of Siena, and Julian of Norwich. Explain that these mystics did their normal life's work, but were always drawn to union with God. Eventually they became united with God in every aspect of their lives. Direct interested students to do more research on Christian mystics.

Catechist's Notes:

_____

_____

_____

_____

_____

_____

_____

_____

_____

Saint James

(first century)

Does your mother ever try to arrange or take care of things for you? It's nothing new! We read in Matthew's Gospel (20:20–28) that the mother of James and John asked Jesus to give her sons a high position in his kingdom. Imagine their conversation:

Mother: Good morning, Master. I would like to talk to you about my two sons. Here they are: fine, strong young men.

Jesus: Yes, they're great guys—both of them. I'm happy they have chosen to be my friends and followers.

Mother: They are your most faithful followers, Master. I love them so much, I want to ask you for a favor. When you set up your kingdom and have your thrones ready, will you let James sit on one side of you and John on the other? They will be a great help to you, I'm sure.

Jesus: *(Looking at James and John)* If you wish to sit on my right and on my left side in the kingdom, you will have to drink the same bitter cup of suffering I am going to drink. Can you do that?

James and John: Oh, yes, Master, of course. We are strong enough to stand with you whatever happens.

Jesus: I want you to share in my sufferings, but only my Father will decide who will sit at my right side and my left side. For now, just stay with me and be my friends.

James and John were the sons of Zebedee, a fisherman in the village of Bethsaida on the Sea of Galilee. They were fishermen too. They were sitting in their boat mending their nets when Jesus called them. James was one of the first disciples Jesus called to follow him. (Matthew 4:21–22). They left their boat and their father, their way of life, and followed Jesus.

James and John were known as *Boanerges,* which means "sons of thunder." Perhaps they had strong tempers. Along with Peter and John, James was one of the three apostles favored to witness the Transfiguration of Jesus, the raising of Jairus's daughter, and Jesus' agony in the Garden of Gethsemane the night before he died.

We do not know very much more about James's life. James did share in the suffering of Jesus, however. Luke records in the Acts of the Apostles: "About that time King Herod laid violent hands upon some who belonged to the church. He had James, the brother of John, killed with the sword" (Acts 12:1–2). James was apparently the first of the apostles to give his life, around the year A.D. 42.

Tradition says James traveled to Spain. There is a famous shrine to St. James, Santiago de Compostela, in Spain. (*Iago* is the Spanish version of "James.") This was one of the most popular pilgrimage places during the Middle Ages. The devotion to Saint James was carried to the New World by Spanish missionaries. The capital city of Chile, Santiago, was named in honor of Saint James, as were many smaller cities.

James is also a popular saint in England. More than 400 churches are dedicated to him there.

DO ON-LINE RESEARCH

Help students to learn more about Santiago de Compostela. Direct them to these Web sites: www.red2000.com/spain/santiago/history.html www.red2000.com/spain/santiago/photo.html

IMAGINE SPECIAL EVENTS

At three special times in his life, Jesus invited only Peter, James, and John to stay with him. Have the students look up Matthew 17:1–8; Mark 14:32; and Luke 8:40–56.

Grades K–2: Have the children choose one story and draw a picture of it. Suggest that they include themselves in the scene.

Grades 3–8: Ask the students to imagine that they are James and write his diary entry for one of these events.

TAKE A POP QUIZ

Test what the students have learned about Saint James with this acrostic puzzle, using the blackline master on page 462.

```
_ _ _ _ _ _ _ A _
      _ P _ _ _
      _ O _ _
  _ _ _ _ S
_ _ _ _ _ _ T _ _ _ _ _ _
    _ _ _ L _ _ _
      _ E _ _ _ _ _
```

- James's work before he became an apostle. *(Fisherman)*

- Country that has a special shrine for James. *(Spain)*

- James's brother. *(John)*

- First apostle to die for Christ. *(James)*

- Nickname for James and his brother. *(Sons of Thunder)*

- Country with more than 400 churches dedicated to James. *(England)*

- James's father. *(Zebedee)*

DISCUSS KINDS OF ANGER

Jesus nicknamed James and John *Boanerges,* "Sons of Thunder." This name may have come from an incident recorded in Luke 9:51–54. A Samaritan village refused to welcome Jesus and his apostles. James and John asked Jesus if he wanted them to call down fire from heaven on the village. They seem to have had strong tempers. Discuss with the students the difference between constructive anger and destructive anger. Have them read Mark 3:1–6 for an example of Jesus' anger. Explain that his anger was constructive because he helped the man and was trying to teach the Pharisees the truth. Then direct the students to look up these examples of destructive anger: Acts 19:23–41, Luke 9:51–56, Luke 15:25–32.

Finally ask students to match Scripture passages with what they tell us about anger. You may use the blackline master on page 463 to make copies of the exercise.

1. People who feel sorry for themselves may get angry at imagined injustice.

2. People may act violently and less than human when they get angry.

3. People who see an injustice may want to correct it with revenge and punishment.

Answers: 1. Luke 15:25–32
2. Acts 19:23–41
3. Luke 9:51–56

Saints Joachim and Ann

July 26

(first century B.C.)

Did you know that your grandparents have patron saints? Well, they do—Saint Joachim and Saint Ann. They were Mary's parents, and so they were the grandparents of Jesus.

We really do not know very much about these saints. The Scriptures never mention them. From Mary's character we can infer that her parents were devout, faithful believers looking forward to the Messiah's coming. Many details we would like to know about them are hidden deep in the past. Tradition has given them names and some stories. A second-century gospel that is not accepted as inspired offers a story about Mary's birth. In the story Ann and Joachim haven't had children. Joachim leaves Ann and goes to the desert to pray. At home Ann also prays. Both are told by angels that they will have a child, and Ann goes out to meet Joachim at the city gate. The story goes on to say that Joachim and Ann take their daughter to the Temple in Jerusalem when she is very young. They understand that Mary is a special child, so they dedicate her to God. This document promoted devotion to Mary and to her parents. Saint Ann is popular in Christian art. She is often shown with Jesus and Mary. One of her two great shrines is St. Anne de Beaupré near Quebec City in Canada.

The name *Ann* means "grace," and the name *Joachim* means "the Lord will judge." Mary certainly had parents, no matter what their names were. They are members of the extended Holy Family.

HAVE A GRANDPARENTS' DAY

Invite grandparents to class. Have the children prepare a song, play, or short program about what they are learning. Invite grandparents to share their memories of religion classes. If possible, involve them in a lesson. Children who do not have grandparents living nearby may invite other older friends, or you may invite older parishioners to pair with these children.

PRAY FOR GRANDPARENTS

Invite children to write a prayer to Saints Joachim and Ann for their grandparents.

INTERVIEW JOACHIM AND ANN

Invite children to think of questions they would like to ask Joachim and Ann.

REFLECT ON FAMILY RELATIONSHIPS

To help the students appreciate what it takes to maintain good family relationships, have them make lists of the qualities of a good mother and of a good father. Then have them compare their two lists. Next have them list the qualities of a good daughter or son. Finally have them find good advice for parents and children in the Book of Proverbs. Possible references are Proverbs 1:8, 4:1, 10:1, 13:1, and 18:22.

COMMUNICATE WITH GRANDPARENTS

Encourage the students to contact their grandparents by e-mail, letter, phone call, invitation to a family meal, or a visit. Allow students to share positive results.

HELP AN EXPECTANT COUPLE

Suggest that the students take baked goods, a little gift, or an offer of an hour's free help to a couple who is expecting a baby.

PLAN A PARTY FOR ELDERS

Let the students plan a party for residents in a nearby home for the elderly. Allow them to decide on a theme, make decorations, and plan entertainment. They should think of activities that they and the residents can do together.

MAKE COLLAGES FOR PARENTS

Have the students make collages of the gifts, talents, and positive Christian qualities of their parents. Direct them to give the finished pieces to their parents.

PLAY A NAME GAME

Let the children unscramble the names of father-mother pairs in the Bible. Challenge the students to name their children too.

    vee / maad
    baramah / rshaa
    brakeeh / acsai
    objca / harcel
    creazahih / bliahetze
    pjoehs / raym

Answers:

    Adam and Eve, whose children were Cain, Abel, and Seth.

    Abraham and Sarah, whose child was Isaac.

    Isaac and Rebekah, whose children were Esau and Jacob.

    Jacob and Rachel, whose children were Joseph and Benjamin.

    Zechariah and Elizabeth, whose child was John the Baptist.

    Joseph and Mary, whose child was Jesus.

Blessed Andrew of Phu Yen

July 26

(c. 1625–1644)

It started out as case of mistaken identity—yet in the end it revealed exactly who Andrew was.

Andrew lived in the province of RanRan, now Phu Yen, in Vietnam. At his mother's request, the boy was allowed to take instructions in the Catholic faith from a French Jesuit missionary priest, Father Alexander de Rhodes. Although Andrew was young, he was very intelligent, and soon went past the older students. When Andrew was about 15, he and his mother were baptized.

Andrew then began to help Father de Rhodes instruct others who were seeking to know Christ. After further studies he joined a catechist association and formally promised to assist the priests in spreading the Gospel.

In 1644 the mandarin who governed the province of RanRan returned with orders from the king to stop the spread of Christianity. He at once sent soldiers to Father de Rhodes's house to arrest a catechist named Ignatius. This man was away at the time; instead they found Andrew. Afraid to return empty-handed, the soldiers arrested Andrew, who was 19 or 20

years old at the time. They beat him, tied him up, and took him to the mandarin's palace. The governor tried to talk Andrew into giving up his "foolish" faith, but Andrew would not budge. This angered the mandarin even more. The next day, July 26, Andrew was brought to a public hearing where he was sentenced to death.

Father de Rhodes and some Portuguese Christians visited Andrew in the house where he was being held. When they told Andrew that they would pray for him, Andrew replied that they should also pray that they, too, might remain faithful. Andrew was confident in his faith, saying, "Let us give love for love to our God, let us give life for life."

That afternoon Father de Rhodes followed as 30 soldiers led Andrew down the street to the place of execution. He witnessed the blows that Andrew received and heard him call out "Jesus!" as the sword fell on his neck.

Andrew was the first martyr of Vietnam. Just as Jesus had given his life for us, Andrew was happy to suffer for the Savior.

ACTIVITIES

STAND TRIAL

Andrew was arrested because of a law against Christianity. Ask the students to imagine they are living under a government that does not allow Christians to practice their faith. Have them make a list of evidence that could be brought against them at a trial.

PRAY FOR FAITH

Andrew said that we should all pray to remain faithful to Christ, to give love for love, life for life. Ask the students to write their own prayer for faith in their journals.

Encourage students to share their prayers at the close of class today.

RESEARCH AND REPORT

"[Be] steadfast in your faith, for you know that your brothers and sisters in all the world are undergoing the same kinds of suffering" (1 Peter 5:9). Let the students research countries where governments have tried to suppress Christianity. Have them find out how the people are keeping their faith alive under such conditions. Ask students to share their findings with the class.

Catechist's Notes:

_____

_____

_____

_____

_____

_____

_____

_____

_____

_____

_____

_____

_____

Saint Martha

(first century)

One of the most precious things in life is to have a home where you can go at any time and find people who accept, love, and understand you. Jesus found such a home in Bethany, at the house of Martha, Mary, and Lazarus. Martha welcomed Jesus and served him, and they developed a special bond of friendship.

Martha lived with her sister Mary. Like many sisters, these two women were very different in personality. Martha was energetic and outspoken, while Mary was quiet and reflective. Jesus loved both of them and appreciated the gifts that each one had. The Gospel of Luke records that once, when Jesus was visiting, Martha came to him with a problem and with her own solution. She was frustrated by all the work she was doing. Her solution was to get her sister Mary to help. After all, Mary was just sitting at the feet of Jesus hanging on every word he said. Martha wanted Jesus to tell Mary to help with the chores. But Jesus saw the situation differently. He showed Martha that because she was worrying so much, she did not have time to enjoy being with him and learning from him.

Another time Martha and Mary sent a message to Jesus that their brother, Lazarus, was ill. They knew Jesus would come and cure him; they trusted in his loving care for them. But when Jesus finally came, Lazarus had already been dead for four days. As soon as she heard that Jesus was nearby, Martha, a woman of action, went out to meet him, while Mary stayed in the house. In her grief over the loss of her brother, Martha told Jesus honestly what she had expected from him. "Lord," she said, "if you had been here, my brother would not have died!" Jesus calmly told Martha that her brother would rise again. He asked Martha to believe that he had power to give eternal life to all who believe in him. Though this is a great mystery, Martha trusted Jesus totally and said, "I believe that you are the Messiah, the Son of God, the one coming into the world" (John 11:27). That day Jesus raised her brother, Lazarus, from the dead to show that he has power over life and death and the power to give eternal life.

The home Jesus found in Bethany was not only in the house but in the faithful heart of a woman named Martha.

JULY

IMAGINE JESUS AS A GUEST

Jesus was a guest at Martha and Mary's house in Bethany. Ask the students what they imagine might happen if Jesus came to visit in their homes. Then direct them to write a story or poem or draw a storyboard about Jesus visiting their homes.

HELP WITH CHORES

Suggest that the children help their sister (or mother) with chores today.

HONOR COOKS

Martha is the patroness of cooks. In honor of Martha, direct the students to carry out one of the following activities:

- Make cards, awards, or decorations for the cafeteria personnel.

- Cook or bake something special for their own families.

- Show special appreciation to the person who prepares the evening meals in their homes.

- Prepare fruit sherbet during class, using the following recipe: Dissolve one cup sugar into two cups whipping cream. Let students take turns stirring. Add one-half cup fruit juice (lemon, grape, cherry, or orange) for flavor. Put in 8" pan and freeze for three hours.

FIND OUT WHAT HAPPENED

Martha lived in Bethany, which was a large town about two miles east of Jerusalem. Have the students look up the following Scripture texts and describe what happened at Bethany in each one:

1. Matthew 26:6–7
   (Woman anoints Jesus at the home of Simon the leper.)

2. Matthew 21:17
   (Jesus spent the night.)

3. Mark 11:11
   (Jesus stayed there during the night.)

4. John 12:1
   (Jesus raised Lazarus from the dead at or near Bethany.)

5. Luke 24:50
   (Jesus ascends.)

MAKE TRAY DECORATIONS

Martha is known for her service to others. As an act of loving service, have the students design tray decorations to send to a hospital or home for the elderly. A simple decoration can be made with scissors, glue, and scraps of paper, as follows:

1. Fold a piece of stiff white paper, 10" × 4", in half lengthwise so that the paper stands independently.

2. Designate one side to be the front.

3. Decide on a symbol of the season, such as a leaf, flower, smiling sun, or little garden, and make the pieces of the symbol from scraps of construction or tissue paper.

4. Glue the symbol on one corner of the front of the paper.

5. Neatly print a line from a psalm or a seasonal message across the front of the paper.

Saint Peter Chrysologus — July 30

(c. 380–450)

Bishop Peter would be very popular today. He found a way to guide Christians to the truth—the short homily.

In 424 Peter, a deacon, was elected bishop of Ravenna, Italy. At this time many Christians in his diocese were following false teachings and living according to unchristian values. Peter became well known as an outstanding preacher, whose brief homilies were filled with suggestions for living a moral life. He often based his homilies on the sections of the Bible that were used in the daily prayer of the Church, the Liturgy of the Hours. He also prepared catechumens for Baptism by explaining the Apostles' Creed and the Lord's Prayer.

Peter also found an opportunity to advise one of these false teachers, Eutyches. At the bishops' meeting in Constantinople in 448, Eutyches firmly denied that Jesus was both God and man.

Finally, unable to convince him of the truth, the bishops refused Eutyches the right to teach his false ideas. Eutyches then went to Peter for help. But Peter said, "In the interest of peace and the faith we cannot judge in matters of faith without the consent of the Roman bishop [the pope]." In this way Peter encouraged Eutyches to accept the authority of the Church.

Peter Chrysologus believed that knowledge is a great support for the Christian faith. He encouraged education as a God-given opportunity and obligation. He urged Christians to learn as much as their capabilities and talents allowed. Thirteen centuries later, Pope Benedict XIII declared him a Doctor of the Church because of his outstanding homilies. He is called *Chrysologus* (meaning "golden words") for his fine preaching. The Church today has preserved 138 of Peter's homilies.

JULY

ACTIVITIES

OVERCOME TEMPTATION

In his short homilies, Peter tried to help Christians turn from sin in order to live in Christ. Have the students list ways of overcoming temptations to sin. You might wish to include the following ideas:

- List all the benefits from overcoming the temptation and all the consequences of failing to overcome the temptation.

- Pray for the strength to overcome temptation.

- Practice acts of penance to gain self-control.

- Get support from someone who wants you to overcome temptation.

- Memorize a line from Scripture and repeat it when faced with temptation. Appropriate passages include: Romans 8:37 and 12:9; 1 Corinthians 10:31; Galatians 5:25; Colossians 2:6 and 3:16; 1 Peter 5:9.

PREPARE A HOMILY BASED ON A NEWS ITEM

Peter was greatly concerned with how Christians could live morally in their society. Have the students look through magazines and newspapers for a moral issue that concerns them. Ask them to cut out a picture or article that could be used as a starter for a Sunday homily. Then have them glue the picture on a sheet of paper, choose a fitting Scripture text, and prepare a short homily to deliver to the class.

TUTOR CHILDREN

Peter held all forms of learning in high esteem. Arrange for the students to tutor younger children in the school for several half-hour sessions. Discuss with them how this can help both the younger children and themselves.

Catechist's Notes:

_____

_____

_____

_____

_____

_____

_____

_____

_____

Saint Maria Venegas de la Torre

(1868–1959)

Have you ever seen a feature in a newspaper or a magazine that lists famous people who were born on that day or in that month? Well, our saint today was born on the birthday of a very famous person—the Virgin Mary. So the baby girl was named Maria Natividad (the birth of Mary). Maria was born in a small village near Zapotlanejo, in the Mexican state of Jalisco.

Like her namesake, Maria showed great holiness even as a child. She received Holy Communion frequently and prayed often in front of the Blessed Sacrament. Her love for God soon led to love of neighbor. Maria cared for the poor and gave religious instructions. Later she joined a community of women who ran the Hospital of the Sacred Heart in Guadalajara. Maria was a competent and caring nurse, most compassionate to the poor. Maria was courteous and attentive not only to the sick, but to the other sisters, to priests and seminarians, and to people in general.

Because of her charity and humility, Maria was elected superior of the little community of women. Maria wrote their rule of life and named them the Congregation of the Daughters of the Sacred Heart of Jesus. She made her vows and took the name Maria de Jesús Sacramentado—Mary of Jesus in the (Blessed) Sacrament.

In 1926 religious persecution by the Mexican government broke out. Maria did not stop caring for the poor and the sick during that dangerous time. Instead she opened two new hospitals in other states in the country.

Maria Venegas de la Torre died in 1959 at the age of 91. She was the first woman from Mexico to be canonized—in May 2000. No doubt many baby girls will be named for her. With God's grace many others will follow her example of love for Jesus in the Eucharist and in the poor and suffering.

SING MARY'S SONG OF PRAISE

Maria possessed the simplicity and humility of Mary, and all generations will call her blessed. Through her the lowly were lifted up and the poor received mercy. Pray Mary's song of praise, the Magnificat (Luke 1:46–55). Divide the class into two groups to alternate the verses. You may use the blackline master on page 452 to make copies for the students.

BE KIND TO MARYS

Encourage the children to do a special act of kindness today for someone who is named for Mary. You may wish to discuss some of the forms of Mary that are popular: Maria, Marie, Mari, Mara, Mae, May, Marian, Marianna, Marietta, Marilyn, Maya, Maureen, Mirelle, Miriam, Moira, Molly. Names that are derived from titles of Mary include Alma, Assunta, Carmella, Consuela, Dolores, Guadalupe, Immaculata, Lili, Lily, Lillian, Lyla, Lourdes, Mercedes, Regina, Renee, Rosaria, Sharon, Stella, Virginia (Ginny, Gina). If the principal, DRE, or someone known by all of the children is named Mary (or a form of Mary), think of an act of kindness the entire class might carry out.

CELEBRATE BIRTHDAYS

Ask the children to make a list of what they would like for their next birthday. Then have them contribute to a master list of what God has already given them: life, parents, faith, freedom, and so on.

CELEBRATE LIFE

Ask the children for ideas on how to celebrate life. Help them put one idea into action. You might contribute these ideas:

- Participate in a fundraiser, publicity event, or membership drive for the local right-to-life group.

- Buy or collect items for babies and young children in family shelters or foster homes.

Catechist's Notes:

_____

_____

_____

_____

_____

_____

_____

_____

Saint Ignatius of Loyola

(1491–1556)

Have you ever daydreamed about being a great hero? Perhaps you see yourself as a paramedic rescuing people from an icy lake. Or as the president making courageous decisions in the face of a national emergency. Perhaps you are a four-star general heroically maneuvering whole regiments to safety while under attack. These dangerous adventures appear very exciting and challenging in dreams. As a young man, Ignatius of Loyola learned that dangerous adventures could become painful experiences.

Ignatius was the youngest son in a noble family. While still a young man, he spent several years as a soldier, fighting in defense of Spain, his native country. At the age of 30, he was seriously wounded. One leg was badly shattered, and the other one was broken. The field surgeons set both legs and sent Ignatius home to the Loyola castle. But one leg was so badly set that it had to be broken again and reset. Since this was in the days before anesthesia, Ignatius suffered terrible pain.

During his long recuperation, Ignatius began to read whatever was available. After the novels he liked, he read a life of Jesus and a book about the saints. This was the beginning of his conversion. Later he spent several days in prayer at the Benedictine monastery in Montserrat. Then he journeyed on to Manresa, where he led a rugged, disciplined life for about a year.

Ignatius, now in his mid-30s, decided to fill in his neglected education. He returned to school with students less than half his age. After 10 hard years, he was ready for the University of Paris. Here he met six young men who joined him in forming a new religious community. The members of the small community offered their service to the pope for whatever he wanted them to do. By this time the group of seven were ordained priests who had taken the three vows of poverty, chastity, and obedience. Ignatius called his community the Company of Jesus. Today they are better known as the Society of Jesus, or the Jesuits.

The Jesuit priests did not wear a special habit, as most other religious orders did. They were trained to work with people wherever people needed them. They were a strong force in fighting false teachings throughout Europe. Their main work was teaching in schools, colleges, and universities, and many became missionaries. One of six original Jesuits was Francis Xavier, who became the great apostle of India and the Far East.

By the time Ignatius died, more than 1,000 Jesuits were working in North and South America, Europe, China, and Japan.

JULY

PRAY FOR THE POPE

Ignatius founded his Society to give the greatest possible service to the Church and to the pope. Today invite the students to pray for the pope, using this prayer:

> Father in heaven, protect our pope, [name]. Fill him with your compassion so that he can live the Gospel in loving service to all people. Lead him in the footsteps of Peter, who, filled with the Holy Spirit, first guided the Church. Amen.

EXERCISE THE SPIRIT

Most people recognize the value of daily physical exercise. Ignatius, a military man, recognized also the need for spiritual strength. He is famous for writing *Spiritual Exercises,* a guide for those who want to live a truly Christian life. Have the students list good forms of physical exercise for people their age. Then have them consider good spiritual exercises for people their age.

EXAMINE YOUR CONSCIENCE

Ignatius encouraged a daily examination of conscience. Have the students try this form of prayer by following these directions:

1. Find a place where you can be quiet for five or ten minutes.

2. Calm the thoughts in your mind.

3. Ask the Holy Spirit for help.

4. Review your thoughts, words, and actions of the day so far.

5. Ask: Are my thoughts, words and actions like those of Christ? Am I the person Jesus expects me to be?

6. Choose one thing to improve on for the rest of the day.

MAKE A JESUIT HALL OF SAINTS

Ignatius had a great zeal for promoting God's glory, for spreading God's Kingdom, and for making this a better world. Other Jesuits besides Ignatius have become saints; among them are Francis Xavier, Isaac Jogues, John de Brebéuf, Edmund Campion, Robert Southwell, Peter Claver, and Robert Bellarmine. Have students pair up, with one student drawing a picture of the saint and the other writing a three-to-five sentence summary of his ministry. Mount the pictures and summaries on bright-colored construction paper and display them as the Jesuit Hall of Saints. You could also have the students prepare displays of Dominican, Franciscan, Benedictine, and Carmelite saints. All of these groups would include both men and women.

LIST WAYS TO BE FAITHFUL

Ignatius valued being faithful to a duty, to what was right, and to principles and beliefs. He stressed fidelity to God, to others, and to self. Help the students realize that they have many opportunities to show fidelity. Put the following list on the board and allow the students to add their own examples:

I show fidelity when I

> am a loyal friend.
>
> obey parents and teachers.
>
> avoid criticism of others behind their backs.
>
> speak out about injustice.
>
> do a job with care.
>
> keep the commandments.

Saint Alphonsus Liguori August 1

(1696–1787)

Do you know anyone who expects to be a lawyer by the time he or she is 16? Probably not. Alphonsus did achieve just that unusual goal. He was born into the rich Liguori family of Naples, Italy. Because he was a very intelligent boy, and because the school system was very different at that time, Alphonsus finished school and began to practice law when he was 16. After 11 years he became so disturbed by the corruption in the courts of Naples that he gave up his career and began to study for the priesthood.

People who were underprivileged now became his clients. Eventually other young men joined Alphonsus in his efforts to meet the spiritual needs of the poor, and he began a religious order of priests known as the Redemptorists. Their goal was to preach and to teach, especially in remote rural areas and in the slums of the cities. His order worked hard to fight Jansenism, a heresy that denied that human beings have free will and advocated an "extremely rigorous code of morals and asceticism." It was responsible for keeping many Catholics from receiving Jesus in the Eucharist. Alphonsus, as a priest and later as a bishop, wrote many sermons, books, and articles to encourage devotion to Jesus in the

Blessed Sacrament. He was also deeply devoted to the Blessed Virgin Mary.

Alphonsus was a friendly, kind man, full of quiet humor. The last years of his life brought him problems of weakening health, misunderstanding, and even a certain amount of failure. But through it all, he kept his awareness of the presence of Christ in his life. In this way he never lost his faith and hope. In 1871 Alphonsus Liguori was declared a Doctor of the Church.

AUGUST

ACTIVITIES

Saint Alphonsus Liguori / August 1

FIND A THOUGHT FOR THE DAY

For his major writing on morality, a three-volume work, Alphonsus mentioned 800 authors in 70,000 references. Have each student find a quotation on the Christian life from a respected author. Direct the students to write their quotations and the authors on slips of paper. Collect the papers. Each day choose a slip and write that quotation on the board as the thought for the day.

CHECK OUT *LIGUORIAN* MAGAZINE

Bring to class copies of *Liguorian,* a magazine published by the Redemptorists and named after Saint Alphonsus. Depending on the number of magazines you have, distribute them to individuals or to groups of students who should examine the magazines with these questions in mind: What subjects are treated? How do the Redemptorists carry on the work of Saint Alphonsus? Have individuals or groups report their findings to the class.

SHARE STORIES ABOUT JUSTICE

As a lawyer Alphonsus showed a keen sense of justice. He gave up being a lawyer because he saw that his clients' causes were often unjust. Have the students share any experiences they have had of taking a stand for justice. Or have them describe incidents when people they knew stood up for justice.

Finally discuss how working for justice is acting as Jesus acted.

VISIT THE BLESSED SACRAMENT

In remembrance of Alphonsus's great devotion to Jesus in the Blessed Sacrament, go with the students to a church or chapel to spend a few minutes in the Lord's eucharistic presence.

LEARN A PRAYER

Alphonsus often spoke and wrote about the overwhelming love of God. Have the students memorize this short prayer, which Alphonsus used in his *Way of the Cross.*

> I love you, my beloved Jesus; I love you more than myself. I repent with my whole heart of having offended you. Never permit me to separate myself from you again. Grant that I may love you always, and then do with me what you will.

COMPOSE MUSIC OR LYRICS

Alphonsus was a person of many talents. Besides writing poetry and books, he was a gifted musician and composed hymns. Have the students, working in small groups, draw upon their own talents and set a psalm to music or compose new lyrics for a familiar melody. Give the groups the opportunity to lead their songs for the class prayer.

Catechist's Notes:

_____

_____

_____

Saint Eusebius of Vercelli   August 2

(d. 371)

Sometimes wrong ideas can really catch on. Early in the fourth century, a dangerous false teaching, or heresy, became very popular. A priest named Arius spread the idea that Jesus was not really divine. Arius taught that Jesus was a good man, but only a man.

In 325 the bishops gathered for a meeting in Nicea and condemned this teaching. At this council the bishops formulated the Nicene Creed, which listed the basic beliefs of the Catholic faith. They drew on an early baptismal creed from Jerusalem. Thirty years later, another council was held in Milan because the Arians were still causing a good deal of trouble. Eusebius, the bishop of Vercelli in northern Italy, attended this meeting. Before the bishops began any discussion, Eusebius insisted that each bishop sign a copy of the Nicene Creed. This act was to strengthen them in their belief in basic Catholic doctrine. At this council the teachings of Arius were condemned again.

The emperor, who favored Arius, became angry and sent Eusebius into exile in Palestine. The Arians in Palestine continued to harass Eusebius, but he held to his convictions, and he was forced to go to Egypt. When the emperor died, Eusebius returned to Italy and continued to fight Arianism for the rest of his life. He was deeply concerned that all priests everywhere should teach the Catholic faith as it had been handed on from the apostles.

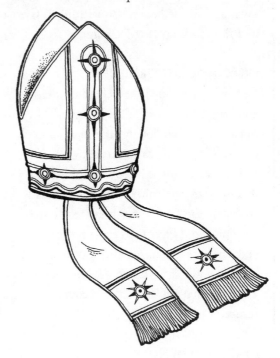

WRITE A PRAYER FOR FAITH

Even during his exile, Eusebius remained loyal to the Church and the Gospel message. Have the students look up the following Scripture quotations on being faithful:

Psalm 119:30

Proverbs 12:22

Luke 16:10

2 Timothy 3:14

Revelation 1:5

Revelation 2:10

Then have the students write prayers of their own, asking for help to be faithful to Christ and the teaching of the Church.

OVERCOMING DISCOURAGEMENT

Eusebius was exiled for defending the truths and true teachers of faith. In exile, Eusebius must have been lonely and discouraged at times. But as soon as he was allowed to return to his own country, he resumed his efforts as defender of the faith. Ask the students to consider the last time they felt lonely or discouraged. Have them explain the situation and their reactions in their journals. Then have them look up Isaiah 41:10–13 and copy a phrase that will give them courage in the future.

MAKE PSALM MOBILES

Eusebius translated a commentary on the psalms. Have the students consider four types of psalms: *praise* psalms, which show wonder or excitement with creation; *thanksgiving* psalms, which show gratitude; *repentance* psalms, which show sorrow for sins and failings; and *wisdom* psalms, which ask for guidance. Have the students work in pairs to find samples of each type of psalm. Then have each pair create a psalm mobile. Distribute index cards and instruct the students to use one card for each type of psalm. They should put the type of psalm and a quotation on one side and cut out a magazine picture that reflects the quotation to put on the other side. Punch holes in each card and attach the cards to a coat hanger with pieces of colored yarn.

DISCUSS JESUS AS HUMAN AND DIVINE

Eusebius risked his life to defend the truth that Jesus is both true God and true man. Have the students discuss how Jesus reflected these two natures in his public life. Then read the following situations taken from the Scriptures and ask the students to stand if the example shows the power of God and to sit if the example shows the human side of Jesus:

- Jesus asks the woman at the well for a drink of water. *(Man)*

- Jesus touches the blind man's eyes, and the man can see. *(God)*

- Jesus falls asleep in the boat. *(Man)*

- Jesus has dinner with a Pharisee. *(Man)*

- Jesus walks on the water. *(God)*

- Jesus tells a man that his sins are forgiven. *(God)*

Let volunteers give other examples to which the class can respond.

PROFESS THE CREED

Eusebius had a strong faith in all that Jesus taught. Have the students, in a spirit of faith, recite the Nicene Creed, which can be found on the blackline master on page 454.

Saint John Vianney

(1786–1859)

August 4

Imagine this scene: It's a warm summer day in the village of Ars, France, in 1850. A stranger strolls up to a fruit stand at the open market.

"Can I help you, sir?" the fruit seller asks.

"Well, yes. I'm looking for the priest, John Vianney. People in my village are saying strange things about him, and I would like to know if the reports are true."

The fruit seller offers the man some grapes and smiles. "What have you heard?" he inquires.

"Someone told me that the devil set fire to his bed a few weeks ago," the visitor replies. "And that he has seen the Blessed Virgin Mary and spoken to her. Are these stories true?"

"Why don't you go over there to his church and get in that long line waiting to go to confession to Father Vianney?"

"Confession? What will that tell me?"

"Try it. Father Vianney will most likely tell you about some secret sins that you committed long ago. Talk to him, and then come back and let me know what you think about him. We call him a saint."

At the age of 19, John Vianney decided to enter a seminary to study for the priesthood. After several months he had to leave because his previous schooling had not prepared him to attend lectures in Latin. He went to live with a friend who was a priest and who was able to tutor him. This priest finally persuaded the bishop to ordain John, not for his learning, but for his holiness.

After a few years, Father Vianney was assigned to Ars, a village of about 50 families in rural France. The people there were careless about practicing their faith, so they were not happy with this new priest who was eager to draw them back to God and the Commandments. Some parish members lied about him, acted violently against him, and refused to cooperate with him. They were hoping that he would give up and leave. But instead, Father Vianney responded with prayers and penance. And God's love began to reach people's hearts.

Gradually people began to come to celebrate the Eucharist and the Sacrament of Penance, and to listen to Father Vianney's simple homilies. Within a few years, Father Vianney was spending 10 hours a day in the confessional during the winter months, and almost 15 hours every day during the summer. People came from all over France, and even from other countries, to consult him and to ask for help. In fact the French government built a special railroad line to Ars just to accommodate all the pilgrims.

Father Vianney paid no attention to these signs of honor. He continued his hard yet simple life of prayer and service to the people. He was strict with his parishioners, but a hundred times more strict with himself. People were calling him a saint long before he died. He was canonized in 1925 and is the patron saint of parish priests.

LOOK THROUGH GOD'S EYES

John lacked proper schooling and a natural ability for learning. Yet he became a priest and a saint. Guide the students to see that God's love for individuals is not based on a person's intelligence, talents, personality, grades, popularity, or money. Help them to appreciate the value that each person has in God's eyes. Have each student write his or her name at the top of a sheet of paper. Direct students to find a partner. Tell them to exchange papers and write down something that they think God loves about the other person. Each student then takes his or her own paper and finds another partner. Repeat the process until each child has partnered with every other child. Give the students time to look over the comments on their papers. Then ask them to write a short prayer thanking God for his love.

SEND PRAYERS AND GREETINGS TO PRIESTS

Father Vianney is the patron of parish priests. Encourage the students to decide on prayers to offer for the priests of the local parish. Have one student design the front of a card for these priests. Guide the class to compose an inside message that mentions the feast of John Vianney, includes a note of encouragement, and explains that prayers have been offered for the priests by the class. Finally have every student sign the card and have a volunteer deliver the card to the priests.

REVIEW THE SACRAMENT OF PENANCE

John heard confessions from midnight to the following evening on a regular basis. He stopped only to celebrate the Eucharist, to pray a lot, and to eat and sleep a bit. Every day he had people waiting in line. John seemed to have the gift of reaching people's hearts and telling them about their past sins. Have the students consider whether they would have chosen to celebrate the Sacrament of Penance with Father Vianney. Then review the steps for celebrating the Sacrament of Penance.

RAISE MONEY FOR THE POOR

John gave away his furnishings, his belongings, and the clothes and food that the neighbors brought him. Once he received a black velvet cape as an award and sold it to buy food for the poor. Tell the students that in 1979 Mother Teresa of Calcutta won the Nobel Peace Prize and used the money to help the poor. Then have the class decide on a project to raise money to help the poor.

DRAW OTHERS TO CHRIST

John drew people to Christ by praying and sacrificing for them. In this way he was a channel through which God's grace could work within the hearts of the people. Encourage the students to think of one person whom they want to draw to Christ. Have them write in their journals a resolution about prayer and sacrifice that they might offer daily for this person.

Dedication of Saint Mary Major

August 5

When you hear the word *church*, what do you think of? Do you think of the priests and people of your own parish? Do you think of a Sunday morning when families of the parish gather to celebrate the eucharistic liturgy? Do you picture a stately building with a round dome, pointed towers, and stained glass windows? The word *church* has a variety of meanings.

Today's feast focuses our attention on a church building, a basilica called St. Mary Major. Tradition says that in August 352 the Blessed Virgin Mary appeared to a wealthy nobleman in Rome. She asked that a church be built on the spot where he would find snow. On that summer day, snow did mysteriously appear and a church was built on the spot and dedicated to Our Lady of the Snows.

Apart from the story, however, we know that a church was built on that spot in the fourth century and was rebuilt in 434. The church was also rededicated to Mary, the Mother of God. This title of Mary was protected by the ecumenical council of Ephesus. Today St. Mary Major is the largest church in the world dedicated to Our Lady. This church is called a patriarchal church, one where the pope officiates on certain occasions. There is a special altar in this church used by the Holy Father and by others with special permission. On a deeper level, this feast reminds us that Mary has been reverenced throughout the history of the Church as our Mother. As she foretold in her prayer, the Magnificat, "All generations will call me blessed" (Luke 1:48).

VISIT A SHRINE

Take the class to a Marian shrine on the property or in the church. Sing a hymn to Mary and pray the Magnificat from Luke 1:46–55. This prayer has become a model prayer of praise for the Church. It might fittingly be used after Communion. You may make copies of the Maginficat for students, using the blackline master on page 452.

REFLECT ON THE PARISH

Have each student mention one good quality of the parish. Then have students give examples of how they, as part of the Church, can help the parish in living out this quality.

HONOR MARY

Have the class list ways in which Christians show love for Mary. The list might include the following practices and/or others the students suggest: wearing a blessed medal; participating in a May crowning; naming a child after Mary; dedicating a school, hospital, or church to Mary; praying the Rosary; becoming a member of the Legion of Mary; remembering to celebrate her feast days. The students might also consult the diocesan directory to find names of religious communities and other organizations that have Mary for a patroness.

RESEARCH MARIAN SHRINES

Have students research shrines of Our Lady, such as the ones in Knock, Ireland; Mexico City; Lourdes, France; Fatima, Portugal; and Czestochowa, Poland. Direct them to share the information and any pictures they find with the class. Encourage the students to look for shrines located in their own diocese or within easy access. They might even plan a pilgrimage to such a nearby shrine.

MAKE A POSTER

Make a large poster on the name of Mary. In the middle of the chart, have a student letter the name *MARY* in decorative script. Then have the students search for the variations of that name in other languages. As they discover a name, have them print it somewhere on the poster. Possible starters are Miriam, Marisa, Maura (Ireland), and Mitzi (Austria).

Catechist's Notes:

_____

_____

_____

_____

_____

_____

_____

Transfiguration

The first three Gospels contain a number of passages that show Jesus' divinity shining through his humanity. One of these is the passage on the Transfiguration. Some time before he died on the cross, Jesus took Peter, James, and John up a high mountain—probably Mount Tabor. There, while the apostles watched, Jesus' face began to shine much more brightly than the sun. His garments became as white as snow.

Suddenly Moses and Elijah appeared, standing on each side of Jesus. The three of them talked together for a brief time about Jesus' coming passion and death. Then Peter exclaimed, "Lord, it is good for us to be here; if you wish, I will make three dwellings here, one for you, one for Moses, and one for Elijah" (Matthew 17:4).

While Peter was still speaking, a bright cloud gathered and covered the apostles with its shadow. Then the apostles heard a voice saying, "This is my Son, the Beloved; with him I am well pleased; listen to him!" (Matthew 17:5). Peter, James, and John fell to the ground because they were so frightened. The next moment Jesus touched them and told them not to fear. When they looked up, there was no one in sight except Jesus, looking like his ordinary self.

As they walked down the mountain, Jesus told the favored three to keep the whole experience a secret. They were permitted to tell others only after he had risen from the dead.

Perhaps Jesus gave these apostles a glimpse of his divine identity in order to strengthen their faith in preparation for the ordeals of his coming passion and death.

AUGUST

ACTIVITIES

Transfiguration / August 6

READ A LETTER

Write the following letter on stationery and put it in an envelope. Open the letter in class, read it to the students, and ask them to guess who could have written a letter like this.

> Dearly Beloved,
> As I am here in prison, awaiting execution, I feel the urge to write to you, pleading with you to be faithful to Christ. I am aware that you have shown loyalty to Christ and his teachings, and I thank God for it; but, still, these few words may raise your spirits when you are tempted to give up. Realize that what we have taught you about the coming of Jesus in glory and power are not figments of our imagination, but actual truths, for we saw Jesus on the mount arrayed in glory and heard the voice from heaven announce, "This is my beloved Son." Let me repeat: Jesus will come again, this time in glory and majesty. Keep this truth in mind when the going is rough. It will be a lamp to light your way through the dark night until the morning star appears and the coming of dawn brings light to your heart. To Jesus be glory.
>
> *(Adapted from 2 Peter 1:12–19)*

After the students have guessed, tell them that this is adapted from Peter's second letter, written while he was in prison. Then guide them to see that Peter used the Transfiguration event to give courage to suffering Christians.

PRESENT A SHADOW PLAY

Have interested students make a shadow play of the Transfiguration event. They may experiment with lighting effects for the play.

DISTINGUISH FIGURATIVE USAGE

In the Bible a cloud may be an actual sign of rain or it may be a symbol to show that God is mysteriously present. Have the students divide into pairs and look up the following quotations. Then have them indicate on a sheet of paper which quotations connect the cloud with weather and which refer to God's presence or glory.

> Exodus 13:21–22 *(presence)*
> Exodus 19:16–20 *(presence)*
> 1 Kings 8:10–13 *(presence)*
> 1 Kings 18:44 *(weather)*
> Isaiah 25:5 *(weather)*
> Matthew 17:5 *(presence)*
> Luke 12:54 *(weather)*
> 1 Corinthians 10:1 *(presence)*
> Jude 12 *(weather)*

MAKE A BOOKMARK

Direct the students to search through song books and to copy sentences that refer to "glory." Then have the students choose a sentence from their list, print it neatly on a strip of poster board, and decorate it to make a bookmark. Encourage them to use the bookmark and to praise the God of glory whenever they see it.

DO A WORD SEARCH

Duplicate the word search on the blackline master on page 464. Challenge the students to find 10 words that refer to the Transfiguration account.

M	J	L	R	E	C	C	B
O	O	Q	U	I	L	H	M
U	H	S	G	L	O	R	Y
N	N	M	F	I	U	I	S
T	S	O	N	C	D	S	T
A	J	S	W	H	I	T	E
I	F	E	A	R	K	E	R
N	R	S	X	W	P	R	Y

The answers are *mountain, John, fear, Moses, glory, cloud, Son, white, Christ, mystery.*

390

Saint Sixtus II and Companions

August 7

(d. 258)

In 257 when Sixtus became pope, he did not know how long he would be able to serve the young Church. Being a Christian had suddenly become dangerous. For a while Emperor Valerius had been gentle and appreciative of Christians. His palace had been filled with Christian high officials. Then overnight he turned against them, accusing Christians of being enemies of the government. In the midst of this new threat, Pope Sixtus struggled for one year to guide the Church through many difficulties, some dealing with false teachers, and some dealing with questions about Baptism.

Because of the persecution, Christians began to gather secretly in the catacombs throughout Rome. The catacombs were damp, dark tunnels used as underground cemeteries. There these brave Christians found strength and joy in their celebration of the eucharistic liturgy. Frequently they would change the particular location or the time so they would not be found by suspicious Roman guards. Then one day during the eucharistic celebration in the catacombs,

Valerius's soldiers appeared. In full view of the community, the soldiers beheaded Sixtus and four deacons who were assisting him. The men were killed simply because they were Christians.

AUGUST

TAKE PART IN A GUIDED MEDITATION

To help students experience the situation of the early Christians, lead them in a guided meditation:

- For the next few minutes, close your eyes and let your imagination do the work.

- Imagine that you are an early Christian walking down a crowded street in Rome. People are rushing past you as you slip behind a building. You are looking for the hidden entrance to one of the catacombs. Earlier in the day, Deacon Lawrence slipped a note into your hand while you were at the market. The note, written in code, warned you that the meeting place had been changed. Some Roman guards had discovered the regular meeting place. Now you are trying to find where Pope Sixtus and the others are gathering for the celebration of the Eucharist. You grope your way through the dark tunnel until your eyes adjust to the darkness. You stop and listen for voices. You are looking forward to greeting your friends and to receiving Christ in the Eucharist. Suddenly your heart stops. Standing before you are Pope Sixtus and the other Christians gathered for worship. All of them are familiar faces to you. BUT . . . they are surrounded by Roman soldiers. Would you turn and run or stay and risk discovery and death?

Allow some silent time for students to complete the story in their own minds. To close the meditation, read this prayer:

Lord, you gave strength and courage to the early Christians. They faced death in order to be loyal to you. For them, you were more important than everything else, including life itself. Now we live as your followers. Give us that same strength. Make us courageous in following you in the face of difficulties and ridicule. Be more important to us than anything else. Amen.

ENCODE A MESSAGE

Have students compose a message that an early deacon might have sent to the Christians, giving the place and time of the next celebration of the Eucharist. Direct students to write the messages in secret code, since Christians were being persecuted. Then tell students to trade papers and decode one another's messages.

MAKE A FISH SYMBOL

Explain or review the meaning of the fish symbol. The first letters of the phrase *Jesus Christ, Son of God, Savior* in Greek spell the word *fish.* So the early Christians used an outline of a fish as a secret identification symbol. Let students draw their own fish symbols on construction paper. Older children can letter the Greek initials ΙΧΘΥΣ on the design using a black felt-tipped marker. Younger children can print the words *Jesus Christ, Son of God, Savior* beneath it.

Saint Dominic

(1170–1221)

"Truth" was Dominic's motto and his goal. He was born in Spain, the youngest of four. He was educated by his uncle, a priest. After further studies Dominic became a priest and joined a religious community similar to the community of the early Christians. Soon he became its prior, or head.

He might have always lived in that monastery if he had not accompanied his bishop to northern Europe in 1204. At that time he met heretics. Their teachings had begun in the town of Albi in France, so the heresy was called Albigensianism. The Albigensians taught that people do not have a free will to do God's will. They taught that marriage was bad and also that suicide and the killing of elderly or fatally ill people could be good. They claimed to be the true church. Many good Christians were confused. They could not see the errors in the heretics' teachings, and they admired the heretics for living strict lives with little comfort.

Dominic saw that missionaries sent by the pope to preach against the heresies slept in hotels, rode in carriages, and ate good meals. Many Christians were not impressed with that lifestyle. So Dominic thought of a new way to fight heresy. Dominic, his bishop, and three monks went from city to city, preaching the truth and using the Bible. They went on foot, depending on donations for food and hospitality for a place to sleep. Dominic's plan changed the attitude of some Christians.

In 1206 Dominic began an order of religious women who would serve women who returned to the Catholic faith. These sisters also were a great help to Dominic. Then events took a turn for the worse. The bishop died, the discouraged monks gave up and went home, and fighting broke out between the heretics and some Church members. The sisters encouraged Dominic to keep trying and prayed that he would be able to touch the hearts of the heretics.

By 1215 a few men had joined Dominic in his work of preaching, and he founded a religious order called the Order of Preachers. Dominic had learned much from his preaching and travels: the importance of education, of praying with Scripture, of living in Christian poverty. Dominic urged his members to study constantly. He knew that if they were not well educated they could be trapped by the arguments of heretics. He encouraged them to pray with Scripture and contemplate the Word of God. Then they would be ready to preach. Dominic also realized that in order to be witnesses of the Gospel, Dominicans had to live in poverty, as Jesus had done. While other monks did manual labor and stayed in the same monastery for life, the Dominicans studied, prayed, traveled, and preached. They lived, defended, and taught the truth that they found in the Christ of the Gospel.

Dominic died while on a preaching mission only six years after he began his community. He was canonized only 13 years later, in 1234.

AUGUST

PRESENT PUBLIC-SERVICE ANNOUNCEMENTS

Dominic was a powerful preacher, who had a way of convincing people of the truth. Challenge the students to write a 30-second public-service announcement to persuade fellow students to follow Christ, to read the Bible, or to participate wholeheartedly in the liturgy. Present the announcements over the school public-address system.

LEARN BIBLE ABBREVIATIONS

Dominicans have always valued the Word of God. Dominic knew most of the Gospel of Matthew and the letters of Paul by memory. Have the students make flash cards with the name of a book of the Bible on one side and the abbreviation of the book on the reverse side. Let them make up games using these cards. Then challenge the students to memorize the names of the books of the Bible in order and recite them in a minute or less. This skill is helpful in looking up a reference.

ANSWER THE NEEDS OF THE TIME

Dominic responded to needs he saw in his own time. Rose Hawthorne was a wealthy American woman who did the same. She used her wealth to begin a community of Dominican sisters who care for incurably ill cancer patients. Ask a volunteer to read Rose Hawthorne's life story and report to the class. Have the students speculate on needs in your city or the world that a new religious community or lay organization might choose to address.

TAKE INVENTORY

Dominic wanted his friars to be well educated and to have a thorough knowledge of religion. To help the students assess their participation in religious classes, distribute a checklist that they can use in each religion class for a week or, if you have weekly classes, for a month. Use the blackline master on page 465 for student copies. Have them use this scale for evaluation: VG = very good; G = good; NI = needs improvement.

Religion Class Check-Up

1. I had the necessary materials when class began: text, pencil, pen, paper.

2. I was paying attention when class began.

3. I participated by asking or answering questions.

4. I actively cooperated in the activities of the lesson.

5. I did the written work neatly and completely.

At the end of the week or month, have the students describe in their journals the results of their survey and suggest some improvements they can make.

Saint Teresa Benedicta of the Cross (Edith Stein)   August 9

(1891–1942)

As she was growing up, Edith prayed at home with her family and went to religious services. While this could be said about many Catholic saints, Edith's family was a little different. She was from a devout Jewish family. Then when Edith was about 13 years old, she gave up faith in God altogether.

Edith grew up in Breslau, Germany, the youngest of seven children. Her father died when Edith was young, so she became very close to her mother. Edith was a very intelligent girl. She was so smart that the teacher sent her home from kindergarten; there was nothing for her to learn there. Edith didn't just study when there was going to be a test in school. She studied because she loved to learn. She always got high marks in everything except math. Edith continued her studies at the university, where she earned a doctorate degree in philosophy.

Then as an inquisitive young woman, she picked up the autobiography of Saint Teresa of Ávila. Edith was so captivated that she couldn't put the book down, and she completed reading it in one night. The next day she bought a Catholic catechism and read it. Edith felt that she had finally found the truth she had been looking for since she was 13.

When Edith was baptized, her mother cried. Edith did not have the heart to tell her mother that she also wanted to be a Carmelite nun. So she waited. She taught school, translated books, and gave lectures—and she prayed. Finally in 1934, she entered the convent and received the name Sister Teresa Benedicta of the Cross. She shared in the domestic work of the nuns, but also continued to write about philosophy.

In 1938 the persecution of Jews became so intense in Germany that it became dangerous for the rest of the sisters in the convent. They could be killed simply for giving shelter to a Jewish person. Edith and her sister Rosa, who had also become Catholic, went to Holland. Four years later Holland was occupied by the Nazis, and one day, without warning, soldiers came to the convent door. They gave Edith and her sister 10 minutes to pack before they put them on a train to Germany. From there they were sent to the concentration camp at Auschwitz in Poland. Two days later, on August 9 or 10, Edith and Rosa died in a gas chamber.

Edith was canonized in 1998. One of her favorite sayings was "Far be it from me to glory except in the Cross of our Lord Jesus Christ." Edith found her glory in the cross.

AUGUST

DO YOUR BEST WORK

Challenge students to search for truth.

- Ask them to do their best work in school today, to look for knowledge rather than just do an assignment.

- Ask each student to complete the sentence: One thing I'd like to know more about is . . . Then make an assignment for each student to research his or her subject and make a short oral or written report.

SHINE IN THE DARKNESS

Tell the children that wherever there is darkness in the world, they can bring the light of Christ. Have them make symbols of the light they share with the world. Give these directions:

1. Draw a large candle, including the flame, on construction paper and cut it out. (You may wish to supply a pattern or precut candles for younger children.)

2. Write your name on the candle and one way you can share the light of Christ with others. (Encourage students to keep it simple and feasible, for example, smile, or say a kind word instead of a putdown.)

3. Cut out the center of the candle flame, being careful to keep an outline of construction paper.

4. Select a small piece of colored cellophane or plastic wrap. Tape or glue the translucent material behind the flame.

5. Display the candles in a classroom window where the light can shine through.

EXPERIENCE SILENCE

Edith Stein found God through study, reflection, prayer, the silence of the Carmelite convent. Help the children become aware of God's presence, near them and in their hearts.

Grades K–2: Ask the children to be very quiet for one minute and just listen for what God wants to tell them.

Grades 3–8: Have students reflect on the following questions:

> Where is there silence in my life? when I take a test in school? in my bedroom at night? during Mass? while I'm waiting in line for something?

> How do I feel when there is silence? peaceful? relaxed? restless? it depends?

Discuss why some people love silence and others prefer to fill up every moment with music or other sounds.

MAKE BOOKMARKS

Edith Stein found God through the words of Saint Teresa. Direct the students to search through religious song books and to copy sentences that refer to *glory*. Then have the students choose a sentence from their list, print it neatly on a bookmark, and decorate the bookmark. Encourage them to use the bookmark and to praise the God of glory whenever they see it.

Saint Lawrence

(d. 258)

August 10

"Where's the money?" demanded the Roman official harshly. Deacon Lawrence looked surprised by the question. "What money?" he asked. "The Church's gold and silver," answered the official. "We know that you're in charge of the treasury, Lawrence. The government has a right to confiscate those funds. Hand them over." The official began to look annoyed. He had seen that Pope Sixtus II and four other deacons had been executed. But he didn't want to kill this deacon until he had the wealth in his hands. Lawrence responded, "Yes, I will show you the real treasures of the Church, but you have to give me time to prepare. Give me three days." Because he suspected that he, too, might be arrested, Lawrence had already sold the gold chalice and the other sacred items and had given the money to the poor.

But Lawrence was true to his promise. In three days the official returned. He saw before his eyes rows and rows of lepers, orphans, widows, and people with disabilities. Lawrence's comment was "These are the treasures of the Church."

This incident that has come down from the early centuries shows how well Lawrence had put on the mind and heart of Christ. That special love he had for the weak, the helpless, and those whom others rejected, and the special dignity he saw in each person made him an excellent deacon. The deacons in the Church were to serve others, especially the poor. Lawrence valued the poor more than he did his own life.

The Roman official was so angry with Lawrence that he had a huge grill built and placed over burning coals. In this way, he hoped that Lawrence would die very slowly and painfully from the burning heat. But Lawrence was filled with good humor and joy while he died. Tradition says that he quipped, "I'm done on this side. Turn me over." The onlookers were amazed. But how could they understand that Lawrence was happy and excited about seeing the most important person in his life face to face—Jesus Christ?

COLLECT TREASURES

Lawrence's attitude toward the poor can be learned from his words and actions. Discuss how the parish or school shows its attitude toward the poor. Decide on a local group that could use help, such as a women's, children's or family shelter or the St. Vincent de Paul society. Make plans to collect the treasures found in closets, drawers, and cabinets that could be used by others. Have the students decorate collection boxes and make signs announcing the collection. Ask for volunteers to gather and deliver the treasure.

START A PEN PALS PROGRAM

Lawrence was a deacon, not a priest, in the early church. The word *deacon* comes from the Greek word *diakonia*, which means "service." Deacons of the early church helped widows, orphans, the poor, and the elderly. Acquire a list of names of senior citizens from a parish minister or home for the elderly. Have each student choose a name and write a letter of introduction as a Christian pen pal. The students might include their pictures, original drawings, poems, or information about their present activities. Send these letters to the club or place of residence of these senior citizens.

LEARN ABOUT DEACONS

Teach the students to distinguish between transitional deacons and permanent deacons. Transitional deacons are preparing for ordination to the priesthood. Permanent deacons are ordained only to the diaconate. Share information about permanent deacons in the parish or young men from the parish who are transitional deacons in the seminary. Invite a deacon, transitional or permanent, to speak to the class about his role of service in the Church.

ACCEPT DIFFICULTIES OF FAITH CHEERFULLY

Lawrence is said to have joked while he was slowly dying. Have the students read 2 Corinthians 9:6–10, which describes a cheerful giver. Point out that they may not be called to die as martyrs for Christ, but they will certainly experience some difficulties in practicing their religion. If they show they honor their parents by obeying a curfew, for example, they might have to suffer the teasing of their friends. Have the students offer additional examples. Then offer a spontaneous prayer asking for courage to be faithful to Jesus.

Catechist's Notes:

_____

_____

_____

_____

_____

Saint Clare

(c. 1193–1253)

August 11

What do you think is the sign of true friendship? Is it loyalty, which keeps friends together through discouraging times as well as through good times? Is it having the same goals, the same values? Is it the ability to help each other become the best person possible? Is it being comfortable together so that no one has to put on an act? Clare and Francis of Assisi had a strong, true friendship that reflected all these qualities. But they had something more—their mutual, deep love of Jesus, which made them want to live according to the Gospel.

Clare was born into a wealthy family of Assisi, Italy. As a teenager she became aware that Francis, the handsome, wealthy leader of the young people in Assisi, had greatly changed. He used to spend a great deal of money having a good time and treating others to a good time. Now he had no money, no possessions, no family to call his own. He dressed in a brown robe, begged for food, and lived on the streets. Yet he seemed to enjoy life more than ever. Clare was puzzled by his behavior. But gradually she saw that the real source of his joy and inner peace was his living in poverty like Jesus. In 1211 Clare left home to join Francis. He cut off her long hair, gave her a rough woolen habit to wear, and took her to stay for a while with the Benedictine sisters. When he found a little house adjoining San Damiano Church, he moved Clare and the other women who had joined her into this little place and guided her in beginning a new religious order.

This small community wanted to live according to the rule of Francis. They slept on the floor each night, went barefoot, kept silence much of the day, and spent hours in prayer. They ate only when food was donated because they had no money to buy their own food. Clare became abbess, the head of this little community. But she did not spend her time giving orders. She eagerly chose the hardest work to do herself. She helped the healthy as well as those who were ill. Her example inspired the others to trust in God. In 1240 and again in 1241, the convent and the whole city were threatened by an invasion of the Saracens from the Middle East. Panic spread. Clare told her sisters not to be afraid but to trust in Jesus. She herself prayed to Jesus in the Blessed Sacrament to save his people. Both times the convent and the whole city were spared.

Clare's dying words were "Blessed may you be, O God, for having created me."

The community that Francis began with Clare is still in existence today. The nuns are called the Poor Clares, and they continue to follow the spirit and the rule of Saint Francis.

ACTIVITIES

CELEBRATE BENEDICTION

When the city of Assisi was threatened by the violence of a Saracen invasion, Clare prayed to Jesus in the Blessed Sacrament for help. If possible, let the students participate in Benediction or pray the Divine Praises. You may use the blackline master on page 455 to make copies of the prayer for the students.

PRAISE GOD IN NATURE

Like her friend Francis, Clare felt wonder and awe at the beauty of nature and the reflection of God in nature.

- Post colorful nature scenes around the room. Ask the students to find appropriate psalm verses to use as captions.

- Have the children draw scenes of their favorite part of nature.

- Together pray St. Francis's Canticle of the Sun, which he composed during his last visit to Clare. You may use the blackline master on page 442.

MAKE FLOWER BASKETS

Have the children make flower baskets for another class, neighbors, or homebound parishioners. Show a sample, using the following directions:

1. Roll a sheet of construction paper (8½" × 11") into a cone and fasten it with staples or glue.

2. Decorate the cone with paper designs, scraps of materials, and ribbon.

3. Attach yarn or ribbon to the top of the cone for a handle.

4. Print a Scripture passage on a small strip of stiff paper (3" × 1½") and tie or staple it to the handle. Good passages to use include Psalm 96:11–12; Psalm 150:8; Isaiah 35:1; Luke 12:27.

5. Fill the cone with real or plastic flowers or flowers made from tissue paper.

The baskets are ready to hang on the doorknobs of people that the students wish to surprise.

THANK GOD FOR BLESSINGS

Clare had a joyful and grateful heart. Use this exercise to help the students reflect on the blessings in their lives. Give these directions:

1. Fold a paper in four parts.

2. Label each part with one of these headings: Persons, Qualities in Myself, Places, Things.

3. List under each heading the things/people for which you are grateful.

4. Choose one item from your list for a class litany of thanksgiving.

For example, a student might say, "For my parents who care for me." As each student reads a prayer, have the class respond, "We thank you, Lord." Close with the Doxology: "Glory be to the Father. . . ."

Saints Pontian and Hippolytus

August 13

(d. 230s)

During the Roman persecution of the early Church, not all Christians were sentenced to death. Some were sentenced to forced labor in metal or salt mines. These Christians convicts marched to the mine shaft two by two, chained together with murderers, political prisoners, thieves, and slaves. Once confined below the ground, the convicts spent their time in endless work. No one came out alive.

How did the Christians keep up their courage in those suffocating places? Their faith in Jesus Christ and the power of his love kept them going. Some of the walls in the mines had words or phrases scratched on them—words that expressed this faith to other suffering Christians. "You will live in Christ . . . You will live forever . . . life . . . life . . . life."

Hippolytus and Pontian were among those sentenced to the mines. Hippolytus was the most influential writer in the Church at that time. But he was also very critical and wanted the Church to be very strict with sinners. When Pope Callistus chose to be forgiving, as Jesus was, Hippolytus became very upset. He gathered his own followers and challenged the pope. When Pontian became pope in 230, Hippolytus still refused to change his position. He caused much unrest and confusion among Christian communities, and Pontian could not seem to change him.

In 235 under the persecution of Maximus, Pontian was sentenced to hard labor in the mines of Sardinia. He resigned as pope so that someone else could lead the Church. Then he went into the mines. That same year Hippolytus was also arrested and condemned to the mines in Sardinia. In that dark, damp prison, the forgiving love of Christ finally penetrated Hippolytus's heart, and he was reconciled to Pontian. The two men died in those mines, united in the love of God. They are martyrs for Christ and recognized as saints in the Church.

AUGUST

DECODE A MESSAGE

The early Christians like Pontian and Hippolytus gladly faced torture and death. Write the following coded message on the board. Have the students decode it to find out the secret of the joy of martyrs. (Hint: Each letter of the message represents the letter that comes directly before it in the alphabet.)

XF IBWF WJDUPSZ UISPVHI KFTVT

The answer is *We have victory through Jesus.*

COUNTERACT CAPITAL SINS

The early Christians lived in a society that admired the capital sins and treated them as popular behavior. Have the students list the capital sins in a column on a sheet of paper: pride, covetousness (greed), lust, anger, gluttony, envy, sloth (laziness). Next to each sin, have them write one action a person could do to avoid that sin (e.g., pride—praise another person's success instead of your own).

HOLD A PRAYER SERVICE

Pontian and Hippolytus witnessed to Christ by their lives in the face of exile and cruel treatment. Celebrate a short prayer service in honor of the early Christian martyrs. Divide the class into three groups and give each group one of the following Scripture references: Matthew 10:17–23; 2 Corinthians 4:7–18; 2 Corinthians 6:3–10. Have each group practice reading the assigned passage aloud, either by having each person take a line to read or by having two sides alternate. Begin with a song such as "Be Not Afraid" (Dufford) from the album *Earthen Vessels* (NALR). Then have each group present its scriptural selection. Conclude with spontaneous petitions to give the students an opportunity to ask for courage and strength for themselves and for other Christians.

Catechist's Notes:

_____

_____

_____

_____

_____

_____

_____

_____

Saint Maximilian Mary Kolbe

August 14

(1894–1941)

Maximilian Kolbe was born in Poland and was named Raymond. His mother told the story that when he was 10 he had a vision of Mary holding out two crowns to him. Mary asked which he wanted, the white crown of purity or the red crown of martyrdom. Raymond answered, "I choose both."

Raymond joined the Franciscans when he was 16 and took the name Maximilian Mary. Maximilian had a great devotion to Mary Immaculate. He worked to spread devotion to her, even traveling to Japan and India to do so. His pockets were always full of miraculous medals to distribute. He published Catholic literature, including a monthly magazine called *The Knight of the Immaculate*. Through this magazine, which had a million subscribers, Father Kolbe taught the Gospel under Mary's protection to all nations. He founded spiritual centers named City of Mary Immaculate. In Japan he established the City at Nagasaki. After the atomic bomb was dropped on Nagasaki, the spiritual center was unharmed.

During World War II, Father Maximilian Kolbe gave shelter to thousands of Polish people, both Christians and Jews, risking his life to help these suffering people. On February 17, 1941, he was arrested and sent to prison in Warsaw. There he was given a convict's uniform and the number 16670. He was sent to the Nazi concentration camp at Auschwitz, where he endured very hard work and beatings that almost killed him. Even then he secretly heard confessions and spoke to the other prisoners about God's love. When food was brought in, he stepped aside for the other prisoners. Sometimes there was nothing left for him.

One day a prisoner escaped from the camp. As a result, the officers said 10 men must die by starvation in an underground pit. They chose 10 men to die. One man cried out, "What will happen to my family?" Father Kolbe stepped forward and offered to take the man's place.

In the pit Father Kolbe led the nine men in prayer and song to Mary, Mother of God. He lifted their spirits. After two weeks, when Father Kolbe was the only one still alive, an executioner killed him with an injection. His body was burned with those of the other prisoners. No doubt Maximilian Kolbe was pleased that his death occurred on August 14, 1941, the vigil of Mary's Assumption, so that now each year this vigil is his feast day. He was canonized in 1982.

AUGUST

PRAY THE ROSARY

Review the Glorious Mysteries of the Rosary, which may be found on the blackline master on page 443. Divide the class into five groups and assign one mystery to each group. Direct the students to write a brief explanation and prayer for their mystery. Then have the class pray the Glorious Mysteries of the Rosary. Before each decade, have a volunteer from the appropriate group read the group's prayer meditation to the class. Remind the students to think about each mystery as they recite the prayers.

Or pray one decade of the Rosary, using the mystery of the Assumption.

EXPLORE WAYS TO HONOR MARY

- Have the class list ways in which Christians today show love for Mary. The list might include wearing a medal; participating in a May crowning; naming a child after Mary; dedicating a school, hospital, or church to Mary; praying the Rosary; and celebrating her feast days.

- Suggest that students consult the diocesan directory to find names of religious communities and other organizations that have Mary for a patroness.

- Have the students find out the story behind the Miraculous Medal.

ASSEMBLE A COLLAGE

Let pairs of students discuss where Father Kolbe found the power to give his life for another. Write out John 15:12–13 on a large poster board. Ask the students to find pictures or articles in newspapers and magazines that show people who are giving their lives out of love for others. Let them make a collage with the pictures and articles. Then invite each of them to write on a colorful strip of paper one way they can give of themselves for another person. Have them add their papers to the collage.

DRAW STRENGTH FROM THE EUCHARIST

During the time of the Roman persecutions, Christians secretly gathered in the catacombs to celebrate the Eucharist. More recently, during World War II, priests like Maximilian Kolbe held Masses secretly in the concentration camps. Guide the students to see that the Eucharist has been a source of strength to Christians of every age, no matter what their surroundings. Have the students write entries in their journals about the Eucharist as a source of strength for them.

Catechist's Notes:

_____

_____

_____

_____

Assumption

One glance at a daily newspaper or a television news show will tell you that some people do not value human life. But this is not news. During the Holocaust of World War II, millions of people were tortured and killed. This terrible tragedy led many people to wonder about human life. How valuable is a single human life? How valuable are the lives of the elderly, the unborn, the terminally ill? Are their lives worth as much as those of people who are healthy and active, working, and raising families?

God creates human life and gives it value. And Jesus gave his life on the cross to redeem each individual human person. By doing this, Jesus said, "Your life is worth my dying to save you." Through his own Resurrection, Jesus showed us the glory of our resurrection and of our living in the Holy Spirit. Jesus promised that the body and soul of a person, separated at death, will be joined together again in glory at the Last Judgment. The person will be whole for all eternity.

The feast of Mary's Assumption is a preview of what our lives will be. At the end of her earthly life, Mary was assumed, or taken up, into heaven body and soul. She did not have to wait for the end of the world, as we do. God granted her this special privilege because of her sinlessness and her fullness of grace.

The Church has always believed in Mary's assumption into heaven. But on November 1, 1950, Pope Pius XII focused the attention of the whole world on the Assumption of Mary as a dogma and mystery of our faith. This mystery shows us that God wants every human person, body and soul, to be in glory forever, just as Mary is now. This dogma shows how important every single human life is. Pope Plus XII hoped that by thinking about Mary's Assumption, people all over the world would develop a deeper respect for their own lives and their own bodies. He also hoped that people would grow in respect for the lives of others.

STUDY VISUAL ARTS

Show various representations of the Assumption of Mary. Ask the students to explain how the artist represented Mary and to imagine why he or she included certain details in the painting. Then compare these depictions with the image of Our Lady of Guadalupe. You may wish to use the blackline master on page 446.

REFLECT ON THE GLORY OF GOD

Mary now experiences the glory of God. Challenge the students to find Scripture passages that refer to God's glory. Write one reference on the board and have the students stand as soon as they locate the exact quotation in their Bibles. Then have one of the standing students read the passage aloud while the others are seated and listening. Put the next reference on the board and repeat the procedure. These are some possible passages to use:

Ephesians 1:17	Habakkuk 2:14
Isaiah 6:3	Romans 1:20
Numbers 14:21	Psalm 19:1
Mark 10:37	Jeremiah 14:21
Psalm 29:1–2	Luke 24:26
1 Samuel 2:8	1 Timothy 3:16

BRAINSTORM IDEAS OF HEAVEN

Give the students one minute to write down all the words they can think of that remind them of heaven. Have the person with the longest list read it to the class. Then discuss with the students why these words may have come to be associated with heaen. Finally read 1 Corinthians 2:9 to the class.

DISCOVER LESSONS OF THE FEAST

In the United States, the Assumption is a holy day of obligation. Catholics gather for the celebration of the Eucharist on the vigil or on the feast day itself. Discuss with the students what lessons the citizens of the United States can learn from this Marian feast.

LEARN ABOUT ROOTS OF THE FEAST

Since the last part of the sixth century, the Eastern Catholic Churches have celebrated the feast of the Dormition of Mary, which eventually led to our feast of the Assumption. The Dormition is the "falling asleep of Mary" at the end of her earthy life. Tell the students that Mary's peaceful crossing over from earthly life to heavenly life is due to Jesus, who died to free her and all of us from the power of death.

SELECT AND SING A HYMN

Divide the class into groups. Give each group several song books and hymnals and a specific time limit. Have them find and list the names of songs that deal with Jesus' Resurrection or his victory over death. Then, as a class, sing one of these hymns.

Saint Stephen of Hungary

August 16

(c. 969–1038)

"Might makes right." "Grab everything you can get." "The strongest person gets the best." "Don't try to cooperate—try to win!" Do you ever hear these attitudes from other kids, or even coaches?

The people who settled near the Danube River in the 10th century thought that way. They were a violent and superstitious people. Often one of these tribes would invade a part of Western Europe, destroying property and stealing anything of value. The tribes themselves were separate from one another and fought among themselves or took revenge for some offense.

The national leader of these people was Geza. When Geza's son, Vajk, was born, people expected the boy to take his father's place as leader of this area called Hungary. Then Geza and his son learned about Jesus Christ and Christianity. They were both baptized. Vajk received Stephen as his baptismal name. As a young adult, Stephen married a girl named Gisela. When Geza died, Stephen had to lead the country. He wanted all the Hungarian people to become Christians. First he asked Pope Sylvester II if he could be a king instead of a national leader like his father. The pope agreed and sent a special crown, which still exists today. In 1000 on Christmas Day, Stephen was crowned the first king of Hungary. Then as king, he made unity a special goal and brought the various tribes into one nation.

Hoping to plant Christianity in the hearts of the Hungarian people, he made three other important decisions. He invited the Benedictine monks of Germany and Italy to come as missionaries to his people. He built churches and had them decorated with sculptures, colorful mosaics, and murals depicting truths of the Catholic faith. He encouraged the people to come to the churches and to value their local priests.

Stephen was very popular with the poor. He often went among them giving donations. One time the crowd of beggars became so excited that they knocked him to the ground. But Stephen laughed and assured them that he would continue to share his wealth with them. Stephen's love for the poor also kept his officials from getting too powerful and abusing the poor and the weak.

Stephen counted on his son Emeric to take his place as king when he died. Stephen is believed to have written *Mirror of Princes* in order to explain to his son how to he a good Christian king. However, young Emeric was killed in a hunting accident, and Stephen faced many family quarrels over who should be the next king. Stephen was buried at the Church of Our Lady of Buda in Hungary. He was an outstanding leader, a dedicated Christian, and a strong defender of the Church. He is the patron saint of Hungary.

ACTIVITIES

FOLLOW GOOD ADVICE

Have the students imagine that they are Emeric and their father is giving them this advice. Read the following selection from *Mirror of Princes* to the class.

> Be humble in this life, that God may raise you up in the next. Be truly moderate and do not punish or condemn anyone immoderately. Be gentle so that you may never oppose justice. Be honorable so that you may never voluntarily bring disgrace on anyone. Be chaste so that you may avoid all the foulness of lust like the pangs of death. All these virtues I have noted above make up the royal crown, and without them no one is fit to rule here on earth or attain to the heavenly kingdom.

Use the blackline master on page 466 to make a copy of the paragraph for each student. Ask them to underline one piece of advice that they think is good advice for themselves. Encourage them to try to follow the advice this week.

RESEARCH AND SHARE HUNGARIAN CUSTOMS

Stephen is recognized as the founder of the state of Hungary. So that the students can see how the Christian influence spread in that country, have them research Hungarian customs and traditions. Let them share their findings with the class.

LEARN DUTIES OF A CATHOLIC

Stephen was a devoted Christian. Give each student a copy of the blackline master on page 467. Have the students make flashcards with a "duty of a Catholic Christian" on one side and a practical example of how that duty is lived on the reverse side. For example:

Duty: To join in the missionary spirit and apostolate of the Church.

Example: Collect rosaries and postage stamps for the missions.

Then have the students pair up and drill each other on the duties of a Catholic Christian. When they finish, have them switch partners and continue the drill.

RESEARCH CHURCH TEACHING ON WORLD PROBLEMS

Stephen realized that Christianity would help his people in all areas of their lives. Explain to the students that Church teachings and documents and the letters of the popes and bishops help all people to apply Christian principles to world problems. Have the students list world problems on the board. Topics might include world hunger, discrimination, the misuse of natural resources, the arms race, abortion, capital punishment, war, immigration, scientific research, and poverty. Let each student choose one to study. Direct the students to use the *Catechism of the Catholic Church* to find out what the Church teaches about the topic. Have them write a report in which they first state the issue and then explain the Church's view of it. Encourage them to discuss their research with their parents.

PRAY FOR LEADERS

Review with the students the names of their local and national leaders. Discuss Christian qualities that these leaders need to do their job well. Lead the students in a litany asking God for a quality that these leaders need. The response to each petition might be "Bless our leaders, Lord."

Saint Jane Frances de Chantal

August 18

(1572–1641)

The early life of Jane Frances Fremyot sounds like a fairy tale. Her family came from nobility, and her father was president of the parliament at Dijon. Tutors came to instruct Jane. She learned to play musical instruments, and she became an excellent hostess. Jane was intelligent, beautiful, and charming. When she was 21, she fell in love and married Christopher de Chantal. Everyone could see how much Jane loved her husband and God. At her request daily Mass was celebrated in the Chantal castle. Not only did she care for her home and four children, but she also cared for sick and elderly people. Beggars were never turned away from her kitchen.

After seven years of marriage, Jane's life was shattered when her husband was killed in a shooting accident. The loss of her husband brought unbearable grief to Jane. In an attempt to get over her depression, Jane sought a spiritual director. Unfortunately the priest she found gave harsh penances and failed to understand her. Then her father-in-law demanded that she come and manage his estate. He threatened to take away her inheritance if she refused. The man was a tyrant, and it took humility to listen to his endless orders without complaining. Jane prayed patiently for hope and strength. And each day she would gather the children and teach them to read, count, and sew. She also told them about God and taught them their prayers. This situation lasted another seven years.

Then her father suggested she spend Lent with her own family. A well-liked bishop, Francis de Sales (feast January 24, p. 179), was giving talks then. Soon he became Jane's new spiritual director. Francis was amazed at Jane's deep faith and courage and her prayer life. Francis encouraged Jane to continue to seek God. Jane returned home with a more positive outlook. She was even able to seek reconciliation with the man who had accidentally caused her husband's death.

Francis de Sales and Jane de Chantal shared a dream of a religious community of women who would pray and help the poor in the cities. In 1610 Francis and Jane opened the first convent that allowed sisters to blend a life of prayer with charitable works. Jane and the 12 women who joined her called themselves the Visitation of Holy Mary. When they tried to open a second convent in Lyons, France, the bishop there protested. The Church was not ready for this new way of life for sisters. Jane and Francis did as the Church asked. The Visitation sisters stayed in their convents and prayed for the world rather than going out to serve it. Before Jane's death, 80 convents were founded.

Jane directed the Visitation Order with the same sensible and compassionate spirit she had shown in directing her home. Once a devoted mother to her husband and children, now she was a devoted mother to her spiritual daughters. She was canonized in 1767.

LIST SAINTLY ACTIONS AND ATTITUDES

Jane Frances de Chantal became a saint both as a mother and as a religious sister. Have students list the saintly actions and attitudes of Jane as a mother and as a religious sister.

PRAY FOR GOD'S GUIDANCE

Jane Frances de Chantal had the courage to change her plans when God asked her to. Close the religion class with a prayer that each student may see God working in everyday events. Have the students pray that they may be aware of God guiding their lives even when their plans are changed.

SERVE OTHERS

Jane wanted to use her energies to serve the poor and sick.

- Provide each student with a paper strip (1" × 5") that will serve as a link for a chain. Have the students write down how they can help someone in their class, neighborhoods, or families. Link the chain together. Hang it on the bulletin board to remind them of how they can help!

- Extend the project to include the whole school or parish program. Challenge all the students to do three acts of service to show their love for others. The next day, or the next week, distribute paper strips of various colors (1" × 5") to all classes. Each student should receive one strip for each act of service he or she did. Direct the students to write down only services that they really did. Then have the classes glue the strips into interlocking loops and form a paper chain. Have classes attach the chains to other class chains. Decorate the halls with these service chains.

REFLECT ON THE STORY

Jane had often reflected on the Visitation. Mary had spent three months with her relative Elizabeth, helping with the household tasks and planning for the birth of Elizabeth's baby. During that time Mary had grown in her love of God as she contemplated the child in her womb. Read the story of the Visitation in Luke 1:39–56 with the class. Ask students to share how they think Mary and Elizabeth felt at this time.

- Have younger children act out the story.

- Ask older students to learn the Magnificat as a prayer they can make their own. You can make copies, using the blackline master on page 452.

Catechist's Notes:

_____

_____

_____

_____

_____

Saint Helena

(c. 250–c. 330)

Helena's life started off like a Cinderella story. She was the daughter of a lowly innkeeper in the city of Drepanum in Bithynia. This was part of the great Roman Empire. Fate smiled on Helena the day Roman general Constantius Chlorus stopped for dinner and a room at the inn. Helena, who was probably hard at work, must have caught his eye. The two were married, and she suddenly enjoyed a position of wealth and honor. A son, Constantine, was born in 274.

Constantius Chlorus's star continued to rise, and in 293 he was proclaimed regent of the western empire under Emperor Maximian. Then, under political pressure, Constantius divorced Helena and married Theodora, the daughter of the emperor. Helena was humiliated by the rejection.

Fourteen years later Constantius died, and his son Constantine was proclaimed regent. Constantine had not forgotten his mother, and he extended her every honor. He brought her to the imperial court, gave her the title of Augusta, had a coin made with her image, and named the city where she had been born Helenopolis.

Constantine also issued the Edict of Milan, which accepted the Christian religion in the empire and released religious prisoners. Under his influence, Helena embraced the Christian faith and was baptized when she was about 63 years old. From then on Helena used her position and wealth in relief of the poor and to build and decorate churches.

When she was about 80 years old, Helena fulfilled her dream of traveling to Palestine to see the holy places where Jesus lived. The Roman emperor Hadrian had built a temple to the Roman goddess Venus at the place of Jesus' crucifixion and burial. Helena had it torn down and supervised the building of a church there.

Helena is most famous for finding the cross on which Jesus died. Though this cannot be confirmed, it is true that she found Jesus. She built churches, cared for the poor, for soldiers, and for prisoners, and prayed much among the women of Jerusalem. She worshiped the King who died on the cross. That is why she is a saint.

The one symbol most often identified with Jesus and the Church is the cross. The meaning of the cross is deeper than any city, any celebration, or any building. The cross is a sign of suffering and death. But for Christians it has become the sign of triumph and victory, the sign of the tremendous love of Jesus Christ.

AUGUST

ACTIVITIES

MAKE CROSSES

Have the students make crosses, using wood, cardboard, foil, pebbles, clay, or other material. Or have them make a clothespin cross.

Materials needed

8 hinged clothespins per student
Craft or wood glue

Directions

1. Remove the metal springs from the clothespins.

2. Lay out vertical beam as indicated in the illustration below. Two side-by-side clothespin halves for the top and bottom (with space in between) are joined and glued in place, using 2 side-by-side clothespin halves in the center of the vertical beam as support.

3. Carefully turn beam to the front. Glue horizontal beam onto vertical beam, using 4 clothespin halves laid in pairs and touching at the center.

4. Form the corpus by turning clothespin halves on their sides. Two halves form the body; two become the legs, and the remaining two are arms.

PRAY BEFORE THE CRUCIFIX

Take the students to the church, chapel, or prayer room for a short prayer or meditation on the cross. You may wish to sing or play appropriate music, such as "Behold the Wood" or "With What Great Love."

Pray the Prayer to Christ Crucified from copies of the blackline master on page 437.

> Good and gentle Jesus,
> I kneel before you.
> I see your five wounds.
> They have pierced your hands and feet;
> They have hurt all your bones.
>
> Fill my heart with faith, hope, and love,
> help me to be sorry for my sins,
> and to turn my life to you. Amen.

LIST TIMES FOR SIGNS OF THE CROSS

Ask the students to name all the times and ways they use the Sign of the Cross. List their ideas on the board. Add any of these they don't mention:

- before prayer, to help fix our minds and hearts on God

- after prayer, to stay close to God.

- in trials and temptations, as a prayer for strength and protection.

- in Baptism as a sign of belonging to Christ.

- when entering church, using holy water as a sign and reminder of Baptism.

LEARN A PRAYER BY HEART

Help the students learn one of these prayers by heart. Say it occasionally at the beginning or end of class. Both prayers may be found on the blackline master on page 437.

> O cross, you are the glorious sign of our victory. Through your power may we share in the triumph of Christ Jesus.
> *(Prayer of Christians)*

> We adore you, O Christ, and we bless you, because by your holy cross you have redeemed the world.
> *(Traditional)*

Saint John Eudes

(1601–1680)

"You always say you're sorry, but you never change." "He has been a problem, he is a problem, and he will be a problem." "We might as well give up trying to help her. She's hopeless."

John Eudes refused to accept comments like these. He believed that every person has value and dignity from God. He believed that God's merciful love is unlimited. His convictions were so strong that he helped many people whose situations might have seemed hopeless to others. He encouraged priests and many other Christians to respond in love to God. His image for divine love was the Sacred Heart of Jesus.

Born in Normandy, France, John was educated by Jesuits at Caen. This training helped prepare him to become a priest and to join a religious community, the Oratorians. Using his outstanding gifts as preacher and confessor, he traveled from parish to parish giving missions, which are similar to parish renewals. His travels convinced him that parish priests needed support in becoming men of prayer and action.

He held frequent conferences for them in which he outlined their duties as shepherds of God's people. Later John started his own society of priests called the Congregation of Jesus and Mary. The members were dedicated to promoting good seminary training, which would form Christlike priests for the parishes.

The love that impelled Jesus to reach out to people with disabilities and to people who were abandoned or rejected also impelled John to feel compassion for the women and young girls who were trying to escape from a life of prostitution. He wanted a place for them to live, a refuge from their former way of life. To serve these women, he established a society of religious women called the Congregation of Our Lady of the Refuge. Through the years this congregation has expanded, and now it serves the needs of troubled girls around the world.

Saint John Eudes has been called the Apostle of the Sacred Heart because he revived this devotion through his writings, his preaching, and his own life of loving service.

ACTIVITIES

MAKE A PRAYER PLAQUE

Because John appreciated the great love of Jesus for everyone, he promoted devotion to the Sacred Heart of Jesus. Make a decorative plaque of the following prayer and display it in the classroom all year. Use it as a class prayer today.

> Jesus, King and Center of our hearts, rule with love in our classroom and in every heart.

DISCUSS SCRIPTURES

John followed the example of Jesus. Jesus showed a prostitute and other outcast women that God loved them. Have students read the following passages: Luke 7:36–50; John 4:5–26, 39–42; John 8:1–11. Discuss these questions in small groups:

1. How did Jesus and the woman meet?

2. How did Jesus treat the woman?

3. How did the woman react to Jesus?

LIST VIRTUES

Early in his career, John gave missions, encouraging people to turn from a life of sin and adopt a life of virtue. List the seven capital sins on the board and ask the students to name the opposite virtue.

    pride—humility
    covetousness (greed)—generosity
    lust—chastity
    envy—friendship
    gluttony—temperance
    anger—gentleness
    sloth (laziness)—discipline

LEARN MORE ABOUT RELIGIOUS COMMUNITIES

Saint Maria Euphrasia Pelletier entered the Congregation of Our Lady of the Refuge in 1814 and then started a new branch, Sisters of Our Lady of Charity of the Good Shepherd. These sisters helped troubled girls get a fresh start in life by believing in their own God-given value. Mother Euphrasia also started a group of contemplative religious dedicated to reparation for sins. Former prostitutes who wanted to follow Christ in religious life were among those who could join this community. Formerly called the Sister Magdalens, the community is now called the Contemplatives of the Cross. Have interested students research these communities or the Congregation of Jesus and Mary and report to the class.

LEARN THE MORNING OFFERING

The Apostleship of Prayer is a spiritual society dedicated to the Sacred Heart of Jesus. The association begun by a Jesuit in France in 1844 has spread throughout the world. Members offer their daily prayers, works, sufferings, and joys to God to make up for sins. Have the students explain the ideas contained in the Morning Offering from the Apostleship of Prayer, which may be found on the blackline master on page 468. Then have the students memorize the prayer by saying it regularly.

Morning Offering
O Jesus, through the Immaculate Heart of Mary, I offer you my prayers, works, joys, and sufferings of this day in union with the Holy Sacrifice of the Mass throughout the world. I offer them for all the intentions of your Sacred Heart: the salvation of souls, reparation for sin, the reunion of all Christians. I offer them for the intentions of our bishops and of all Apostles of Prayer, and in particular for those recommended by our Holy Father this month.

Saint Bernard of Clairvaux

August 20

(1090–1153)

Have you ever surprised your parents? Bernard did! At the age of 22, Bernard decided to become a monk. Bernard lived in France where the Benedictine monastery at Cluny was thriving. The monks were known for holiness, and the place was alive with young, enthusiastic men. Bernard surprised everyone by choosing to enter a poor, crumbling monastery called Citeaux. Those monks, most of them elderly, followed the holy Rule of Saint Benedict, as did the monks at Cluny. However, the monks at Citeaux lived a stricter life of prayer, silence, and penance. Bernard was so eager about his choice that 31 other men decided to enter with him, among them four of his brothers, his uncle, and cousin.

These new people brought vitality to Citeaux. Within three years the place was flourishing, and Bernard was sent to start a new monastery—Clairvaux. As abbot, Bernard wanted to establish a lifestyle opposite to the worldly, powerful ways of the rich. In the first year, he was very strict about meals (sometimes the only food was barley bread and boiled beech leaves), work, prayers, and sleep. Then he became sick and thus learned to be more understanding about human needs. After that, the monastery thrived.

Bernard often longed for solitude and time to live a simple monk's life. However, almost daily he received visitors and letters asking for advice and help. He gave time and effort to each request. Because of his ability to settle disputes, Bernard was also called on to travel to other countries to give advice on important affairs of Church and of government. He was fearless in giving his opinion and highly respected for his insight into difficult problems.

In 1130 the newly elected Pope Innocent II faced the popularity of an antipope named Anacletus, whose claim to be pope threatened to split the Church. Bernard went to various countries, asking government and Church leaders to support the true pope. Finally Anacletus lost his power, and Innocent II returned as official bishop of Rome.

As an official preacher for the Second Crusade, Bernard inspired many soldiers and pilgrims to join the cause for Christ. However, the Crusade failed because of the cruelty and greed of some of those in the group, and Bernard was unjustly blamed.

Bernard has many titles. For his reforms at Citeaux and Clairvaux, he is known as the founder of the Cistercian Order. For his good advice and inspiring preaching, he has been called the "honey-tongued teacher." Because he was influential in government and Church matters, he is known as "the man of the twelfth century." He has been named a Doctor of the Church for his many theological writings.

AUGUST

SHARE GOOD EXAMPLES

Ask the children to tell a good thing they'd like to do that might surprise their families.

Grades K–5: Have a children draw a picture of themselves doing something that would give a good example to their families.

Grades 6–8: Have the students write a paragraph about a time when someone in their own families set a good example, and other family members were inspired to do something good too. Be sure to write your own paragraph to share with the class and allow volunteers to share theirs as well.

SHINE A LIGHT

The monastery of Clairvaux came to be known as the "monastery of light." Bernard wanted the monks to shine as the light of Christ in a dark world.

- Have the students memorize the Beatitudes, which reflect the happiness of life according to God's values.

- Light a candle for prayer during class today. Sing a song about light, for example, "This Little Light of Mine" or "We Are the Light of the World."

- Let the children perform a shadow play showing ways they can share the light of Christ.

RESEARCH RELATED ORDERS

Direct interested students to research how these orders are related: Benedictines, Cistercians, Trappists. Have the students find out if there are any monasteries of these religious nearby.

GROUP GOSPEL STUDY

Bernard loved the Scriptures and taught that we can reach God by studying Christ's life in the New Testament. Explain to the students that each Gospel writer presents Jesus from a different point of view. Divide the class into four groups. Give each group an assignment and let them share their findings with the class.

Group 1: Find five examples from Matthew's Gospel that show that Jesus is a teacher.

Group 2: Find five examples from Mark's Gospel that show Jesus' sufferings.

Group 3: Find five examples from Luke's Gospel that show Jesus as a loving savior to the poor, to women, and to the Gentiles.

Group 4: Count the number of times that the terms *Son, Son of the Father, Son of God,* or *only Son of God* are used in John's Gospel in referring to Christ.

CHOOSE GROUP PATRONS

Bernard is often pictured with a beehive as an emblem, and he has been chosen by beekeepers as a patron. Some chandlers (candle makers) also have Bernard as a patron.

- Have students look up the definition of *patron* in the Glossary on page 472. Discuss why such associations are fitting for Saint Bernard.

- Have the students consider the idea of choosing patrons for special school activities this year: yearbook or class newspaper, school play, sports teams, other groups, clubs, or activities.

- Direct pairs of students to name five saints and decide on a group of people, a career, or an institution for which each saint might be chosen as patron.

Saint Pius X

(1835–1914)

"I was born poor, I lived poor, I will die poor." These words were part of the will that Pope Pius X left at his death.

Giuseppe Melchiorre Sarto lived in the village of Riese, Italy, where his father was a poor parish clerk and his mother worked as a seamstress. At 11 Giuseppe was admitted to the high school. Every day he walked the five miles to school and back. Then at the age of 15, he began attending the local seminary. When his father died, Giuseppe wanted to leave school, come home, and help with the family. He realized that his mother would face even greater poverty than she had when his father was alive. However, his mother would not let him give up studying for the priesthood.

Giuseppe was ordained at the age of 23, and he worked as a parish priest for the next 17 years. He believed his call was to encourage the poor to lead strong Christian lives and to help them overcome financial problems. But the bishop had other ideas. Recognizing his gifts and talents, the bishop named Giuseppe spiritual director of the major seminary and chancellor of the diocese. Later he became a bishop and then a cardinal.

In 1903 in a surprising turn of events, this little-known cardinal was elected pope by a ballot of 50 out of 62 votes. As Pope Pius X, he took his motto, "Restore all things in Christ," from Paul's letter to the Ephesians. Pope Pius X tried to fulfill his motto in many ways. He emphasized how important the Eucharist is in the life of all Christians and recommended frequent Mass attendance and even daily Communion. He directed that children as young as seven, who have reached the age of reason, should be allowed to receive Jesus in the Eucharist. He initiated important changes in Church music and public worship. To promote study of the Scriptures, he began a biblical institute. He gave the first official impetus and pastoral direction to the modern liturgical renewal, which flowered at the Second Vatican Council.

Pope Pius X believed that real order and peace among individuals, groups, and nations could be achieved only through social justice and charity. He sponsored and sheltered refugees with his own resources. In 1912 he wrote an encyclical encouraging the Latin American bishops to make efforts to improve the treatment of Indians working on plantations. Tirelessly he worked to stop the world from going to war. When Europe entered World War I, Pius X was heartbroken, saying, "I would gladly give my life to save my poor children from this ghastly scourge." Just a few weeks after the war started, Pope Pius X died. All his life he had been poor. Now, having used all his money to help the poor, he really did die poor. He commonly used the expression "I am a poor man and Jesus Christ is all."

MAKE POSTERS ON THE EUCHARIST

Pope Pius X is called the Pope of the Eucharist. Have the students design posters to encourage reverence and prayerful preparation for receiving Jesus in the Eucharist. They may use lyrics from a eucharistic song or prayer and symbols of the Eucharist. Display these posters in the school hall or in the church entrance.

MAKE LITURGICAL FLOWCHARTS

Pope Pius X was interested in public worship. Have small groups of students make flowcharts to show how the liturgical seasons follow in the Church year. Tell them to include Advent, Christmas, Epiphany, Ordinary Time, Lent, Easter Triduum, Easter, Pentecost, and Season of Ordinary Time after Pentecost.

CHOOSE A MOTTO FROM SCRIPTURE

Pope Pius X chose a verse of Scripture as his motto. Have the students think of a verse of Scripture or look through the letters of the New Testament for a motto that they could adopt. Direct them to print this motto in their journals and design the page.

PRESENT A CHORAL READING

Pope Pius X had a great love and appreciation for the psalms of the Old Testament. He wished that in the Liturgy of the Hours, all the psalms could be prayed aloud within a week. Choose a psalm and have the students practice it as a choral reading. Divide the class into sides and choose four speakers. You may wish to use the following arrangement of Psalm 100. You may make copies for the students, using the blackline master on page 469.

Side 1: Make a joyful noise to the LORD, all the earth.

Side 2: Worship the LORD with gladness;

All: come into his presence with singing. Know that the LORD is God.

Speaker 1: It is he that made us,

Speakers 1, 2: and we are his;

Speakers 1, 2, 3, 4: we are his people,

All: and the sheep of his pasture.

Girls: Enter his gates with thanksgiving,

All: and his courts with praise.

Boys: Give thanks to him, bless his name.

Side 1: For the LORD is good;

Side 2: his steadfast love endures forever,

All: and his faithfulness to all generations.

Girls: Glory be to the Father, and to the Son, and to the Holy Spirit.

Boys: As it was in the beginning, is now, and ever shall be, world without end. Amen.

Catechist's Notes:

_____

_____

_____

Queenship of Mary

In 1954 Pope Pius XII declared a feast day honoring Mary as queen of heaven and earth. But "queen" is one of the oldest titles given to Mary in Christian tradition. When Elizabeth spoke of Mary as "the mother of my Lord" (Luke 1:43), she used the words that mean "queen mother" in the Old Testament.

Jesus is the Lord and King of heaven and earth. So Mary, who was chosen by the Father, was filled with the Holy Spirit, and became the mother of Christ, can be considered queen. Like a queen, she stood at the cross on Calvary, supporting her kingly Son's sacrifice with her love, faith, and obedience.

After being raised body and soul to heaven, Mary now sits in splendor at the right hand of her Son. There she intercedes for us. We ponder this whenever we pray the Fifth Glorious Mystery of the Rosary, Mary's coronation as Queen of Heaven.

Mary's power as queen is manifested in the tenderness of a loving mother who cares for her children. Saint Bernard of Clairvaux (feast day August 20, page 415), who had a great devotion to Mary, often wrote books and sermons that inspired his listeners to turn to her. For example:

> In dangers, in doubts, in difficulties, think of Mary, call upon Mary . . . with her for guide, you shall never go astray; while invoking her, you shall never lose heart; so long as she is in your mind, you are safe from deception; while she holds your hand, you cannot fall; under her protection you have nothing to fear. . . .

Artists depict Mary being crowned by her Son, or sometimes by God the Father. In either case, as Mother of the King of Kings and by her role in redemption, Mary is Queen of the Universe.

AUGUST

MAKE CROWNS FOR MARY

Direct each student to cut out a crown (6" × 10") from construction paper. On the crowns have the students neatly print a title of Mary that begins "Mary, Queen of _____." The students may create their own titles or choose titles given in this excerpt from the Litany of Loreto:

Queen of Angels
Queen of Patriarchs
Queen of Prophets
Queen of Apostles
Queen of Martyrs
Queen of Confessors
Queen of Virgins
Queen of All Saints
Queen Conceived Without Original Sin
Queen Assumed into Heaven
Queen of the Most Holy Rosary
Queen of Peace

With some ceremony, invite the children to display their crowns around a statue or picture of Mary as a way of honoring her as queen. Together pray the Hail Mary; Hail, Holy Queen; or Litany of Loreto.

IDENTIFY THE WORDS OF MARY

Ask the students to listen carefully as you read the words of Mary recorded in Scripture. Then have them identify to whom she is speaking, in what place she is speaking, and what event is happening.

- "Let what you have said be done to me" (Luke 1:38). *Angel Gabriel; Nazareth; Annunciation*

- "My soul proclaims the greatness of the Lord" Luke (1:46). *Elizabeth; Judah; Visitation*

- "See how worried your father and I have been, looking for you" (Luke 2:48). *Jesus; Jerusalem; finding in the Temple*

- "They have no wine" (John 2:3). *Jesus; Cana; wedding feast*

- "Do whatever he tells you" (John 2:5). *servants; Cana; wedding feast*

BE KIND TO MARYS

Encourage the students to do a special act of kindness today for a person who has Mary or a form of Mary for a name. (Some of these names are listed on page 378.)

PRAY FOR PEACE

Mary has been given the title of Queen of Peace. Have the students discuss the reasons why this title is so important at the present time. Then remind them that in various appearances, such as at Fatima, Our Lady has reminded Christians to pray and to make sacrifices for world peace. Direct each student to write an original petition related to world peace. Then lead the class in a litany for peace. Use this response: "Queen of Peace, lead us to peace."

MAKE RESOLUTIONS TO WORK FOR PEACE

Help the students understand that they can work for world peace by beginning with themselves. Encourage them to make a class resolution to be kind and considerate to others at home and at school. Let them think of specific things they will do to be peacemakers.

Saint Rose of Lima

August 23

(1586–1617)

Some saints have traveled around the world. Rose of Lima became a saint without ever leaving her backyard.

Gaspar de Flores and his wife, Maria de Olivia, were very proud of their little daughter, born on April 20, 1586. On Pentecost of that year, she was baptized Isabel de Flores, named after an aunt who was also her godmother. One day a household maid, amazed at the great beauty of the tiny baby, exclaimed that she looked just like a rose. Isabel's mother agreed and declared firmly that this child would be called Rose from then on. At the age of 14, she was confirmed, taking Rose as her Confirmation name.

Through her childhood and youth, Rose did not have the opportunity to attend school. She stayed at home and worked in the garden, growing a variety of beautiful flowers. Rose delighted in the butterflies, birds, and flowers that surrounded her because they reminded her of God's beauty. She also learned to embroider on silk and create designs, usually of flowers.

Rose took Saint Catherine of Siena as the model for her life. Even as a child, she wanted to live only for Jesus. She looked for difficult things to do to show her love for him. She also built a prayer hut for herself in the backyard so she could have a place to be alone and pray. Her parents' financial difficulties presented Rose with a real conflict. She wanted to enter a convent, become a sister, and live a life offered to God. Her parents wanted her to marry so that they would have a son-in-law to help them financially. Finally Rose found an answer to this problem. To help her parents, she stayed home and sold her needlework and the flowers that she raised in the garden. At the same time, she joined the Third Order of Saint Dominic. She wore the white habit and black veil of the Dominican sisters. She spent many more hours a day in her prayer hut. Eventually she began to live in that hut. But her love for God also led her to love the poor. In her parents' home, she set up one room as a free medical clinic for poor children and elderly people who were ill. This free service became the beginning of social service in Peru.

In the last years of her life, Rose became very ill, and she died on August 24, 1617. She was widely known and loved by both rich and poor. Huge crowds gathered when they heard about her death. She was buried privately in the cloistered part of St. Dominic's Church.

DISPLAY ROSES IN THE CLASSROOM

Rose saw God's beauty in nature and often put fresh roses around her veil to please her mother. If fresh flowers are available in local gardens, bring some to class and display them for the day in honor of Saint Rose. Or bring a potted plant to keep in the classroom.

WRITE ABOUT FRIENDSHIP

Rose of Lima was a close friend of Saint Martin de Porres (feast day November 3, page 77). Have the students find out more about Saint Martin and compare and contrast the two saints. Ask them to write essays on what they think friendship really means. Post the essays in the hall or publish them in the school newspaper.

LEARN ABOUT SERVICES TO THE POOR

In Rose's time there were hospitals and medical services. One hospital even bordered on her family's property. But Rose insisted that the people offer free medical help for the poor. Through such charity, Rose made the people of the city aware of the needs of the poor. Have the students bring in articles from magazines or newspapers that show how organizations such as Catholic Relief Services and Catholic Charities are drawing attention to the needs of the poor.

LEARN ABOUT THIRD ORDERS

Rose joined the Third Order of St. Dominic. Invite someone from a third order to speak to the class about the role of third orders in the Church.

CREATE A "PRAYER HUT"

Rose built a prayer hut so she could have a place to be alone and pray. Suggest that students create a corner in their home that can be their own special "prayer hut." Encourage them to gather religious articles and books for this special space and set aside time to spend with God.

Catechist's Notes:

_____

_____

_____

_____

_____

_____

_____

Saint Bartholomew

(first century)

Bartholomew is mentioned by name only four times in the whole New Testament. In the Gospels of Matthew and Luke, he is one of the twelve apostles called by Jesus. Mark's Gospel states that Bartholomew is one of the twelve apostles appointed to be Jesus' companions, to preach, and to cast out devils. The Acts of the Apostles lists the people who are in the upper room in Jerusalem waiting for the Holy Spirit to come. Bartholomew is in the list of apostles who are waiting there with several women, including Mary, Jesus' mother. Of the four evangelists, John alone does not mention Bartholomew by name. John does, however, list Nathanael as an apostle. Some scholars feel that Bartholomew and Nathanael are two names for the same person. If this is the case, then John's Gospel gives us a detailed account of Nathanael's (or Bartholomew's) first meeting with Jesus.

According to this report, Philip was so excited about meeting Jesus that he asked his friend Nathanael to come to meet him also. Nathanael, who was from Cana, was scornful when he heard that Jesus was from Nazareth. He thought that Nazareth was unimportant and that nothing good could come from such a place. Philip did not argue. Arguments don't bring people to Christ. Meeting Christ and getting to know him is the way that people learn to love and follow him. So Philip told Nathanael to come and see for himself.

On seeing Nathanael, Jesus recognized a person who was not proud, prejudiced, or scheming. Jesus told Nathanael that he was a man without deceit in his heart. "How could Jesus make a snap decision about my personality?" Nathanael must have thought. But Jesus showed that he had a supernatural knowledge about people and things. When Nathanael realized that Jesus knew him in a very deep way, he began to praise Jesus as the real Messiah.

Even if Nathanael and Bartholomew are not the same person, we still know that Bartholomew was one of the twelve apostles. Whenever the twelve were assembled for some event, he was present also. Shortly after Pentecost, Bartholomew became a missionary in a foreign land. Armenians honor him as the apostle of their country.

DO GOSPEL PANTOMIMES

Divide the class into three groups. Give each group three of the following Scripture references from the Gospel of John: 2:1–10; 2.13–22; 4:46–54; 5:1–9; 6:5–15; 9:1–7; 12:1–8; 12:12–17; 20:24–29; 21:1–14. Allow the students five or ten minutes to plan a pantomime for all three of their stories. Then have each group present its pantomimes, one at a time, while the rest of the class tries to guess the story.

PLAN TO BE AN APOSTLE

As an apostle, Bartholomew was sent to bring the Good News of Jesus to others. Have the students research Scripture texts to discover what the apostles and disciples needed and did on their earliest missionary journeys: Matthew 10:1–42, Luke 9:1–6, Luke 9:57–82, Luke 10:1–20. Then ask the students to use this information to plan how they can answer their own call to be apostles. Give each a large sheet of paper. Have them divide it into three columns with the following heads: What I Will Need, Where I Will Go, What I Will Do. They may write or sketch their responses.

PRAY THE APOSTLES' CREED

Have students read aloud Acts 5:34–39. Discuss with the class how the Church has lasted through these past 2,000 years and how it can be traced back to Jesus and the apostles. Finally, to deepen the students' awareness of their bond with the past, pray the Apostles' Creed with them.

MAKE MODELS

Direct the students to create models of various scenes from the Acts of the Apostles. Have them make figures out of colored pipe cleaners. Provide a variety of paper and materials and let them design scenery and props out of scraps and found objects.

PLAY AN APOSTLE GUESSING GAME

Have the students look up the occasions when Bartholomew is mentioned in the Scriptures: Matthew 10:3; Mark 3:18; Luke 6:14; Acts of the Apostles 1:13. Then distribute small slips of paper to each student. Direct the students to go through the New Testament and find clues about each of the apostles. Have them write one clue on each slip of paper in the following way: "I am the apostle who _____." Collect the slips and put them in a box or an envelope. Then have students draw a slip, read the clue, and name the apostle who fits the clue. This game could be brought out again for the feast of other apostles throughout the year.

Catechist's Notes:

_____

_____

_____

_____

Saint Louis of France

August 25

(1214–1270)

Louis was a husband, a father, a soldier, a king, a peacemaker, and a saint. When King Louis VIII and Blanche of Castille married, they expected one of their children to become the next king of France. Of the 12 children they had, it was Louis who succeeded his father.

Young Louis became king of France at the age of 12. However, his mother made most of the important decisions for the kingdom until her death. In 1234 Louis married Marguerite of Provence, and they had 10 children. In 1244 King Louis began preparations for a Crusade to the Holy Land. Though the Crusade failed, many soldiers remembered Louis's example. They remembered how he chose to share all the dangers and hardships of an ordinary soldier when, as the king-commander of the troops, he could have given himself privileges and had an easier time of it. They recalled how each decision he made was based on the moral principle of justice. But Louis's efforts to achieve justice, mercy, and peace can best be seen in the way he ruled France.

As king, Louis had a great love for God and for the people of his kingdom. He built a chapel in Paris and an abbey in Royaumont. He supported the Cistercians, the Franciscans, and the Dominicans, religious orders that served the French people. He also built hospitals and encouraged learning. He reformed some of the social structures that were promoting injustice. His reforms helped the legal system in France to provide fair laws and just trials.

Until he died, Louis tried to follow the advice that he gave to his son, the future king of France:

> Dear Son, let your heart be gentle, compassionate, and charitable toward the poor, the feeble, the unfortunate, toward everyone you think to be suffering in mind or in body. . . . Maintain the good customs of your kingdom, suppress those which are bad. Do not covet your people's goods, and do not oppress them with duties or taxes.
>
> *(Saint Louis's "Testament")*

WRITE LETTERS OR INTERVIEW FATHERS

Besides ruling France, Louis was the father of 10 children.

- Have the students discuss the responsibilities fathers have toward their families. Together pray the Our Father for all fathers.

- Have the students write letters to their fathers, grandfathers, godfathers, or uncles expressing appreciation for the fatherly things these men have done for them.

- Have the students interview their fathers (or those who are like fathers to them) on being a father. Give them time in class to brainstorm for possible interview questions, such as

    What is it like to be a father?

    What goals do you have for your children?

    What do you see as a father's role in handing on the Christian faith to his children?

DEFINE PEACE

In France Louis promoted peace. Ask the students to brainstorm for various definitions of peace. Then have a student print the words "Peace Is . . ." at the top of a long piece of shelf paper. Have each student contribute one definition to the list. Post the list and encourage the students to continue to add ideas as they find them.

PERFORM AN ACT OF KINDNESS

Louis had a great interest in serving the physical, intellectual, and social needs of the people of France. Have the students resolve to perform a kind act for someone who cannot return the kindness.

LOOK FOR JUSTICE

Louis tried to help individual people, and he also worked to make the structures of society more just. Have the students discuss how each of the following unjust situations could be changed to a just situation:

- A system where imported products are inexpensive because factory workers in the exporting country are getting a very low wage

- A system where fruits and vegetables are less expensive because migrant workers live in subhuman conditions

- A system in which Native Americans have suffered by losing their land and having their treaties broken

WRITE ABOUT FAMILY PEACE

As king, Louis dealt with issues of war and peace on an international level. As a parent, Louis was concerned that his children live peacefully together. Have the students choose one of the following sentences as a topic sentence and write a paragraph on family peace. Then have volunteers read their compositions to the class.

- Brothers and sisters should get along better than people who are unrelated.

- Brothers and sisters have a harder time apologizing to each other than to other people.

Saint Monica

(331–387)

Have you ever wondered if God answers prayers? Through her life Monica shows us how faithfully God answers prayers. Monica lived in Tagaste, Numidia, in Africa. She and her sisters were raised by an elderly servant.

As a young girl, Monica had a shocking experience. According to the custom of the time, her parents would ask her to bring up wine from the cellar for them. Once Monica took a little sip of the wine before she brought it up. After that she gradually began to drink just a little more each day. She thought no one knew about her secret action. Then one day, Monica quarreled with the servant who used to accompany her to the cellar. The angry servant accused Monica of drinking too much wine. Young Monica was stunned. But she realized that the maid, while trying to win a quarrel, had really helped her to face this temptation. She decided at this time to stop drinking, and she did stop. Overcoming this weakness helped Monica become a caring wife and mother.

When she was old enough, Monica was married to a pagan official named Patricius. They had at least three children: Navigius, Perpetua, and Augustine. Patricius was a man with a terrible temper. Gradually Monica learned to be patient and wait for the right moment to discuss matters with him or to explain her actions. By her constant forgiveness and love, she hoped to draw her husband to Christ. Before he died Patricius was baptized a Christian! Because she and her husband seemed to get along so well, other wives with marriage problems asked Monica for advice. In this way she often used her painful experiences to help others.

Because of rumors spread by unhappy servants, Monica's mother-in-law turned against her during the early part of her marriage. Using patient forgiveness, Monica won her cooperation. Another source of worry was her son Augustine. He was not yet baptized and was living an immoral life. Monica tried to get through to her wild teenage son. She once attempted a dangerous ocean voyage in order to advise him. She prayed and fasted persistently for him. She even asked the local bishop to speak to her son. But the bishop told Monica, "Not yet, he is not ready and would not listen." But he did promise her, "Surely the son of so many tears will not perish."

Clinging to these comforting words, Monica continued to pray and sacrifice year after year. Slowly Augustine did change. With the help of the Holy Spirit, he began to realize that God loved him. When he finally gained courage to be baptized, his mother was one of the first persons he told, for she was with him in Milan at the time. In the fall of 387, after his Baptism, Augustine planned to return to Tagaste with his mother, but she died at Ostia on the coast of Italy where they were waiting to embark. Their last conversation was a beautiful sharing of longing for heaven.

ACTIVITIES

THANK HELPERS

Monica was raised by a wise woman who was highly respected by Monica's parents. This woman made a great impact on Monica's life. Have the students make thank-you cards or paper corsages for the women who work in or for the school or parish program. Direct the students to present these gifts with a reference to the feast of Saint Monica.

THANK MOTHERS

Monica is an example for all mothers who want their families to enjoy eternal life in Christ. Have the students make cards or write letters of appreciation to their mothers, grandmothers, or godmothers. Encourage the students to contribute to class prayers by offering spontaneous prayers for their mothers and all mothers.

MAKE MEAL PRAYER CARDS

As a wife and mother, Monica was probably concerned about family meals. Have the students write before-meal and after-meal prayers on a card that will stand on the family dinner table. Encourage them to pray with family members before and after each meal.

TACKLE TEMPTATIONS AND BAD HABITS

Talk about how Monica recognized and responded to a temptation in her youth. Tell the students that their mothers or other adults in their lives can help them see a weakness or a fault. Ask the students to consider what their mothers or teachers most often try to correct in them. Suggest that the students make a resolution to change their behavior. Tell them you will pray for them that they will be strong in choosing what is good.

Catechist's Notes:

Saint Augustine

(354–434)

Saint Monica prayed for many years for her wayward son Augustine. Here is proof that God does answer prayers: Today is the feast of Saint Augustine.

Augustine grew up in Tagaste, Numidia, in Africa. It was clear to his pagan father, Patricius, and his Christian mother, Monica, that Augustine was a very intelligent but restless child. As a student he put all his energy into finding the meaning of real love and of life. He tried wild parties, sex, philosophy, and a popular heresy. None of these satisfied him.

Augustine was first a teacher in Rome and then a professor in Milan. In Milan he listened to the sermons of Ambrose, the bishop. Through them, Augustine learned to read the Scriptures prayerfully. He enrolled as a catechumen in the Catholic Church. However, he feared that he was too weak to follow Christ. He wavered back and forth about being baptized.

Then one day Augustine heard a voice like that of a child chanting repeatedly, "Take up and read." Augustine opened the Bible and read the first words his eyes fell upon: "Let us live honorably as in the day, not in reveling and drunkenness, not in debauchery and licentiousness, not in quarreling and jealousy. Instead, put on the Lord Jesus Christ, and make no provision for the flesh, to gratify its desires" (Romans 13:13–14). At that moment Augustine realized real love and the meaning of life. When he was 33 years old, Augustine was baptized.

Augustine decided to return to Africa with his mother, Monica. While they were waiting for the ship to embark, Monica died. Eventually he reached Tagaste, gave away all he had, and settled down to a quiet, prayerful life.

However, while visiting in the African city of Hippo, Augustine heard the bishop, Valerius, preaching on the shortage of priests. Suddenly people in the crowd shouted, "Let Augustine be our priest!" Valerius was happy about the way God showed his will for Augustine and ordained him a priest. In 396 when Valerius died, Augustine became the bishop of Hippo.

Augustine dearly loved his land and the people. He worked hard to counteract the false religious teachings that were popular in Africa, to protect the people from corrupt government officials and foreign invaders, and to care for the sick, the poor, and those in prison. His many writings reflect his deep love for God.

In 430 Vandals invaded the African province. People panicked because it seemed that the whole world was being destroyed. For the next three months, the elderly Augustine continued to inspire Christian hope in his people. He reminded them that they belonged to Christ and no Vandal could rob them of true life. On August 28, Augustine died of a high fever. His influence continues to this day.

REFLECT ON THEIR OWN SEARCH FOR GOD

Throughout his life Augustine was searching for the God of love. Augustine summed up his long search for God in the famous words: "You have made us, O God, for yourself, and our hearts shall find no rest until they rest with you."

In their journals, have the students answer the following questions about their own lives:

> When you were a small child, what did you think about God? What was Jesus like for you?

> How do you see God now? Has your image of Jesus changed? How?

> What do you hope for your friendship with God in the future?

LIST DISTRACTIONS AND ATTRACTIONS

Augustine was influenced by the culture he lived in. Have the students list the things they think distract young people today from following Christ. Also have them list the things that draw young people to following Christ.

SHARE INSPIRATIONS

Augustine was influenced by listening to the sermons of Ambrose. Have the students recall a homily they have heard that impressed them. Invite them to share one thought from that homily that they have or could put into practice.

WRITE AUTOBIOGRAPHIES

In his famous autobiography, *Confessions,* Augustine of Hippo told the story of his struggle to find God. Direct the students to write short autobiographies. They may wish to interview their parents for information about their earliest days. Encourage them to add anecdotes and photographs.

MEDITATE ON THE GOSPEL

When Augustine opened the Bible and read Romans 13:13–14, he felt that the words of Scripture applied directly to his own life. A similar story was told about Saint Anthony of Egypt, a story Augustine most likely knew. Anthony happened to be in church one day and heard the Gospel reading of the rich young man. When Anthony heard the words from Luke 18:22–23, he sold all he had and became a monk. Have the students spend a few minutes silently reading a passage from the New Testament. Then have them write how the passage they read could apply to their own lives.

Catechist's Notes:

_____

_____

_____

_____

Martyrdom of John the Baptist

August 29

John, the relative and forerunner of Jesus, was so brave, so fearless, that some people thought he was crazy!

As a youth John had gone into the desert to fast and pray in order to learn what God wanted him to do with his life. Then one day, following the inspiration of God, he began to walk along the bank of the Jordan River, preaching to anyone who would listen. Like the prophets of the Old Testament, his message was always the same—turn from your sins, repent, and live for God.

John saw clearly how people can fool themselves into choosing evil actions. Fearlessly he confronted people with their behavior. Sometimes he even pointed out their sins. Always he gave them hope and the challenge to live according to God's law. He did not recommend that people live in the desert or eat wild locusts, as he had done. Rather he told people to be honest and loving, to avoid violence, and to do their jobs well. As a sign of their sincere repentance for sin, John would baptize them in the Jordan River.

John was not afraid of wealthy religious leaders or powerful political officials. When the ruler Herod Antipas married his brother's wife Herodias, John publicly warned him about the evil of adultery. Herodias wanted to kill John because she was so angry with him. But Herod Antipas respected and admired John for his courageous honesty. Unfortunately Herod Antipas was also weak. He had John arrested and chained in prison so John could no longer speak out against him.

John's time in prison might have dragged on indefinitely if it had not been for a huge banquet Herod gave on his birthday. As entertainment, Salome, Herodias's daughter, danced for the guests. Herod Antipas was so impressed that he promised to give the young girl whatever she wanted. Her mother persuaded her to ask for only one thing—the head of John the Baptist on a platter.

Herod Antipas was too embarrassed to admit before his guests that he had made a foolish promise. He could not change his mind. Because he was afraid of what others would think, he had John executed and the head brought in on a platter.

John knew that it was dangerous to challenge the authority of the king. That's how fearless John the Baptist was!

ROLE-PLAY

Read aloud Luke 3:3–18. Then ask the students to role-play conversations in which John gives advice to a banker, a farmer, a teacher, a factory worker, or a person of the student's choice.

SHARE A SCRIPTURE STUDY

John's approach to his mission was that Jesus must increase in the people's estimation and he must decrease. Divide the students into study groups. Have them look up and read together the Scripture passages that tell what John said about Jesus: Mark 1:7–8, John 1:29–34; John 3:28–30. Then have them read what Jesus said about John: Luke 7:24–30. Have the students compose a group summary of the readings and write it on the board.

WRITE A MONOLOGUE

After announcing the arrival of the Messiah, John spent his last months in prison. Have the students read Mark 6:17–29 and Matthew 11:2–6. Encourage them to imagine how difficult it must have been for John to have been chained in prison. Then have them write a monologue of what John might have thought while he was alone in prison.

SING OUT JOHN'S MESSAGE

Sing with the students a song that refers to John's message of filling in valleys and bringing down mountains. Possible songs are "Exult, You Just Ones" (O'Connor), "Let the Valleys Be Raised" (Schutte), and "Every Valley" (Dufford).

CREATE A DESIGN

Have the students create a patterned design using symbols of John the Baptist. First direct students to read Matthew 3:1–11 and John 1:6–8. Next ask them to think of a symbol that represents John the Baptist or something he said or did. This symbol may be an image that is in the actual Scripture text or an image that could be drawn from the passage. Give the students clean plastic-foam trays from the produce or meat department of a grocery store. Have each student carve a design on the bottom of a tray with a pencil. Instruct the students to press hard but not to carve all the way through the tray. Then have them use a paintbrush or sponge to apply tempera paint carefully within the design. They can then use the tray as a stamp. Have them press repeatedly on a sheet of paper to make a patterned design. After the paint on the paper is dry, direct them to letter one of the Scripture passages over the design with a black felt-tipped marker.

Catechist's Notes:

_____

_____

_____

Blackline Masters

Liturgical Colors
for Feasts and Seasons

Feasts and Seasons	Color of Vestments	Meaning of Color
Feasts of martyrs, apostles; Pentecost, Holy Cross, Passion Sunday, Good Friday, Confirmation	Red	Fire, love, blood, sacrifice, Holy Spirit
Advent, Lent	Violet*	Expectation, repentance
Easter, Feasts of Mary, Jesus, non-martyr saints, votive Masses, weddings and funerals	White	Joy, purity, glory
Sundays and weekdays in Ordinary Time	Green	Hope, growth

* On some solemn occasions, silver or gold vestments may be substituted for any color above except violet. Rose is used at times on the Third Sunday of Advent and the Fourth Sunday of Lent. It expresses joy.

Prayer for Missionaries

For love of you, Lord,
    they walk among new family
        on a distant path.
Bless their minds and thoughts,
    bless the words they say,
    so that in hearing their voices
        your Word will be known.
Bless the work they do
and the love they give,
    so that your own care will be seen
    as they heal the sorrows and
        mend the pain of your poor ones
Bless them with the gift of
    seeing the Gospel come to new life
        as their people learn the meaning
        of the peace of Christ.
For love of you, Lord,
    they walk among new family
        on a distant path.
Help me to walk with them
        each day in prayer.

(Society for the Propagation of the Faith)

Prayers to Mary

Hail Mary

Hail Mary, full of grace,
the Lord is with you!
Blessed are you among women,
and blessed is the fruit of your womb,
　Jesus.
Holy Mary, Mother of God,
pray for us sinners,
now and at the hour of our death.
Amen.

Memorare

Remember, O most loving
　Virgin Mary,
that never was it known
that anyone who fled to
　your protection
implored your help, or sought
　your intercession
was left unaided.

Inspired with this confidence,
we turn to you,
O Virgin of virgins our Mother.
To you we come, before you we kneel,
sinful and sorrowful.

O Mother of the Word Incarnate,
do not despise our petitions
but in your mercy hear and answer us.
Amen.

(Saint Bernard of Clairvaux)

Hail, Holy Queen

Hail, holy Queen, Mother of mercy,
hail, our life, our sweetness,
　and our hope.
To you we cry, the children of Eve;
to you we send up our sighs,
mourning and weeping in this
　land of exile.
Turn, then, most gracious advocate,
your eyes of mercy toward us;
lead us home at last
and show us the blessed fruit
　of your womb, Jesus:
O clement, O loving,
　O sweet Virgin Mary.

Act of Consecration to Mary

My Queen, my Mother! I give myself
entirely to you, and to show my
devotion to you I consecrate to you my
eyes, my ears, my mouth, my heart and
my whole being. Wherefore, good
Mother, as I am your own, keep me,
guard me, as your property and
possession.
Amen

Prayers Before the Cross

Good and gentle Jesus,
I kneel before you.
I see your five wounds.
They have pierced your hands and feet;
They have hurt all your bones.

Fill my heart with faith, hope, and love,
help me to be sorry for my sins, and to turn my life to you.

Amen.

(A Prayer to Christ Crucified)

†

O cross, you are the glorious sign of our victory.
Through your power may we share in the triumph of Christ Jesus.

(Prayer of Christians)

†

We adore you, O Christ, and we bless you,
because by your holy cross,
you have redeemed the world.

(Traditional)

Good King Wenceslas

Good King Wenceslas looked out
On the feast of Stephen
When the snow lay round about
Deep and crisp and even.
Brightly shone the moon that night,
Though the frost was cruel,
When a poor man came in sight,
Gathering winter fuel.

"Hither, page, and stand by me,
If thou know'st it, telling,
Where and what his dwelling?"
"Sir, he lives a good league hence,
Underneath the mountain,
Right against the forest fence,
By St. Agnes' fountain."

"Bring me flesh and bring me wine,
Bring me pine-logs hither:
Thou and I will see him dine,
When we bear them thither."
Page and monarch forth they went,
Forth they went together;
Through the rude wind's wild lament
And the bitter weather.

"Sire, the night is darker now,
And the wind blows stronger;
Fails my heart, I know not how,
I can go no longer."
"Mark my footsteps, good my page;
Tread thou in them boldly;
Thou shalt find the winter's rage
Freeze thy blood less coldly."

In his master's step he trod,
Where the snow lay dinted;
Heat was in the very sod
Which the saint had printed.
Therefore, Christian men, be sure,
Wealth and rank possessing,
Ye who will now bless the poor,
Shall yourselves find blessing.

Words by J. M. Neale (1818-1866)
Traditional tune

Prayer to St. Michael

St. Michael the Archangel,
defend us in the day of battle;
guard us against the wickedness
    and tricks of the devil.
By the power of God,
throw into hell Satan
    and all the other evil spirits
who prowl about the world
    seeking the ruin of souls. Amen.

Crossword Puzzle

Name _____ **Date** _____

Down

1. Who was the archangel sent to communicate God's message to Daniel, Zachary, and Mary?

2. Who is the archangel whose name means "Who is like God?"

4. What job was Raphael hired to do for Tobias on the journey? to be a _____

6. To whom did Gabriel announce the Incarnation?

Across

3. What type of angel has God given to each person to protect him or her on the way to heaven?

5. Who is the archangel who was a companion to Tobias?

7. What kind of angel carries out important missions for God?

8. Against whom did Michael wage war?

Prayers to Your Guardian Angel

Angel of God
my guardian dear,
to whom God's love
commits me here,
Ever this day
be at my side,
to light and guard,
to rule and guide.
Amen.

† † † † † † † † † † † † † † † †

Angel sent by God to guide me,
be my light and walk beside me;
be my guardian and protect me;
on the paths of life direct me.
Amen.

O most high, almighty, good Lord
  God,
O most high, almighty, good Lord
  God,
to you belong praise, glory, honor,
and all blessing!

Praised be my Lord God
through all his creatures;
and especially our brother the sun,
who brings us the day,
and who brings us the light;
fair is he, and shining
with a great splendor:
O Lord, to us he signifies you!

Praised be my Lord for our sister the
  moon,
and for the stars, which he has set
clear and lovely in heaven.

Praised be my Lord for our brother
  the wind,
and for air and cloud, calms and all
  weather,
by which you uphold in life all
  creatures.

Praised be my Lord for our sister
  water,
who is very serviceable, and humble,
and precious, and clean.

Praised be my Lord for our brother
  fire,
through whom you give us light
in the darkness;

and he is bright, and pleasant,
and very mighty, and strong.

Praised be my Lord for our mother
  the earth,
which sustains us and keeps us,
and brings forth fruits,
and flowers of many colors, and grass.

Praised be my Lord for all those who
  pardon
one another for his love's sake
and who endure weakness and
  tribulation;
blessed are they
who peaceably shall endure,
for you, O most Highest,
shall give them a crown!

Praised be my Lord for our sister,
the death of the body, from whom
no man escapes.
Woe to him who dies in mortal sin!
Blessed are they who are found
  walking
by your most holy will,
for the second death shall have no
  power
to do them harm.

Praise you, and bless you the Lord,
and give thanks to him,
and serve him with great humility.

(Saint Francis of Assisi)

The Mysteries of the Rosary

The Joyful Mysteries

1. *The Annunciation*
   The angel Gabriel announces to Mary that she has been chosen to be the Mother of Jesus.

2. *The Visitation*
   Mary visits her relative Elizabeth.

3. *The Nativity*
   Jesus is born in Bethlehem.

4. *The Presentation*
   Mary and Joseph present the baby Jesus to God in the Temple at Jerusalem.

5. *The Finding in the Temple*
   Mary and Joseph find the child Jesus with the teachers in the Temple.

The Luminous Mysteries

1. *Jesus' Baptism in the Jordan River*
   Jesus is baptized by John the Baptist.

2. *The Wedding Feast at Cana*
   Jesus performs his first miracle at Mary's request.

3. *Proclamation of the Kingdom of God*
   Jesus announces the Kingdom and calls for conversion.

4. *The Transfiguration of Jesus*
   Jesus reveals the glory of his divinity to Peter, James, and John.

5. *The Institution of the Eucharist*
   Jesus offers us his body and blood as spiritual food under the signs of bread and wine.

The Sorrowful Mysteries

1. *The Agony in the Garden*
   Jesus prays and suffers in the Garden of Gethsemane on the night before he dies.

2. *The Scourging*
   Jesus is whipped.

3. *The Crowning with Thorns*
   Jesus wears a crown of thorns.

4. *The Carrying of the Cross*
   Jesus carries his cross to Calvary.

5. *The Crucifixion*
   Jesus is crucified and dies on the cross.

The Glorious Mysteries

1. *The Resurrection*
   Jesus is raised from the dead.

2. *The Ascension*
   Jesus ascends to his Father in heaven.

3. *The Coming of the Holy Spirit*
   The Holy Spirit comes upon the disciples at Pentecost.

4. *The Assumption*
   Mary is taken into heaven, body and soul.

5. *The Crowning of Mary*
   Mary is crowned Queen of Heaven and Earth.

The Huron Christmas Carol

Father Brébeuf wrote this hymn in Quebec, while he was recuperating from a broken clavicle. He set the words to the tune of a 16th-century French folk tune. One of the last Jesuit missionaries to the Huron, Father de Villeneuve, wrote the old Huron words to the carol and later translated it into simple French.

Iesous Ahatonnia (Jesus, He Is Born)

Have courage, you who are humans;
Jesus, he is born.
Behold, the spirit who had us as prisoners has fled.
Do not listen to it, as it corrupts the spirits of our minds.
Jesus, he is born.

They are spirits, sky people, coming with a message for us.
They are coming to say, "Rejoice (Be on top of life)."
Marie, she has just given birth. Rejoice.
Jesus, he is born.

Three have left for such, those who are elders.
Tichion, a star that has just appeared on the horizon leads them there.
He will seize the path, he who leads them there.
Jesus, he is born.

As they arrived there, where he was born,
the star was at the point of stopping, not far past it.

Having found someone for them, he says, "Come here!"
Jesus, he is born.

Behold, they have arrived there and have seen Jesus,
They praised (made a name) many times, saying "Hurrah, he is good in nature."
They greeted him with reverence (greased his scalp many times), saying: "Hurrah"
Jesus, he is born.

We will give to him praise for his name,
Let us show reverence for him as he comes to be compassionate to us.
It is providential that you love us and wish, "I should adopt them."
Jesus, he is born.

This is a literal translation of the Huron carol from the Huron. Translation by John Steckley/Hechon.

Litany to Mary, Mother of the Church

Lord, have mercy.
Lord, have mercy.

Christ, have mercy.
Christ, have mercy.

Lord, have mercy.
Lord, have mercy.

God our Father in heaven,
have mercy on us.

God the Son, our Redeemer,
have mercy on us.

God the Holy Spirit,
have mercy on us.

Holy Trinity, one God,
have mercy on us.

Holy Mary,
pray for us.

Mother of God
pray for us.

Woman of faith,
pray for us.

Most honored of all virgins,
pray for us.

Joy of Israel,
pray for us.

Honor of our people,
pray for us.

Model of prayer and virtue,
pray for us.

Incentive to trust,
pray for us.

Temple of the Holy Spirit,
pray for us.

Spouse of Joseph,
pray for us.

Mother of Jesus,
pray for us.

Faithful follower of Jesus,
pray for us.

Mother of the Church,
pray for us.

Image of the Church at prayer,
pray for us.

Our Lady of Guadalupe, patroness of the Americas,
pray for us.

Mary Immaculate, patroness of the United States,
pray for us.

Advocate of life,
pray for us.

Guide for the young,
pray for us.

Friend of the single,
pray for us.

Companion of the married,
pray for us.

Voice for the unborn,
pray for us.

Mother of mothers,
pray for us.

Support of the family,
pray for us.

Comforter of the sick,
pray for us.

Nurse of the aged,
pray for us.

Echo of the suffering,
pray for us.

Consoler of the widowed,
pray for us.

Strength of the broken-hearted,
pray for us.

Hymn of the joyful,
pray for us.

Hope of the poor,
pray for us.

Example of detachment for the rich,
pray for us.

Goal of pilgrims,
pray for us.

Resort of the traveler,
pray for us.

Protector of the exile,
pray for us.

Woman most whole,
pray for us.

Virgin most free,
pray for us.

Wife most loving,
pray for us.

Mother most fulfilled,
pray for us.

Queen of love,
pray for us.

Lamb of God, you take away the sins of the world:
have mercy on us.

Lamb of God, you take away the sins of the world:
have mercy on us.

Lamb of God, you take away the sins of the world:
have mercy on us.

(Rev. Medard P. Laz and James E. Wilbur)

Our Lady of Guadalupe

I'm Glad You're You Coupon

Because I'm GLAD YOU'RE YOU,

I want to make this day special for you by

_____

_____

Signed,

_____

"Two-Second" Prayers

Not my will but yours be done. (Luke 22:42)

Have mercy on us, Son of David. (Matthew 9:27)

Lord, you have the words of eternal life. (John 6:68)

Truly you are the Son of God. (Matthew 14:33)

Lord, help me. (Matthew 15:25)

My Lord and my God. (John 20:28)

I believe; help my unbelief! (Mark 9:24)

Lord, you know that I love you. (John 21:15)

Here am I, the servant of the Lord; let it be with me according to your word. (Luke 1:38)

My soul magnifies the Lord. (Luke 1:46)

Lord, teach us to pray. (Luke 11:1)

Come, Lord Jesus! (Revelation 22:20)

Prayers in Latin

Sign of the Cross
In nomine Patris,
et Filii,
et Spiritus Sancti.
Amen.

The Lord's Prayer
Pater noster, qui es in caelis:
sanctificétur nomen tuum:
advéniat regnum tuum:
fiat volúntas tua, sicut in caelo, et in terra.
Panem nostrum cotidiánum da nobis hódie;
et dimítte nobis débita nostra,
sicut et nos dimíttimus debitóribus nostris.
Et ne nos indúcas in tentatiónem:
sed líbera nos a malo.
Amen.

Hail Mary
Ave María, grátia plena, Dóminus tecum,
benedicta tu in muliéribus,
et benedíctus fructus ventris tui, Jesus.
Sancta María, Mater Dei, ora pro nobis
peccatóribus,
nunc et in hora mortis nostrae.
Amen.

Glory Be
Glória Patri,
et Filio,
et Spirítui Sancto,
Sícut érat in princípio,
et nunc et sémper:
et in sáecula saeculórum.
Amen.

Sign of the Cross
In the name of the Father,
and of the Son,
and of the Holy Spirit.
Amen.

The Lord's Prayer
Our Father, who art in heaven,
hallowed be thy name;
thy kingdom come;
thy will be done on earth as it is in heaven.
Give us this day our daily bread;
and forgive us our trespasses
as we forgive those who trespass against us;
and lead us not into temptation,
but deliver us from evil.
Amen.

Hail Mary
Hail Mary, full of grace, the Lord is with you!
Blessed are you among women,
and blessed is the fruit of your womb, Jesus.
Holy Mary, Mother of God, pray for us
sinners,
now and at the hour of our death.
Amen.

Glory Be
Glory be to the Father,
and to the Son,
and to the Holy Spirit.
As it was in the beginning,
is now, and ever shall be,
world without end.
Amen.

Sioux Indian Prayer

Mother Katharine Drexel met the great Sioux Chief Red Cloud when she visited South Dakota.

O Great Spirit
Whose voice I hear in the winds,
And whose breath gives life to all the world,
   Hear me! I am small and weak,
   I need your strength and wisdom.

Let me walk in beauty and make my eyes
   ever behold the red and purple sunset!
Make my hands respect the things you have made
   and my ears sharp to hear your voice.

Make me wise that I may understand
   all things you have taught my people.
Let me learn the lessons
   you have hidden in every leaf and rock.

I seek strength, not to be greater than my brother,
   but to fight my greatest enemy, myself.
Make me always ready to come to you with
   clean hands and straight eyes.

So when my life fades, as the fading sunset,
   my spirit may come to you without shame.

Breastplate of Saint Patrick

I bind unto myself today
The power of God to hold and lead.
His eye to watch, his might to stay,
His ear to listen to my need,
The wisdom of my God to teach.
His hand to guide, his shield to protect,
The word of God to give me speech.
His heavenly messengers to be my guard.

Christ be with me, Christ within me,
Christ behind me, Christ before me,
Christ beside me, Christ to win me,
Christ to comfort and restore me,
Christ beneath me, Christ above me,
Christ in quiet, Christ in danger,
Christ in the hearts of all who love me,
Christ in the mouth of friend or stranger.

I bind unto myself the name,
The strong name, of the Trinity
By calling on the same,
The Three in One, the One in Three,
From whom all nature has creation:
Eternal Father, Spirit, Word.
Praise to the Lord of my salvation.
Salvation is of Christ the Lord. Amen.

The Magnificat—
Mary's Song of Praise

My soul magnifies the Lord,
and my spirit rejoices in God my Savior,
for he has looked with favor
on the lowliness of his servant.
Surely, from now on all
generations will call me blessed;
for the Mighty One
has done great things for me,
and holy is his name.
His mercy is for those who fear him
from generation to generation.
He has shown strength with his arm;
he has scattered the proud
in the thoughts of their hearts.
He has brought down the powerful
from their thrones,
and lifted up the lowly;
he has filled the hungry with good things,
and sent the rich away empty.
He has helped his servant Israel,
in remembrance of his mercy,
according to the promise he made
to our ancestors,
to Abraham and to his descendants forever.

(Luke 1:46-55)

Te Deum

You are God: we praise you;
You are the Lord: we acclaim you;
You are the eternal Father:
All creation worships you.

To you all angels, all the powers of heaven,
Cherubim and Seraphim, sing in endless praise:
Holy, holy, holy Lord, God of power and might,
heaven and earth are full of your glory.

The glorious company of apostles praise you.
The noble fellowship of prophets praise you.
The white-robed army of martyrs praise you.

Throughout the world the holy Church acclaims you:
Father, of majesty unbounded,
our true and only Son, worthy of all worship,
and the Holy Spirit, advocate and guide.

You, Christ, are the king of glory,
the eternal Son of the Father.

When you became man to set us free
you did not spurn the Virgin's womb.

You overcame the sting of death,
and opened the kingdom of heaven to all believers.

You are seated at God's right hand in glory.
We believe that you will come, and be our judge.
Come then, Lord, and help your people,
bought with the price of your own blood,
and bring us with your saints
to glory everlasting.

The Nicene Creed

We believe in one God,
  the Father, the Almighty,
  maker of heaven and earth,
  of all that is seen and unseen.

We believe in one Lord, Jesus Christ,
  the only Son of God,
  eternally begotten of the Father,
  God from God, Light from Light,
  true God from true God,
  begotten, not made, one in Being with the Father.
  Through him all things were made.
  For us men and for our salvation
  he came down from heaven:
  by the power of the Holy Spirit
  he was born of the Virgin Mary, and became man.

For our sake he was crucified under Pontius Pilate;
  he suffered, died, and was buried.
  On the third day he rose again
  in fulfillment of the Scriptures;
  he ascended into heaven
  and is seated at the right hand of the Father
He will come again in glory
  to judge the living and the dead,
  and his kingdom will have no end.

We believe in the Holy Spirit, the Lord, the giver of life,
  who proceeds from the Father and the Son.
  With the Father and the Son he is worshiped and glorified.
  He has spoken through the prophets.
  We believe in one holy catholic and apostolic Church.
  We acknowledge one baptism for the forgiveness of sins.
  We look for the resurrection of the dead,
  and the life of the world to come.
Amen.

The Divine Praises

Blessed be God.

Blessed be his holy name.

Blessed be Jesus Christ, true God and true man.

Blessed be the name of Jesus.

Blessed be his most sacred heart.

Blessed be his most precious blood.

Blessed be Jesus in the most holy sacrament of the altar.

Blessed be the Holy Spirit, the Paraclete.

Blessed be the great mother of God, Mary most holy.

Blessed be her holy and immaculate conception.

Blessed be her glorious assumption.

Blessed be the name of Mary, virgin and mother.

Blessed be Saint Joseph, her most chaste spouse.

Blessed be God in his angels and in his saints.

Liturgical Checklist

Name _____ **Date** _____

Check the ways you can participate in the eucharistic liturgy.

_____ planning the liturgy

_____ playing an instrument

_____ presenting the gifts

_____ giving to the collection

_____ singing and giving responses at Mass

_____ being a lector

_____ reading the general intercessions

_____ designing a banner for the liturgy

Word Search

Name _____   **Date** _____

Find and cross out these terms:

- perjury
- cursing
- blasphemy
- profanity
- obscene language

```
S E T B B L A S P H E M Y D D
W W X A C A E B R C U L G K L
O B P D F F B L O B S A T N A
V U E A I I D M F S Y O F M N
O P R C R O F P A T Z U G O T
A D J C U R S I N G A B H L M
T F U A D U N R I W E C I Q V
H I R P D C H G T M O W S R W
S I Y O M J I Z Y X I D J S X
O B S C E N E L A N G U A G E
```

Benedictus

Blessed be the Lord God of Israel,
for he has looked favorably on his people and redeemed them.

He has raised up a mighty savior for us
   in the house of his servant David,
as he spoke through the mouth of his holy prophets from of old,
   that we would be saved from our enemies
   and from the hand of all who hate us.

Thus he has shown the mercy promised to our ancestors,
   and has remembered his holy covenant,
the oath that he swore to our ancestor Abraham,
   to grant us that we, being rescued from the hands of our enemies,
   might serve him without fear,
   in holiness and righteousness before him all our days.

And you, child, will be called the prophet of the Most High;
   for you will go before the Lord to prepare his ways,
to give knowledge of salvation to his people
   by the forgiveness of their sins.

By the tender mercy of our God,
   the dawn from on high will break upon us,
to give light to those who sit in darkness and in the shadow of death,
   to guide our feet into the way of peace.

(Luke 1:68-79)

Prayer from the Mass for the Progress of Peoples

Father,
you have given all peoples one common origin,
and your will is to gather them as one family in yourself.
Fill the hearts of all men with the fire of your love
and the desire to ensure justice for all their brothers
    and sisters.
By sharing the good things you give us
may we secure justice and equality for every human being,
an end to all division,
and a human society built on love and peace.

We ask this through our Lord Jesus Christ, your Son,
who lives and reigns with you and the Holy Spirit,
one God, for ever and ever.
Amen.

Mountain Matching

Name _____   **Date** _____

Mountains are frequently referred to in both the Old and New Testaments as places to meet God, places to pray, and places to seek refuge. Match each Scripture reference with the name of a mountain or with an event that occurred on a mountain. Write the letter of the correct answers on the lines.

1. Matthew 21:1 _____
2. Matthew 4:8 _____
3. Mark 3:13 _____
4. Matthew 17:1 _____

5. Matthew 5:1 _____
6. Mark 6:46 _____
7. Luke 4:29 _____
8. Hebrews 12:22 _____

(a) Mount Zion

(b) Jesus prays

(c) Transfiguration of Jesus

(d) Temptation of Jesus

(e) Mount of Olives

(f) Sermon on the Mount

(g) Jesus is almost killed

(h) Call of the disciples

Prayer to Mary Magdalene

Father,
your Son first entrusted to Mary Magdalene
the joyful news of his resurrection.
By her prayers and example
may we proclaim Christ as our living Lord
and one day see him in glory,
for he lives and reigns with you and the Holy Spirit.
one God, for ever and ever. Amen.

Saint James Acrostic

Name _____   **Date** _____

Use the clues below to fill in the puzzle.

```
_ _ _ _ _ _ _ A _

        _ P _ _ _

        _ O _ _

      _ _ _ _ S

_ _ _ _   _ _ T _ _ _ _ _ _

      _ _ _ L _ _ _

        _ E _ _ _ _ _
```

- James's work before he became an apostle

- Country that has a special shrine for James

- James's brother

- First apostle to die for Christ

- Nickname for James and his brother

- Country with more than 400 churches dedicated to James

- James's father

462

Why Get Angry?

Name _____ **Date** _____

Look up each of these Scripture passages. Match each with what it tells you about anger. Then think of a present-day example of each type of anger and write it on the lines below.

Luke 9:51–56

Luke 15:25–32

Acts 19:23–41

_____ 1. People who feel sorry for themselves may get angry at imagined injustice.

_____ 2. People may act violently and less than human when they get angry.

_____ 3. People who see an injustice may want to correct it with revenge and punishment.

1. _____

   _____

   _____

2. _____

   _____

   _____

3. _____

   _____

   _____

Word Search

Name _____   **Date** _____

Find 10 words that refer to the Transfiguration account. Circle the words and list them below.

```
M  J  L  R  E  C  C  B
O  O  Q  U  I  L  H  M
U  H  S  G  L  O  R  Y
N  N  M  F  I  U  I  S
T  S  O  N  C  D  S  T
A  J  S  W  H  I  T  E
I  F  E  A  R  K  E  R
N  R  S  X  W  P  R  Y
```

_____   _____

_____   _____

_____   _____

_____   _____

_____   _____

Religion Class Check-up

Name _____ **Date** _____

Fill in the initials of the days of the week or the dates of your religion classes across the top.

Use this scale for evaluation: VG = very good; G = good; NI = needs improvement.

Day/date:					
1. I had the necessary materials when class began: text, pencil, pen, paper.					
2. I was paying attention when class began.					
3. I participated by asking or answering questions.					
4. I actively cooperated in the activities of the lesson.					
5. I did the written work neatly and completely.					

Mirror of Princes

Name _____ **Date** _____

Read the following paragraph from *Mirror of Princes* by Saint Stephen of Hungary. Underline a piece of advice that would be a good one for you to follow. Then in the space below, write how you will try to do this in the coming week.

> Be humble in this life, that God may raise you up in the next. Be truly moderate and do not punish or condemn anyone immoderately. Be gentle so that you may never oppose justice. Be honorable so that you may never voluntarily bring disgrace on anyone. Be chaste so that you may avoid all the foulness of lust like the pangs of death. All these virtues I have noted above make up the royal crown, and without them no one is fit to rule here on earth or attain to the heavenly kingdom.

_____

_____

_____

_____

_____

_____

_____

_____

_____

_____

_____

Duties of Catholic Christians

1. To take part in the Eucharist every Sunday and holy day; to do no unnecessary work on Sunday.

2. To lead a sacramental life: To receive the sacrament of Penance at least once a year. To receive Holy Communion at least during the Easter Season.

3. To study Catholic teaching; to be confirmed.

4. To observe the marriage laws of the Church; to give religious training to one's children.

5. To contribute to the support of the Church.

6. To do penance, including abstaining from meat and fasting from food on the appointed days.

7. To join in the missionary spirit and apostolate of the Church.

Morning Offering

O Jesus, through the Immaculate Heart of Mary, I offer you my prayers, works, joys, and sufferings of this day in union with the Holy Sacrifice of the Mass throughout the world. I offer them for all the intentions of your Sacred Heart: the salvation of souls, reparation for sin, the reunion of all Christians. I offer them for the intentions of our bishops and of all Apostles of Prayer, and in particular for those recommended by our Holy Father this month.

(from the Apostleship of Prayer)

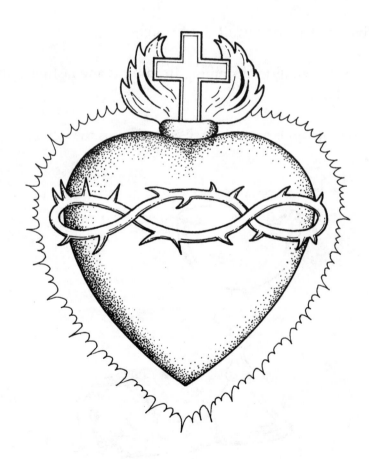

Psalm 100

Side 1: Make a joyful noise to the LORD, all the earth.

Side 2: Worship the LORD with gladness;

All: come into his presence with singing.
Know that the LORD is God.

Speaker 1: It is he that made us,

Speakers 1, 2: and we are his;

Speakers 1, 2, 3, 4: we are his people,

All: and the sheep of his pasture.

Girls: Enter his gates with thanksgiving,

All: and his courts with praise.

Boys: Give thanks to him, bless his name.

Side 1: For the LORD is good;

Side 2: his steadfast love endures forever,

All: and his faithfulness to all generations.

Girls: Glory be to the Father, and to the Son, and to the Holy Spirit.

Boys: As it was in the beginning, is now, and ever shall be, world without end. Amen.

About the Illustrations

Page 3: The hawthorn is often called "Mary's Flower of May."

Page 9: The Jerusalem cross represents spreading the Gospel to the "four corners" of the earth.

Page 11: The lily of the valley symbolizes Mary's tears at the foot of the cross.

Page 71: Saint Simon's shield represents a "fisher of men" and Saint Jude's a missionary ship.

Page 75: In Mexican tradition, the "Day of the Dead" is observed with elaborate symbolism.

Page 83: The crosier, in the form of a shepherd's crook, symbolizes a bishop's authority.

Page 93: The Sacred Heart of Jesus has long been the object of devotion.

Page 101: St. Peter's basilica is on the left and St. Paul's on the right.

Page 103: The white snowdrop is a symbol of Mary's purity.

Page 107: The keys are a symbol of the authority Jesus gave to Peter as the first head of the Church.

Page 109: The ship is often used to symbolize the Church, which is carrying us safely toward heaven.

Page 117: The crown is a symbol of Christ's sovereignty.

Page 175: The *agnus dei* reminds us that Christ is the Lamb of God.

Page 277: Saint Philip's shield refers to the feeding of the 5,000; that of James the Less reflects the violent death he met at the hands of enemies.

Page 283: Shown here is a version of the Coptic cross; the Coptic church has existed in North African countries such as Ethiopia and Egypt since apostolic times.

Page 289: The tiara, a headpiece made up of three crowns, is worn by the pope.

Page 303: "Blessed are you among women" was Elizabeth's greeting to Mary.

Page 305: We honor Mary by devotion to her Immaculate Heart.

Page 309: Early Christians in Rome often met for worship among the underground tombs of the catacombs, and many martyrs were buried there.

Page 329: The archangel Gabriel is frequently portrayed as God's messenger.

Page 349: The cross of the Benedictines is shown here.

Page 357: The cross of the Franciscans is shown here.

Page 365: The crown of thorns directs our attention to the Passion of Jesus.

Page 369: This Temple stood in Jerusalem at the time Jesus and John were born.

Page 381: A monstrance such as this one holds the Blessed Sacrament before us.

Page 383: The shape of the mitre worn by bishops represents the flames of Pentecost.

Page 387: St. Mary Major is the largest church in the world that is dedicated to Our Lady.

Glossary

abbess. The superior of a community of nuns.

abbot. The superior of a community of monks.

antipope. One who claims to be pope but is not validly elected.

apostle. The word comes from a Greek word meaning "to be sent." Jesus called twelve men to be his apostles and sent them to bring the message of salvation to all. Paul of Tarsus was called to be his apostle to the Gentiles. Others are sometimes called apostle, for example, Francis Xavier as the apostle to India and Japan.

Arianism. A heresy, preached by Arius in the fourth century, that denied the divinity of Christ, claiming that Jesus of Nazareth was simply a good man.

beatify. To declare that a person may be called Blessed and honored in the liturgy. It is a step toward canonization as a saint of the Church and involves a thorough investigation into a person's life and, except in the case of martyrs, a miracle worked through the intercession of the person.

Benedictine. A member of a religious order that follows the Rule of Saint Benedict.

canonize. To declare that a person is now in heaven and is worthy of honor and imitation of virtue. The pope canonizes a holy person as a saint after a detailed study of the person's life, writings, and holiness.

Carmelite. A member of the Order of Our Lady of Mount Carmel, a community founded in the 12th century with roots in the first monks or hermits who lived on Mount Carmel in the Holy Land. Teresa of Ávila and John of the Cross reformed the Carmelite Order in Spain in the 16th century.

catacombs. Underground cemeteries, especially around Rome, that were used as burial places for early martyrs and Christians. Catacombs also served as secret places for celebration of the Eucharist during times of persecution.

catechist. A person who instructs others in Christian doctrine and guides their spiritual formation.

catechumen. A person preparing for Baptism and full membership in the Church through a program of instruction and spiritual formation.

cloister. The part of a convent or monastery reserved for and accessible only to members of a religious order; a religious house in which contemplative monks or nuns live entirely enclosed from the outside world.

contemplation. A form of prayer that is an intimate and profound awareness of God.

contemplative. A person who seeks union with God through a life of deep prayer and penance.

convent. A gathering of sisters, or nuns, in community life.

council. An assembly of Church officials called together to discuss important issues of the Church.

Doctor of the Church. The title Doctor means that a particular saint's writing or preaching is outstanding in guiding the faith of Christians.

doctrine. The beliefs and teachings of the Church.

Dominican. A member of a religious order founded by Saint Dominic.

Father of the Church. A title given to writers and bishops of the early Christian Church who faithfully passed on the teaching of the apostles; also called apostolic father.

feast. A day of celebration on which the Church observes the feast day of a saint; usually on the day of his or her death because that is his or her birthday in heaven.

founder. One who establishes or sets up a religious order, institution, or organization.

Glossary

Franciscan. A member of a religious order founded by Saint Francis.

friar. A member of a religious order that ministers in the world, for example, Franciscans and Dominicans, as opposed to a monastic order.

heresy. A false teaching that denies or distorts the truth of Church teaching.

heretic. A baptized person who publicly denies a belief of the Church.

Jesuit. A member of the Society of Jesus, an order founded by Ignatius of Loyola in 1540. The Society has been particularly active in the field of education, founding many colleges and universities.

martyr. A person who gives public witness to his or her faith and dies for it.

mission. The work of the Church in teaching the message of Christ; also a place where this work is carried out.

missionary. A person who carries out the teaching mission of the Church, especially to the poor or unchurched.

monk. A member of a religious order of men who take vows of poverty, chastity, and obedience and live apart from the world in a monastery.

mystic. A person who has received a special gift of prayer from God. Because this type of prayer is a free gift given to the persons whom God chooses, no one can control it or earn it. Mystical prayer is an experience of a special union with God in love.

nun. A member of a religious order of women who has taken solemn vows.

patron or patroness. A particular saint chosen as a protector and intercessor by a person, place, or group of people.

penance. Any prayer, sacrifice, good deed, kindness, or other action offered to God in order to make up for sin by doing something good.

primacy. Being first in pastoral authority. The pope, as Bishop of Rome, has primacy over other bishops because he is the successor of Peter, to whom Christ gave authority over the entire Church.

prior. The main assistant to the abbot of a monastery.

prioress. The main assistant to the abbess of a convent.

reform. To return to the original form, focus, or purpose.

Reformation. An attempt in the 1500s to cleanse the Church of abuses and human errors that resulted in the division of the Catholic Church, the establishment of Protestant churches, and the Council of Trent.

religious order. A group of vowed men or women who live and work together to serve Christ and the Church in a particular way.

sister. A member of a religious order of women who has made simple vows of poverty, chastity, and obedience.

spiritual director. Someone, usually a priest, who guides a person in his or her spiritual life and growth.

tertiary. A lay member of a religious order.

venerate. To show love, devotion, or respect to the Blessed Mother or the saints. Similar respect can also be shown toward relics and sacred objects.

vision. A spiritual gift by which one is able to see and talk to Jesus, Mary, or the saints.

vow. A deliberate and free promise made to God to do something good.

witness. The passing on to others, by our words and by our actions, the faith we have been given. Every Christian has the duty to give witness to the good news about Jesus Christ that they have come to know.

Bibliography

Bunson, Matthew, Margaret, and Stephen. *John Paul II's Book of Saints*. Huntington, Indiana: Our Sunday Visitor, 1999.

_____. *Our Sunday Visitor's Encyclopedia of Saints*. Huntington, Indiana: Our Sunday Visitor, 1998.

Delaney, John J. *Pocket Dictionary of Saints (Abridged)*. Garden City, New York: Doubleday & Company, Inc., 1983.

_____, ed. *Saints for All Seasons*. Garden City, New York: Image Books (a division of Doubleday & Company, Inc.), 1978.

Dollen, Charles, ed. *Prayer Book of the Saints*. Huntington, Indiana: Our Sunday Visitor, 1984.

Ellsberg, Robert. *All Saints: Daily Reflections on Saints, Prophets and Witnesses for Our Time*. New York: The Crossroad Publishing Company, 1997.

Finley, Mitch. *The Seeker's Guide to Saints*. Chicago: Loyola Press, 2000.

Foley, Leonard, O.F.M., ed. *Saint of the Day*. 4th Revised ed. Cincinnati, Ohio: St. Anthony Messenger Press, 2001.

Jones, Kathleen, ed. *Butler's Lives of the Saints*. Collegeville, Minnesota: The Liturgical Press, 2000.

_____. *Women Saints: Lives of Faith and Courage*. Maryknoll, New York: Orbis Books, 1999.

Lodi, Enzo. *Saints of the Roman Calendar*. New York: Alba House, 1992.

McBride, Alfred. *Saints Are People*. Dubuque, Iowa: Wm. C. Brown, 1981.

McGinley, Phyllis. *Saint-Watching*. New York: Doubleday, 1982.

Moran, Patrick R. *Day by Day with the Saints*. Huntington, Indiana: Our Sunday Visitor, 1985.

Nevins, Albert J. *A Saint for Your Name (Boys)* Huntington, Indiana: Our Sunday Visitor, 1980. revised and updated by Ann Ball, 1991.

_____. *A Saint for Your Name (Girls)*. Huntington, Indiana: Our Sunday Visitor, 1980. Revised and updated by Ann Ball, 1991.

Ransom, Ed. *Saints for Our Time*. Mystic, Connecticut: Twenty-Third Publications, 1998.

Sandoval, Annette. *The Dictionary of Saints: A Concise Guide to Patron Saints*. New York: Signet (a division of Penguin Books USA, Inc.), 1996.

Self, David. *The Loyola Treasury of Saints: From the Time of Jesus to the Present Day*. Chicago: Loyola Press, 2004.

Sheehan, Thomas. *Dictionary of Patron Saints Names*. Huntington, Indiana: Our Sunday Visitor, 2001.

Wallace, Susan Helen, F.S.B., ed. *Saints for Young Readers for Every Day*. 2nd revised ed. Boston: Pauline Books & Media, 1995.

Walsh, Michael, ed. *Butler's Lives of the Saints*. Concise edition. New York: HarperCollins, 1991.

Water, Mark. *A Year with the Saints*. Ligouri, Missouri: Ligouri Publications, 1997.

Wellborn, Amy. *Loyola Kids Book of Saints*. Chicago: Loyola Press, 2001.

Woodward, Kenneth L. *Making Saints: How the Catholic Church Determines Who Becomes a Saint, Who Doesn't, and Why*. New York: Touchstone Books, 1996.

Saints Kit by Mary Kathleen Glavich, S.N.D., and other Sisters of Notre Dame is available from Loyola Press (toll free: 800–621–1008). It contains 201 illustrated lives of the saints and suggested student activities on cards. The material is adapted for students from *Saints and Feast Days*.

Index

Index